GATE PREP SERIES

GATE

Graduate Aptitude Test in Engineering

2020

Geology & Geophysics

Solved Papers

(2009-2019)

GATE PREP SERIES

GATE

Graduate Aptitude Test in Engineering

2020

Geology & Geophysics

Solved Papers

(2009-2019)

G. K. PUBLICATIONS (P) LTD.

CL MEDIA (P) LTD.

Edition : 2020

ISBN : **978-81-93975-68-8**

Typeset by : *CL Media DTP Unit*

Administrative and Production Offices

Published by : **CL Media (P) Ltd.**

A-45, Mohan Cooperative Industrial Area,
Near Mohan Estate Metro Station,
New Delhi - 110044

Marketed by : **G.K. Publications (P) Ltd.**

A-45, Mohan Cooperative Industrial Area,
Near Mohan Estate Metro Station,
New Delhi - 110044

For product information :

Visit ***www.gkpublications.com*** or email to ***gkp@gkpublications.com***

Contents

- **Preface** (vii)
- **About GATE** (ix)
- **GATE Syllabus** (xvii)

PREVIOUS YEARS SOLVED PAPERS

2019	....	1-17
2018	....	1-24
2017	....	1-20
2016	....	1-20
2015	....	1-16
2014	....	1-22
2013	....	1-16
2012	....	1-18
2011	....	1-19
2010	....	1-16
2009	....	1-20

GATE
Graduate Aptitude Test in Engineering

IIT Institutes

Indian Institute of Technology, Mumbai

Indian Institute of Technology, Kharagpur

GATE 2020 will be conducted by
Indian Institute of Technology, Delhi

GATE 2019 conducted by
Indian Institute of Technology, Chennai

Indian Institute of Technology, Guwahati

Indian Institute of Technology, Roorkee

Indian Institute of Technology, Kanpur

Preface

The Graduate Aptitude Test in Engineering (GATE) is an online exam conducted by the IITs for admissions to PG courses in IITs, IISc Bangalore, NITs and many state run universities as well as private universities. Also there are more than 37 PSUs that use GATE score for recruitments. A large number of corporates are also using GATE score as a tool to screen students for placements.

GK Publications is well known as the "publisher of choice" to students preparing for GATE and other technical examinations in the country. We published the first set of books in 1994 when GATE exam, both objective and conventional, was conducted in the paper and pencil environment, and used as a check point for entry to post graduate courses in IITs and IISCs. At that time, students had little access to technology and relied mainly on instructor led learning followed by practice with books available for these examinations.

A lot has changed since then!

Today, GATE is conducted in an online only mode with multiple choice and numerical based questions. The score is valid for three years and is used not only for post graduate courses but is also used by major PSUs for recruitment. Today's students have easy access to technology and the concept of a monologue within the classroom has changed to dialogue where students come prepared with concepts and then discuss topics. They learn a lot of things on the go with their mobile devices and practice for mock tests online.

We, as a leading publisher of GATE books, have also embraced change. Today, our books are no more guides and papers only but come with a fully supported mobile app and a web portal. The mobile app provides access to video lectures, short tests and regular updates about the exam. The web portal in additional to what is available on the app provides full length mock tests to mimic the actual exam and help you gauge your level of preparedness. The combination of practice content in print, video lectures, and short and full length tests on mobile and web makes this product a complete courseware for GATE preparation.

This book includes previous years GATE questions along with detailed solution of each question for better understanding. It will help the GATE aspirants to know an idea about the pattern of questions asked in GATE examination.

We also know that improvement is a never ending process and hence we welcome your suggestions and feedback or spelling and technical errors if any. Please write to us at gkp@gkpublications.com

We hope that our small effort will help you prepare well for the examination.

We wish you all the best!

GK Publications Pvt. Ltd.

About GATE

The Graduate Aptitude Test in Engineering (GATE) conducted by IISc and IITs has emerged as one of the bench mark tests for engineering and science aptitude in facilitating admissions for higher education (M.Tech./Ph.D.) in IITs, IISc and various other Institutes/Universities/ Laboratories in India. With the standard and high quality of the GATE examination in 23 disciplines of engineering and science subjects, it identifies the candidate's understanding of a subject and aptitude and eligibility for higher studies. During the last few years, GATE score is also being used as one of the criteria for recruitment in Government Organizations such as Cabinet Secretariat, and National/State Public Sector Undertakings in India. Because of the importance of the GATE examination, the number of candidates taking up GATE exams has increased tremendously. GATE exams are conducted by the IITs and IISc as a computer based test having multiple choice questions and numerical answer type questions. The questions are mostly fundamental, concept based and thought provoking. From 2017 onwards GATE Exam is being held in Bangladesh, Ethiopia, Nepal, Singapore, Sri Lanka and United Arab Emirates. An Institute with various nationalities in its campus widens the horizons of an academic environment. A foreign student brings with him/her a great diversity, culture and wisdom to share. Many GATE qualified candidates are paid scholarships/assistantship, especially funded by Ministry of Human Resources Development, Government of India and by other Ministries. Indian Institute of Technology Delhi is the Organizing Institute for GATE 2020.

New in GATE 2019 Onward

A new paper Statistics (ST) is added in GATE 2019

Why GATE?

Admission to Post Graduate and Doctoral Programmes

Admission to postgraduate programmes with MHRD and some other government scholarships/ assistantships in engineering colleges/institutes is open to those who qualify through GATE. GATE qualified candidates with Bachelor's degree in Engineering/Technology/Architecture or Master's degree in any branch of Science/Mathematics/Statistics/Computer Applications are eligible for admission to Master/Doctoral programmes in Engineering/Technology/Architecture as well as for Doctoral programmes in relevant branches of Science with MHRD or other government scholarships/assistantships. Candidates with Master's degree in Engineering/ Technology/Architecture may seek admission to relevant PhD programmes with scholarship/ assistantship without appearing in the GATE examination.

Financial Assistance

A valid GATE score is essential for obtaining financial assistance during Master's programs and direct Doctoral programs in Engineering/Technology/Architecture, and Doctoral programs in relevant branches of Science in Institutes supported by the MHRD or other Government agencies. As per the directives of the MHRD, the following procedure is to be adopted for admission to the post-graduate programs (Master's and Doctoral) with MHRD scholarship/ assistantship. Depending upon the norms adopted by a specific institute or department of the Institute, a candidate may be admitted directly into a course based on his/her performance in GATE only **or** based on his/her performance in GATE **and** an admission test/interview conducted by the department to which he/she has applied **and/or** the candidate's academic record. If the candidate is to be selected through test/interview for post-graduate programs, a minimum of 70% weightage will be given to the performance in GATE and the remaining 30% weightage will be given to the candidate's performance in test/interview and/or academic record, as per MHRD guidelines. The admitting institutes could however prescribe a minimum passing percentage of marks in the test/interview. Some colleges/institutes specify GATE qualification as the mandatory requirement even for admission without MHRD scholarship/assistantship.

To avail of the financial assistance (scholarship), the candidate must first secure admission to a program in these Institutes, by a procedure that could vary from institute to institute. Qualification in GATE is also a minimum requirement to apply for various fellowships awarded by many Government organizations. Candidates are advised to seek complete details of admission procedures and availability of MHRD scholarship/assistantship from the concerned admitting institution. The criteria for postgraduate admission with scholarship/assistantship could be different for different institutions. The management of the post-graduate scholarship/assistantship is also the responsibility of the admitting institution. Similarly, reservation of seats under different categories is as per the policies and norms prevailing at the admitting institution and Government of India rules. *GATE offices will usually not entertain any enquiry about admission, reservation of seats and/or award of scholarship/assistantship.*

PSU Recruitments

As many as 37 PSUs are using GATE score for recruitment. It is likely that more number of PSUs may start doing so by next year. Below is the list of PSUs:

MDL, BPCL, GAIL, NLC LTD, CEL, Indian Oil, HPCL, NBPC, NECC, BHEL, WBSEDCL, NTPC, ONGC, Oil India, Power Grid, Cabinet Secretariat, Govt. of India, BAARC, NFL, IPR, PSPCL, PSTCL, DRDO, OPGC Ltd., THDC India Ltd., BBNL, RITES, IRCON, GHECL, NHAI, KRIBHCO, Mumbai Railway Vikas Corporation Ltd. (MRVC Ltd.), National Textile Corporation, Coal India Ltd., BNPM, AAI, NALCO, EdCIL India.

Important :

1. Admissions in IITs/IISc or other Institutes for M.Tech./Ph.D. through GATE scores shall be advertised separately by the Institutes and GATE does not take the responsibility of admissions.
2. Cabinet Secretariat has decided to recruit officers for the post of Senior Field Officer (Tele) (From GATE papers of EC, CS, PH), Senior Research Officer (Crypto) (From GATE papers of EC, CS, MA), Senior Research Officer (S&T) (From GATE papers EC, CS, CY, PH, AE, BT) in the Telecommunication Cadre, Cryptographic Cadre and Science & Technology Unit respectively of Cabinet Secretariat. The details of the scheme of recruitment shall be published in National Newspaper/Employment News by the concerned authority.
3. Some PSUs in India have expressed their interest to utilize GATE scores for their recruitment purpose. The Organizations who intend to utilize GATE scores shall make separate advertisement for this purpose in Newspapers etc.

Who Can Appear for GATE?

Eligibility for GATE

Before starting the application process, the candidate must ensure that he/she meets the eligibility criteria of GATE given in Table.

Eligibility Criteria for GATE 2020

Qualifying Degree	Qualifying Degree/Examination (Descriptive)	Description of Eligible Candidates	Year of qualification cannot be later than
B.E./B.Tech./ B.Pharm.	Bachelor's degree holders in Engineering/ Technology (4 years after 10+2 or 3 years after B.Sc./Diploma in Engineering/ Technology)	Currently in the final year or already completed	2020
B. Arch.	Bachelor's degree holders of Architecture (Five years course)	Currently in the final year or already completed	2020
B.Sc. (Research)/ B.S.	Bachelor's degree in Science (Post-Diploma/4 years after 10+2)	Currently in the 4th year or already completed	2020
M. Sc./ M.A./MCA or equivalent	Master's degree in any branch of Science/Mathematics / Statistics / Computer Applications or equivalent	Currently in the final year or already completed	2020
Int. M.E. / M.Tech. (Post-B.Sc.)	Integrated Master's degree programs in Engineering / Technology (Four year program)	Currently in the 2nd/3rd/4th year or already completed	2022
Int. M.E./ M.Tech. or Dual Degree(after Diploma or 10+2)	Integrated Master's degree program or Dual Degree program in Engineering / Technology (Five year program)	Currently in the 4th/5th year or already completed	2021
Int. M.Sc./ Int. B.S.-M.S.	Integrated M.Sc. or Five year integrated B.S.-M.S. program	Currently in the final year or already completed	2020
Professional Society Examinations (equivalent to B.E./B.Tech./B.Arch.)	B.E./B.Tech./B.Arch. equivalent examinations, of Professional Societies, recognized by MHRD/UPSC/AICTE (e.g., AMIE by Institution of Engineers-India, AMICE by the Institute of Civil Engineers-India)	Completed section A or equivalent of such professional courses	NA

In case a candidate has passed one of the qualifying examinations as mentioned above in 2019 or earlier, the candidate has to submit the degree certificate / provisional certificate / course completion certificate / professional certificate / membership certificate issued by the society or institute. In case, the candidate is expected to complete one of the qualifying criteria in 2020 or later as mentioned above, he/she has to submit a certificate from Principal or a copy of marks card for section A of AMIE.

Certificate From Principal

Candidates who have to submit a certificate from their college Principal have to obtain one from his/her institution beforehand and upload the same during the online submission of the application form.

Candidates With Backlogs

Candidates, who have appeared in the final semester/year exam in 2020, but with a backlog (arrears/failed subjects) in any of the papers in their qualifying degree should upload a copy of any one of the mark sheets of the final year,

OR

obtain a declaration from their Principal along with the signature and seal beforehand and upload the same during the online submission of the application form.

GATE Structure

Structure of GATE

For the GATE examination, a candidate can apply for only one of the 23 papers listed in Tables below. The syllabus for each of the papers is given separately. Making a choice of the appropriate paper during GATE application is the responsibility of the candidate. Some guidelines in this respect are suggested below.

The candidate is expected to appear in a paper appropriate to the discipline of his/her qualifying degree. However, the candidate can choose any paper according to his/her admission plan, keeping in mind the eligibility criteria of the institutions in which he/she wishes to seek admission. For more details regarding the admission criteria in any particular institute, the candidate is advised to refer to the website of that institute.

List of GATE Papers and Corresponding Codes

Paper	Code	Paper	Code
Aerospace Engineering	AE	Geology and Geophysics	GG
Agricultural Engineering	AG	Instrumentation Engineering	IN
Architecture and Planning	AR	Mathematics	MA
Biotechnology	BT	Mechanical Engineering	ME
Civil Engineering	CE	Mining Engineering	MN
Chemical Engineering	CH	Metallurgical Engineering	MT
Computer Science and Information Technology	CS	Petroleum Engineering	PE
		Physics	PH
Chemistry	CY	Production and Industrial Engineering	PI
		Statistics	ST
Electronics and Communication Engineering	EC	Textile Engineering and Fibre Science	TF
Electrical Engineering	EE	Engineering Sciences	XE*
Ecology and Evolution	EY	Life Sciences	XL**

*XE Paper Sections	Code	**XL Paper Sections	Code
Engineering Mathematics (Compulsory)	A	Chemistry (Compulsory)	P
Fluid Mechanics	B	Biochemistry	Q
Materials Science	C	Botany	R
Solid Mechanics	D	Microbiology	S
Thermodynamics	E	Zoology	T
Polymer Science and Engineering	F	Food Technology	U
Food Technology	G		
Atmospheric and Oceanic Sciences	H		

*XE (Engineering Sciences) and **XL (Life Sciences) papers are of general nature and will comprise of Sections listed in the above table. More detailed explanation is given as following pages.

General Aptitude Questions

All the papers will have a few questions that test the General Aptitude (Language and Analytical Skills), apart from the core subject of the paper.

XE Paper

A candidate appearing in the XE paper has to answer the following

1. Section A – Engineering Mathematics

2. GA – General Aptitude

3. Any two of XE sections B to H

The choice of two sections from B to H can be made during the examination after viewing the questions. Only two optional sections can be answered at a time. A candidate wishing to change midway of the examination to another optional section must first choose to deselect one of the previously chosen optional sections (B to H).

XL Paper

A candidate appearing in the XL paper has to answer the following

1. Section P – Chemistry

2. GA – General Aptitude

3. Any two of XL sections Q to U

The choice of two sections from Q to U can be made during the examination after viewing the questions. Only two optional sections can be answered at a time. A candidate wishing to change midway of the examination to another optional section must first choose to deselect one of the previously chosen optional sections (Q to U).

Duration and Examination Type

The GATE examination consists of a single paper of **3-hour** duration that contains **65** questions carrying a maximum of **100 marks**. The question paper will consist of both multiple choice questions (MCQ) and numerical answer type (NAT) questions. The pattern of question papers is discussed in following paragraphs.

The examination for all the papers will be carried out in an ONLINE Computer Based Test (CBT) mode where the candidates will be shown the questions in a random sequence on a computer screen. The candidates are required to either select the answer (for MCQ type) or enter the answer for numerical answer type question using a mouse on a virtual keyboard (keyboard of the computer will be disabled). Each candidate will be provided with a scribble pad for rough work. The scribble pad has to be returned after the examination. At the end of the 3-hour window, the computer will automatically close the screen from further actions.

Pattern of Question Papers

In all the papers, there will be a total of 65 questions carrying 100 marks, out of which 10 questions carrying a total of 15 marks will be on General Aptitude (GA).

In the papers bearing the codes AE, AG, BT, CE, CH, CS, EC, EE, IN, ME, MN, MT, PE, PI, TF and XE, the Engineering Mathematics will carry around **15% of the total marks**, the General Aptitude section will carry **15% of the total marks** and the **remaining 70% of the total marks** is devoted to the subject of the paper.

In the papers bearing the codes AR, CY, EY, GG, MA, PH and XL, the General Aptitude section will carry **15% of the total marks** and the **remaining 85% of the total marks** is devoted to the subject of the paper.

GATE 2020 would contain questions of two different types in various papers:

(*i*) **Multiple Choice Questions (MCQ)** carrying 1 or 2 marks each in all papers and sections. These questions are objective in nature, and each will have a choice of four answers, out of which the candidate has to mark the correct answer(s).

(*ii*) **Numerical Answer Questions** of 1 or 2 marks each in all papers and sections. For these questions the answer is a real number, to be entered by the candidate using the virtual keypad. No choices will be shown for this type of questions.

Marking Scheme

For **1-mark** multiple-choice questions, **1/3** mark will be deducted for a wrong answer. Likewise, for **2-mark** multiple-choice questions, **2/3** mark will be deducted for a wrong answer. **There is NO negative marking for numerical answer type questions**.

Consult syllabus before proceeding

General Aptitude (GA) Questions

In all papers, GA questions carry a total of **15 marks**. The GA section includes 5 questions carrying **1-mark** each (sub-total **5 marks**) and 5 questions carrying **2-marks** each (sub-total **10 marks**).

Question Papers other than GG, XE and XL

These papers would contain **25** questions carrying **1-mark** each (sub-total **25 marks**) and **30** questions carrying **2-marks** each (sub-total **60 marks**). The question paper will consist of questions of multiple choice and numerical answer type. For numerical answer questions, choices will not be given. Candidates have to enter the answer (which will be a real number, signed or unsigned, e.g., 25.06, – 25.06, 25, – 25 etc.) using a virtual keypad. An appropriate range will be considered while evaluating the numerical answer type questions so that the candidate is not penalized due to the usual round-off errors.

GG (Geology and Geophysics) Paper

Apart from the General Aptitude (GA) section, the GG question paper consists of two parts: Part A and Part B. Part A is common for all candidates. Part B contains two sections: Section 1 (Geology) and Section 2 (Geo-physics). Candidates will have to attempt questions in Part A and either Section 1 or Section 2 in Part B.

Part A consists of **25** multiple-choice questions carrying **1-mark** each (sub-total **25 marks** and some of these may be numerical answer type questions). Each section in Part B (Section 1 and Section 2) consists of **30** multiple choice questions carrying **2-marks** each (sub-total **60 marks** and some of these may be numerical answer type questions).

XE Paper (Engineering Sciences)

In XE paper, Engineering Mathematics section (Section A) is **compulsory**. This section contains **11** questions carrying a total of **15 marks**: 7 questions carrying **1-mark** each (sub-total **7 marks**), and 4 questions carrying **2-marks** each (sub-total **8 marks**). Some questions may be of numerical answer type questions.

Each of the other sections of the XE paper (Sections B through H) contains 22 questions carrying a total of **35 marks**: 9 questions carrying **1-mark** each (sub-total **9 marks**) and 13 questions carrying **2-marks** each (sub-total **26 marks**). Some questions may be of numerical answer type.

XL Paper (Life Sciences)

In XL paper, Chemistry section (Section P) is **compulsory**. This section contains **15** questions carrying a total of **25 marks**: 5 questions carrying **1-mark** each (sub-total **5 marks**) and 10 questions carrying **2-marks** each (sub-total **20 marks**). Some questions may be of numerical answer type.

Each of the other sections of the XL paper (Sections Q through U) contains 20 questions carrying a total of **30 marks**: 10 questions carrying **1-mark** each (sub-total **10 marks**) and 10 questions carrying **2-marks** each (sub-total **20 marks**). Some questions may be of numerical answer type.

Note on Negative Marking for Wrong Answers

For a wrong answer chosen for the **multiple choice questions** (MCQs), there would be negative marking. For **1-mark** multiple choice questions, **1/3** mark will be deducted for a wrong answer. Likewise, for **2-mark** multiple choice questions, **2/3** mark will be deducted for a wrong answer. However, there is **NO negative marking for a wrong answer in numerical answer type questions**.

GATE Score

After the evaluation of the answers, the raw marks obtained by a candidate will be converted to a normalized GATE Score.

The GATE score will be computed using the formula given below.

Calculation of Normalized Marks for CE, CS, EC, EE and ME papers (multi-session papers)

In GATE, examination for some papers may be conducted in multi-sessions. Hence, for these papers, a suitable normalization is applied to take into account any variation in the difficulty levels of the question papers across different sessions. The normalization is done based on the fundamental assumption that "in all multi-session GATE papers, the distribution of abilities of candidates is the same across all the sessions". This assumption is justified since the number of candidates appearing in multi-session papers in GATE is large and the procedure of allocation of session to candidates is random. Further it is also ensured that for the same multi-session paper, the number of candidates allotted in each session is of the same order of magnitude.

Based on the above, and considering various normalization methods, the committee arrived at the following formula for calculating the normalized marks for the multi-session papers.

Normalization mark of jth candidate in the ith session $\widehat{M_{ij}}$ is given by

$$\widehat{M_{ij}} = \frac{\bar{M}_t^g - M_q^g}{\bar{M}_{ti} - M_{iq}}(M_{ij} - M_{iq}) + M_q^g$$

where

M_{ij} : is the actual marks obtained by the jth candidate in i^{th} session

$\bar{M}_t^g$: is the average marks of the top 0.1% of the candidates considering all sessions

M_q^g : is the sum of mean and standard deviation marks of the candidates in the paper considering all sessions

$\bar{M}_{ti}$: is the average marks of the top 0.1% of the candidates in the ith session

M_{iq} : is the sum of the mean marks and standard deviation of the ith session

After evaluation of the answers, normalized marks based on the above formula will be calculated corresponding to the raw marks obtained by a candidate and the GATE Score will be calculated based on the normalized marks.

For all papers for which there is only one session, actual marks obtained will be used for calculating the GATE Score.

Calculation of GATE Score For All Papers

GATE 2020 score will be calculated using the formula

$$\text{GATE Score} = S_q + (S_t - S_q)\frac{(M - M_q)}{(\bar{M}_t - M_q)}$$

In the above formulae

M : marks obtained by the candidate (actual marks for single session papers and normalized marks for multi-session papers)

M_q : is the qualifying marks for general category candidate in the paper

$\bar{M}_t$: is the mean of marks of top 0.1% or top 10 (whichever is larger) of the candidates who appeared in the paper (in case of multi-session papers including all sessions)

S_q : 350, is the score assigned to M_q

S_t : 000, is the score assigned to $\bar{M}_t$

In the GATE 2020 score formula, M_q is usually 25 marks (out of 100) or + s, whichever is larger. Here μ is the mean and s is the standard deviation of marks of all the candidates who appeared in the paper.

After the declaration of results, GATE Scorecards can be downloaded by

(a) All SC/ST/PwD candidates whose marks are greater than or equal to the qualifying mark of SC/ST/PwD candidates in their respective papers, and

(b) All other candidates whose marks are greater than or equal to the qualifying mark of OBC (NCL) candidates in their respective papers.

There is no provision for the issue of hard copies of the GATE Scorecards

The GATE Committee has the authority to decide the qualifying mark/score for each GATE paper. In case any claim or dispute arises in respect of GATE, the Courts and Tribunals in Bangalore alone shall have the exclusive jurisdiction to entertain and settle any such dispute or claim.

GATE Syllabus

GENERAL APTITUDE

Verbal Ability: English grammar, sentence completion, verbal analogies, word groups, instructions, critical reasoning and verbal deduction.

Numerical Ability: Numerical computation, numerical estimation, numerical reasoning and data interpretation.

PART A

COMMON SECTION

Earth and Planetary system - size, shape, internal structure and composition of the earth; concept of isostasy; elements of seismology – body and surface waves, propagation of body waves in the earth's interior; Gravitational field of the Earth; geomagnetism and paleomagnetism; continental drift; plate tectonics – relationship with earthquakes, volcanism and mountain building; continental and oceanic crust – composition, structure and thickness.

Weathering and soil formation; landforms created by river, wind, glacier, ocean and volcanoes. Basic structural geology - stress, strain and material response; brittle and ductile deformation; nomenclature and classification of folds and faults. Crystallography – basic crystal symmetry and concept of point groups. Mineralogy – silicate crystal structure and determinative mineralogy of common rock forming minerals. Petrology – mineralogy and classification of common igneous, sedimentary and metamorphic rocks. Geological time scale - geochronology and absolute time. Stratigraphic principles; major stratigraphic divisions of India. Geological and geographical distribution of mineral, coal and petroleum resources of India.

Introduction to remote sensing. Engineering properties of rocks and soils. Ground water geology.

Principles and applications of gravity, magnetic, electrical, electromagnetic, seismic and radiometric methods of prospecting for oil, mineral and ground water; introductory well logging.

PART B (SECTION-1)

GEOLOGY

Geomorphic processes and agents; development and evolution of landforms; slope and drainage; processes in deep oceanic and near-shore regions; quantitative and applied geomorphology.

Mechanism of rock deformation; primary and secondary structures; geometry and genesis of folds, faults, joints and unconformities; cleavage, schistosity and lineation; methods of projection; tectonites and their significance; shear zones; superposed folding; basement-cover relationship.

Crystallography - symmetry, forms and twinning; crystal chemistry; optical mineralogy, classification of minerals, diagnostic physical and optical properties of rock - forming minerals.

Cosmic abundance of elements; meteorites; geochemical evolution of the earth; geochemical cycles; distribution of major, minor and trace elements in crust and mantle; elements of geochemical thermodynamics; isotope geochemistry; geochemistry of waters including solution equilibria and water-rock interaction.

Igneous rocks – classification, forms and textures; magmatic differentiation; binary and ternary phase diagrams; major and trace elements as monitors of partial melting and magma evolutionary processes. Sedimentary rocks – texture and structure; sedimentary processes and environments, sedimentary facies, provencance and basin analysis. Metamorphic rocks – structures and textures.

Physico-chemical conditions of metamorphism and concept of metamorphic facies, grade and baric types; metamorphism of pelitic, mafic and impure carbonate rocks; role of fluids in metamorphism; metamorphic P-T-t paths and their tectonic significance. Association of igneous, sedimentary and metamorphic rocks with tectonic setting. Igneous and metamorphic provinces and important sedimentary basins of India.

Morphology, classification and geological significance of important invertebrates, vertebrates, plant fossils and microfossils.

Principles of Stratigraphy and concepts of correlation – lithostratigraphy, biostratigraphy and chronostratigraphy. Indian stratigraphy – Precambrian and Phanerozoic. Overview of Himalayan Geology.

Ore-mineralogy and optical properties of ore minerals; ore forming processes vis-à-vis ore-rock association (magmatic, hydrothermal, sedimentary, supergene and metamorphogenic ores); fluid inclusions as an ore genetic tool. Coal and petroleum geology; marine mineral resources. Prospecting and exploration of economic mineral deposits - sampling, ore reserve estimation, geostatistics, mining methods. Ore dressing and mineral economics. Origin and distribution of mineral, fossil and nuclear fuel deposits in India.

Engineering properties of rocks and soils; rocks as construction materials; role of geology in the construction of engineering structures including dams, tunnels and excavation sites; natural hazards. Ground water geology – exploration, well hydraulics and water quality. Basic principles of remote sensing – energy sources and radiation principles, atmospheric absorption, interaction of energy with earth's surface, aerial-photo interpretation, multispectral remote sensing in visible, infrared, thermal IR and microwave regions, digital processing of satellite images. GIS – basic concepts, raster and vector mode operations.

PART B (SECTION-2)

GEOPHYSICS

The earth as a planet; different motions of the earth; gravity field of the earth, Clairaut's theorem, size and shape of earth; geomagnetic field, paleomagnetism; Geothermics and heat flow; seismology and interior of the earth; variation of density, velocity, pressure, temperature, electrical and magnetic properties of the earth; earthquakes-causes and measurements, magnitude and intensity, focal mechanisms, earthquake quantification, source characteristics, seismotectonics and seismic hazards; digital seismographs,

Scalar and vector potential fields; Laplace, Maxwell and Helmholtz equations for solution of different types of boundary value problems in Cartesian, cylindrical and spherical polar coordinates; Green's theorem; Image theory; integral equations in potential theory; Eikonal equation and Ray theory.

Absolute and relative gravity measurements; Gravimeters, Land, airborne, shipborne and bore-hole gravity surveys; various corrections for gravity data reduction – free air, Bouguer and isostatic anomalies; density estimates of rocks; regional and residual gravity separation; principle of equivalent stratum; data enhancement techniques, upward and downward continuation; derivative maps, wavelength filtering; preparation and analysis of gravity maps; gravity anomalies and their interpretation – anomalies due to geometrical and irregular shaped bodies, depth rules, calculation of mass.

– Elements of Earth's magnetic field, units of measurement, magnetic susceptibility of rocks and measurements, magnetometers, Land, airborne and marine magnetic surveys, Various corrections applied to magnetic data, IGRF, Reduction to Pole transformation, Poisson's relation of gravity and magnetic potential field, preparation of magnetic maps, upward and downward continuation, magnetic anomalies-geometrical shaped bodies, depth estimates, Image processing concepts in processing of magnetic anomaly maps; Interpretation of processed magnetic anomaly data. Applications of gravity and magnetic methods for mineral and oil exploration.

Conduction of electricity through rocks, electrical conductivities of metals, non-metals, rock forming minerals and different rocks, concepts of D.C. resistivity measurement, various electrode configurations for resistivity sounding and profiling, application of filter theory, Type-curves over multi-layered structures, Dar-Zarrouck parameters, reduction of layers, coefficient of anisotropy, interpretation of resistivity field data, equivalence and suppression, self-potential and its origin, field measurement, Induced polarization, time and frequency domain IP measurements; interpretation and applications of IP, ground-water exploration, mineral exploration, environmental and engineering applications.

Basic concept of EM induction in the earth, Skin-depth, elliptic polarization, inphase and quadrature components, Various EM methods, measurements in different source-receiver configurations,. Earth's natural electromagnetic field, tellurics, magneto-tellurics; geomagnetic depth sounding principles, electromagnetic profiling, Time domain EM method, EM scale modeling, processing of EM data and interpretation. Geological applications including groundwater, mineral and hydrocarbon exploration.

Seismic methods of prospecting; Elastic properties of earth materials; Reflection, refraction and CDP surveys; land and marine seismic sources, generation and propagation of elastic waves, velocity – depth models, geophones, hydrophones, recording instruments (DFS), digital formats, field layouts, seismic noises and noise profile analysis, optimum geophone grouping, noise cancellation by shot and geophone arrays, 2D and 3D seismic data acquisition, processing and interpretation; CDP stacking charts, binning, filtering, dip-moveout, static and dynamic corrections, Digital seismic data processing, seismic deconvolution and migration methods, attribute analysis, bright and dim spots, seismic stratigraphy, high resolution seismics, VSP, AVO. Reservoir geophysics.

Geophysical signal processing, sampling theorem, aliasing, Nyquist frequency, Fourier series, periodic waveform, Fourier and Hilbert transform, Z-transform and wavelet transform; power spectrum, delta function, auto correlation, cross correlation, convolution, deconvolution, principles of digital filters, windows, poles and zeros.

Principles and techniques of geophysical well-logging, SP, resistivity, induction, gamma ray, neutron, density, sonic, temperature, dip meter, caliper, nuclear magnetic, cement bond logging, micro-logs. Quantitative evaluation of formations from well logs; well hydraulics and application of geophysical methods for groundwater study; application of bore hole geophysics in ground water, mineral and oil exploration.

Radioactive methods of prospecting and assaying of mineral (radioactive and non radioactive) deposits, half-life, decay constant, radioactive equilibrium, G M counter, scintillation detector, semiconductor devices, application of radiometric for exploration, assaying and radioactive waste disposal.

Basic concepts of forward and inverse problems, Ill-posedness of inverse problems, condition number, non-uniqueness and stability of solutions; L1, L2 and Lp norms, overdetermined, underdetermined and mixed determined inverse problems, quasi-linear and non-linear methods including Tikhonov's regularization method, Singular Value Decomposion, Backus-Gilbert method, simulated annealing, genetic algorithms and artificial neural network.

SOLVED PAPER - 2019

GENERAL APTITUDE (GA)

Q. 1 - Q. 5 carry one mark each.

1. The fishermen, __________ the flood victims owed their lives, were rewarded by the government.

(*a*) whom (*b*) to which

(*c*) to whom (*d*) that

2. Some students were not involved in the strike.

If the above statement is true, which of the following conclusions is/are logically necessary?

1. Some who were involved in the strike were students.
2. No student was involved in the strike.
3. At least one student was involved in the strike.
4. Some who were not involved in the strike were students.

(*a*) 1 and 2 (*b*) 3

(*c*) 4 (*d*) 2 and 3

3. The radius as well as the height of a circular cone increases by 10%. The percentage increase in its volume is __________ .

(*a*) 17.1 (*b*) 21.0

(*c*) 33.1 (*d*) 72.8

4. Five numbers 10, 7, 5, 4 and 2 are to be arranged in a sequence from left to right following the directions given below:

1. No two odd or even numbers are next to each other.
2. The second number from the left is exactly half of the left-most number.
3. The middle number is exactly twice the right-most number.

Which is the second number from the right?

(*a*) 2 (*b*) 4

(*c*) 7 (*d*) 10

5. Until Iran came along, India had never been __________ in kabaddi.

(*a*) defeated

(*b*) defeating

(*c*) defeat

(*d*) defeatist

Q. 6 - Q. 10 carry two marks each.

6. Since the last one year, after a 125 basis point reduction in repo rate by the Reserve Bank of India, banking institutions have been making a demand to reduce interest rates on small saving schemes. Finally, the government announced yesterday a reduction in interest rates on small saving schemes to bring them on par with fixed deposit interest rates.

Which one of the following statements can be inferred from the given passage?

(*a*) Whenever the Reserve Bank of India reduces the repo rate, the interest rates on small saving schemes are also reduced

(*b*) Interest rates on small saving schemes are always maintained on par with fixed deposit interest rates

(*c*) The government sometimes takes into consideration the demands of banking institutions before reducing the interest rates on small saving schemes

(*d*) A reduction in interest rates on small saving schemes follow only after a reduction in repo rate by the Reserve Bank of India

7. In a country of 1400 million population, 70% own mobile phones. Among the mobile phone owners, only 294 million access the Internet. Among these Internet users, only half buy goods from e-commerce portals. What is the percentage of these buyers in the country?

(*a*) 10.50 (*b*) 14.70

(*c*) 15.00 (*d*) 50.00

8. The nomenclature of Hindustani music has changed over the centuries. Since the medieval period *dhrupad* styles were identified as *baanis*. Terms like *gayaki* and *baaj* were used to refer to vocal and instrumental styles, respectively. With the institutionalization of music education the term *gharana* became acceptable. *Gharana* originally referred to hereditary musicians from a particular lineage, including disciples and grand disciples.

Which one of the following pairings is NOT correct?

(*a*) *dhrupad, baani* (*b*) *gayaki,* vocal

(*c*) *baaj,* institution (*d*) *gharana,* lineage

9. Two trains started at 7AM from the same point. The first train travelled north at a speed of 80 km/h and the second train travelled south at a speed of 100 km/h. The time at which they were 540 km apart is ________ AM.

(*a*) 9 (*b*) 10
(*c*) 11 (*d*) 11.30

10. "I read somewhere that in ancient times the prestige of a kingdom depended upon the number of taxes that it was able to levy on its people. It was very much like the prestige of a head-hunter in his own community."

Based on the paragraph above, the prestige of a head-hunter depended upon

(*a*) the prestige of the kingdom
(*b*) the prestige of the heads
(*c*) the number of taxes he could levy
(*d*) the number of heads he could gather

PART-A (Common Part)

Q. 1 - Q. 25 carry one mark each.

1. On the present-day global plate tectonic map, the Reunion hotspot is located in the ________ .

(*a*) Indian Plate (*b*) Australian Plate
(*c*) African Plate (*d*) Antarctic Plate

2. Which one of the following statements about the planetary motion of the Solar system is INCORRECT?

(*a*) The orbital-radius of planets sweep out equal areas in equal intervals of time.
(*b*) The orbital speed of planets is constant throughout their respective orbits.
(*c*) Planets revolve in anticlockwise direction relative to a point above the plane of planetary motion.
(*d*) At least one focus of the elliptical orbit of each planet lies at the same point.

3. Choose the CORRECT combination for the following two statements

Statement-I: The correct order of magnetic chrons from the oldest to the youngest is Gilbert-Gauss-Matuyama-andBruhnes.

Statement -II: Magnetic chrons Gilbert and Matuyama are reverse whereas Gauss and Bruhnes are normal.

(*a*) Both statements I and II are correct.
(*b*) Both statements I and II are incorrect.
(*c*) Statement I is correct and statement II is incorrect.
(*d*) Statement I is incorrect and statement II is correct.

4. Body waves ________ .

(*a*) can travel through vacuum
(*b*) have cylindrical wavefronts
(*c*) are mechanical waves
(*d*) are known as ground roll

5. The acceleration due to gravity (g) begins to fall sharply towards the centre of the Earth from the ________ discontinuity.

(*a*) Conrad (*b*) Mohorovicic
(*c*) Gutenberg (*d*) Lehmann

6. Which one of the following lists ONLY kinematic parameters?

(*a*) Force, translation, rotation.
(*b*) Translation, rotation, distortion.
(*c*) Stress, distortion, translation.
(*d*) Force, stress, strain.

7. The plunge of the normal to the axial planes of vertical and upright folds is.

(*a*) 0° (*b*) 45°
(*c*) 60° (*d*) 90°

8. Which one of the following rocks is associated with metamorphic thermal aureoles?

(*a*) Chlorite schist (*b*) Amphibolite
(*c*) Hornfels (*d*) Glaucophane schist

9. Which one of the following clay minerals contain potassium (K)?

(*a*) Illite (*b*) Kaolinite
(*c*) Montmorillonite (*d*) Vermiculite

10. Which one of the following sequences of minerals CORRECTLY list an increasing rate of dissolution during chemical weathering?

(*a*) Olivine-Quartz-Pyroxene-Orthoclase
(*b*) Quartz-Orthoclase-Pyroxene-Olivine
(*c*) Olivine-Pyroxene-Orthoclase-Quartz
(*d*) Quartz-Olivine-Orthoclase-Pyroxene

11. Which one of the following combination of reservoir and cap rock respectively, is suitable for oil accumulation?

(*a*) Limestone-Sandstone
(*b*) Dolomite-Evaporite
(*c*) Sandstone-Conglomerate
(*d*) Shale-Limestone

12. Bituminous coal is found in ________ .

(*a*) Neyveli (*b*) Panandhro
(*c*) Singareni (*d*) Vastan

13. Extinction of Trilobites is associated with which one of the following geological time boundaries?

(*a*) Ordovician-Silurian

(*b*) Permian-Triassic

(*c*) Triassic-Jurassic

(*d*) Cretaceous-Palaeogene

14. Transmissivity of an aquifer is the product of __________ .

(*a*) saturated thickness and storitivity

(*b*) hydraulic conductivity and storitivity

(*c*) saturated thickness and hydraulic conductivity

(*d*) saturated thickness and hydraulic head

15. Which one of the following is only a correction and not a reduction in the computation of gravity anomalies with respect to a datum?

(*a*) Free air (*b*) Bouguer

(*c*) Terrain (*d*) Isostatic

16. The difference in the mobility of ions in the electrolyte and electrons in metallic conductors in the sub-surface due to applied external electric field gives rise to __________ .

(*a*) electrode polarization

(*b*) membrane polarization

(*c*) electro-kinetic potential

(*d*) electro-chemical potential

17. A high frequency acoustic wave propagating in a gas saturated sandstone formation exhibits an increase in __________ .

(*a*) frequency (*b*) velocity

(*c*) wavelength (*d*) wave number

18. Which one of the following logging methods uses a radioactive source in the sonde?

(*a*) Natural Gamma ray

(*b*) Gamma-Gamma

(*c*) Natural Gamma ray spectroscopy

(*d*) Nuclear Magnetic Resonance (NMR)

19. Isodynamic contours of the geomagnetic field represent lines of equal .

(*a*) inclination (*b*) declination

(*c*) total field intensity (*d*) magnetic potential

20. A Very Low Frequency (VLF) electromagnetic survey is conducted for the delineation of 2-D conducting mineralization located at 50 m depth from the surface with different geological formations as the overburden layer. For which of the following geological overburden layers given below, will the VLF method fail to yield response?

(*a*) Granite

(*b*) Snow

(*c*) Dry sand

(*d*) Saline water saturated sand

21. Assuming Airy isostatic compensation, the depth to the Moho from a point located 2 km above the mean sea level is _____ km. (round off to 1 decimal place).

(The depth of compensation T for the crust at mean sea level is 30 km, the density of crust and upper mantle are 2.67 gm/cc and 3.30 gm/cc, respectively).

22. On Survey of India Toposheet number $45\frac{D}{16}$, the distance between two points is 18 cm.

The actual ground distance between these two points is __________ km.

23. For a dam site investigation, drilling was carried out up to a depth of 20 m. The total length of recovered core pieces, each over 100 mm, add up to 16 m. The Rock Quality

Designation (RQD) of the foundation rock mass is __________ %.

24. Given that $\left(\frac{^{18}O}{^{16}O}\right)_{V-SMOW} = 2005.2 \times 10^{-6}$, the $\left(\frac{^{18}O}{^{16}O}\right)$ of a sample whose $(\delta^{18}O)_{V-SMOW} = +25‰$ is __________ $\times 10^{-6}$ (round off to 1 decimal place).

25. The shear wave velocity in an igneous rock with a density of 2.7 gm/cc and rigidity modulus of 24.3 GPa is _____ km/s. (round off to 1 decimal place).

PART-B
GEOLOGY

Q. 26 - Q. 55 carry two marks each.

26. Stream power is the product of specific weight of water with __________ .

(*a*) hydraulic radius and Manning roughness coefficient

(*b*) wetted perimeter and slope

(*c*) slope and discharge

(*d*) discharge and Manning roughness coefficient

27. Match the landforms given in Group I to the causative process in Group II

Group I	Group II
P. Seif	1. Coastal
Q. Spit	2. Aeolian
R. Levee	3. Glacial
S. Drumlin	4. Fluvial

(*a*) P-2; Q-3; R-1; S-4 (*b*) P-1; Q-2; R-4; S-3

(*c*) P-4; Q-3; R-1; S-2 (*d*) P-2; Q-1; R-4; S-3

28. In a thrust fault exhibiting ramp and flat geometry which one of the following pairs defines a **Flat**?

Fault dip	**Bedding dip**
(I) 0°	20°N
(II) 30°N	30°S
(III) 40°S	40°N
(IV) 60°N	60°N

(*a*) I (*b*) II

(*c*) III (*d*) IV

29. In the given diagram, which one of the combinations CORRECTLY lists structures typically developed at I, II, III, IV?

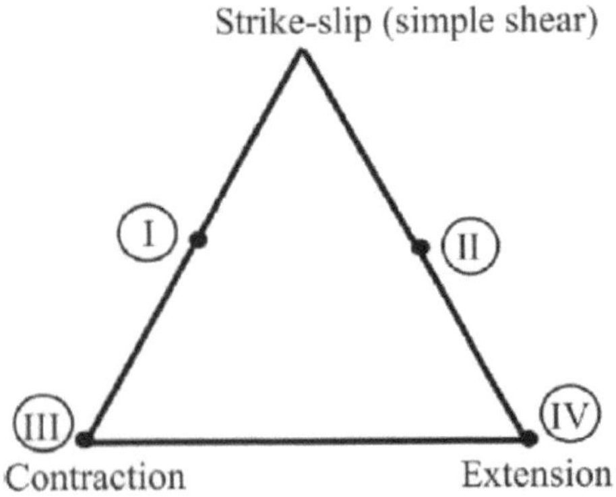

(*a*) I-pressure ridge, II-thrust, III-horst, IV-pull-apart basin

(*b*) I- pull-apart basin, II-thrust, III-horst, IV-pressure ridge

(*c*) I-pressure ridge, II-pull-apart basin, Ill-thrust, IV-horst

(*d*) I- pull-apart basin, II- pressure ridge, III-horst, IV-thrust

30. The best developed lineation and foliation traces in a L-S tectonite will be observed on a plane _____ .

(*a*) parallel to the lineation and foliation

(*b*) perpendicular to the lineation and foliation

(*c*) perpendicular to the foliation but parallel to the lineation

(*d*) perpendicular to the lineation but parallel to the foliation

31. Match the type of twinning (Group I) with the mineral (Group II) that best exhibits it

Group I	**Group II**
P. Carlsbad	1. Rutile
Q. Pericline	2. Quartz
R. Brazil	3. Orthoclase
S. Geniculated (elbow)	4. Plagioclase

(*a*) P-3, Q-4, R-2, S-4

(*b*) P-2, Q-4, R-1, S-3

(*c*) P-3, Q-1, R-2, S-4

(*d*) P-2, Q-1, R-3, S-4

32. On inserting a first order red interference filter in SE-NW direction, the interference figure of quartz shows

(*a*) blue in NE, SW quadrants and yellow in NW, SE quadrants.

(*b*) yellow in NE, SW quadrants and blue in NW, SE quadrants.

(*c*) blue in NE, NW quadrants and yellow in SW, SE quadrants.

(*d*) yellow in NE, NW quadrants and blue in SW, SE quadrants.

33. Choose the CORRECT combination for the following two statements.

Statement I: Four elements that make up about 90% of the bulk Earth are Fe, O, Si and Mg (in decreasing order of wt % abundance).

Statement II: The four most abundant elements in the Earth's crust (in decreasing order of wt % abundance) are O, Si, Al and Fe.

(*a*) Both Statements I and II are correct.

(*b*) Both Statements I and II are incorrect.

(*c*) Statement I is correct and Statement II is incorrect.

(*d*) Statement I is incorrect and Statement II is correct.

34. Choose the CORRECT combination for the following four statements.

Statement I: Anhydrous partial melting of peridotites produces basaltic magma.

Statement II: Hydrous melting of peridotites produces andesitic magma.

Statement III: Congruent melting of minerals produces liquids of compositions identical to the minerals.

Statement IV: Incongruent melting of minerals produces liquids of different compositions and new solids.

(*a*) All the four statements I to IV are correct.

(*b*) Statements I, II and III are correct but statement IV is incorrect.

(*c*) Statements I and II are correct but statements III and IV are incorrect.

(*d*) All the four statements I to IV are incorrect.

35. The value of salinity, in terms of wt.% NaCl equivalent, of an aqueous saline bi-phase liquid-vapour fluid inclusions is determined by measurement of____ during microthermometry.

(*a*) last ice-melting temperature

(*b*) dissolution temperature of halite

(*c*) eutectic temperature

(*d*) homogenization temperature

36. Which of the following case (s) represent (s) textural inversion in sandstone?

Case I: Rounded grains in clayey matrix.

Case II: Rounded, but poorly sorted grains.

(*a*) Only case I.

(*b*) Only case II.

(*c*) Both cases I and II.

(*d*) Neither case I nor case II.

37. Which one of the following set of statements regarding the overall nature of marine shelf succession is CORRECT?

Statement I: Transgressive systems tract deposit is deepening upward Statement II: Highstand systems tract deposit is deepening upward Statement III: Falling stage systems tract deposit is deepening upward Statement IV: Lowstand systems tract deposit is overall shallowing upward

(*a*) I and II (*b*) II and III

(*c*) III and IV (*d*) I and IV

38. Which of the following set of statements is CORRECT?

Statement I: A well sorted sandstone bed showing current ripple, planar laminae, convolute laminae and prod marks.

Statement II: A poorly sorted sandstone bed showing wave ripples, dish structure, pillar structure and groove casts.

Statement III: A well sorted sandstone bed showing desiccation cracks, current crescent planar laminae and convolute laminae.

Statement IV: A poorly sorted sandstone bed showing current ripple, planar laminae, skip marks and load casts.

(*a*) 1,11 and III (*b*) 11,111 and IV

(*c*) I, III and IV (*d*) I, II and IV

39. In metamafites, which one of the following mineral assemblages is stable under green schist facies conditions?

(*a*) Albite + Chlorite + Actinolite + Epidote

(*b*) Andesine + Biotite + Hornblende

(*c*) Oligoclase + Biotite + Hornblende

(*d*) Oligoclase + Epidote + Biotite + Hornblende

40. Match the type of metamorphism listed in Group I with their products in Group II.

Group I	**Group II**
P. Contact metamorphism	1. Impactite
Q. Shear zone metamorphism	2. Spillite
R. Ocean floor metamorphism	3. Mylonite
S. Shock metamorphism	4. Skarn

(*a*) P-4, Q-3, R-2, S-1 (*b*) P-2, Q-3, R-4, S-1

(*c*) P-3, Q-1, R-2, S-4 (*d*) P-1, Q-2, R-3, S-4

41. Glaucophane schist forms in .

(*a*) subduction zones (*b*) pull-apart basins

(*c*) continental rifts (*d*) mid-oceanic ridges

42. Which one of the following statements is CORRECT about bivalve habitat?

(*a*) *Gryphaea* is a burrowing variety.

(*b*) *Pholas* is a free lying form.

(*c*) *Lucina* is a boring variety.

(*d*) *Mytilus* is a bysally attached form.

43. Match foraminifera in Group I with its wall structure in Group II

Group I	**Group II**
P. *Fusulina*	1. Hyaline
Q. *Cibicides*	2. Porcellaneous
R. *Textularia*	3. Microgranular
S. *Quinqueloculina*	4. Agglutinated

(*a*) P-1, Q-2, R-3, S-4 (*b*) P-3, Q-2, R-4, S-1

(*c*) P-4, Q-3, R-2, S-1 (*d*) P-3, Q-1, R-4, S-2

44. Which one of the following stratigraphic units represents the CORRECT order of younging?

(*a*) Trichinopally Group - Uttatur Group - Ariyalur Group - Niniyur Group

(*b*) Kopili Formation - Sylhet Formation - Barail Formation - Boka Bil Formation

(*c*) Chinji Formation - Nagri Formation - Dhok Pathan Formation - Tatrot Formation

(*d*) Barakar Formation - Talchir Formation - Barren Measures - Raniganj Formation

45. Match the Formation names in Group I with their dominant lithology in Group II

Group I	**Group II**
P. Hanseran Formation	1. Sandstone
Q. Nagthat Formation	2. Limestone
R. Bijli Formation	3. Evaporite
S. Shahbad Formation	4. Volcanics

(*a*) P-3, Q-2, R-1, S-4 (*b*) P-2, Q-1, R-3, S-4

(*c*) P-3, Q-1, R-4, S-2 (*d*) P-4, Q-1, R-2, S-3

46. Match the economic deposits in Group I with their occurrence in stratigraphic units in Group II

Group I	**Group II**
P. Phosphate	1. Sargur Group
Q. Manganese	2. Nallamalai Group
R. Chromite	3. Udaipur Formation
S. Barite	4. Mansar Formation

(*a*) P-1, Q-3, R-4, S-2 (*b*) P-3, Q-4, R-2, S-1
(*c*) P-2, Q-1, R-4, S-3 (*d*) P-3, Q-4, R-1, S-2

47. Match the basin type in Group I with Indian example provided in Group II

Group I	**Group II**
P. Foreland basin	1. Kerala-Konkan
Q. Passive margin	2. Cambay
R. Fore-arc	3. Ganga
S. Failed rift	4. Andaman

(*a*) P-3, Q-2, R-4, S-1 (*b*) P-3, Q-1, R-4, S-2
(*c*) P-4, Q-1, R-3, S-2 (*d*) P-1, Q-2, R-4, S-3

48. Choose the CORRECT set of statements.

Statement I: The hydrocarbon source rock in Cambay basin is of Jurassic age.

Statement II: Borholla field is in Assam basin.

Statement III: Toulene is an aromatic hydrocarbon.

Statement IV: Porosity of a reservoir rock increases with increase in sorting.

(*a*) I, II and III (*b*) II, III and IV
(*c*) I and IV (*d*) I and III only

49. The figure given below represents a scatter plot of Digital Numbers (DN) of Band 4 and Band 5 of a satellite imagery. The fields of Class A and Class B are indicated by the rectangular boxes along with their class means (open circles). Class assignment for the point P by Minimum Distance to Mean (MDM) and Nearest Neighbour (NN) algorithms are _____ .

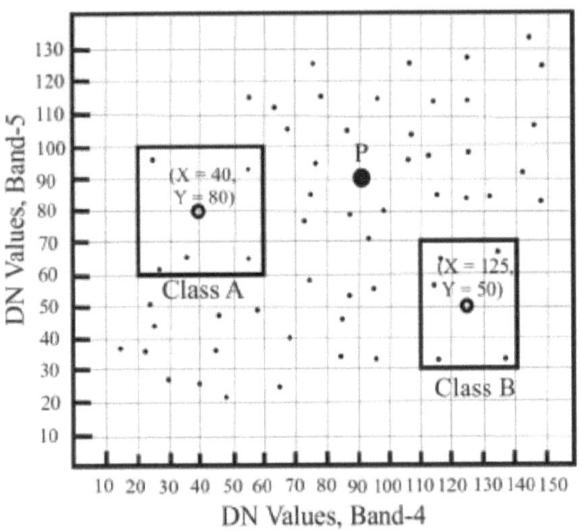

(*a*) Class A by MDM and class B by NN
(*b*) Class A by NN and class B by MDM
(*c*) Class A by both MDM and NN
(*d*) Class B by both MDM and NN

50. Hydrogeological setup of a hypothetical alluvial area (where contact X-Y between two sands is vertical) is given in the schematic section. Hydraulic heads are indicated as hi, h2 and hydraulic conductivities as Kl and K2. The hydraulic head at the contact (X-Y) is _______ m. (round off to 2 decimal places).

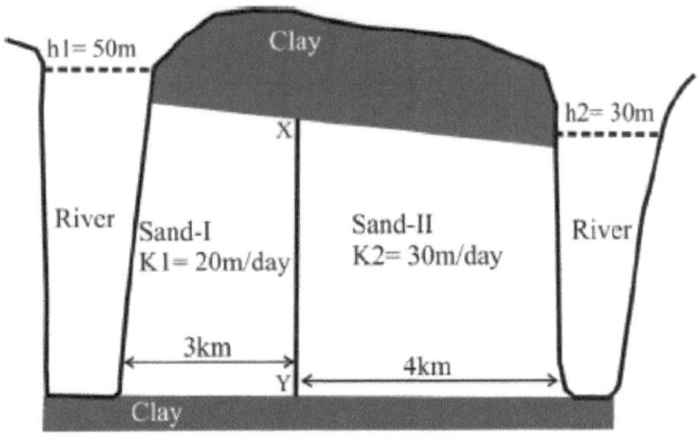

51. The normalized longitudinal profile of a river is given below. The Concavity Index of the river is ____ %.

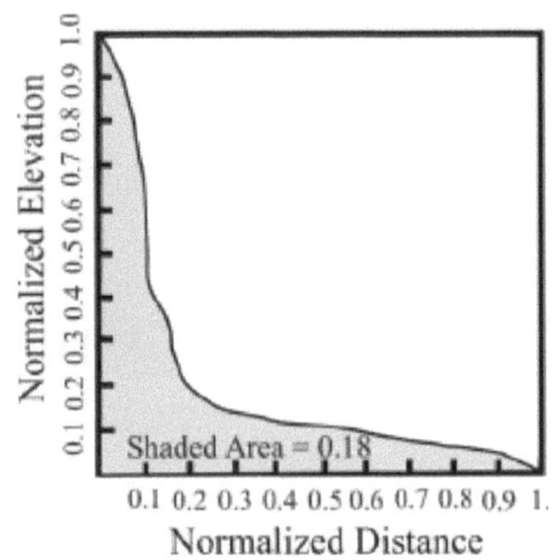

52. For producing 1 kg of gold from an ore having an assay of 2 ppm Au, _________ $\times 10^3$ kg of ore needs to be processed.

53. A cylindrical core of granite with a radius of 25 mm was subjected to point load test. The load was applied parallel to the diameter of the core and the failure load was 20 kN. The unconnected point load strength index isMPa.

54. A hypothetical garnet peridotite composed of 60% olivine, 25% orthopyroxene, 10% clinopyroxene and 5% garnet undergoes 10% batch melting described by $\frac{C_L}{C_O} = \frac{1}{F + D - F * D}$ where F is degree of melting and D is bulk partition coefficient. The ratio of Ce in the melt to the original rock will be ________ . (round off to 2 decimal places).

(The K_D values of Ce for olivine, orthopyroxene, clinopyroxene and garnet are 0.001, 0.003, 0.10 and 0.02, respectively)

55. ^{87}Rb decays to ^{87}Sr with a decay constant $\lambda = 1.42$ 10^{-11} per year. If at the time of formation, a system contains 8×10^4 atoms of ^{87}Rb and 10^3 atoms of ^{87}Sr, the number of ^{87}Sr atoms in this system at the end of 4 half-lives will be _______ $\times 10^3$. Assume close system evolution for parent-daughter pair.

GEOPHYSICS

Q. 56 - Q. 85 carry two marks each.

56. The Young's modulus 'E' is related to the Lame's parameter 'A,' for a Poisson solid as

(a) $E = 2.5\lambda$, (b) $E = 1.5\lambda$

(c) $E = \lambda$ (d) $E = 0.5\lambda$

57. Which one of the following seismic phases is the earliest arrival in the P shadow zone?

(a) PKiKP (b) PPP

(c) P_{diff} (d) PKIKP

58. A reversed refraction survey was done over a two layered medium with the interface between them dipping at an angle of 15°. The velocities in the upper and lower medium are V_1 and V_2 respectively, with $V_2 > V_1$. If the critical angle is 45°, then, which one of the following is CORRECT? (V_u and V_d are updip and downdip velocities).

(a) $V_1 = V_d = V_u$ (b) $V_u > Vd > V_1$

(c) $V_1 > V_d < V_u$ (d) $V_u < V_d > V_1$

59. In a migrated seismic time section _______ .

(a) both synclines and anticlines appear tighter

(b) both synclines and anticlines appear broader

(c) synclines appear tighter and anticlines appear broader

(d) synclines appear broader and anticlines appear tighter

60. Which one of the following is CORRECT for the density porosity (ϕ_D) and neutron porosity (ϕ_N) estimated for a finely interbedded organic-rich, shaly sandstone formation relative to those for a shale-free sandstone formation at shallow depths?

(a) ϕ_N decreases and ϕ_D increases.

(b) ϕ_N increases and ϕ_D decreases.

(c) Both ϕ_N and ϕ_D decrease.

(d) Both ϕ_N and ϕ_D increase.

61. Which one of the following statements is INCORRECT with regard to Nuclear Magnetic Resonance (NMR) logging? (ϕ_{NMR} - NMR derived total porosity, ϕ_D - Density porosity)

(a) The relaxation time (T2) decreases with decrease in pore size.

(b) The ϕ_{NMR} is greater than ϕ_D in a water saturated sandstone formation.

(c) The NMR logs provide lithology independent measurement of total porosity.

(d) The ϕ_{NMR} is less than ϕ_D in a gas saturated shaly sandstone formation.

62. A 3-D seismic tomography experiment was carried out with an inter-station spacing of 'X' km. The subsurface velocity perturbations in three dimensional blocks were estimated with block size of '2X'km and '0.5X'km in case 1 and case 2, respectively. Which one of the following statements is CORRECT?

(a) The spatial resolution is poor and variance is small for case 1.

(b) The spatial resolution is good and variance is small for case 2.

(c) The spatial resolution is good and variance is large for case 1.

(d) The spatial resolution is poor and variance is large for case 2.

63. A shallow focus, Great earthquake with seismic moment of 2.5×10^{40} dyne-cm is recorded at an epicentral distance of 50°. The body wave magnitude (mb), surface wave magnitude (Ms) and moment magnitude (Mw) were estimated. Which one of the following is CORRECT?

(a) mb > Ms > Mw

(b) mb = Ms = Mw

(c) mb < Ms < Mw

(d) mb < Ms > Mw

64. A pair of current electrodes C1 (+1) and C2 (–1) is placed 50m apart (shown in the figure below) over a homogeneous structure of resistivity 100 Ωm and 1 Ampere current flows through the subsurface. Which one of the following is CORRECT for the potential (V_p) and horizontal component of electric field (Ex) at a point P located exactly below the midpoint between Cl and C2 at a depth of 10 m?

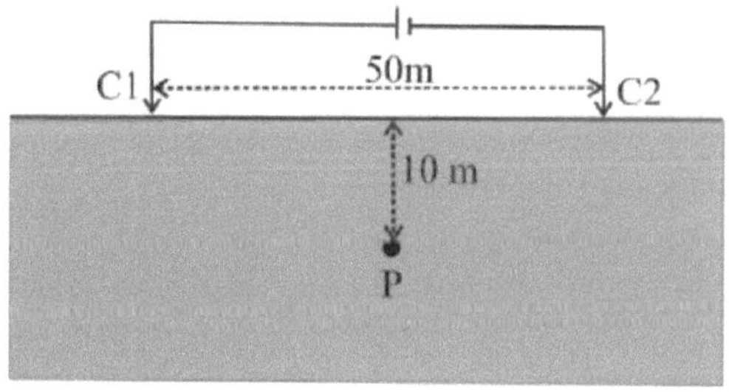

(a) $V_p = 0$ and $E_x = 0$

(b) $V_p = 0$ and $E_x \neq 0$

(c) $Vp \neq 0$ and $E_x = 0$

(d) $V_p \neq 0$ and $E_x \neq 0$

65. A massive sulphide body in the subsurface is partially above the water table. According to the pH variation hypothesis for the origin of Self Potential, which one of the following statements is CORRECT for such a body?

(*a*) Acidic above and basic below the water table.

(*b*) Basic above and acidic below the water table.

(*c*) Acidic above and below the water table.

(*d*) Basic above and below the water table.

66. The phase difference between the input and output signals for a 'Compensator device' used in electromagnetic prospecting to nullify the effect of primary field at the receiver coil is ________.

(*a*) 0° (*b*) 45°

(*c*) 90° (*d*) 180°

67. In an electromagnetic scale modeling experiment in the lab, the relation between the field and lab geometrical scaling factor (n) with the field and lab resistivity (p_f & p_m) as well frequencies (f_f & f_m) will be ________ .

(subscripts f and m refer to field and lab systems and n >> 1)

(*a*) $n^2 = \left(\frac{\rho_f}{\rho_m}\right)\left(\frac{f_m}{f_f}\right)$ (*b*) $n^2 = \left(\frac{\rho_f}{\rho_m}\right)\left(\frac{f_f}{f_m}\right)$

(*c*) $n^2 = \left(\frac{\rho_f}{\rho_f}\right)\left(\frac{f_m}{f_f}\right)$ (*d*) $n^2 = \left(\frac{\rho_m}{\rho_f}\right)\left(\frac{f_f}{f_m}\right)$

68. If G(ω) is the Fourier transform of *g*(*t*), then the Fourier transform of *g*(*t* + *ln* 2) will be ________ .

(*a*) *e*-2*i0*/*G*(*a*>) (*b*) e2jwG(w)

(*c*) 2eJWG(w) (*d*) 2*e*-*Ja*>*G*(*a*>)

69. The primary objective of 'Regularization' in geophysical inversion is to________.

(*a*) improve the resolution

(*b*) reduce the non-uniqueness

(*c*) enhance the condition number

(*d*) stabilize the inversion process

70. P is a point on the Earth's surface defined by radius (r), colatitude (θ), and longitude (ϕ) in spherical coordinate system. The three components of the magnetic induction 'B' at P in Cartesian coordinate system are B_x, B_y and B_z (x-North, y-East and z-downward). For the relation B = –∇V (V is the magnetic potential), the B_x, B_y, and B_z can be expressed in spherical coordinate system as ________.

(*a*) $B_x = \frac{\partial V}{\partial \theta}, \; B_y = -\frac{1}{r\sin\theta}\frac{\partial V}{\partial \varnothing}, \; B_z = \frac{1}{r}\frac{\partial V}{\partial r}$

(*b*) $B_x = \frac{1}{r}\frac{\partial V}{\partial r}, \; B_y = -\frac{1}{r\sin\theta}\frac{\partial V}{\partial \varnothing}, \; B_z = \frac{\partial V}{\partial \theta}$

(*c*) $B_x = \frac{1}{r}\frac{\partial V}{\partial \theta}, \; B_y = -\frac{1}{r\sin\theta}\frac{\partial V}{\partial \varnothing}, \; B_z = \frac{\partial V}{\partial r}$

(*d*) $B_x = \frac{\partial V}{\partial \theta}, \; B_y = \frac{1}{r\sin\theta}\frac{\partial V}{\partial \varnothing}, \; B_z = \frac{1}{r}\frac{\partial V}{\partial r}$

71. In gravity anomalies, the 'Indirect effect' mainly arises from________.

(*a*) the sources outside the area of investigation

(*b*) improper instrument drift

(*c*) effect of mass lying between the geoid and ellipsoid

(*d*) short-wavelength uncompensated masses in the subsurface

72. For defining the axial geocentric magnetic dipole of the Earth's magnetic field using the spherical harmonic expression for magnetic potential, the three non-zero Gauss coefficients for n = 1 are____.

(*a*) g_0^0, g_1^0, h_1^0 (*b*) g_1^0, g_1^1, h_1^1

(*c*) g_1^0, g_1^1, h_1^0 (*d*) g_1^0, g_1^1, h_0^0

73. The flexural rigidity (*d*) of the oceanic lithosphere (assuming no secondary thermal perturbations) ________.

(*a*) increases with both age and plate cooling

(*b*) decreases with age and increases with plate cooling

(*c*) increases with age and decreases with plate thickness

(*d*) decreases with both age and plate thickness

74. If ΔJ and Δσ are the uniform magnetization and density contrasts respectively, of a point source, the relation between the vertical components of the gravity (g_z) and magnetic (T_z) anomalies can be expressed (neglecting long-wavelength component) as ________.

(G is Gravitational constant)

(*a*) $T_z = G\frac{\Delta J}{\Delta\sigma}\frac{\partial g_z}{\partial z}$ (*b*) $T_z = \frac{G}{2\pi}\frac{\Delta J}{\Delta\sigma}\frac{\partial g_z}{\partial z}$

(*c*) $T_z = \frac{1}{G}\frac{\Delta J}{\Delta\sigma}\frac{\partial g_z}{\partial z}$ (*d*) $T_z = \frac{1}{G}\frac{\Delta\sigma}{\Delta J}\frac{\partial g_z}{\partial z}$

75. Which one of the following statements about the gravity anomalies on land is CORRECT?

(*a*) Free-air and Bouguer anomalies are always positively correlated with elevation

(*b*) Isostatic anomalies are not useful to understand the crustal heterogeneities

(*c*) Vertical derivatives are used to enhance the gravity effects of deep-seated bodies

(*d*) X-horizontal gradient $\left(\frac{\partial g}{\partial x}\right)$ map enhances / sharpens anomalies of bodies trending N-S (X-East, Y-North, Z-downward).

76. An aeromagnetic survey is conducted over an area with outcropping magnetic sources. The aircraft is flying at a height of 250 m with a speed of 200 km/hour. In order to fully define the magnetic anomalies along the flight path, the largest sampling rate of measurement by a Proton Precession Magnetometer will be _______ seconds, (round off to the nearest integer).

77. In an abandoned mine-site, three hollow spherical cavities are located below the surface centered at depths of 50, 100 and 150 metres. Assuming that residual gravity is low due to each one of these cavities are small (~ 0.05 mGal), do not interfere and can be detected by the gravimeter, the most ideal (largest) grid spacing for carrying out the gravity surveys in order to correctly delineate these cavities is _________ metres, (round off to the nearest integer).

78. A split-spread reflection survey is carried out along a profile in the direction of the dipping interface. The difference in arrival times of the reflected waves from the interface at two geophones with an offset distance of 1000 m from the shot-point on both sides is 20 msec. If the velocity of the layer above the dipping interface is 3000 m/s, then the dip of the bed is _______ degrees, (round off to 1 decimal place).

(Assumption 2d >> X, where 'd' is depth below the shot-point normal to the interface and X is the source-geophone spacing)

79. The bulk resistivity of a carbonate formation having 10% porosity which is 75% saturated with hydrocarbons is 500 Ωm. The bulk resistivity of the formation when the porosity is doubled and 100% saturated with water is ______ ohm-metres, (round off to 1 decimal place).

(Assume the tortuosity, cementation factor and saturation exponent to be 1, 2 and 2, respectively).

80. In a seismogram of a shallow focus (h = 5 km) earthquake, the difference between the arrival times of the S and P phases is 1.34 s. Assuming the average P wave velocity of the crust to be 6.0 km/s and the Poisson's ratio to be 0.27, the epicentral distance is ________ kilometres, (round off to 1 decimal place)

81. A Two-electrode array is placed over a vertical contact (2-D) as shown in the given figure (strike of contact is perpendicular to the plane of paper). If 1 Amp current flows through the subsurface, then the potential at the potential electrode PI will be ________ millivolts. (round off to the nearest integer).

(Consider structures with resistivity ρ1 and ρ2 to be laterally extending to infinity on both sides of the contact and also in the downward direction, C2 and P2 are grounded at infinity) (Use $\pi = 3.14$)

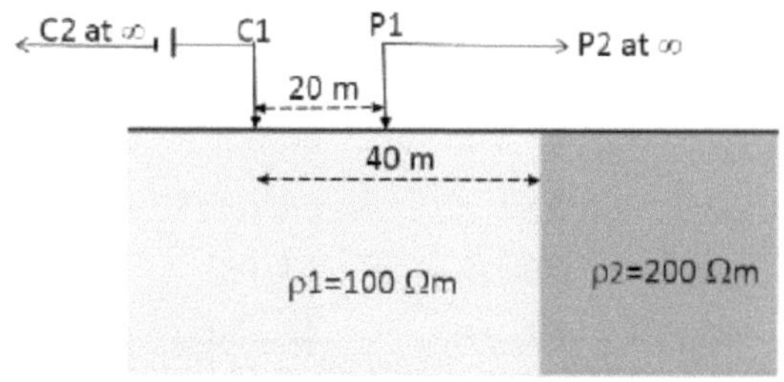

82. In an electrical resistivity imaging survey, Axial Dipole-dipole array is placed over an inhomogeneous structure. The centers of current and potential dipoles are separated by a distance of 100 m. The length of each dipole is 10 m. If 5 Amp current flows through the subsurface and 50 mV potential difference is measured across the potential dipole then apparent resistivity will be ________ ohm-metres, (round off to the nearest integer) (Use $\pi = 3.14$)

83. In an electromagnetic land survey, the resultant field (primary and secondary) at any point P makes an angle of 60° from the vertical. A 30 mV signal is observed in the receiver coil placed in a horizontal position at point P. The magnitude of the signal in the receiver coil when the plane of the receiver coil is perpendicular to the resultant field is ________ milli Volts.

84. A vibroseis source sweeps acoustic signal in the frequency range 10 Hz – 100 Hz. The maximum sampling interval to correctly recover the recorded signal will be _________ milliseconds.

85. The abundance of ^{234}U in secular equilibrium with its parent ^{238}U will be ________ $\times 10^{-3}$ %.

(Given Half-life ($T_{1/2}$) of ^{238}U and ^{234}U are 4.467×10^9 y and 2.44×10^5 y, respectively, and abundance of ^{238}U is 99.28%)(round off to 2 decimal places)

ANSWERS

(General Aptitude)

1. (*c*) **2.** (*c*) **3.** (*c*) **4.** (*c*) **5.** (*a*) **6.** (*c*) **7.** (*a*) **8.** (*c*)
9. (*b*) **10.** (*d*)

PART A (Common Part)

1. (*c*) **2.** (*b*) **3.** (*a*) **4.** (*c*) **5.** (*c*) **6.** (*b*) **7.** (*a*) **8.** (*c*)
9. (*a*) **10.** (*b*) **11.** (*b*) **12.** (*c*) **13.** (*b*) **14.** (*c*) **15.** (*c*) **16.** (*a*)
17. (*c*) **18.** (*b*) **19.** (*c*) **20.** (*d*) **21.** (40.47) **22.** (9 km) **23.** (80%)
24. (2055.33) **25.** (3 km/s)

PART-B (Geology)

26. (*c*) **27.** (*d*) **28.** (*d*) **29.** (*c*) **30.** (*c*) **31.** (*a*) **32.** (*a, b*) **33.** (*a*)
34. (*a*) **35.** (*a*) **36.** (*c*) **37.** (*d*) **38.** (*d*) **39.** (*a*) **40.** (*a*) **41.** (*a*)
42. (*d*) **43.** (*d*) **44.** (*c*) **45.** (*c*) **46.** (*d*) **47.** (*b*) **48.** (*b*) **49.** (*a*)
50. (39.40) **51.** (64) **52.** (500) **53.** (8 MPa) **54.** (8.99) **55.** (75.97)

(Geophysics)

56. (*a*) **57.** (*c*) **58.** (*b*) **59.** (*d*) **60.** (*d*) **61.** (*b*) **62.** (*a*) **63.** (*c*)
64. (*b*) **65.** (*a*) **66.** (*d*) **67.** (*a*) **68.** (*c*) **69.** (*d*) **70.** (*c*) **71.** (*c*)
72. (*b*) **73.** (*a*) **74.** (*c*) **75.** (*d*) **76.** (2 to 2) **77.** (38 to 39) **78.** (1.6 to 18)
79. (7.7 to 7.9) **80.** (8.8 to 9.2) **81.** (880 to 890) **82.** (305 to 315)
83. (60 to 60) **84.** (5 to 5) **85.** (5.40 to 5.44)

EXPLANATIONS

(GENERAL APTITUDE SECTION)

1. Inthis question the award is given to dead fishermen so To whom is fitting correct here.

2. Using Venn diagram.

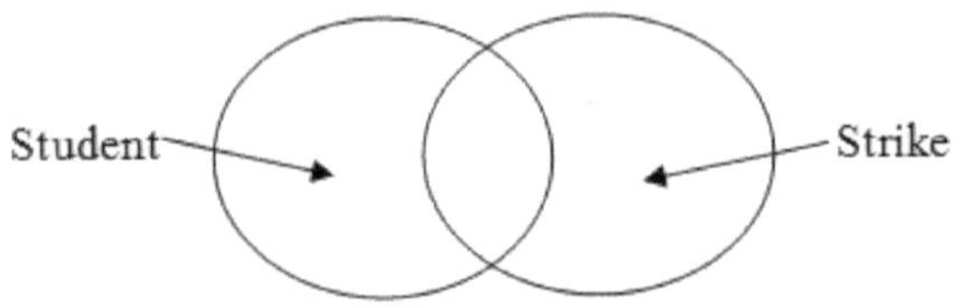

Therefore, some students who were not involve in the strike were students is logically true.

3. Initial volume of cone is $(1/3)\pi r^2 h$

After 10% increment in height and radius of the cone,

The new volume will be $(1/3)\,\pi\,(1.1r)^2(1.1h)$.

Now % increment in volume

= (final volume – initial volume)/ initial volume

$= ((1/3)\,\pi\,(1.1r)^2(1.1h) - (1/3)\pi r^2 h) * 100 /(1/3)\pi r^2 h$

= 33.11%

4. Afterarranging all the numbers in the given order

10, 5, 4, 7, 2

7 is the 2nd place number from right according to question.

5. The sentence is in past form where never is used so defeated is correct filling the position.

6. Statements A and B absolute statements. It was only after the demand banking institutions that the interest rates on small saving schemes were reduced.

Option B is also incorrect, since, had the interest rates on small savings schemes been always maintained on par with fixed interest rates, there would have been no need for the banks to demand deductions in their rates.

Option D is not conclusively derived from the passage given i.e. A reduction in interest rates on small saving schemes can also happen independently of a change in repo rate by the RBI.

Hence only option C is possible under these conditions.

7. **Step 1** – Number of mobile owners = 70% of 1400 million = 980 million

   Step 2 – out of 980 million mobile owners 294 million access internet

   Step 3 – half of 294 million ie. 147 million buy goods from e-commerce portals

   Step 4 – Percent of these buyers in the country

   = (peoples who buy goods from e-commerce portals)/(total population of the country) * 100

   = (147 million/ 1400 million) * 100

   = 10.5%

8.

Medieval nomenclature	Contemporary meaning
Dhrupad	Baani
Gayaki	Vocal
Baaj	Instrumental style
Gharana	lineage

Therefore, Baaj, institution is the only incorrect pair given in the options.

9. Trains are running in opposite direction with 80 km/h in north direction and 100 km/h in south direction respectively from same location at 7 AM.

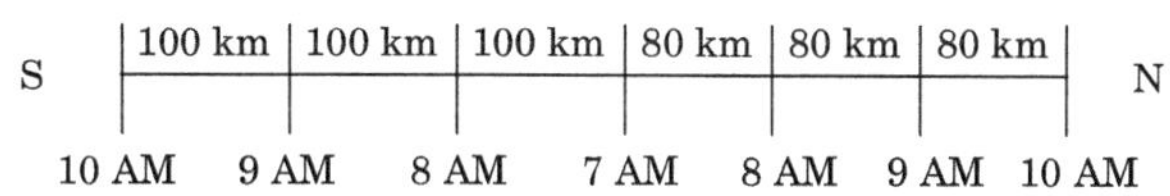

At 10 AM both trains will be 540 km away from each other.

10. Because here the head hunter dependent only on the number of heads that he can bring.

PART A (COMMON PART)

1.

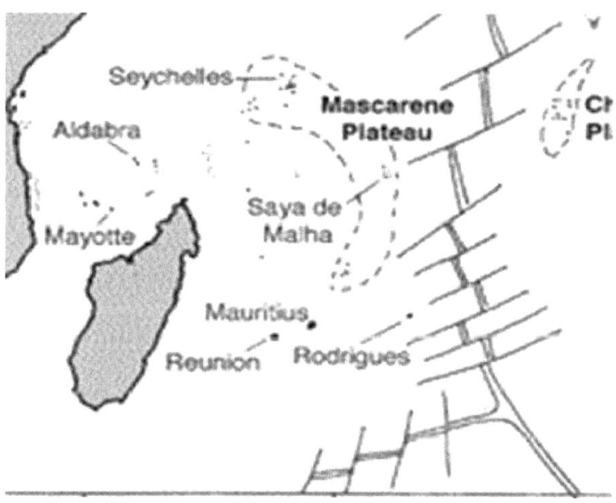

Presently, Reunion is located near to Madagascar and Mauritius.When Reunion hot spot activity took place in past geological time. It sent India on its journey towards the north and remain in the African tectonic plate.

2. When the planets revolve around the sun in an orbital plane they faces successive perigee and apogee. At perigee the speed of planets higher than the speed at apogee.

3. The given order Gilbert-Gauss –Matuyama-Bruhnes is correct sequence from older to younger And after magnetic survey it was found that Gilbert and Matuyama shows Reversal polarity while Gauss and Bruhnes shows Normal magnetic chrons.

4. Body waves travel through the interior of the Earth along paths controlled by the material properties in terms of density and modulus (stiffness). The density and modulus, in turn, vary according to temperature, composition, and material phase. This effect resembles the body waves as mechanical waves.

5. At this discontinuity the gravity falls because of presence of liquid outer core at Gutenberg boundary.

6. A study of the motion causing the geometries within rocks is called kinematicskinematic parameters involves only deformational phases but not force or any stress.

7. Certical upright fold have 0 degree plunge as their axial plane is vertical and no inclination with the imaginary horizontal plane.

8. Hornfels is a metamorphic rock formed by the contact between mudstone / shale, or other clay-rich rock, and a hot igneous body, and represents a heat-altered equivalent of the original rock. This process is termed contact metamorphism. In contact aureoles due to rapid reaction between the country rock and the pluton hornfels rock formed.

9. Illite has chemical composition in which potassium (K+) ion present in high amount. It forms at the early stage of chemical weathering.

10.

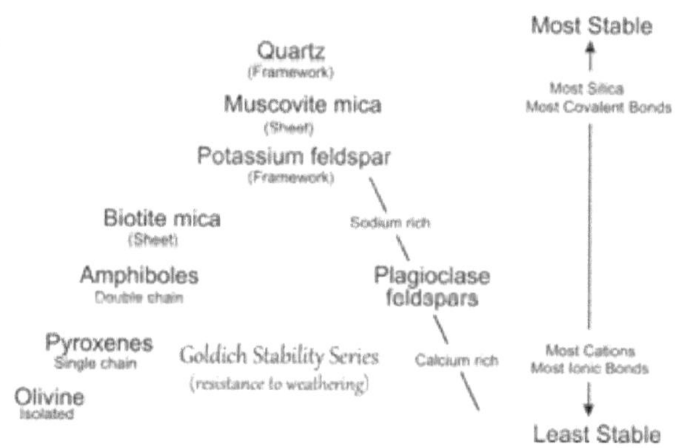

Quartz is more stable and olivine is least stable. Bowen's reaction series shows the mineral which forms first is least stable to chemical weathering.

11. Dolomitization of pre-existing limestones commonly enhances permeability and improves porosity. Dolomitization may have a "homogenizing" effect on a carbonate reservoir, so that vertical and lateral permeability within the reservoir is improved. Because of its low ductility relative to limestone (and sandstone), the reservoir characteristics of dolomite often are enhanced by fracturing.

The ability of evaporites to form highly efficient seals is clearly demonstrated by consideration of the number of hydrocarbon reserves that are sealed by evaporites. Even though evaporites constitute less than 2% of the world's sedimentary rocks (compared to mudstones and shales which comprise 65%), 14 of the world's 25 largest oil fields and 9 of the world's 25 largest gas fields are sealed by evaporites (Grunau, 1987; Warren, 2007).

12. All the coals from lower gondwana is of bituminous quality but remaining is the example of lignite coal. Singareni coal field is located in Andhra Pradesh in Godavari.

13. Trilobites Extinct but not a failure. The trilobitesmay have gone **extinct** (along with 95% of marine species) during the mass **extinction** at the end of the Permian period at the Permian-Triassic boundary which leads to the disappearance of trilobites.

14. Transmissivity of an aquifer is calculated by the following formula.

S = kb, where k = hydraulic conductivity andb

= saturated thickness of the aquifer

15. A **correction** applied to observed values obtained in geophysical surveys in order to remove the effect of variations in the observations due to the topography near observation sites.this correction is always added in gravity correction.

16. In electrochemistry, polarization is a collective term for certain mechanical side-effects (of an electrochemical process) by which isolating barriers develop at the interface between electrode and electrolyte.

17. A high frequency acoustic wave propagating in a gas saturated sandstone formation exhibits an increase in wavelength.

18. This consists of a gamma ray source (e.g. Cesium-137) and a detector so shieldedthat it records only back scattered gammarays - i.e. the Compton scatter. Because the back scatteredradiation depends on electron density.

19. The variation of the magnetic field over the Earth's surface is best illustrated by isomagnetic charts—that is, maps on which lines are drawn through points at which a given magnetic element has the same value. Contours of equal intensity in any of the elements X, Y, Z, H or F are called "isodynamic."

20. The VLF method uses relatively simple instruments and can be a useful reconnaissance tool. Potential targets include tabular conductors in a resistive host rock such as faults in limestone or igneous terrain. The depth of exploration is limited to about 60% to 70% of the skin depth of the surrounding rock or soil. Therefore, the high frequency of the VLF transmitters means that in more conductive environments, the exploration depth is quite shallow; for example, the depth of exploration might be 10 to 12 m in 25-?m material.

Additionally, the presence of conductive overburden seriously suppresses response from basement conductors, and relatively small variations in overburden conductivity or thickness can themselves generate significant VLF anomalies. For this reason, VLF is more effective in areas where the host rock is resistive and the overburden is thin.

So saline water saturated sand is correct answer.

21. Applying Airy hypothesis

$$R = H\ \rho c/(\rho m - \rho c)$$

$$R = 2 * 2.67/(3.30 - 2.67)$$

$$R = 8.47$$

The depth to the Moho from the given point

$$= H + T + R$$

$$= 2 + 30 + 8.47$$

$$= 40.47 \text{ km}$$

22. Using geological scale of 1:50,000 for given Toposheet no.

Scale = map distance / ground distance

1/50000 = 18/ground distance

Ground distance = 18 * 50000

= 9, 00,000 cm

= 9 km

23. RQD = sum of the Length of core samples (more than 10 cm) * 100/total drill length

= 16*100/20

RQD = 80%.

24. VSMOW

= (Oxygen isotope ratio in sample – Oxygen isotope ratio in standard) * 1000/(Oxygen isotope ratio in standard)

Let oxygen isotope ratio in sample is A. putting all the values in the given equation.

+25%= (A – 2005.2 × 10^ – 6) * 1000/2005.2 × 10^ – 6

A = 0.025 * 2005.2 * 10^6 + 2005.2 * 10^ -6

A = (0.025 * 2005.2 + 2005.2) * 10^ – 6

= 2055.33*10^ – 6

25. Shear wave velocity is govern by the following formula:

$$V_s = \sqrt{\mu/\rho}$$

Putting the values in above equation:

$$V_s = \sqrt{(2.43 * 10^9/2.7)}$$

$$V_s = 3 \text{ km/s}$$

PART-B (GEOLOGY)

26. Stream power is defined by the following equation.

Stream power (Ω) = ρg * slope * discharge

Where ρg is the specific weight of water.

Hence slope and discharge are two other products of stream power.

27. Seif landform is formed in Aeolian environment, spit is associated with coastal region, levee is commonly found in fluvialand Drumlin is the glacial landform. So the option D is correct.

28. In a thrust system which shows a Flat geometry the dip of the fault plane and bedding must be equal. So the option D is correct.

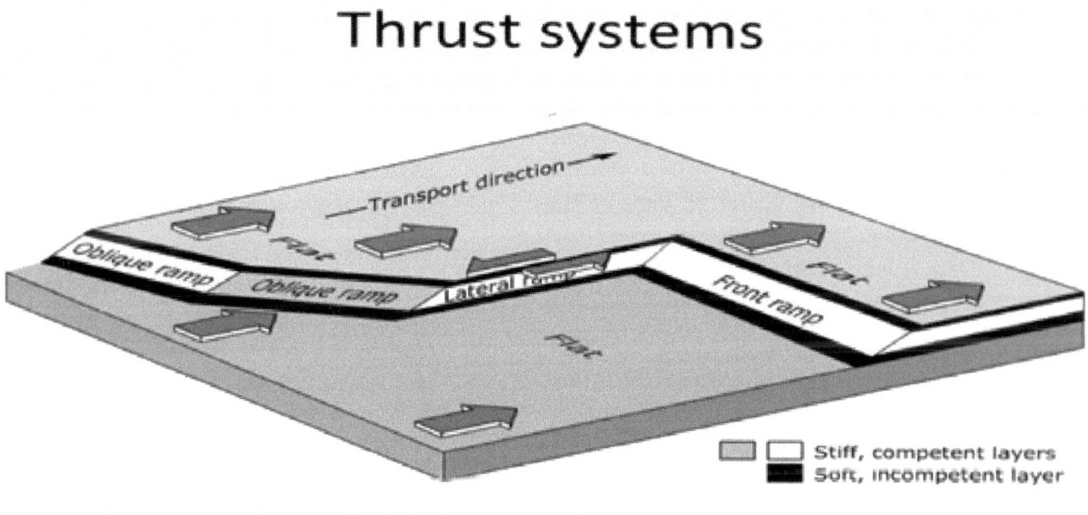

Lateral ramps act like transform faults → also called tear faults

29. In compression zone the development of thrust took place while in extension zone formation of horst and Graben takes place while pull apart basin formed in combination withextension and strike slip boundary. So the option C is right.

30. L-S tectonites have equally developed linear and planar fabric elements and may indicate a plane strain deformation. Many mylonites are L-S tectonites consistent with a simple shear deformation.L-S Tectonites (Plain strain) indicate both elongation and flattening strain.L-S taconites viewed perpendicular to the plane of the S fabric.

31. **Carlsbad** twinning is found in **orthoclase** and **pericline** twinning is found in plagioclase, while **Brazil** twinning is the characteristic of **quartz** and **geniculate** twinning is typically of **Rutile** mineral.

32.

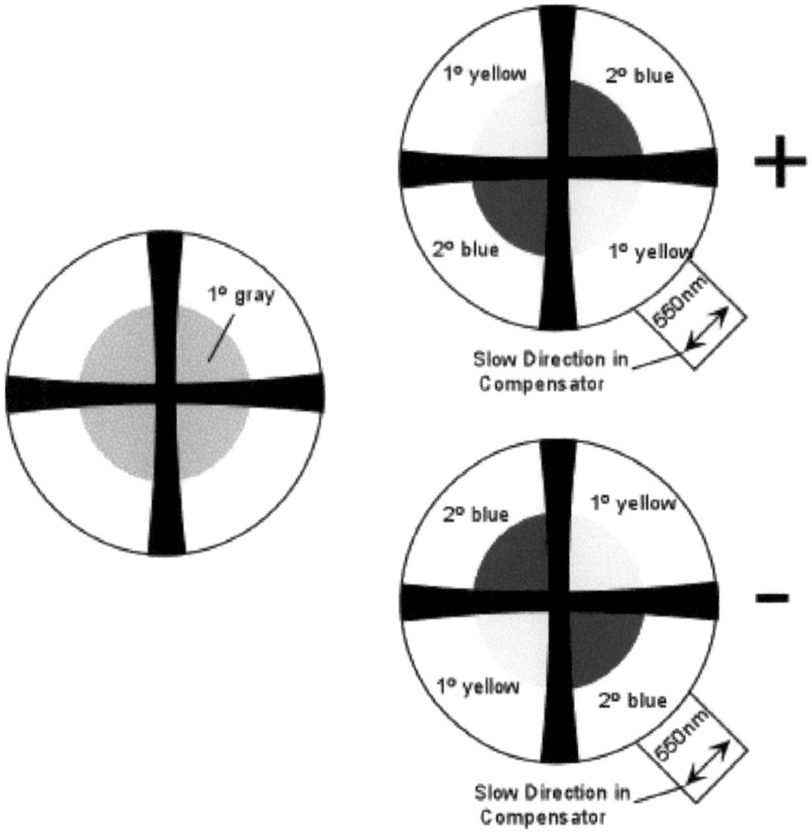

Interference figure for Quartz.

33. The four most abundant elements (O, Mg, Si, and Fe) make up 94.19% of the total primitive mantle mass. Fe-Ni alloy accounts for 87.90 wt% of the total mass of the core, and the major light elements in the core are Si, O, S, C, Cr, Mn, P, Co, Na, Mg and H in order of decreasing abundance.

The mass-abundance of the nine most abundant elements in the Earth's crust is approximately: oxygen 46%, silicon 28%, aluminium 8.2%, iron 5.6%, calcium 4.2%, sodium 2.5%, magnesium 2.4%, potassium 2.0%, and titanium 0.61%. Other elements occur at less than 0.15%.

So the option A is true.

34. Congruent melting occurs during melting of a compound when the composition of the liquid that forms is the same as the composition of the solid. It can be contrasted with incongruent melting. This generally happens in two-component systems.Incongruent melting occurs when a solid substance does not melt uniformly. During melting a new solid (of different composition) forms.

The peridotite compositions studied are equivalent to 'Hawaiian' pyrolite and a more depleted spinel lherzolite (Tinaquillo peridotite) and in both cases the experimental studies used peridotite 40% olivine compositions.

So the more appropriate option A is correct.

35. Salinity of the fluids,the stage is cooled with the help of liquid N2 during which time phase changes in the inclusion are carefully monitored. After the liquid in the inclusion completely solidifies, the stage is heated slowly while the inclusion is observed. The temperature at which the last piece of solid melts (Tmf) is then recorded (Fig. 6). This will correspond to the freezing temperature of the inclusion. Knowing the freezing points of pure H2O and CO2, the recorded freezing point (Tmf) is "plugged" into an equation of state (one of the form: PV= nRT), and the freezing point depression for the system in question is then directly related to the amount of "impurities" in this system, providing us with some information on the concentration of salts in this fluid (i.e. salinity of the fluid).

36. Textural inversion occurs in a red bed horizon of the Lower Jurassic Ardon Formation at Makhtesh Ramon. This texture consists of highly spherical, well rounded very well-sorted, coarse quartz grains, dispersed within an argillaceous silty micrite.

37. With the help of the following figure it can be seen the different system tracts.

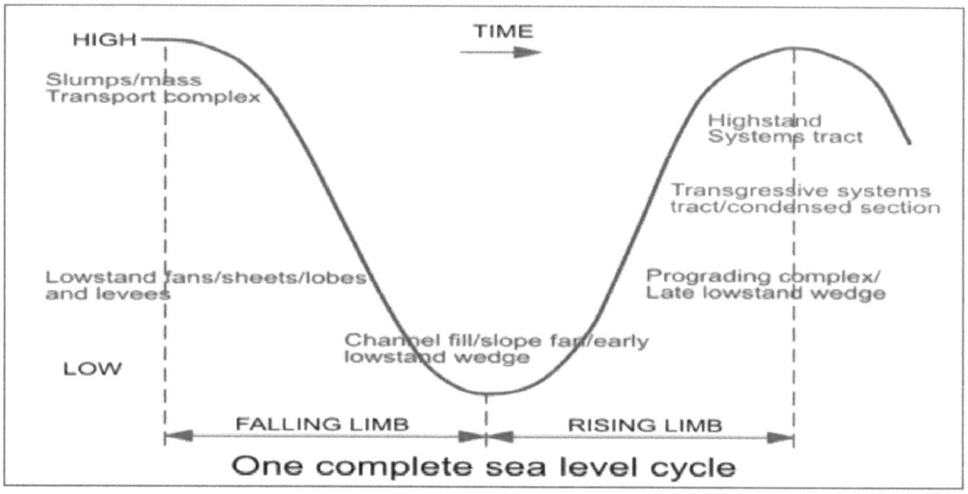

38. Dessication cracks are found in fine grained shales, and not in sandstone.

Dish and pillar structure generally seen in syn-sedimentary rocks like turbidites which are poorly sorted.

39. Albite, chlorite, actinolite and epidote are the characteristic mineral assemblage in stable metamorphic condition for green schist facies group of rocks.

40. Most **skarns** form when carbonate rocks such as limestone, dolostone or marble are intruded by a magma body and altered by contact metamorphism and metasomatism. At thetime of intrusion, the heat of contact metamorphism is the primary agent of change.

Mylonite – Mylonites can be found in places call mylonite zones. These zones are located along major fault zones called shear zones, and can range in lengths of hundreds of kilometers, and can also be several kilometres thickstrongly deformed rock that has undergone grain size reduction due to plastic deformation. Mylonites are separated into three subgroups depending on how much of the original matrix is still intact.

Spilite – It is a metasomatic rock with a microscopic or very-fine grain size produced by hydrothermal alteration of basalt, and composed of albite or oligoclase, together with chlorite, epidote, calcite, and actinolite.

Impactite – 1850 my ago, there was a huge impact crater formed at Sudbury, Ontario, 500 km E of Negaunee. This was a huge meteorite, similar to the Hadean bombardment, although it happened in the Archean. This great event seems to have ended the period of banded iron formation

41. Blueschists are typically found within orogenic belts as terranes of lithology in faulted contact with green schist or rarely eclogite faciesrocks.

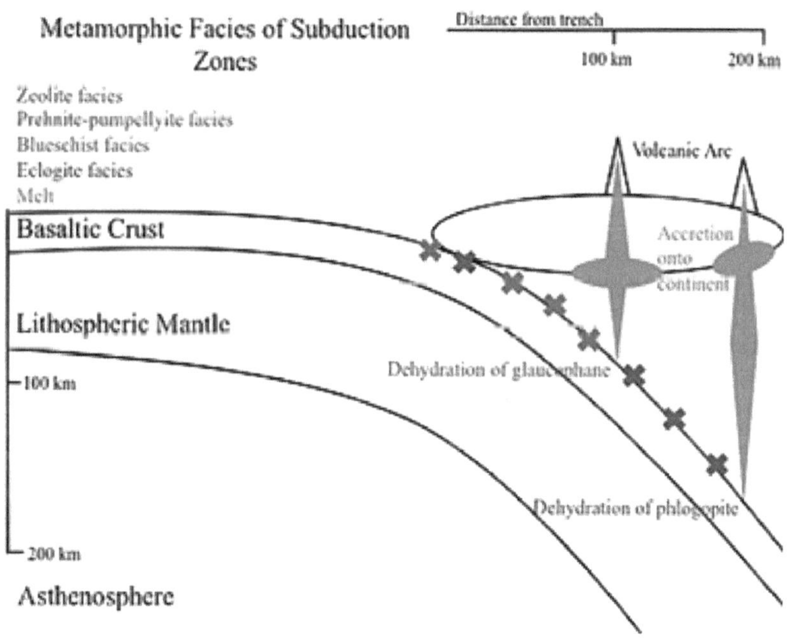

42. The following figure shows the presence of byssus thread in Mytillus which help to attached with the floor.

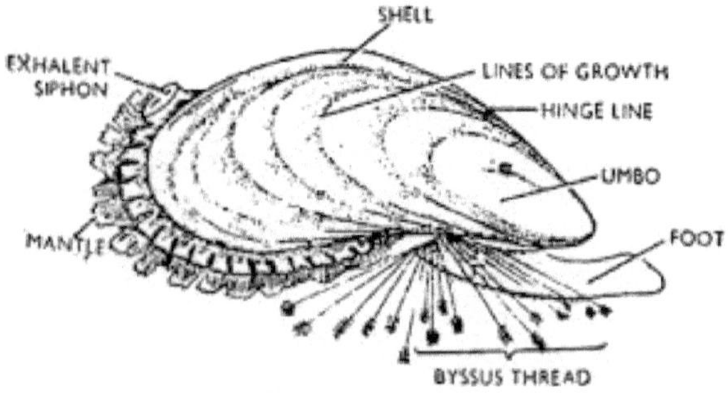

43. Fusulina have wall structure of micro granular

The wall composition of Cibicides is composed of Hyaline.

The wall of Textularia is composed of agglutinated

Quinqueloculina have wall composition of porcellenite.

So the option D is correct.

44. The following table shows the correct chronological order from older at the bottom and younger at the top.

Potwar Formations	The Siwali group	The Siwalik zone
Upper siwalik fms.	Upper siwalik subgroup	Boulder conglomerate zone
		Pinjor zone
		Tatrot zone
Dhok pathan	Middle siwalik subgroup	Dhok pathan zone
Nagri		Nagri zone
Chinji	Lower siwalik subgroup	Chinji zone
Kamlial		Kamlial zone

45. Hanseran formation is the evaporates, Nagthat formation is contain sandstone, Bijli formation is the rhyolite which formed due to volcanic eruption, Shahbad formation consist of limestone.

So the option C is correct.

46. Phosphate – Regional Distribution-almost entire production of rock phosphate of the country is obtained from two states of Rajasthan (93.9%) and Madhya Pradesh (16.1%). Rajasthan-Rajasthan is the largest producer accounting for 93.9 per cent of the total production of rock phosphate in the country.

Manganese – Manganese silicate rocks, interbanded with manganese oxide orebodies, constitute an important stratigraphic horizon in the Mansar formation of the Sausar Group of Precambrian age in India. The manganese silicate rocks of Gowari Wadhona occupy the westernmost flank of the manganese belt of the Sausar Group.

Chromite – Chromite layers and chromite-bearing ultamafic rocks exposed in the Byrapur area form a part of layered ultramafic-gabbro complex which is emplaced in to the Sargur group of Nuggihalli schist belt in the Hassan district of Dharwar craton.

Barite – One of the largest baryte deposits of the world, is considered to have formed through precipitation from volcanic vapours under submarine conditions and sub aerial showering of ash and molten baryte lapilli. The deposit occurs in the Pullampet Formation of the Nallamalai Group of the Cuddapah Supergroup.

47. Foreland basin - A foreland basin is a structural basin that develops adjacent and parallel to a mountain belt. ... Examples include the North Alpine Foreland Basin of Europe, or the Ganges Basin of Asia.

For arc – The Andaman Sea is a marginal sea of the eastern Indian Ocean separated from the Bay of Bengal. It is caused by the ongoing subduction of the India plate beneath the Andaman island arc, which forces magma to rise in this location of the Burma.

Failed rift – the result of rifting of India from Madagascar and later from. Laccadive Ridge, Kerala-Konkan Basin, Laccadive Basin and Arabian Basin are possibility of a failed rift in the basin.

Passive margin – The western margin of India such as the Cambay, Narmada and Tapi, comprising passive continental margin is thought to have developed.

48. Statement I is wrong and combination is not well with the other options. So marks to all is given.

49. Based on the statistics of remote sensing it is classified that class A by MDM and class B by NN

50. Using Darcy flow equation.

$D = K\ dh/dl$

Let the height of water at location x is H

Darcy velocity forporous sand I

$D1 = K1 * dh/dl = 20 * (50 - H)/3$

Darcy velocity for porous sand II

$D2 = K2 * dh/dl = 30 * (H - 30)/4$

Darcy velocity would be same throughout the porous media

So D1 = D2, putting all the values in equations and simplifying:

$20 * (50\text{-}H)/3 = 30 * (H - 30)/4$, $H = 6700/170$

$= 39.4$ m.

51. Concavity index

= (triangular area – area of the basin) / triangular area of half square

= (0.5 – 0.18) * 100/0.5

= 64

52. 2 parts of gold is present in 1 million parts of the ore i.e. 2 kg of gold is present in 1 million kg of ore.

Hence, 1 kg gold will be present in (1/2) million kg of ore

= 0.5 * 1000000 = 500 * 1000 kg of ore.

53. The point load strength index is calculated by following formula

$Is_{50} = P/De^2$

Where Is_{50} = point load strength index

P = Failure Load in KN and De^2 = Equivalent core diameter

Putting all the given values in the defined equation by normalizing at 50mm.

Is = 20 * 1000/(50 * 50) = 8 MPa.

54. First we need to calculate the bulk distribution coefficient by the following formula

D = k_d of olivine * wt % of olivine + kd of orthopyroxene * wt % of orthopyroxenes + kd of clinopyroxenes * wt % of clinopyroxenes + kd of garnet * wt % of garnet.

D = 0.001 * 0.6 + 0.003 * 0.25 + 0.1 * 0.1 + 0.05 * 0.02

= 0.01235

Now using equation of batch melting.

Cl/Co = 1/(F + D (1 – F))

= 1/(0.1 + 0.01235(1 – 0.1))

Cl/Co = 1/(0.111115) = 8.99

55. Using radioactive decay equation.

N = No $e^{-\lambda t}$ for small value of λt, $e^{\lambda t} = \lambda t$

Now N = No/λt, putting the values in this equation.

N = 8 * 104/1.42 * 10 – 11 * 4

= 1.3199 * 104 * 1011

Now total no. of Sr isotopes present at 4 half-lives are

D = Do + D*

D = 10^3 + Nλt

= 10^3 + 1.3199 * 10^4 * 10^11 * 1.42 * 10^ – 11 * 4

= 75.97*103

(GEOPHYSICS)

57.

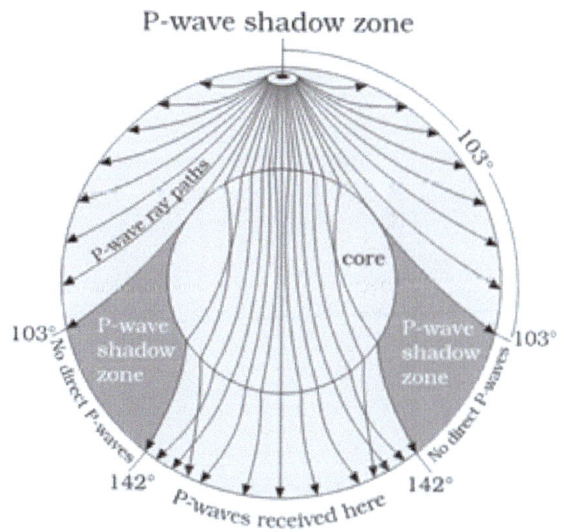

59. **Justification :** The maximum dip on the **seismic section** of 45ocorresponds to a reflector dip of 90o. By taking a semicircular arc equal to the travel **time** from each of the recorded positions and constructing a line at tangent to the arcs the true **migrated** position of the reflector is discovered

SOLVED PAPER - 2018

GENERAL APTITUDE (GA)

Q. 1 – Q. 5 carry one mark each.

1. "When she fell down the _______, she received many _______ but little help." The words that best fill the blanks in the above sentence are

(*a*) stairs, stares (*b*) stairs, stairs

(*c*) stares, stairs (*d*) stares, stares

2. "In spite of being warned repeatedly, he failed to correct his _________ behaviour." The word that best fills the blank in the above sentence is

(*a*) rational (*b*) reasonable

(*c*) errant (*d*) good

3. For $0 \le x \le 2\pi$, sin x and cos x are both decreasing functions in the interval ________.

(*a*) $\left(0, \frac{\pi}{2}\right)$ (*b*) $\left(\frac{\pi}{2}, \pi\right)$

(*c*) $\left(\pi, \frac{3\pi}{2}\right)$ (*d*) $\left(\frac{3\pi}{2}, 2\pi\right)$

4. The area of an equilateral triangle is $\sqrt{3}$. What is the perimeter of the triangle?

(*a*) 2 (*b*) 4

(*c*) 6 (*d*) 8

5. Arrange the following three-dimensional objects in the descending order of their volumes:

(i) A cuboid with dimensions 10 cm, 8 cm and 6 cm

(ii) A cube of side 8 cm

(iii) A cylinder with base radius 7 cm and height 7 cm

(iv) A sphere of radius 7 cm

(*a*) (i), (ii), (iii), (iv) (*b*) (ii), (i), (iv), (iii)

(*c*) (iii), (ii), (i), (iv) (*d*) (iv), (iii), (ii), (i)

Q. 6 – Q.10 carry two marks each.

6. An automobile travels from city A to city B and returns to city A by the same route. The speed of the vehicle during the onward and return journeys were constant at 60 km/h and 90 km/h, respectively. What is the average speed in km/h for the entire journey?

(*a*) 72 (*b*) 73

(*c*) 74 (*d*) 75

7. A set of 4 parallel lines intersect with another set of 5 parallel lines. How many parallelograms are formed?

(*a*) 20 (*b*) 48

(*c*) 60 (*d*) 72

8. To pass a test, a candidate needs to answer at least 2 out of 3 questions correctly. A total of 6,30,000 candidates appeared for the test. Question A was correctly answered by 3,30,000 candidates. Question B was answered correctly by 2,50,000 candidates. Question C was answered correctly by 2,60,000 candidates. Both questions A and B were answered correctly by 1,00,000 candidates. Both questions B and C were answered correctly by 90,000 candidates. Both questions A and C were answered correctly by 80,000 candidates. If the number of students answering all questions correctly is the same as the number answering none, how many candidates failed to clear the test?

(*a*) 30,000 (*b*) 2,70,000

(*c*) 3,90,000 (*d*) 4,20,000

9. If $x^2 + x - 1 = 0$ what is the value of $x^4 + \frac{1}{x^4}$?

(*a*) 1 (*b*) 5

(*c*) 7 (*d*) 9

10. In a detailed study of annual crow births in India, it was found that there was relatively no growth during the period 2002 to 2004 and a sudden spike from 2004 to 2005. In another unrelated study, it was found that the revenue from cracker sales in India which remained fairly flat from 2002 to 2004, saw a sudden spike in 2005 before declining again in 2006. The solid line in the graph below refers to annual sale of crackers and the dashed line refers to the annual crow births in India. Choose the most appropriate inference from the above data.

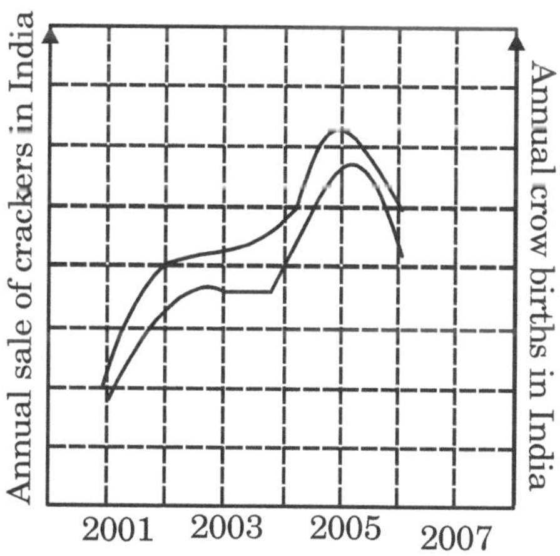

(a) There is a strong correlation between crow birth and cracker sales.

(b) Cracker usage increases crow birth rate.

(c) If cracker sale declines, crow birth will decline.

(d) Increased birth rate of crows will cause an increase in the sale of crackers.

PART-A (Common Part)

Q. 1 – Q. 25 carry one mark each.

1. Which one of the following periods has the longest time duration?

(a) Ordovician (b) Cretaceous

(c) Jurassic (d) Silurian

2. A siliciclastic sedimentary rock consisting predominantly of the same type of gravel-sized clasts is called

(a) Polymict conglomerate.

(b) Arkose.

(c) Oligomict conglomerate.

(d) Petromict conglomerate.

3. Brown coal that has high moisture content and commonly retains many of the original wood fragments is called

(a) Anthracite (b) Bituminous coal

(c) Lignite (d) Peat

4. The speed of revolution of the Earth around the Sun is

(a) maximum at Perihelion.

(b) minimum at Perihelion.

(c) maximum at Aphelion.

(d) equal at Aphelion and Perihelion.

5. The geometrical factor for the following electrode configuration is

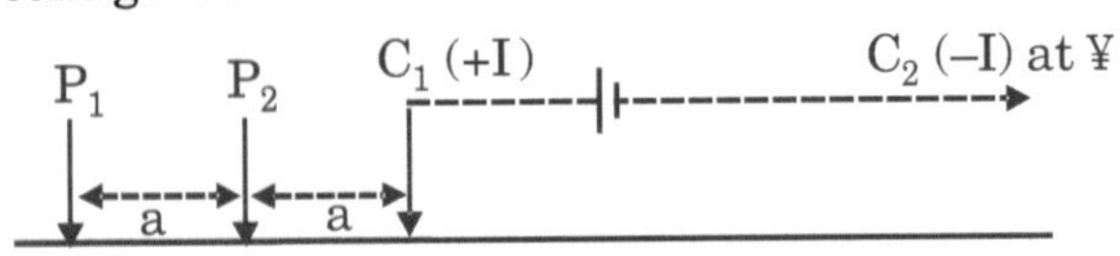

(a) πa (b) $2\pi a$

(c) $3\pi a$ (d) $4\pi a$

6. Which one of the following geophysical methods uses the physical property 'Dielectric Constant'?

(a) Gravity

(b) Ground Penetrating Radar

(c) Seismic

(d) Self-Potential

7. Pascal second is a unit of

(a) seepage force (b) dynamic viscosity

(c) kinematic viscosity (d) permeability

8. Which one of the following statements is CORRECT?

(a) Strength of a rock decreases with increase in confining pressure.

(b) Strength of a rock increases with increase in temperature.

(c) Strength of a rock increases with increase in strain rate.

(d) Strength of a rock increases with increase in pore water pressure.

9. The geomorphic feature 'horns' are formed by

(a) wind erosion (b) river erosion

(c) wind deposition (d) glacial erosion

10. A melanocratic porphyritic rock containing phenocrysts of biotite, with feldspar restricted to the groundmass, is called

(a) trachyte (b) dacite

(c) andesite (d) lamprophyre

11. The supercontinent that existed in the late Mesoproterozoic to early Neoproterozoic time was

(a) Kenorland (b) Columbia

(c) Rodinia (d) Pangaea

12. The figure below shows the triple junction between three plates A, B and C. The boundary between the plates A and B is a ridge with a half-spreading rate of 4 cm/year. The A-C and B-C boundaries are collinear and orthogonal to the A-B ridge. The A-C boundary is a dextral transform fault with a relative velocity of 6 cm/year. The boundary between plates B and C is a

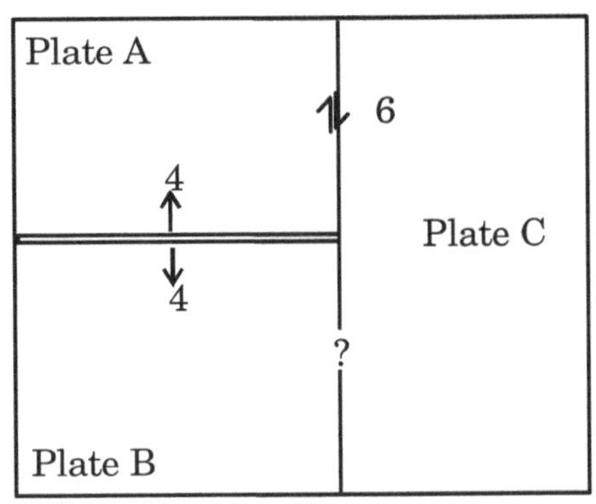

(a) dextral transform fault with a relative velocity of 10 cm/year.

(b) dextral transform fault with a relative velocity of 2 cm/year.

(c) sinistral transform fault with a relative velocity of 2 cm/year.

(d) sinistral transform fault with a relative velocity of 6 cm/year.

13. A rock follows Mohr-Coulomb failure criterion. Which one of the Mohr-Coulomb failure en-velopes shown below allows failure of the rock under stress state Y, but not under stress state X?

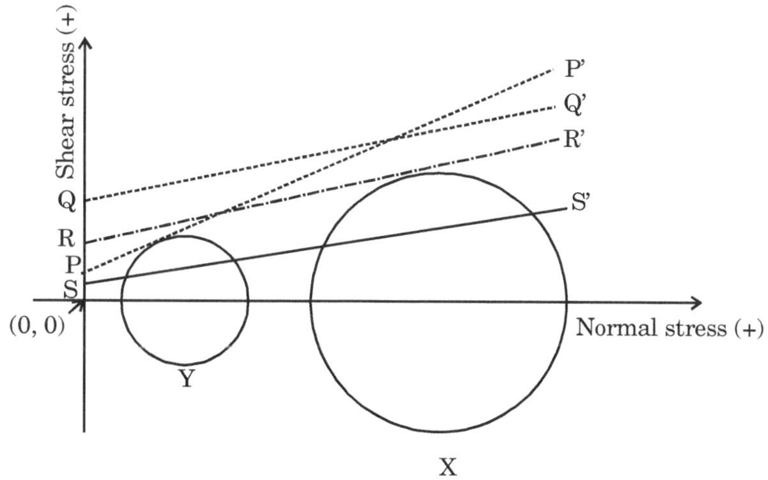

(a) PP' (b) QQ' (c) RR' (d) SS'

14. The maximum and the minimum principal stresses are denoted by σ_1 and σ_3, respectively. The differential stress can have an absolute value greater than σ_1 when

(a) σ_1 and σ_3 are both compressive.

(b) σ_1 is compressive and σ_3 is tensile.

(c) σ_1 and σ_3 are equal.

(d) σ_1 and σ_3 are both tensile.

15. The geoid can be best defined as

(*a*) an oblate spheroid that best approximates the shape of the earth.

(*b*) a surface over which the value of gravity is constant.

(*c*) the physical surface of the earth.

(*d*) an equipotential surface of gravity of the earth.

16. For a layered isotropic medium with a flat horizontal free surface, match the wave types listed in Group-I with their corresponding polarizations listed in Group II.

Group I	Group II
P. P-waves	1. Particle motion is transverse to the direction of wave propagation.
Q. S-waves	2. Particle motion is transverse to the direction of wave propagation and confined to the horizontal plane.
R. Rayleigh waves	3. Particle motion is parallel to the direction of wave propagation.
S. Love waves	4. Intermediate floor
	5. Particle motion is elliptical.

(*a*) P-1; Q-3; R-4; S-2 (*b*) P-3; Q-1; R-4; S-2

(*c*) P-3; Q-1; R-2; S-4 (*d*) P-2; Q-3; R-1; S-4

17. A 'gentle' fold with an interlimb angle equal to 160° appears tight (apparent interlimb angle equal to 20°) in horizontal section. According to the plunge of the fold axis, it can also be classified as

(a) horizontal fold.

(b) gently plunging fold.

(c) steeply plunging fold.

(d) vertical fold.

18. The unit of shear modulus (rigidity modulus) is

(*a*) kg m^{-1} s^{-2} (*b*) m^2 s^{-2}

(*c*) kg m^{-2} s^{-2} (*d*) m^{-1}

19. With increasing activity of silica, the CORRECT order of appearance of minerals in a weathering environment with constant ratio of activities of K^+ and H^+ is

(*a*) gibbsite → kaolinite → pyrophyllite

(*b*) gibbsite → pyrophyllite → kaolinite

(*c*) kaolinite → gibbsite → pyrophyllite

(*d*) pyrophyllite → gibbsite → kaolinite

20. Match the items listed in Group-I with those listed in Group-II.

Group I	Group II
P. Mica	1. Beldih
Q. Uranium	2. Koderma
R. Phosphate	3. Agucha
S. Zinc	4. Gogi

(*a*) P-2,Q-3, R-4, S-1 (*b*) P-2, Q-4, R-1, S-3

(*c*) P-4, Q-2, R-3, S-1 (*d*) P-3, Q-1, R-4, S-2

21. Which one of the following corrections is always added during reduction of the observed gravity data?

(*a*) Latitude (*b*) Free-air

(*c*) Bouguer (*d*) Terrain

22. The magnitudes of the total geomagnetic field at the equator and pole are denoted by B_E and B_P, respectively. Which one of the following is TRUE?

(*a*) $B_P \approx 4 B_E$ (*b*) $B_P \approx 2 B_E$

(*c*) $B_P \approx B_E$ (*d*) $B_P \approx \frac{1}{2} B_E$

23. Assume a flat earth with crustal thickness of 35 km and average crustal and upper mantle P-wave velocities of 6.4 km.s^{-1} and 8.1 km.s^{-1}, respectively. The minimum distance from the epicenter of a near surface earthquake at which P_n -waves are observed is _______ km.

24. Given that the velocity of P-waves in a sandstone matrix is 5600 m/s and that in oil is 1200 m/s, the velocity of P-wave propagation in oil saturated sandstone with 30% porosity is __________ m/s. (Use Wyllie time average equation.)

25. If the total porosity of a soil is 20%, its void ratio (%) is _________.

PART-B
GEOLOGY

Q. 26 to Q. 55 carry two marks each.

26. Which one of the following Himalayan lithounits predates India-Eurasia collision?

(*a*) Kasauli sandstone

(*b*) Rangit Pebble Slat

(*c*) Annapurna granite

(*d*) Lower Karewa sandstone

27. Which one of the following ore minerals shows internal reflection?

(*a*) Orpiment (*b*) Magnetite

(*c*) Pyrite (*d*) Molybdenite

28. Which one is CORRECT for the following equilibrium reaction between quartz and magnetite:

$$Si^{16}O^{16}O + Fe_3{}^{16}O_3{}^{18} = Si^{16}O^{18}O + Fe_3{}^{16}O_4\ ?$$

(*a*) $1000 \ln \alpha = \Delta_{qtz\text{-}mag}$ where $\alpha = K^{\frac{1}{n}}$ (K is the equilibrium constant at the specified temperature and n is a constant quantity)

(*b*) $1000 \ln \alpha = \Delta_{qtz\text{-}mag}$ where $\alpha = K^n$ (K is the equilibrium constant at the specified temperature and n is the number of exchangeable atomic sites)

(*c*) $\left(\ln \frac{\alpha}{1000}\right) = \Delta_{qtz-mag}$ where $\alpha = K^{\frac{1}{n}}$ (K is the equilibrium constant at the specified temperature and n is a constant quantity)

(*d*) $1000 \ln \alpha = \Delta_{qtz\text{-}mag}$ where $\alpha = K^{\frac{1}{n}}$ (K is the equilibrium constant at the specified temperature and n is the number of exchangeable atomic sites)

29. Match the modes of life (listed in Group I) with the corresponding bivalve genera (listed in Group II).

Group I	Group II
P. Burrowing	1. Mytilus
Q. Recumbent unattached	2. Pecten
R. Byssally attached	3. Mya
S. Swimming	4. Gryphaea

(*a*) P-4, Q-3, R-2, S-1 (*b*) P-3, Q-4, R-1, S-2

(*c*) P-2, Q-3, R-1, S-4 (*d*) P-3, Q-1, R-4, S-2

30. Based on the hypothetical litholog given below that shows a continuous succession of sedimentary rocks, which one of the following statements is CORRECT?

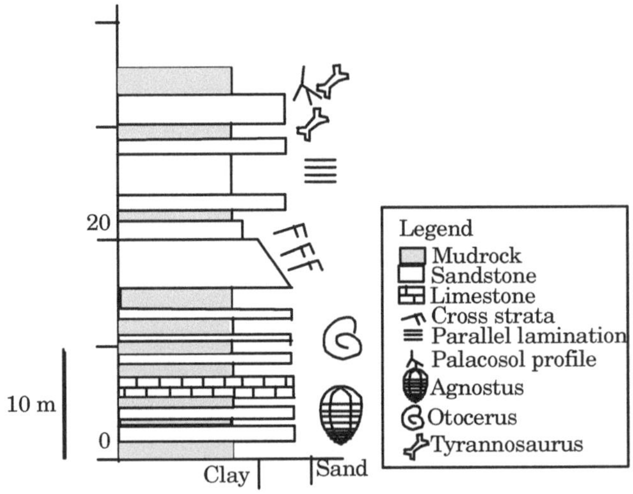

(*a*) The rocks range from Cambrian to Cretaceous and show change in depositional environment from marine to continental.

(*b*) The rocks range from Cambrian to Triassic and show change in depositional environment from marine to continental.

(*c*) The rocks range from Cambrian to Cretaceous and show change in depositional environment from continental to marine.

(*d*) The rocks are Palaeozoic in age and show change in depositional environment from marine to continental.

31. Which one of the following cladograms shows the CORRECT interrelationships among the major groups of vertebrates?

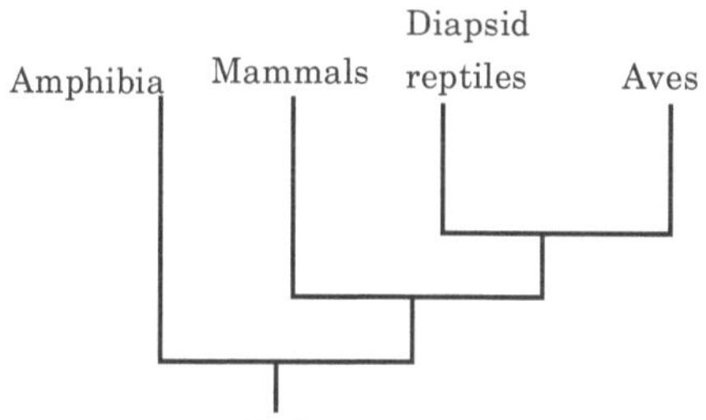

Cladogram I

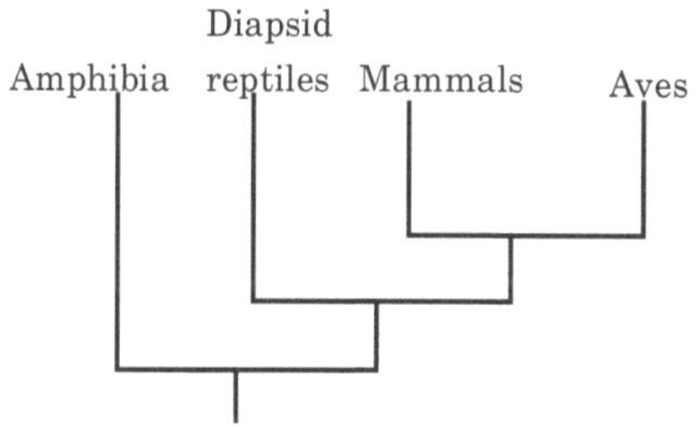

Cladogram II

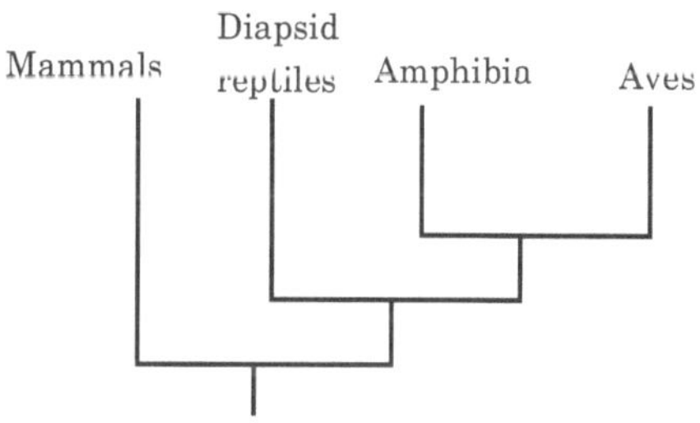

Cladogram III

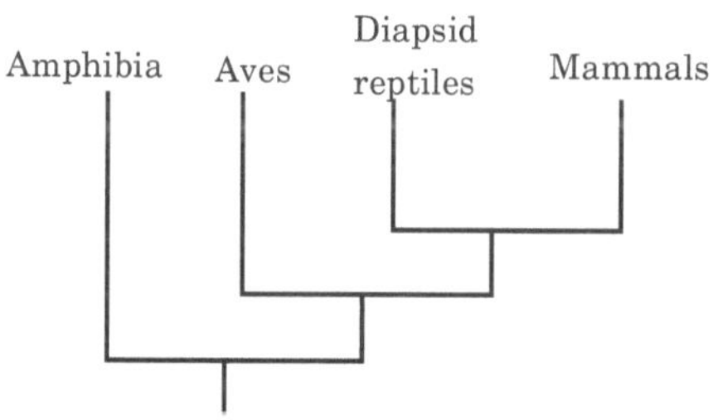

Cladogram IV

(*a*) Cladogram I (*b*) Cladogram II
(*c*) Cladogram III (*d*) Cladogram IV

32. Which one of the following stratigraphic successions is in the CORRECT chronological order (from older to younger)?

(*a*) Rajmahal, Dubrajpur, Barakar
(*b*) Fenestella Shale, Muth Quartzite, Syringothyris Limestone
(*c*) Bagh Bed, Lameta Formation, Deccan Traps
(*d*) Singhbhum Granite, Kolhan Group, Older Metamorphic Gneiss

33. Match the items listed in Group I with their appropriate description listed in Group II.

Group I	Group II
P. Peloids	1. Grains containing nucleus surrounded by irregular, non-concentric laminae.
Q. Ooids	2. Small micritic grains without internal structure
R. Oncoids	3. Rounded grains with a thin coating of micrite.
S. Cortoids	4. Spherical grains consisting of regular laminae in concentric rings

(*a*) P-3, Q-1, R-4, S-2 (*b*) P-2, Q-4, R-1, S-3
(*c*) P-3, Q-4, R-1, S-2 (*d*) P-2, Q-3, R-4, S-1

34. Which one of the following is an image rectification technique?

(*a*) Histogram equalization
(*b*) Density slicing
(*c*) Histogram normalization
(*d*) Rubbersheeting

35. Match the items listed in Group I with those in Group II.

Group I	Group II
P. Determination of coefficient of com-pressibility of soils	1. Brazilian test
Q. A method of slope stabilization	2. Overcoring
R. A method of in situ stress determination	3. Oedometer test
S. Determination of indirect tensile strength of rocks	4. Shotcreting

(*a*) P-4, Q-2, R-3, S-1 (*b*) P-1, Q-4, R-2, S-3
(*c*) P-3, Q-2, R-1, S-4 (*d*) P-3, Q-4, R-2, S-1

36. Match the items listed in Group I with those listed in Group II.

Group I	Group II
P. Crevasse	1. river
Q. Yardang	2. Groundwater
R. Mesa y	3. Wind
S. Stalactite	4. Glacier

(*a*) P-4, Q-3, R-1, S-2
(*b*) P-3, Q-1, R-4, S-2
(*c*) P-4, Q-2, R-3, S-1
(*d*) P-1, Q-2, R-3, S-4

37. In the hypothetical isobaric ternary liquidus projection diagram given below, solid phases A, B, C, D and E exist in equilibrium with liquid. The reaction taking place at the isobaric invariant point **W** is

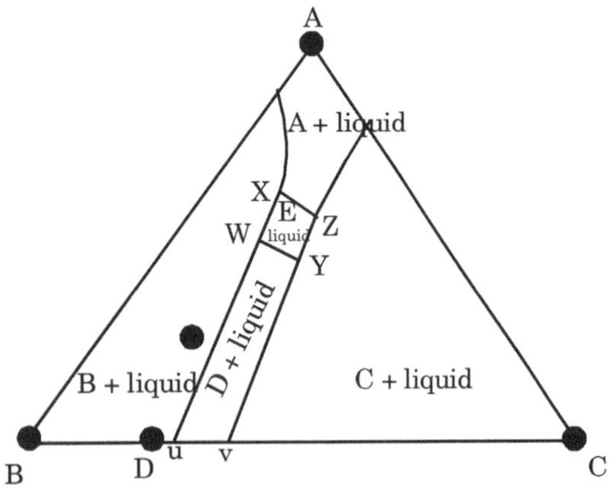

(*a*) Liquid (at W) = B + D + E

(*b*) Liquid (at W) = A + B + D

(*c*) Liquid (at W) + E = B + D

(*d*) Liquid (at W) + B + D = E

38. Match the optical properties listed in Group I with the corresponding mineral in Group II.

Group I	**Group II**
P. Brown colour, very high refractive index, very high bire-fringence, biaxial positive	1. Apatite
Q. Colourless, very high refractive index, low bire-fringence, uniaxial negative	2. Rutile
R. Deep reddish-brown colour, very high refractive index, very high birefringence, uniaxial positive	3. Zircon
S. Colourless, very high refractive index, very high birefringence, uniaxial positive	4. Titanitei

(*a*) P-4, Q-1, R-2, S-3 (*b*) P-1, Q-2, R-4, S-3

(*c*) P-3, Q-4, R-1, S-2 (*d*) P-4, Q-1, R-3, S-2

39. The reaction

muscovite + quartz = K-feldspar + sillimanite + water

(*a*) takes place within the greenschist facies.

(*b*) takes place within the amphibolite facies.

(*c*) takes place within the eclogite facies.

(*d*) takes place within the granulite facies.

40. Match the items listed in Group I with those in Group II.

Group I

P. Diopside-tre-molite-forsterite

Q. Talc-phengite-kyanite

R. Hornblende-cummingtonite-plagioclase

S. Andalusite-cordierite-biotite

Group II

1. Pelite (low P, high T)
2. Metabasite (low P, high T)
3. Calc-silicate (moderate P, T)
4. Pelite (high P, low T)

(*a*) P-3, Q-4, R-1, S-2 (*b*) P-1, Q-2, R-4, S-3

(*c*) P-3, Q-4, R-2, S-1 (*d*) P-1, Q-2, R-3, S-4

41. The figure below is a schematic section showing the initial stages of development of a thrust fault (FF') having a typical ramp and flat geometry, with the thrust sheet being transported from east to west. With respect to the synform and antiform created in Stage 2, which one of the options below is CORRECT for the next increment of movement on the fault plane?

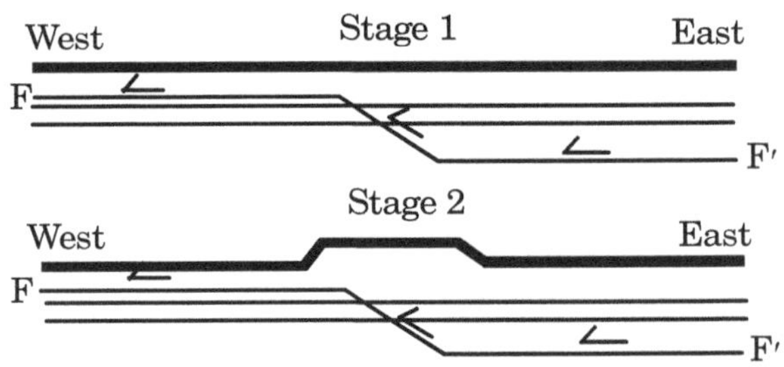

(*a*) The synform and the antiform will both move westward.

(*b*) The synform will remain in position, while the antiform will grow in amplitude.

(*c*) Both synform and antiform will grow in amplitude.

(*d*) The geometry will remain unchanged.

42. Which one of the following is the CORRECT chronological sequence for Iron formations?

(*a*) Algoma type > Superior type > Rapitan type > Minette type

(*b*) Superior type > Algoma type > Rapitan type > Minette type

(*c*) Rapitan type > Minette type > Algoma type > Superior type

(*d*) Algoma type > Minette type > Superior type > Rapitan type

43. **Assertion (a) :** High-temperature, low-pressure metamorphism occurs on the over-riding plate near convergent plate margins.

Reason (r) : Partial melting in the mantle wedge generates magmas that rise to form the arc.

(*a*) (a) is true but (r) is false.

(*b*) (a) is false but (r) is true.

(*c*) Both (a) and (r) are true and (r) is the correct reason for (a).e

(*d*) Both (a) and (r) are true and (r) is not the correct reason for (a).

44. Two coeval primary aqueous biphase fluid inclusions, X (liquid-rich) and Y (vapour-rich), occur in the same grain of the host mineral. Which one of the following situations most likely indicates boiling of the fluid?

(*a*) X homogenizes to liquid and Y homogenizes to vapour at different temperatures.

(*b*) Both homogenize to liquid at the same temperature.

(*c*) Both homogenize to vapour at the same temperature

(*d*) X homogenizes to liquid and Y homogenizes to vapour at the same temperature.

45. During bench blasting in a quarry, 50 kg of an explosive with a yield of 5 MegaJoule/kg is required to break 100 m^3 of marble. In this case, the energy expended in breaking a unit volume of marble in MegaNewton/m^2 would be _____.

46. The stretching lineation on the axial plane (S_2) of a reclined fold on the S_1 foliation makes an angle of 30° with the $\frac{S_1}{S_2}$ intersection lineation. The rake of the stretching lineation on the axial plane in degrees is _____________.

47. A basaltic magma has an initial nickel concentration of 300 ppm. Olivine crystallizes from this magma by equilibrium crystallization (Case I) or fractional crystallization (Case II).

Then, the absolute value of the difference between the nickel concentrations of the liquids remaining after 25% crystallization in these two cases is _____________. (Use $K_{D,Ni}$ olivine/melt = 10).

48. The difference in the number of faces in forms {hkl} and {111} in the holosymmetric class of the isometric system is _____________.

49. An inclined cylindrical confined aquifer has coefficient of permeability of 40 m/day. The horizontal distance between two vertical wells penetrating the aquifer is 800 m. The water surface elevations in the wells are 50 m and 45 m above a common horizontal datum. The absolute value of Darcy flux through the aquifer is ______ m/day.

50. The mass and volume of a natural soil sample are 2.1 kg and 1×10^{-3} m^3, respectively. When fully dried, the mass of the soil sample becomes 2 kg without any change in volume.

Assuming the specific gravity of soil particles to be 2.5, and water density of 1000 kg/m^3, the degree of saturation of the natural soil sample is _____________%.

51. For a granitic rock mass, joint set number (Jn) = 9, joint water reduction factor (Jw) = 1, joint alteration number (Ja) = 1, stress reduction factor (SRF) = 1, rock quality designation (%) = 84 and joint roughness number (Jr) = 3. The Q-value as per Barton's Q-system of rock mass classification (year 1974) is _____________.

52. A sun synchronous satellite is at an altitude of 300 km and the spectrometer makes an angular coverage angle of 12°. The Swath (GFOV) of the satellite is ____________ km.

53. The stability field boundary between two minerals A and B is linear with a positive slope in P-T space. The molar entropy of A and B are 85.5 and 92.5 Joules K^{-1}, respectively and their respective molar volumes are 35.5 and 38.2 cc. The slope of the phase boundary in P-T space is _____ bar K^{-1}.

54. Five moles of gas A (volume V1) and 3 moles of gas B (volume V2) were kept in separate containers. These two gases are completely transferred to a new container of volume V.

Assuming isothermal condition, and that the work done is only mechanical, the entropy change of the system is ___________ Joules K^{-1}. (R = 8.3 J K^{-1} $mole^{-1}$)

55. The value of Eh corresponding to the upper limit of natural surface aqueous environment at pH of 8.0 is ___________ V.

GEOPHYSICS

Q. 56 – Q. 85 carry two marks each.

56. The maximum number of linearly independent rows of an m × n matrix G where m > n is

(*a*) m (*b*) n

(*c*) m – n (*d*) 0

57. The impulse response of the Kirchhoff pre-stack time migration operator for non-zero offsets in a homogeneous and isotropic medium is _________.

(*a*) a circle (*b*) a parabola

(*c*) a hyperbola (*d*) an ellipse

58. A solution to the eikonal equation $|\nabla_\tau| = \frac{1}{v_0}$ for homogeneous and isotropic medium in cartesion coordinates is

(*a*) $\tau = \frac{\sqrt{x^2+y^2+z^2}}{v_0}$ (*b*) $\tau = \frac{1}{v_0}$

(*c*) $\tau = \frac{x+y+z}{v_0}$ (*d*) $\tau = \frac{xyz}{v_0}$

59. The formula for the 'forward' Fourier transform is $F(\omega) = \int_{-\infty}^{\infty} F(\omega)\, e^{-\omega t}\, dt$ and the for the 'inverse' Fourier transform is $F(t) = \int_{-\infty}^{\infty} F(\omega)\, e^{-\omega t}\, d\omega$.

Then the forward Fourier transform of the function $F(\omega)e^{-2i\omega}$. Then, the forward Fourier transform of the function $F(\omega)e^{-2i\omega}$ is

(*a*) $2\delta(t)$ (*b*) $\delta(2t)$

(*c*) $\delta(t+2)$ (*d*) $\delta(t-2)$

60. Which one of the following rock types has the highest bulk magnetic susceptibility value?

(*a*) Gabbro (*b*) Marble

(*c*) Orthoquartzite (*d*) Limestone

61. Figure 1 is a schematic diagram of four seismic events in t-x (time-offset) domain and Figure 2 is the result of transformation from t-x domain to f-kx (frequency-horizontal wavenumber) domain. Match the events in t-x domain in Figure 1 with their counterparts in f-kx domain in Figure 2.

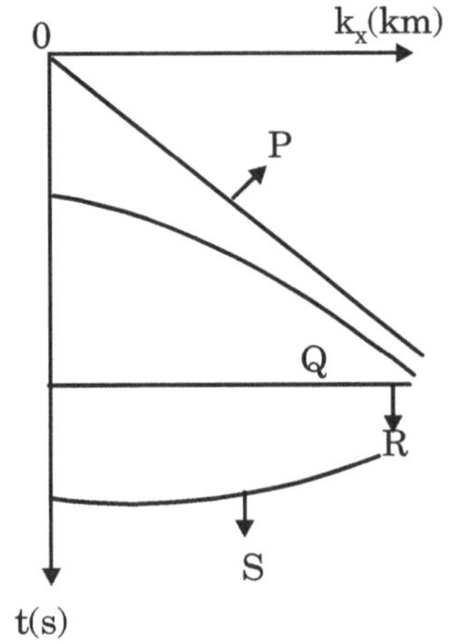

Figure 1

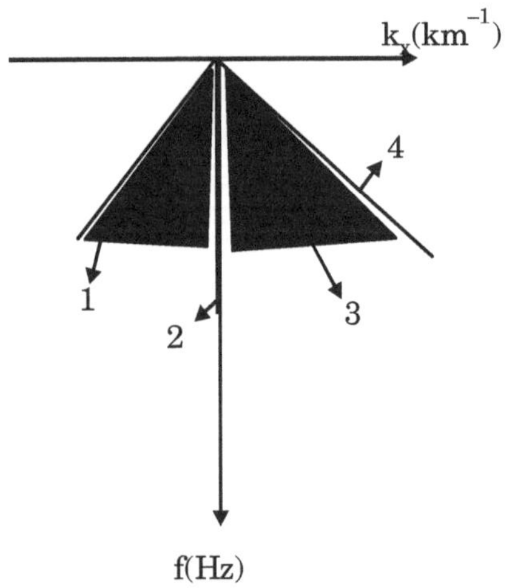

Figure 2

(*a*) P-1; Q-2; R-3; S-4 (*b*) P-1; Q-3; R-2; S-4

(*c*) P-4; Q-3; R-2; S-1 (*d*) P-4; Q-2; R-3; S-1

62. There is a change in the values of the bulk modulus and density across the Gutenberg discontinuity (from mantle to outer core). Which one of the following statements is CORRECT?

(*a*) Both bulk modulus and density increase.

(*b*) Both bulk modulus and density decrease.

(*c*) Bulk modulus decreases and density increases.

(*d*) Bulk modulus increases and density decreases.

63. Multi-electrode resistivity survey is carried out by placing 10 equispaced electrodes (denoted by arrows in the figure below) on the surface of the earth. The points of observations in the distance-apparent depth plane are marked as solid dots in the figure shown below. Considering the mid-point of the 4-electrode array as the point of observation in the lateral direction, identify the CORRECT electrode configuration used for the survey.

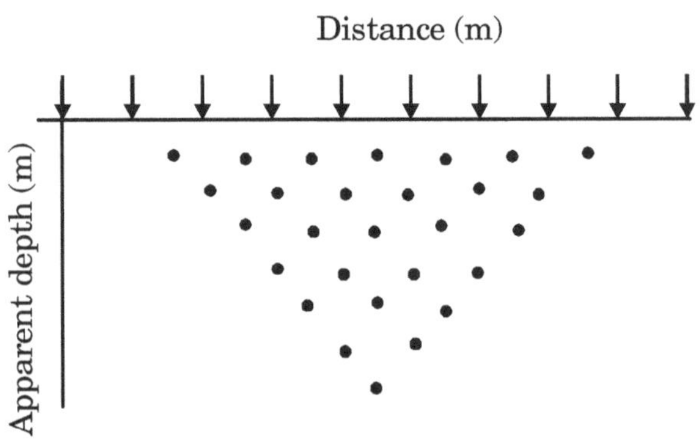

(*a*) Multi-electrode Wenner array.

(*b*) Multi-electrode Axial Dipole-dipole array.

(*c*) Multi-electrode Wenner-Schlumberger array.

(*d*) Multi-electrode Axial Pole-dipole array.

64. Match the Electromagnetic methods in Group I with the corresponding quantity measured by them given in Group II.

Group I	Group II
P. AFMAG method	1. Decay of secondary field
Q. Time domain EM method	2. Real and imaginary components
R. TURAM method	3. Dip angle
S. Slingram method	4. Amplitude ratio and phase difference
	5. Ellipticity of polarization ellipse

(*a*) P-3, Q-2, R-4, S-5

(*b*) P-2, Q-1, R-4, S-3

(*c*) P-3, Q-1, R-4, S-2

(*d*) P-1, Q-2, R-5, S-3

65. Dip angle electromagnetic response measured along a profile over multiple conductors is shown in the figure below. Which of the crossover points P, Q and R represent the CORRECT locations of conductors beneath them?

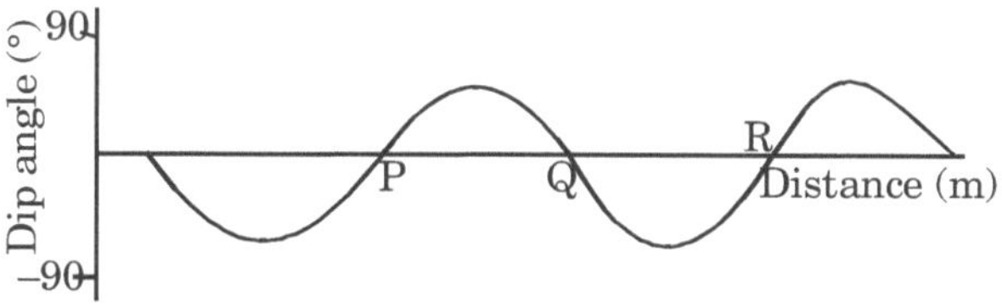

(*a*) P, Q and R (*b*) Q and R

(*c*) P and R (*d*) P and Q

66. The effect of small scale near surface inhomogeneities can be removed from magnetic data by

(*a*) upward continuation.

(*b*) downward continuation.

(*c*) second vertical derivative.

(*d*) reduction to pole.

67. The frequencies of the primary magnetic field generated by worldwide thunderstorm activity vary in the range

(*a*) 10^{-6} Hz – 10^{-3} Hz

(*b*) 10^{-3} Hz – 1 Hz

(*c*) 1 Hz – 10^{-3} Hz

(*d*) 10^{3} Hz – 10^{6} Hz

68. Assertion (a) : The Static Self-Potential for a thick, clean freshwater bearing sandstone formation is positive.

Reason (r) : Resistivity of the formation water is less than the resistivity of salt water mud-filtrate.

(*a*) Both (a) and (r) are true and (r) is the correct reason for (a).

(*b*) Both (a) and (r) are true and (r) is not the correct reason for (a)

(*c*) Both (a) and (r) are false.

(*d*) (a) is true but (r) is false.

69. Which one of the following well log responses characterizes an overpressured zone in the subsurface?

(*a*) High velocity and high resistivity.

(*b*) Low velocity and low density.

(*c*) High velocity and low resistivity.

(*d*) Low velocity and high density.

70. The angle of inclination of the remanent magnetization measured on a basalt flow at a location P (28°N 85°E) is 40°. The palaeomagnetic latitude of the basalt flow is _______ °N.

71. Using the Gutenberg-Richter recurrence relationship, the mean annual rate of exceedance of earthquake occurrence in a seismic belt is 0.3 per year for an earthquake of magnitude 6.0. The return period for an earthquake of magnitude 6.0 in this belt is ______ years.

72. In the figure below, Z denotes the depth to the center of a buried sphere from the surface and $X_{\frac{1}{2}}$ denotes the half-width of the profile at half the maximum value of gravity. Then, the ratio $\frac{Z}{X_{\frac{1}{2}}}$ is ________.

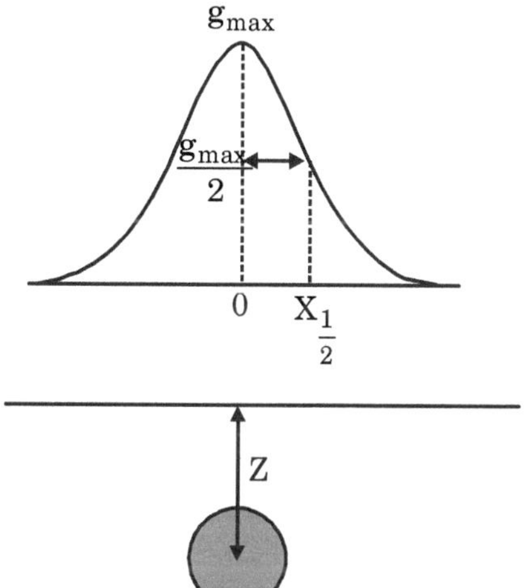

73. Two survey vessels with shipborne gravimeters are cruising towards each other at a speed of 6 knots each along an east-west course. The difference in gravity readings of the two-gravimeters is 63.5 mGal at the point at which the survey vessels cross each other. The latitude along which the survey vessels are cruising is ______ °N

74. A gravity reading is taken in a stationary helicopter hovering 1 km above mean-sea level at a particular location. The difference in the value of g measured in the helicopter and at mean sea level vertically beneath the helicopter is ____________ mGals.

75. The P-wave velocity and the Poisson's ratio for a homogeneous and isotropic sedimentary rock are 2500 m/s and 0.3, respectively. The S-wave velocity for the rock is ________m/s.

76. A plane electromagnetic (EM) wave travelling vertically downwards with a frequency of 1000 Hz in a homogeneous medium has a skin depth of 100 m. The ratio of the amplitude of the EM wave at a depth of 75 m with respect to the amplitude at the Earth's surface is ___________.

77. A student interpreted a four layer Schlumberger resistivity sounding data and obtained the resistivities (ρ) and thicknesses (h) as follows: $\rho_1 = 100\ \Omega m$, $\rho_2 = 20\ \Omega m$, $\rho_3 = 1500\ \Omega m$ and $\rho_4 = 50\ \Omega m$; $h_1 = 50$ m, $h_2 = 10$ m and $h_3 = 20$ m. The same data is interpreted by another student who obtains $\rho_3 = 2000\ \Omega m$. Then, according to the principle of equivalence, the value of h_3 interpreted by the second student is ________m. (All other model parameters estimated by both the students are the same.)

78. The apparent resistivities obtained at 0.1 Hz and 10 Hz in the frequency domain I.P. measurement are 100 Ωm and 80 Ωm, respectively. The Percentage Frequency Effect is ________.

79. A 15 Volt power supply is applied across a cylindrical container (diameter = 0.20 m and length = 0.50 m). Currents of 750 mA and 500 mA are measured when the container is filled with (i) brine only, and (ii) rock sample fully saturated with brine, respectively. The formation factor of the rock sample is ________.

80. The ratio of the number of daughter nuclides to the number of parent nuclides after a decay period of 3 half-lives is ________..

81. Consider a laterally homogeneous and isotropic earth model with a flat horizontal surface and three horizontal layers underlain by a half-space. A seismic reflection survey was simulated on this model with the sources and receivers placed on the surface. The table below lists the root mean square (rms) velocities, V rms, and zero-offset two-way traveltimes t_0 for the three reflection events from the bottom of each of the three layers observed in a pre-stack CDP (CMP) gather. The interval velocity of the second layer is ______ m/s.

Reflection Event	V_{rms}	t_0
1	1500 m/s	0.2 s
2	1600 m/s	0.3 s
3.	1700 m/s	0.4 s

82. A spherically symmetric vector field $\overline{g(r)}$ is defined by the relationship $\nabla . \overline{g(r)} = -r$. The flux of the vector field through a sphere of unit radius is ________.
(Use π = 3.14)

83. A horizontally travelling surface wave with a wavelength of 20 m is attenuated by a linear and uniform receiver array consisting of 4 receivers if the minimum receiver spacing is ________ m.

84. An end-on marine survey is carried out with equal and uniform shot and receiver spacing. If the total number of shots fired is 50 and a total of 10000 traces are recorded, the maximum fold for the survey is ______.

85. The highest singular value of the matrix $G = \begin{pmatrix} 1 & 2 & 1 \\ -1 & 2 & 0 \end{pmatrix}$ is ________.

ANSWERS

(General Aptitude)

1. (a)	**2.** (c)	**3.** (b)	**4.** (c)	**5.** (d)	**6.** (a)	**7.** (c)	**8.** (d)	**9.** (c)	**10.** (a)

PART A (Common Part)

1. (b)	**2.** (c)	**3.** (c)	**4.** (a)	**5.** (d)	**6.** (b)	**7.** (b)	**8.** (c)	**9.** (d)	**10.** (d)
11. (c)	**12.** (c)	**13.** (a)	**14.** (b)	**15.** (d)	**16.** (b)	**17.** (b)	**18.** (a)	**19.** (a)	**20.** (b)
21. (d)	**22.** (b)	**23.** (*)	**24.** (*)	**25.** (*)					

PART-B (Geology)

26. (b)	**27.** (a)	**28.** (d)	**29.** (b)	**30.** (a)	**31.** (a)	**32.** (c)	**33.** (b)	**34.** (d)	**35.** (d)
36. (a)	**37.** (d)	**38.** (a)	**39.** (b)	**40.** (c)	**41.** (b)	**42.** (a)	**43.** (c)	**44.** (d)	**45.** (*)
46. (*)	**47.** (*)	**48.** (*)	**49.** (*)	**50.** (*)	**51.** (*)	**52.** (*)	**53.** (*)	**54.** (*)	**55.** (*)

(Geophysics)

56. (b)	**57.** (d)	**58.** (a)	**59.** (c, d)	**60.** (a)	**61.** (c)	**62.** (a)	**63.** (b)	**64.** (c)	**65.** (c)
66. (a)	**67.** (c)	**68.** (d)	**69.** (b)	**70.** (*)	**71.** (*)	**72.** (*)	73. (*)	**74.** (*)	**75.** (*)
76. (*)	**77.** (*)	**78.** (*)	**79.** (*)	**80.** (*)	**81.** (*)	**82.** (*)	**83.** (*)	**84.** (*)	**85.** (*)

EXPLANATIONS

(GENERAL APTITUDE SECTION)

1. When she fell down the stairs, she received many stares but little help."

   Stare means 'a long fixed or vacant look'.

2. "In spite of being warned repeatedly, he failed to correct his errant behaviour ."

   errant is the most suitable word in this question

3. 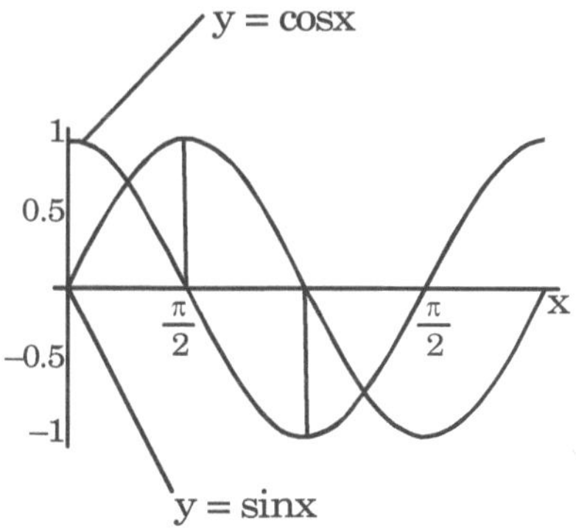

   Both functions are decreasing in the interval $\left(\frac{\pi}{2}, \pi\right)$

4. Area of equilateral triangle is given by

   $\frac{\sqrt{3}}{4}a^2 = \sqrt{3}$ [As per question]

   $\therefore a = 2$

   Now, Perimeter = $3a$ = 6

5. The Volume of each object is given as

   (i) $V_{cuboid} = L \times B \times H = 10 \times 8 \times 6 = 480 \text{ cm}^2$

   (ii) $V_{cube} = a^3 = 8^3 = 512 \text{ cm}^2$

   (iii) $V_{cylinder} = \pi r^2 h = \pi \times 7^2 \times 7 = 1077.56 \text{ cm}^2$

   (iv) $V_{sphere} = \frac{4}{3}\pi r^3 = \frac{4}{3} \times \pi \times 7^3 = 1436.76 \text{ cm}^2$

   Therefore, the descending order is (iv), (iii), (ii), (i).

6. 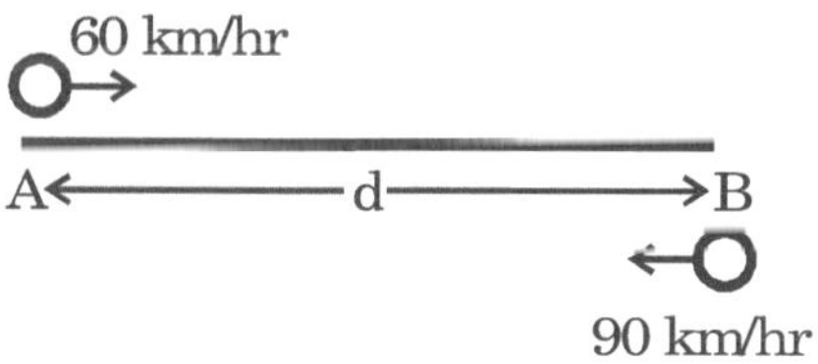

   Average Speed = $\frac{\text{Distance}}{\text{Time taken}}$

   Total distance travelled = $2d$

   Total time taken = Time taken from A + B + Time taken from B to a = $\frac{d}{60} + \frac{d}{90}$

   Average speed = $\frac{2d}{\frac{d}{60} + \frac{d}{90}} = \frac{2d \times 180}{5d} = 72$ km/hr

7. If we choose any 2 of the 4 lines and any 2 of the 5 lines we will get a parallelogram. This way we can count all the possibilities.

   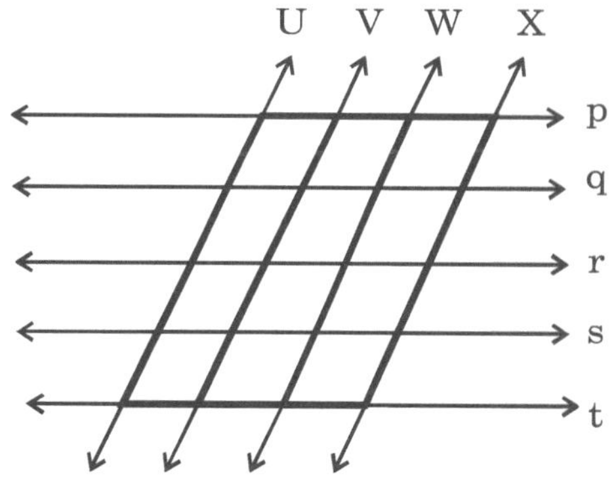

   $\binom{4}{2} \times \binom{5}{2} = 6 \times 10 = 60$

   Here, the first term is the ways of choosing 2 lines out of 4 parallel lines, and the second term is for choosing 2 lines out of 5 parallel lines.

8. Let us consider that the number of students who answered correctly is x.

   Now, as per question,

   The equation using inclusion exclusion principle,

   $63000 - x = 330000 + 250000 + 260000 - 100000 - 900000 - 800000 + x$

   $\Rightarrow x = 30000$

   As per question t pass the student needs to answer atleast 2 out of 3 question

   Thus, those who answered one answer correctly is also considered fail.

   Only A answered correctly 330000 − 100000 − 80000 + 30000 = 180000

   Only B answered correctly 250000 − 100000 − 90000 + 30000 = 90000

   Only C answered correctly 260000 − 80000 − 90000 + 30000 = 120000

   Therefore, total failed student 180000 + 90000 + 120000 + 30000 = 420000

9. $(x^2 + x - 1) = 0$

   $\Rightarrow (x^2 - 1) = -x$

   Squaring both sides

   $\Rightarrow (x^2 - 1)^2 = (-x)^2$

$$\Rightarrow x^4 - 2x^2 + 1 = x^2$$

$$\Rightarrow x^4 + 1 = 3x^2$$

Again, Squaring both sides

$$\Rightarrow \left(x^4 + 1\right)^2 = \left(3x^2\right)^2$$

$$\Rightarrow x^8 + 2x^4 + 1 = 9x^4$$

$$\Rightarrow x^8 + 1 = 7x^4$$

Dividing by x^4 on both sides, we get,

$$x^4 + \frac{1}{x^4} = 7$$

10. In the graph in the given question, during the period 2002 to 2004, there was relatively no crow birth. Whereas, cracker sales also remain flat from 2002 to 2004.

In between 2004 to 2005, there was a sudden spike in crow birth, and in this period, cracker sales increase.

In 2006, crow birth decreases, cracker sale also decreases.

Therefore, we can say that there was a strong correlation between crow birth and cracker sales.

PART A (COMMON PART)

1. Geologic time correlates rocks and time. The longest divisions of geologic time are the eras. Most geologic time scales recognize four eras, three of which have been named for the fossils in the associated strata. Thus, the Paleozoic Era refers to "ancient life," the Mesozoic Era to "medieval life" and the Cenozoic Era to "modern life." Rocks older than Paleozoic generally lack diagnostic fossils and are widely known as belonging to the Precambrian Era.

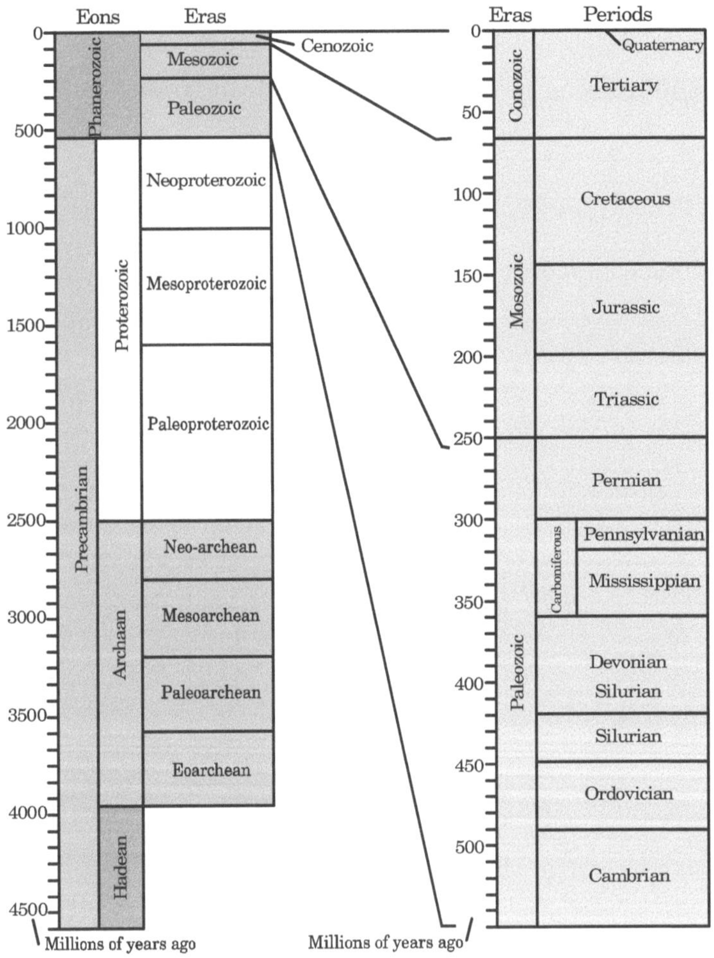

2. A siliciclastic sedimentary rock consisting predominantly of the same type of gravel-sized clasts is called Oligomict congomerates.

Conglomerates are very special in the sedimentary record for two reasons:

- They are always associated with high energy systems.
- They bring large chunks of material right to your feet. Thus, they more often preserve properties of bulk source rock, in addition to the minerals of which it consisted.

As such, they are very helpful in reconstructing provenance of the hinterland, as they consist of sediments that generally have not been transported far, and are often linked to nearby tectonic activity. Together these comprise 1 - 2% of sedimentary rocks.

Conglomerates may be named and classified by the:

- Amount and type of matrix present
- Composition of gravel-size clasts they contain
- Size range of gravel-size clasts present

A sedimentary rock composed largely of gravel is first named according to the roundness of the gravel. If the gravel clasts that comprise it is largely well rounded to subrounded, it is a conglomerate. If the gravel clasts that comprise it are largely angular, it is a breccia.

Conglomerates are also classified according to the composition of their clasts. A conglomerate or any clastic sedimentary rock that consists of a single rock or mineral is known as either a monomict, monomictic, oligomict, or oligomictic conglomerate. If the conglomerate consists of two or more different types of rocks, minerals, or combination of both, it is known as either a polymict or polymictic conglomerate.

3. **Types of Coal :** Based on the degree to which the original plant material has been transformed into carbon and percent of carbon content, coal is classified into different types:
   - **Lignite coal :** Lignite is brownish black, has a high moisture content (up to 45 %), and a high suphur content. Lignite is more like soil than a rock and tends to disintegrate when exposed to the weather. Lignite is also called brown coal.
   - **Subbituminous coal :** Subbituminous coal is also called black lignite. Subbituminous coal black and contains 20-30 % moisture. Subbituminous coal is used for generating electricity and space heating.
   - **Bituminous coal :** Bituminous coal is a soft, dense, black coal. Bituminous coal often has bands of bright and dull material in it. Bituminous coal is the most common coal and has a moisture content less than 20%. Bituminous coal is used for generating electricity, making coke, and space heating.
   - **Anthracite coal :** Often referred to as hard coal, anthracite is hard, black and lustrous. Anthracite is low in suplhur and high in carbon. It is the highest rank of coal. Moisture content generally is less than 15 %.

4. The velocity of an object at some distance r from the Sun is given as,

$$V = \sqrt{GM \times \left(\frac{2}{r} - \frac{1}{a}\right)}$$

where G is the universal gravitationa, constant,

M is the mass of Sun,

R is the distance between Sun and earth

And a is the planet's semimajor axis.

At perihelion, Earth's distance from the Sun is $r = a(1-e)$ and at aphelion, it's $r = a(1+e)$.

Also, $G = 6.673 \times 10^{-11}$ N m^2/kg^2

$M = 1.989 \times 10^{30}$ kg

$a = 1.496 \times 10^{11}$ m

$e = 0.017$

The speed at perihelion is therefore 30,300 m/s and at aphelion it's 29,300 m/s.

Therefore, it is maximum at perihelion.

5. For the given configuration in the figure this is a case of pole-dipole, the geometrical factor is given as

$$\rho = 2\pi an(n+1)\frac{V}{I}$$

As per figure, $n = 1$

$$\therefore \rho = 2\pi a1(1+1)\frac{V}{I} = 4\pi a\frac{V}{I}$$

6. **Ground Penetrating Radar:** One of the other main applications for ground-penetrating radars is for locating underground utilities. Standard electromagnetic induction utility locating tools require utilities to be conductive. These tools are ineffective for locating plastic conduits or concrete storm and sanitary sewers. Since GPR detects variations in dielectric properties in the subsurface, it can be highly effective for locating non-conductive utilities.

7. Pascal second (Ns/m^2) is the unit of dynamic viscosity which is also known as the absolute viscosity of the fluid.

8. Increasing confined pressure has an effect of increasing the value of yield stress and the specimen has an overall increase in its strength, all the other variables being constant. Therefore, option A is not correct.

   Increasing the temperature can decrease the yield stress (the strength that stress needs to exceed for deformation to go from elastic to becoming permanent). Option B is also not correct.

   Decreasing the strain rate decreases a rocks strength, causing it to become more ductile and vice versa. Thus, Option C is correct.

Pore-fluid pressure occurs because water is trapped within the pores of rocks. Like confining pressure, it also acts equally in all directions, but counteracts the effects of confining pressure i.e. on an increase in pore-fluid pressure, the strength of the rock decreases. Therefore, Option D is also not correct.

9. A glacial horn is a feature created by glaciers and what exactly this term means is intricately linked with how it formed. A horn is a peak that forms from three arêtes. It is also known as a pyramidal peak.

10. Option A- **Trachyte** is an extrusive rock, belonging to the alkali series of intermediate volcanic rocks. The major mineral component of trachyte is alkali feldspar (e.g. orthoclase), and it generally contains no quartz. Trachyte often displays trachytic texture, where acicular to tabular feldspar phenocrysts align in one direction, suggestive of flow prior to cooling.

Option B - **Dacite** is a felsic extrusive rock, intermediate in composition between andesite and rhyolite. It is often found associated with andesite, and forms lava flows, dikes, and, in some cases, massive intrusions in the centers of old volcanoes. Dacite is the volcanic equivalent of granodiorite.

Option C - **Andesite** is an extrusive rock intermediate in composition between rhyolite and basalt. Andesite lava is of moderate viscosity and forms thick lava flows and domes. The word andesite is derived from the Andes Mountains in South America, where andesite is common. Andesite is the volcanic equivalent of diorite.

Option D – **Lamprophyre** is a group of dark gray to black intrusive igneous rocks that generally occur as dikes (tabular bodies inserted in fissures). Such rocks are characterized by a porphyritic texture in which large crystals (phenocrysts) of dark, iron-magnesium (mafic) minerals are enclosed in a fine-grained to dense matrix (groundmass). The abundance, large size, well-formed crystal outline, and brilliantly reflecting cleavage faces of the mafic phenocrysts give the rock a striking appearance.

11. **Rodinia** meaning, "to give birth", is the name of a supercontinent. It had most or all of Earth's landmass when the Neoproterozoic era began. Rodinia existed between 1.1 billion and 750 million years ago. It formed from parts of the older supercontinent, Columbia. Rodinia broke up in the first period of the Neoproterozoic, the Tonian. Later its continental fragments were re-assembled to form Pangaea 300–250 million years ago. In contrast with Pangaea, little is known yet about the exact position and history of Rodinia.

The extreme cooling of the global climate around 700 million years ago (the so called Snowball Earth of the Cryogenian period) and the rapid evolution of primitive life during the following Ediacaran and Cambrian periods may have been triggered by the breaking up of Rodinia.

12. As per figure, the boundary between plates B and C is a sinistral transform fault and the relative velocity is given as 6 – 4 = 2 cm/year.

13. As per Mohr – Coulomb failure criterion for the rock under stress state Y the PP' line touches the Y stress Mohr circle which indicates the failure of the rock.

14. The maximum and the minimum principal stresses are denoted by σ_1 and σ_3, respectively.

The differential stress can have an absolute value greater than σ_1 when σ_1 is compressive and σ_3 is tensile.

Differential stress, $\sigma_d = \sigma_1 - \sigma_3$

$\Rightarrow \sigma_3 = \sigma_1 - \sigma_d$

As $\sigma_d > \sigma_1$, σ_3 must be –ve.

Thus, σ_3 is tensile.

15. **Geoid**: The equipotential surface of the Earth's gravity field which best fits, in a least squares sense, global mean sea level.

16. Types of seismic waves

- Body waves — travel through interior
- Surface waves — travel on surface of earth

➢ **P wave** - Deformation propagates. Particle motion consists of alternating compression and dilation. Particle motion is parallel to the direction of propagation (longitudinal). Material returns to its original shape after wave passes.

➢ **S wave** - Deformation propagates. Particle motion consists of alternating transverse motion. Particle motion is perpendicular to the direction of propagation (transverse). Transverse particle motion shown here is vertical but can be in any direction.

➢ **Rayleigh wave** - Deformation propagates. Particle motion consists of elliptical motions (generally retrograde elliptical) in the vertical plane and parallel to the direction of propagation. Amplitude decreases with depth. Material returns to its original shape after wave passes.

➢ **Love wave** - Deformation propagates. Particle motion consists of alternating transverse motions. Particle motion is horizontal and perpendicular to the direction of propagation (transverse). Amplitude decreases with depth. Material returns to its original shape after wave passes.

The definition provide P-3; Q-1; R-4; S-2 to match.

17. A 'gentle' fold with an interlimb angle equal to appears tight (apparent interlimb angle equal to) in horizontal section. According to the plunge of the fold axis, it can also be classified as gently plunging fold.

18. Shear modulus or modulus of rigidity, denoted by G, or sometimes S or ¼, is defined as the ratio of shear stress to the shear strain. The derived SI unit of shear modulus is the pascal (Pa)

Its dimensional form is $M^1L^{-1}T^{-2}$

Therefore, the unit of shear modulus is kg/ms^2 or $kg\ m^{-1}s^{-2}$.

19. With increasing activity of silica, the correct order of appearance of minerals in a weathering environment with constant ratio of activities of K^+ and H^+ is

Gibbsite $\left(Al(OH)_3\right) \rightarrow$ Kaolinite

$\left(Al_2Si_2O_5(OH)_4\right) \rightarrow$ Pyrophyllite

$\left(Al_2Si_4O_{10}(OH)_2\right)$

20. Group I contains of names of minerals and Group II contains place where these minerals are found.

Beldih is an important location for apatite mining and is exactly located along south Purulia shear zone (SPSZ). Geological study suggests that Beldih **phosphate mine** lies near the SPSZ.

During a random radiometric survey, nuclear radiation was detected near exposed rocks in an open-pit phosphatemine at Beldih (Purulia, W.B.), India.

Kodarma (also spelled as Koderma) is a city and a notified area in Koderma district in the Indian state of Jharkhand. The Koderma district and the Lokai-Indarwa area covers the southern part of Great **Mica-Belt** of Jharkhand, Bihar and India. Previously the Mica belt was known as Bihar mica belt, which extends for a distance of 160 km having an average width of 25 kms. The mica belt strenches from Gurpa in Gaya district in the west through Nawada, Koderma, Hazaribag, Giridih in Jharkhand and Jamui as well as Bhagalpur district of the Bihar state in the east. Its maximum width is about 40 km at Koderma-Hazaribagh-Nawada area. The whole belt encompasses roughly 4,000 sq. km. around area, lies on the north fringe of Chotanagpur plateau, and runs in an east-north east to west-southwest direction.

Rampura Agucha is a **zinc** and **lead** mine located on a massive sulfide deposit in the Bhilwara district of Rajasthan, India. Rampura-Agucha zinc-lead deposit, located 15 km southeast of Gulabpura in Bhilwara District, Rajasthan, forms a part of pre-Aravalli Banded Gneissic Complex (3.2 to 2.5 billion years old) consisting of gneisses. schists and intrusives of acidic and basic igneous rocks, that occupy predominantly the southeastern plain of Ajmer and Bhilwara.

21. Terrain correction is always added during reduction of the observed gravity data.

22. The total geomagnetic field at equator is twice that of the total geomagnetic at poles and is given as

$B_P \approx 2B_E$

That magnetic force at the poles (ends) of a dipole is stronger because it is "concentrated." The force that is along the axis between the poles of the dipole (between the poles (or ends) is less dense (concentrated) than the poles. Interestingly a cone shaped magnet has a stronger field at the tip than the base (depending on the design, it can be very much stronger).

23. Given,

Crustal Thickness, h = 35 km

Average crustal P wave velocity,

$V_{P_{crust}} = 6.4$ km/s

$V_{P_{mantle}} = 8.1$ km/s

Minimum distance from the epicenter at which the P-waves will be observed is equal to the distance at which the internally reflected wave at critical angle reaches the surface.

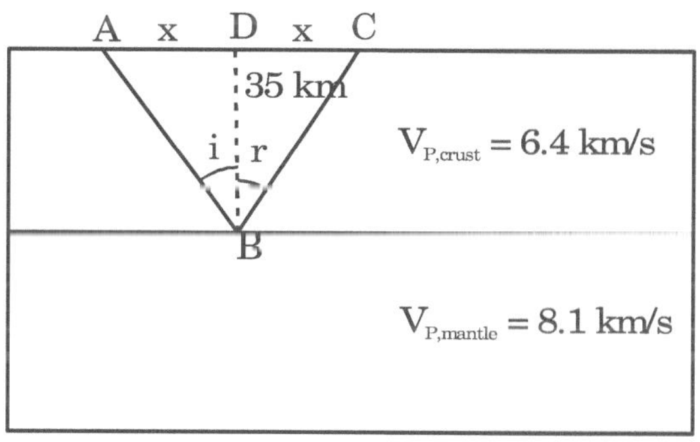

Using snell's law

$$\frac{\sin i}{\sin r} = \frac{V_{P_{crust}}}{V_{P_{mantle}}}$$

where, 'i' is incident ray

and 'r' is refracted ray

$$\therefore \frac{\sin i}{\sin r} = \frac{6.4}{8.1}$$

At critical angle of refraction, $r_c = 90°$

Therefore, $\sin r_c = 1$

Now, As per figure

$$\frac{\sin i}{\sin r_c} = \frac{x}{AB}$$

$$\Rightarrow \frac{6.4}{8.1} = \frac{x}{\sqrt{x^2 + (35)^2}}$$

$$\Rightarrow 64(x + 35) = 81x$$

$$\Rightarrow 64x + 2240 = 81x$$

$$\Rightarrow 2240 = 81x - 64x$$

$$\Rightarrow 2240 = 17x$$

$$\Rightarrow x = 131.76\ km$$

Minimum distance at which P_n observed

$= 2x = 263.52$ km

24. Given,

Porosity, $\phi = 30\%$

Velocity of sandstone matrix, $V_S = 5600$ m/s

Velocity of oil, $V_0 = 1200$ m/s

Now, As per Wyllie time average equation, given as

$$\frac{1}{V} = \frac{\phi}{V_o} + \frac{1-\phi}{V_s}$$

$\therefore$ As per question

$$\frac{1}{V} = \frac{0.3}{1200} + \frac{0.7}{5600}$$

$$\Rightarrow \frac{1}{V} = \frac{3}{8000}$$

$$\Rightarrow V = \frac{8000}{3} = 2666.67\ \text{m/s}$$

25. The relationship between porosity and void ratio are given as,

$$e = \frac{V_V}{V_s} = \frac{V_V}{V_T - V_V} = \frac{\phi}{1-\phi}$$

where,

ϕ is the porosity

e is the void ratio

V_v is the volume of voids

V_s is the volume of solids

V_T is the bulk volume

Now, As per question,

Given, $\phi = 20\ \% = 0.2$

$$\therefore e = \frac{0.2}{1-0.2} = 0.25 = 25\%$$

PART-B (GEOLOGY)

26. Rangit Pebble Slate: To the south of the Central crystalline zone of the Darjeeling Himalayas, in the interior parts of the frontal zone of the nappes, a sequence of the Lower Gondwana rocks occurs in a window, overlain by the tectonic cover of the Daling-Darjeeling group of metamorphites. A prominent marine fauna bearing pebble-slate horizon is developed at the base of this sequence. The stratigraphy and lithologic characters of this horizon are described in detail, and are considered significant in the context of the palaeogeography and tectonic evolution of this part of Himalaya.

27. Orpiment is a photosensitive mineral and will eventually dull and develop a white powdery film upon prolonged exposure to light. Due to the instability of Orpiment, specimens should be stored enclosed and covered to prevent their exposure to light. Occasional exposure to look at a specimen will not cause damage; only prolonged or repeated exposure will cause deterioration.

28. Equilibrium reaction between quartz and magnetite:

Si16O16O + Fe316O318O = Si16O18O + Fe316O4

(K is the equilibrium constant at the specified temperature and n is the number of exchangeable atomic sites)

29. The burrowing success of recently transported juvenile softshell clams (Mya arenaria) was studied in a laboratory flume under a wide range of hydrosedimentary environments. Juvenile individuals (5–20 mm) were observed under a simulated 30 min slack tide before initiating the flow for a period of 60 min.

Gryphaea (or Devil's Toenail) : This is an extinct genus of bivalve that is thought to have existed roughly 150 million years ago. It is believed to have been an unattached recumbent recliner on the sea floor, with its very own self-righting mechanism if a strong current knocked it out of the sediment.

The colour of the body of Pecten maximus is pink or red with the mantle marbled brown and white. When young they are attached to the substrate by a byssus but mature animals are capable of swimming by the opening and rapid closing of the valves.

30. As per the hypothetical litholog that shows succession of sedimentary rocks in the question,

The rocks range from Cambrian to Cretaceous and show change in depositional environment from marine to continental.

31. A cladogram is a diagram used to represent a hypothetical relationship between groups of animals, called a phylogeny. A scientist studying phylogenetic systematics to visualize the groups of organisms being compared, how they are related, and their most common ancestors uses a cladogram.

As per given figure in the question, Cladogram I shows the correct interrelationships among the major group of vertebrates.

32. Chronological order (order to younger)

Bagh Bed (older)

↓

Lameta Formation,

↓

Deccan Traps (younger)

33. Peloids are allochems that are composed of micrite, irrespective of size, shape, or origin. The two primary types of peloids are pellets and intraclasts. Another type of peloid is pseudo-oolith.

Ooids are small (commonly d"2 mm in diameter), spheroidal, "coated" (layered) sedimentary grains, usually composed of calcium carbonate, but sometimes made up of iron- or phosphate-based minerals. Ooids usually form on the sea floor, most commonly in shallow tropical seas.

Oncoids: Grains containing nucleus surrounded by irregular, non- concentric laminae.

The cortoids are coated with micrite similar to that which comprises the ooid cortices, and may be finely laminated or dense and cloudy in nature.

34. Rubbersheeting refers to the process by which a layer is distorted to allow it to be seamlessly joined to an adjacent geographic layer of matching imagery, such as satellite imagery which are digital maps. This is sometimes referred to as image-to-vector conflation. Often this has to be done when layers created from adjacent map sheets are joined together. Rubber-sheeting is necessary because the imagery and the vector data will rarely match up correctly due to various reasons, such as the angle at which the image was taken, the curvature of the surface of the earth, minor movements in the imaging platform (such as a satellite or aircraft), and other errors in the imagery.

35. The one-dimensional compression and swelling characteristics of a soil may be measured in the laboratory using the oedometer test. A cylindrical specimen of soil enclosed in a metal ring is subjected to a series of increasing static loads, while changes in thickness are recorded against time. From the changes in thickness at the end of each load stage the compressibility of the soil may be observed, and parameters measured such as Compression Index (Cc) and Coefficient of Volume Compressibility (mv).

Shotcrete figures prominently among several methods for slope stabilization due to its versatility, durability, early resistance and its capacity to adhere to/ adherence to the subtract. Because shotcrete is applied pneumatically, the material is compacted against the surface to fill cracks and fissures and prevent loose material from falling. Shotcrete can therefore act both as a protective coating over the slope's surface, but also as an 'anchoring surface' onto which bolts and other support systems can be fastened.

In-situ rock stress measurement by overcoring from the surface, using a specialised equipment commonly referred to as an IST (In-situ Stress Testing) tool, provides a means of stress measurement technique on virgin or exploration grounds. Stress measurement depths of up to 750 meters from surface have been achieved, where the rock strata may have differing stiffness.

Indirect tension tests using Brisbane tuff Brazilian disc specimens under standard Brazilian jaws and various loading arcs were performed. The standard Brazilian indirect tensile tests caused catastrophic, crushing failure of the disc specimens, rather than the expected tensile splitting failure initiated by a central crack. This led to an investigation of the fracturing of Brazilian disc specimens and the existing indirect tensile Brazilian test using steel loading arcs with different angles. The results showed that the ultimate failure load increased with increasing loading arc angles.

36. A crevasse is a deep crack, or fracture, found in an ice sheet or glacier, as opposed to a crevice that forms in rock. Crevasses form because of the movement and resulting stress associated with the shear stress generated when two semi-rigid pieces above a plastic substrate have different rates of movement. The resulting intensity of the shear stress causes a breakage along the faces.

A yardang is a streamlined protuberance carved from bedrock or any consolidated or semiconsolidated material by the dual action of wind abrasion by dust and sand, and deflation, which is the removal of loose material by wind turbulence.

Mesa is the American English term for tableland, an elevated area of land with a flat top and sides that are usually steep cliffs. It takes its name from its characteristic tabletop shape. It may also be called a table hill, table-topped hill or table mountain. It is larger than a butte, which it otherwise resembles closely.

A stalactite is a type of formation that hangs from the ceiling of caves, hot springs, or manmade structures such as bridges and mines.

37. The system in the given figure is a peritectic type reaction system. Here, W is an invariant point and B, D and E are available solids.

The reaction at point W can be found out by dividing the diagram into triangular regions.

AT W, outside triangle ABE and BDE lies the liquid composition and inside triangle AEC. Thus, the solid B and D cannot crystallize. Only solid E can crystallize out. Therefore, the reaction would be Liquid (at W) +B + D = E

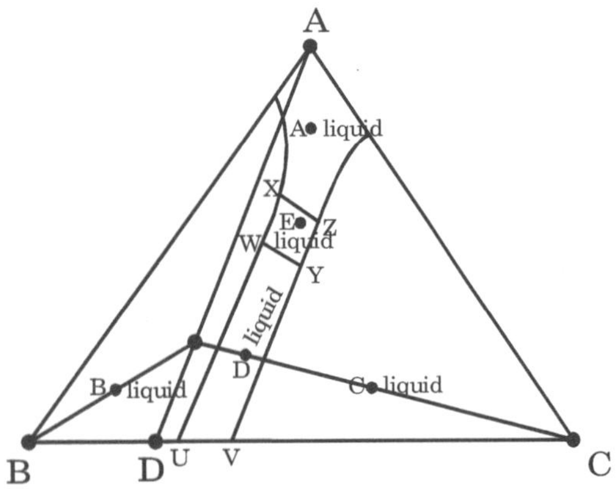

38.

Optical properties	Minerals
Brown colour, very high refractive index, very high birefringence, biaxial positive	Titanite
Colourless, very high refractive index, low birefringence, uniaxial negative	Apatite
Deep reddish-brown colour, very high refractive index, very high birefringence, uniaxial positive	Rutile
Colourless, very high refractive index, very high birefringence, uniaxial positive	Zircon

39. Given,

The reaction

muscovite + quartz = K-feldspar + sillimanite + water

The above reaction takes place within the amphibolite facies.

40.

Group-I	Group-II
P. Diopside-tremolite-forsterite	Calc-silicate (moderate P, T)
Q. Talc-phengite-kyanite	Pelite (high P, low T)
R. Hornblende-cummingtonite-plagioclase	Metabasite (low P, high T)
S. Andalusite-cordierite-biotite	Pelite (low P, high T)

41. The figure shown in Stage 2 with respect to the creation of the synform and antiform. For the next increment of movement on the fault plane, the synform will remain in position, while the antiform will grow in amplitude. Anticline grows in amplitude and the synform remains in position as the fold grows.

42. For Iron formations

Algoma type > Superior type > Rapitan type > Minette type

Algoma type is the oldest Archaean and seems to be associated with volcanics arcs.

Superior type formed on stable continental shelves during the paleo- Proterozoic.

Rapitan type formed due to environmental changes associated with glaciation during the neo-Proterozoic.

Minette type formed during the Jurassic in fluvial/marine setting.

43. Assertion (a): High-temperature, low-pressure metamorphism occurs on the over-riding plate near convergent plate margins.

Reason (r): Partial melting in the mantle wedge generates magmas that rise to form the arc.

The magma generated by partial melting of the subduction plate rises to the over-riding plate and produces high temperature and low-pressure metamorphism. Therefore,

Both (a) and (r) are true and (r) is the correct reason for (a).

44. The co-existence of liquid phase and gaseous phase is possible at same temperature, during boiling. Either a liquid-rich (X) or a vapour-rich (Y) inclusion can be trapped during boiling. During cooling, this inclusion will subsequently separate into two phases. Thus, during homogenization, X will homogenize into liquid and Y will homogenize to vapour at the same temperature.

45. Given,

Mass of explosive, $m = 50$ kg

Yield = 5 MegaJoule/kg

Total Volume = 100 m^3

Now, Total energy expended = mass × yield

= 50 × 5 MegaJoules

Energy required for breaking a unit volume

$$= \frac{50 \times 5}{100} = 2.5 \text{ MegaNewton/m}^2$$

46. The stretching lineation on the axial plane (S2) of a reclined fold on the S1 foliation makes an angle of 30° with the S1/S2 intersection lineation. As the fold is a reclined fold, the hinge line dips along the axial plane with the same plunge as the dip of the axial plane. Thus, the intersection of the foliation S1 and the axial plane S2 is basically the hinge line. Therefore, the rake of the stretching lineation on the axial plane is 60°.

47. During equilibrium crystallization the newly formed crystals are in equilibrium with the melt and the crystal composition keeps on varying until the crystallization has reached completion. In contrast, during fractional crystallization the crystals are removed from the system as soon as they are formed.

Case–I

Equilibrium crystallization model is described by the same equation as that of batch melting,

$$\frac{C_L}{C_O} = \frac{1}{D_i(1-F)+F}$$

where F is weight fraction of solid, and is equal to 1 - weight fraction of liquid

For 0.25 liquid fraction, F = 1 – 0.25 = 0.75

$$\frac{C_L}{300} = \frac{1}{10(1-0.75)+0.75}$$

$$\Rightarrow C_L = \frac{300}{3.25} = 92.30$$

Case–II

Fractional Crystallization model equation

$$\frac{C_L}{C_O} = F^{(D_i-1)}$$

$$\frac{C_L}{300} = 0.75^{(10-1)}$$

$$\Rightarrow C_L = 300 \times 0.075 = 22.52$$

Difference in $C_L = 92.30 - 22.52 = 69.78$

48. The Isometric crystal system has three equivalent crystallographic axes perpendicular to each other. The objects of this crystal system appear as if they could be fit into a sphere. This system has 6 crystal classes. The holosymmetric class is characterized by following symmetry operations: 4/m3 * 2/m

The {1 1 1} class is an octahedron possessing 8 faces.

The {h k 1} class is a hexakisoctahedron possessing 48 faces.

The difference in the number of faces in forms {hkl} and {111} in the holosymmetric class of the isometric system = 48 – 8 = 40

49. Given,

Coefficient of permeability, $K = 40$ m/day

Distance between aquifer, $\Delta L = 800$ m

Elevations, $h_1 = 45$ m and $h_2 = 50$ m

Now, As per Darcy's equation,

$$\frac{Q}{A} = \frac{K(h_2 - h_1)}{\Delta L}$$

where, $\frac{Q}{A}$ is the darcy flux

As per question,

$$\frac{Q}{A} = \frac{40(50-45)}{800} = 0.25 \text{ m/day}$$

50. Given,

Mass of soil, $m_{soil} = 2.1$ kg

Volume of soil, $V_{soil} = 1 \times 10^{-3}$ m^3

Mass of dry soil, $m_{day} = 2$ kg

Water density, $\rho_{water} = 1000$ kg/m^3

Specific gravity of soil, $\gamma_{soil} = 2.5$

Now, $m_{soil} = m_{dry} + m_{void}$

where, voids are filled with water and air, thus

$m_{soil} = m_{dry} + m_{water} + m_{air}$

$m_{water} = \rho_{water} \times V_{water} = \rho_{water} \times V_{void} \times S_w$

where, S_w is degree of saturation

$m_{water} = 100(V_{soil} - V_{dry})S_w$

Also, $m_{water} = m_{soil} - m_{dry} - m_{air}$

$1000(V_{soil} - V_{dry})S_w = 2.1 - 2 - 0$

$$\Rightarrow 1000\left(10^{-3} - \frac{2}{2500}\right)S_w = 0.1$$

$$\Rightarrow 0.2S_w = 0.1$$

$$\Rightarrow S_w = \frac{1}{2} = 0.5 = 50\ \%$$

51. Given,

Joint set number, $J_n = 9$

Joint water reduction factor, $J_w = 1$

Joint alteration number, $J_a = 1$

Stress Reduction factor, $SRF = 1$

Rock quality designation (%), $RQD = 84$

Joint Roughness Number, $J_r = 3$

The Q-value as per Barton's Q-system of rock mass classification is given as

$$Q = \frac{RQD}{J_n} \times \frac{J_r}{J_a} \times \frac{J_w}{SRF}$$

Now, As per question

$$Q = \frac{84}{9} \times \frac{3}{1} \times \frac{1}{1} = 28$$

52. Given,

Altitude, $h = 300$ km

Angular coverage angle, $\theta = 12°$

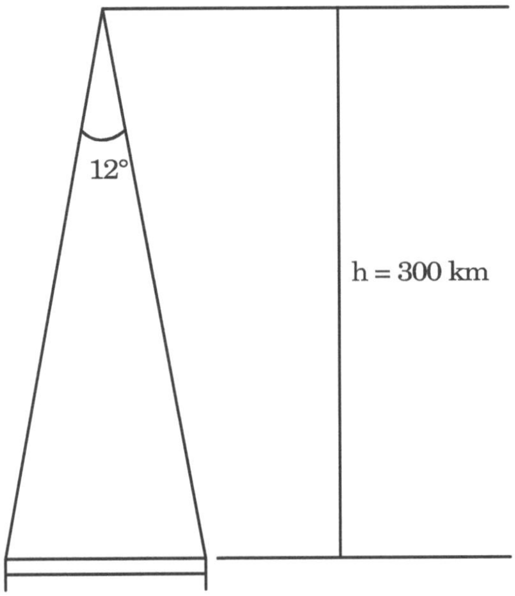

Now, The Swath of the satellite is given as,

$GFOV = h \times \tan\theta = 300 \times \tan 12 = 63.77$ km

53. Given,

Molar entropy

$S_A = 85.5$ Joules K^{-1}

$S_B = 92.5$ Joules K^{-1}

Molar Volumes

$V_A = 35.5$ cc

$V_B = 38.2$ cc

Now, According to Clapeyron equation,

$$\frac{dP}{dT} = \frac{\Delta S}{\Delta V}$$

$\therefore$ Slope of phase boundary in P–T space

$$= \frac{\Delta S}{\Delta V} = \frac{92.5 - 85.5}{38.2 - 35.5} = \frac{7}{2.7} \times 10^6 \ Pa$$

$$= 2.59 \times 10^6 \ Pa \ K^{-1}$$

$\because 1 \ bar = 10^5 \ Pa$

Thus, Slope = 25.9 bar K^{-1}

54. For isothermal expansion of gas, the change in entropy of the system is given as,

$$\Delta S = nR \ln\left(\frac{V_2}{V_1}\right)$$

where, V_2 is final volume

and V_1 is initial volume

For gas *A*, entropy change is

$$\Delta S_A = 5 \times 8.3 \times \ln\left(\frac{5+3}{5}\right) = 24.4 \ JK^{-1}$$

For gas *B*, entropy change is

$$\Delta S_B = 3 \times 8.3 \times \ln\left(\frac{5+3}{5}\right) = 19.5 \ JK^{-1}$$

$$\Delta S_{total} = \Delta S_A + \Delta S_B = 24.4 + 19.5 = 43.9 \ JK^{-1}$$

55. The Eh

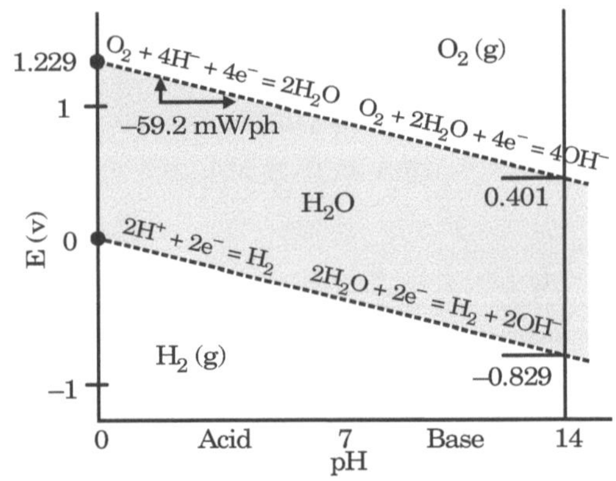

The pourbaix diagram gives the stability region of water. Below the lower limit, water is reduced to hydrogen according to the equation,

$$2H_2O + 2e^- \geq H_2 + 2OH^-$$

Above the upper limit, water is oxidized to equation according to the equation,

$$O_2 + 2H_2O + 4e^- \geq 4OH^-$$

The equation of the straight line marking the upper limit is

$$Eh = (1.229 - 0.0591 \times pH) \text{ volts}$$

Given, $pH = 8$

$$\therefore Eh = (1.229 - 0.0591 \times 8) = 0.7562 \text{ volts}$$

(GEOPHYSICS)

56. Given,

A matrix G where $m > n$

The maximum number of linearly independent rows in a matrix G is called the row rank of G, and the maximum number of linarly independent columns in G is called the column rank of G. If G is an m by n matrix, i.e., if G has m rows and n columns, then it is obvious that

row rank of G $\leq$ m

and, column rank of G $\leq$ n

This is true when, the row rank of G = the column rank of G. In case of inequalities

$$rank\left(A_{\min}\right) \leq \min(m,n)$$

Where min (m,n) denotes the smaller of the two numbers m and n.

In the given question, m > n

Therefore, the maximum number of linearly independent rows of an $m \times n$ matrix G is n.

57. An ellipse is the impulse response of the Kirchhoff pre-stack time migration operator for non-zero offsets in a homogeneous and isotropic medium.

58. For given eikonal equation $|\nabla \tau| = 1/v_0$

For a homogeneous and isotropic medium in cartesian coordinates is

$$\tau = \frac{\sqrt{x^2+y^2+z^2}}{v_0}$$

59. Given,

$$F(\omega) = e^{-2i\omega}$$

Now, As per formula of forward transform

$$F(\omega) = \int_{-\infty}^{\infty} f(t)e^{-i\omega t}dt$$

and for inverse Fourier transform

$$f(t) = \int_{-\infty}^{\infty} F(\omega)e^{i\omega t}d\omega$$

Applying inverse fourier transform to find $f(t)$

$$f(t) = \int_{-\infty}^{\infty} e^{-2i\omega}e^{i\omega t}d\omega$$

$$= \int_{-\infty}^{0} (0)e^{i\omega t}d\omega + \int_{0}^{\infty} e^{-2i\omega}e^{i\omega t}d\omega$$

$$= \int_{0}^{\infty} e^{i\omega(t-2)}d\omega = \delta(t \pm 2)$$

60. A table summarizing typical susceptibilities of common materials follows:

Material	Susceptibility x 10^{-3} (SI)
Air	about 0
Quartz	-0.01
Rock Salt	-0.01
Calcite	-0.011
Sphalerite	0.4
Pyrite	0.05 - 5
Hematite	0.5 - 35
Illmenite	300 - 3500
Magnetite	1200 - 19,200
Limestones	0 - 3
Sandstones	0 - 20
Shales	0.01 - 15
Schist	0.3 - 3
Gneiss	0.1 - 25
Slate	0 - 35
Granite	0 - 50
Gabbro	Jan-90
Basalt	0.2 - 175
Peridotite	90 - 200

61.

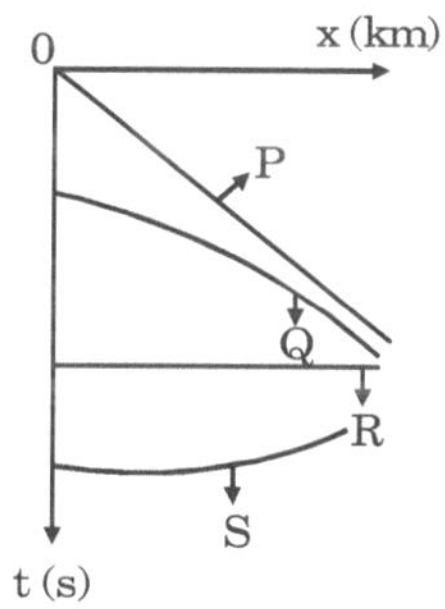

Figuro 1

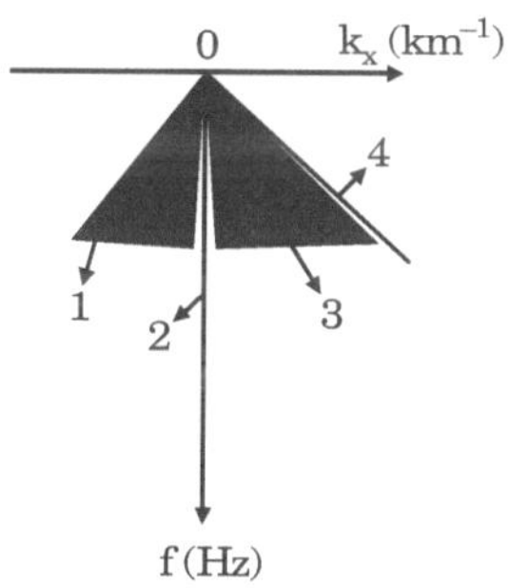

Figuro 2

Figure 1 is a schematic diagram of four seismic events in t-x (time-offset) domain and Figure 2 is the result of transformation from t-x domain to f-kx (frequency-horizontal wavenumber) domain.

The events in t-x domain in Figure 1 with their counterparts in f-kx domain in Figure 2 is given by P-4; Q-3; R-2; S-1

62. Across the Gutenberg discontinuity i.e., from the mantle to outer core the density increases. The bulk modulus also increases. As pressure increases, the minerals should become more compressed, and consequently their incompressibility (Bulk Modulus) should become greater. As rocks become more compressed, their densities increase.

63. The figure in the question, which has multi-electrode resistivity survey is carried out by placing 10 equispaced electrodes on the surface of the earth. Now, considering the mid-point if the 4-electrode array as the point of observation in the lateral direction. This type of electrode configuration is used for multi-electrode axial dipole-dipole array. This method provides information pertaining to both the depth and lateral extent of electrical resistivity variations The survey is usually conducted by introducing current into the subsurface with a current dipole and measuring the resulting ground voltage along a survey line using a potential dipole.

64.

Electromagnetic methods	Quantity measured
AFMAG method	Dip angle
Time domain EM method	Decay of secondary field
TURAM method	Amplitude ratio and phase difference
Slingram method	Real and imaginary components

65. In frequency domain EM, depth and size of the conductor primarily affect the amplitude of the secondary field. In the given figure, the crossover points indicating positive angle of dip represents the locations of conductors beneath them, here the crossover points are P and R.

66.

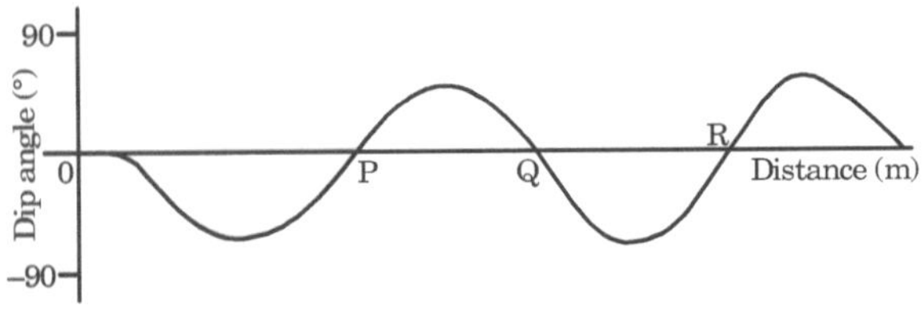

Upward continuation can be used to remove the effect of small scale near surface inhomogeneities from magnetic data.

67. Primary magnetic field generated by worldwide thunderstorm activity have frequencies in the range 1 Hz – 10^3 Hz.

68. For a thick, clean freshwater bearing sandstone formation, the static self-potential is positive. Whereas resistivity of the formation water is more than the resistivity of salt-water mud filtrate.

The resistivity of formation water is around 10 Ωm and resistivity of salt-water mud filtrate is 0.1 Ωm. Thus, (a) is true but (r) is false.

69. Low velocity and low density well log responses characterizes an overpressured zone in the subsurface.

70. Given,

Angle of inclination, $I = 40°$

Now, As per formula

$$\tan I = 2\tan\lambda$$

where, λ is the palaeomagnetic latitude of the basalt flow.

Therefore, $\tan\left(40^o\right) = 2\tan\lambda$

$$\Rightarrow \lambda = \tan^{-1}\left(\tan 40/2\right) = 22.7^o\ N$$

71. Given,

The mean annual rate of exceedance of earthquake occurrence in a seismic belt, $\lambda_m = 0.3$/year

An earthquake of magnitude, $M = 6$

The reciprocal of the annual rate of exceedance for a particular magnitude is commonly referred to as the return period of earthquakes exceeding that magnitude.

Therefore, The return period for an earthquake of magnitude 6.0 in this belt $= \dfrac{1}{\lambda_m} = \dfrac{1}{0.3} = 3.3$ years.

72.

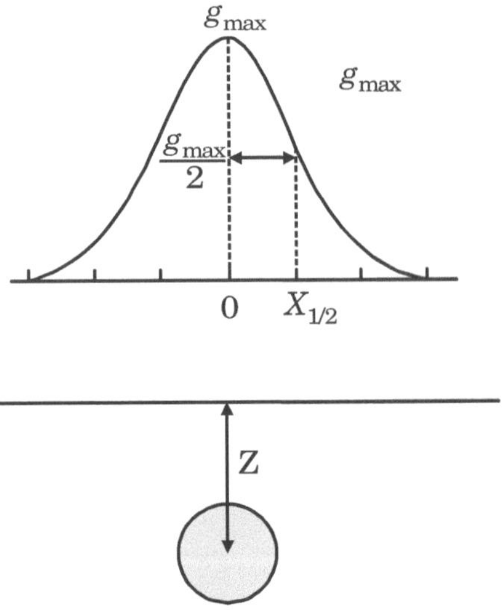

As per figure,

The depth to the center of a spherical body from its gravity anomaly is given as,

$$Z = 2 \times 0.652 \times X_{1/2}$$

$$\Rightarrow \frac{Z}{X_{1/2}} = 1.304$$

73. Given,

Velocity, $V = 6$ knots

$\Delta g = 63.5$ mGal

Now, As per formula

Thelatitude along which the survey vessels are cruising is

$$\phi = \cos^{-1}\left(\frac{7.503 \times V \times \sin\alpha}{\Delta g - 0.004154 \times V^2}\right)$$

Here, $\alpha = 90^o$

$$\therefore \phi = \cos^{-1}\left(\frac{7.503 \times 6 \times \sin(90)}{63.5 - 0.004154 \times 6^2}\right) = 44.7^o\ N$$

74. Given,

Gravity reading is taken in a stationary helicopter hovering, h = 1 km = 1000 m

Now, The difference in the value of g measured in the helicopter and at mean sea level vertically beneath the helicopter is

$$\Delta g_{diff} = 0.3086 \times h = 0.3086 \times 1000 = 308$$

75. Given,

Velocity of P wave, V_P = 2500 m/s

Poisson's ratio, σ = 0.3

Relation between Velocity of P wave, S wave and Poisson ratio is given as

$$\frac{V_P}{V_S} = \left[\frac{2(1-\sigma)}{1-2\sigma}\right]^{1/2}$$

$$\Rightarrow \frac{V_P}{V_S} = \left[\frac{2(1-0.3)}{1-2\times 0.3}\right]^{1/2}$$

$$\Rightarrow \frac{2500}{V_S} = 1.87$$

$$\Rightarrow V_S = \frac{2500}{1.87} = 1336.89 \text{ m/s}$$

76. Given,

Frequency of EM wave, f = 1000 Hz

Skin depth, δ = 100 m

Depth, z = 75 m

The amplitude of an EM wave for depth 'z' is given as

$$A(z) = A_0 e^{-\beta z}$$

where, β is constant decay, $\beta = \frac{1}{\delta}$

Here, $\beta = \frac{1}{100}$

The ratio of the amplitude of the EM wave at a depth of 75 m with respect to the amplitude at the Earth's surface is given as,

$$\frac{A(75)}{A(0)} = \frac{A_0 e^{-\frac{75}{100}}}{A_0 e^0} = 0.472$$

77. Given,

For student – 1

resitivities (ρ) and thickness (h)

$\rho_1 = 100\ \Omega m\ , h_1 = 50\ m$

$\rho_2 = 20\ \Omega m, h_2 = 10\ m$

$\rho_3 = 1500\ \Omega m, h_3 = 20\ m$

For student – 2

$\rho_3 = 1500\ \Omega m$, *find* h_3

Now, We know, Trasverse resistance, $T = \sum_{i=1}^{n} \rho_i h_i$

According to the principle of equivalence,

$T_1 = T_2$

Since, all other model parameters estimated by both the students are the same

Therefore,

$$(\rho_1 h_1 + \rho_2 h_2 + \rho_3 h_3)_{\text{student}-1} = (\rho_1 h_1 + \rho_2 h_2 + \rho_3 h_3)_{\text{student}-2}$$

$$\rightarrow 100 \times 50 + 20 \times 10 + 1500 \times 20 = 100 \times 50 + 20 \times 10 + 2000 \times h_3$$

$$\Rightarrow h_3 = \frac{1500 \times 20}{2000} = 15$$

78. Given,

Apparent resistivity at frequency 0.1 Hz,

$$\rho_{0.1} = 100\ \Omega m$$

Apparent resistivity at frequency 10 hz,

$$\rho_{10} = 80\ \Omega m$$

Therefore, The Percentage Frequency Effect is given as

$$\text{PFE} = 100\left(\frac{\rho_{10} - \rho_{0.1}}{\rho_{0.1}}\right)$$

$$\therefore \text{PFE} = 100\left(\frac{100 - 80}{80}\right) = 25$$

79. Given,

Volt, V = 15 V

Diameter of clindrical container, d = 0.20 m

Length of clindrical container, l = 0.50 m

Current measured when container is filled with saturated sample with brine, I_{sample} = 500 mA

Current measured when container is filled with brine solution, I_w = 750 mA

Now, by using Archie's first equation

$$\rho_0 = F\rho_w$$

where, ρ_w is the resistivity of brine solution ρ_0 is resistivity of the sample fully saturated with brine solution and F is the formation factor of the rock sample.

$$\therefore F = \frac{\rho_0}{\rho_w} = \frac{V \times A}{I_{sample} \times l} \times \frac{I_w \times l}{V \times A}$$

$$= \frac{I_w}{I_{sample}} = \frac{750}{500} = 1.5$$

80. Given,

$t_{1/2} = 3$

Now, as per formula relating the fraction of nuclide with the original nuclide with half life

$$\lambda = \frac{0.693}{t_{1/2}} = \frac{0.693}{3} = 0.231$$

Now, As per formula,

the rati of the number of daughter nuclides to the number of parent nuclides is given as,

$$\frac{N_t}{N_0} = e^{(-\lambda t)} = e^{\left(-0.693 \times \frac{t}{t_{1/2}}\right)} = \left(\frac{1}{2}\right)^{\frac{t}{t_{1/2}}}$$

here, $\frac{N_t}{N_0} = \left(\frac{1}{2}\right)^3 = \frac{1}{8} = 0.125$

81. Given,

$V_{rms,1} = 1500$ m/s and $t_{0,1} = 0.2$ s

$V_{rms,2} = 1600$ m/s and $t_{0,2} = 0.3$ s

$V_{rms,3} = 1700$ m/s and $t_{0,3} = 0.4$ s

Now, Using Dix equation to compute the interval velocity for layer 2,

$$V_2 = \sqrt{\left[\frac{V_{rms,2}^2 t_{0,2} - V_{rms,1}^2 t_{0,1}}{t_{0,2} - t_{0,1}}\right]}$$

$$\Rightarrow V_2 = \sqrt{\frac{1600^2 \times 0.3 - 1500^2 \times 0.2}{0.3 - 0.2}} = 1783.25 \text{ m/s}$$

82. Given,

$\overrightarrow{\nabla g(r)} = -r$

For a spherically symmetric vector field

$g_r = f(r), g_\theta = g_\phi = 0$

Now, Flux is given as

$$\iint_S g(r).\hat{n}\, dS = \iiint_D \nabla.g(r) dV$$

For unit radios i.e., $r = 1$

$$\iiint_D \nabla.g(r) dV = (-r) \times \frac{4}{3}\pi \times \frac{r^3}{4} \times 3 = -\pi = -3.142$$

83. Given,

Wavelength = 20 m

Receiver = 4 receivers

$\therefore$ The minimum receiver spacing $= \frac{20}{4} = 5$

84. Given,

Total number of shot fired, $n = 50$

Total number of traces, $N = 10000$

now, As per formula

Maximum fold recorded $= \frac{N}{2n} = \frac{10000}{2 \times 50} = 100$

85. Given,

$$G = \begin{bmatrix} 1 & 2 & 1 \\ -1 & 2 & 0 \end{bmatrix}$$

To construct G into a square matrix.

we compute G^TG

$$\therefore G^TG = \begin{bmatrix} 1 & -1 \\ 2 & 2 \\ 1 & 0 \end{bmatrix} \begin{bmatrix} 1 & 2 & 1 \\ -1 & 2 & 0 \end{bmatrix} = \begin{bmatrix} 2 & 0 & 1 \\ 0 & 8 & 2 \\ 1 & 2 & 1 \end{bmatrix}$$

Now, the eigen values are given as,

$\det(G^TG - \lambda I) = 0$

here, $\begin{bmatrix} 2-\lambda & 0 & 1 \\ 0 & 8-\lambda & 2 \\ 1 & 2 & 1-\lambda \end{bmatrix}$

$\Rightarrow (2-\lambda)\{(8+\lambda^2 - 8\lambda - \lambda) - 4\} - (8-\lambda) = 0$

$\Rightarrow (2-\lambda)\{\lambda^2 - 9\lambda + 4\} - 8 + \lambda = 0$

$\Rightarrow 2\lambda^2 - 18\lambda + 8 - \lambda^3 + 9\lambda^2 - 4\lambda - 8 + \lambda = 0$

$\Rightarrow -\lambda^3 - 21\lambda + 11\lambda^2 = 0$

$\Rightarrow -\lambda(\lambda^2 - 11\lambda + 21) = 0$

$\Rightarrow \lambda = 0, 8.54, 2.45$

Therefore, Singular value of non zero eigen values

$\sigma = \sqrt{\lambda}$

here, $\sigma = 2.92, 1.56$

$\therefore$ The largest singular value is 2.92.

SOLVED PAPER - 2017

PART-A (Common Part)

1. Which one of the following is a continental hotspot?

(a) Reunion (b) Macdonald

(c) Hawaii (d) Afar

2. The diagram given below shows a Mohr circle for two-dimensional stress with points numbered as shown. The mean stress and the maximum shear stress are given by which one of the following number pairs?

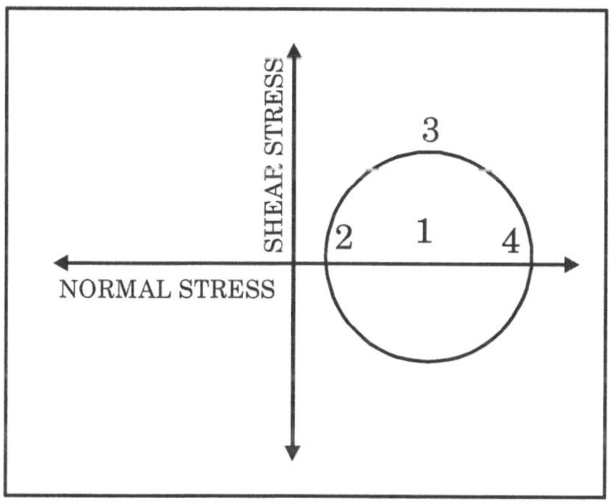

(a) 1, 2 (b) 1, 3

(c) 1, 4 (d) 2, 3

3. Which type of fault is developed in the setting shown in the figure below? Velocity vectors on either side of the fault are given in the figure.

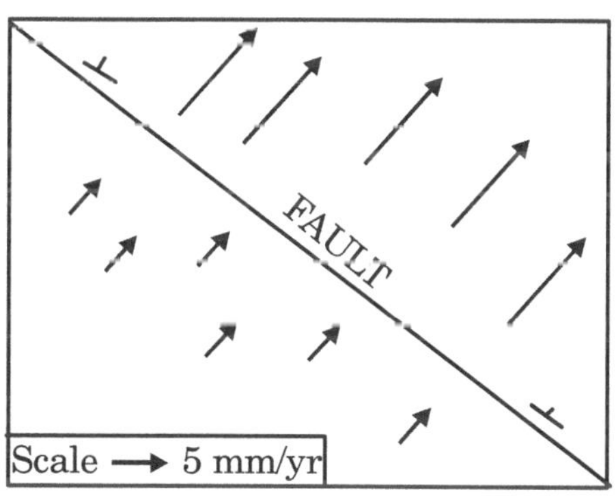

(a) Normal

(b) Dextral strike-slip

(c) Sinistral strike-slip

(d) Thrust

4. The age of most of the bituminous coal seams of India is

(a) Silurian (b) Miocene

(c) Carboniferous (d) Permian

5. The time equivalent of the time-stratigraphic team 'Series' is

(a) Epoch (b) Period

(c) Age (d) Stage

6. Match the following stratigraphic units of India (Group-I) with their age (Group-II)

Group I	Group II
P. Barakar Formation	1. Miocene
Q. Warkalli (Varkala) Formation	2. Cretaceous
R. Bagh Beds	3. Proterozoic
S. Bhander Limestone	4. Eocene
	5. Permian

(a) P-5, Q-1, R-2, S-3 (b) P-1, Q-4, R-2, S-5

(c) P-5, Q-4, R-2, S-3 (d) P-2, Q-3, R-1, S-4

7. Universal Transverse Mercator (UTM) is a type of

(a) conical projection

(b) gnomonic projection

(c) orthogonal projection

(d) cylindrical projection

8. The groundwater flow equation

$$\frac{\partial^2 h}{\partial x^2} + \frac{\partial^2 h}{\partial y^2} + \frac{\partial^2 h}{\partial z^2} = 0,$$

where h refers to the hydraulic head and x, y, z are coordinates, is valid when the flow condition is

(a) steady state in isotropic media.

(b) unsteady state in isotropic media.

(c) steady state in anisotropic media.

(d) unsteady state in anisotropic media.

9. Los Angeles abrasion test was conducted for a granite aggregate with an initial weight of 4800 grams. After the test, the aggregate weighed 3504 grams. The Los Angeles abrasion value is _____%.

10. Brightness temperature is a function of surface temperature and

(a) transmittance (b) reflectance

(c) refractive index (d) emissivity

11. Which one of the following minerals has poor cleavage in all directions?

(a) Fluorite (b) Orthoclase
(c) Quartz (d) Muscovite

12. The figure below shows the intercepts of the plane HKL with the crystallographic axes a, b, c. The Miller index of the plane HKL is

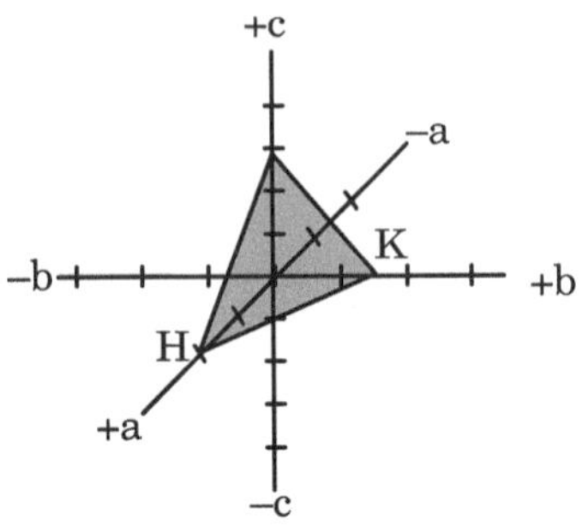

(a) (243) (b) (342)
(c) (436) (d) (634)

13. Match the rocks listed in Group-I with the corresponding general rock classification listed in Group-II

Group I	Group II
P. Granite	1. Extrusive igenous rock
Q. Basalt	2. Biochemical sedimentary rock
R. Gneiss	3. Intrusive igneous rock
S. Sandstone	4. Metamorphic rock
	5. Clastic sedimentary rock

(*a*) P-1; Q-3; R-5; S-2 (*b*) P-4; Q-5; R-1; S-2
(*c*) P-3; Q-1; R-4; S-5 (*d*) P-3; Q-4; R-1; S-5

14. Which one of the following oceanic ridges is known to be aseismic?

(a) Carlsberg (b) Mid Atlantic
(c) Ninety East (d) Southwest Indian

15. Isogonic lines are contours of equal magnetic

(*a*) inclination
(*b*) declination
(*c*) total field intensity
(*d*) horizontal field intensity

16. Match the geophysical terms in Group-I their corresponding units of measurements in Group-II

Group I	Group II
P. Transit time	1. mGal
Q. Conductivity	2. nano Tesla
R. Gravity anomaly	3. siemens
S. Magnetic field intensity	4. millivolt
	5. microsecond per feet

(*a*) P-5; Q-4; R-2; S-1 (*b*) P-5; Q-4; R-3; S-2
(*c*) P-5; Q-3; R-1; S-2 (*d*) P-4; Q-3; R-2; S-1

17. The Maxwell's equation based on Ampere's low is

(a) $\nabla \times E = -\frac{\partial B}{\partial t}$ (b) $\nabla \times H = j + \frac{\partial D}{\partial t}$

(c) $\nabla . B = 0$ (d) $\nabla . E = \frac{\rho}{\varepsilon}$

18. The normal gravity formula (for e.g. GRS80) is a function of

(*a*) geocentric latitude (*b*) geodetic latitude
(*c*) longitude (*d*) altitude

19. A seismic reflection survey was carried out over a subsurface consisting of a stack of horizontal isotropic layers. In the common midpoint (CMP) domain, the moveout (travel time v/s offset) curve for any primary reflection event is best approximated by

(*a*) an ellipse (*b*) a parabola
(*c*) a circle (*d*) a hyperbola

20. Assertion (a) : Magnetic stripes are observed around mid-oceanic ridge regions.

Reason (r) : The earth's magnetic field undergoes reversals of polarity.

(*a*) (a) is true but (r) is false
(*b*) (a) is false but (r) is true
(*c*) Both (a) and (r) are true and (r) is one of the correct reasons for (a)
(*d*) Both (a) and (r) are true but (r) is not the correct reason for (a)

21. A seismic gap refers to a

(*a*) time gap between two great earthquakes.
(*b*) distance gap between the epicenters of two great earthquakes.
(*c*) segment of an active belt where a historical great earthquake has no occurred.
(*d*) wide gap in the earth created by a great earthquake

22. The travel time difference between the arrival times of a shear wave (S) and primary wave (P) observed on a seismogram recorded at an epicentral distance of 100 km from a near surface earthquake is _________s.

(Assume the average P and S wave velocities to be 6.0 km/s and 3.5 km/s, respectively).

23. The percentage increase in P-wave velocity (km/s) across the Mohorovicic discountinuity from the lower crust to the upper mantle beneath craton is approximately __________(%)

24. Which one amongst the following logging tools has the alrgest depth of investigation?

(*a*) Density (*b*) Laterolog 3
(*c*) Laterolog 8 (*d*) Neutron

25. The most abundant radioactive isotope in the continental crust is

(*a*) ^{40}K (*b*) ^{232}Th

(*c*) ^{235}U (*d*) ^{238}U

PART-B
GEOLOGY

26. Stylolitic foliation developed during diagenetic processes is typically

(*a*) parallel to bedding

(*b*) perpendicular to bedding

(*c*) oblique to bedding

(*d*) vertical

27. A coal seam with a attitude 0.90°, 50°S outcrops at an elevation of 1400 m in an area that has flat topography. A vertical exploratory drill hole will intersect the seam

(*a*) north of the outcorp at elevations greater than 1400 m

(*b*) north of the outcorp at elevations less than 1400 m

(*c*) south of the outcrop at elevations less than 1400 m

(*d*) south of the outcrop at elevations greater than 1400 m

28. Earthquakes result in the formation of which one of the following features?

(*a*) Prophyroblast (*b*) Porphyroclast

(*c*) Pseudotachylite (*d*) Pressure shadow

29. In a bilaterally symmetrical brachiopod fossil, the angle between the hinge line and the median line changes to 45° after deformation. The shear strain observed in the deformed fossil is _______.

30. The empirical probability distribution of gold (Au) grades shows a unimodal distribution with mode = 2g/t, mediuan = 3 g/t, and mean = 5 g/t. This probability distribution is

(*a*) positively skewed (*b*) negatively skewed

(*c*) platykurtic (*d*) platykurtic

31. A limb of a non-plunging fold with an attitude 070°, 40°S is rotated about its fold axis 30° clockwise (looking towards ENE). The plunge amount of the pole to the fold limb after rotation is ____ degrees.

32. The bulk Silicate Earth (BSE) is best approximated by the average

(*a*) enriched upper mantle composition

(*b*) mantle and continental crust composition

(*c*) depleted mantle composition

(*d*) primitive upper mantle composition

33. Which one of the following is the stable minerals assemblage in metamorphism of a rock with peltic bulk composition under graulite facies?

(*a*) staurolite + muscovite + sillimanite + K feldspar

(*b*) phengite + garnet + chloritoid + biotite

(*c*) garnet + orthopyroxene + clinopyroxene + plagioclase

(*d*) garnet + cordierite + K-feldspar +d sillimanite

34. The given P-T diagram shows four distinct metamkorphic paths designated as 1, 2, 3 and 4. Which one of these P-T paths represents crustal thickening in a collisional tectonic setting?

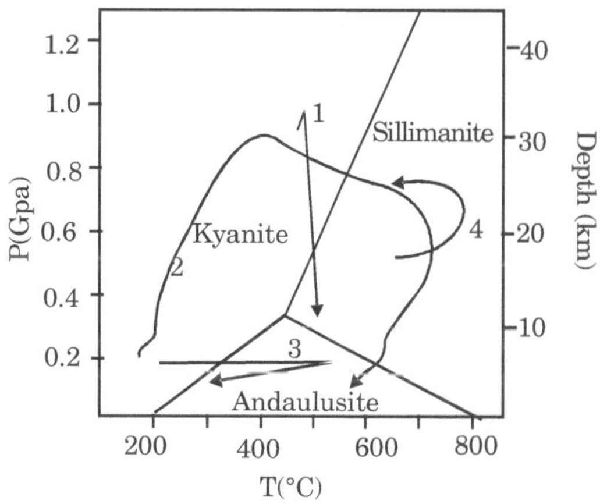

(*a*) 1 (*b*) 2

(*c*) 3 (*d*) 4

35. The pressure on a rock overlain by a 7 km thick basaltic crust ($\rho = 3100\ kgm^{-3}$) is ________ kilobar. (Use $g = 9.8\ ms^{-2}$, 10^5 Pa = 1 bar)

36. The given T-X diagram shows the phase relations in the olivine soild solution at 1 bar pressure. If 'P' is the initial position of melt, the proportion of melt at 1500°C is ________%.

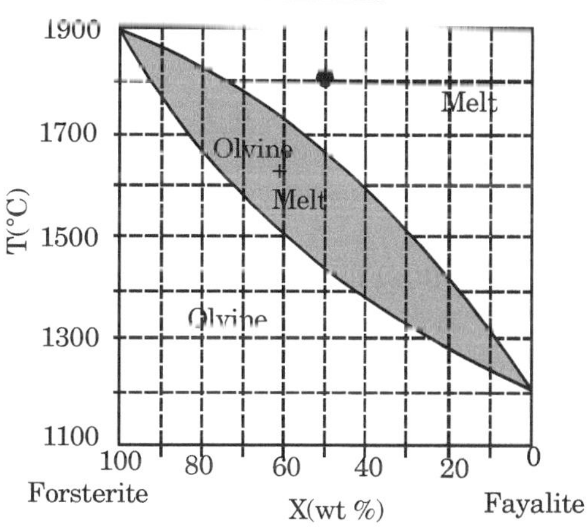

37. Fluorite crystal (CaF_2) adopts face-centered cubic structure with lattice parameter a = 5.463 Å. If the ionic radius of anion (F^-) is 1.71 Å, the ionic radius of cation (Ca^{+2}) is ______Å.

38. The diagram below shows the interference figure of a mineral. The mineral is

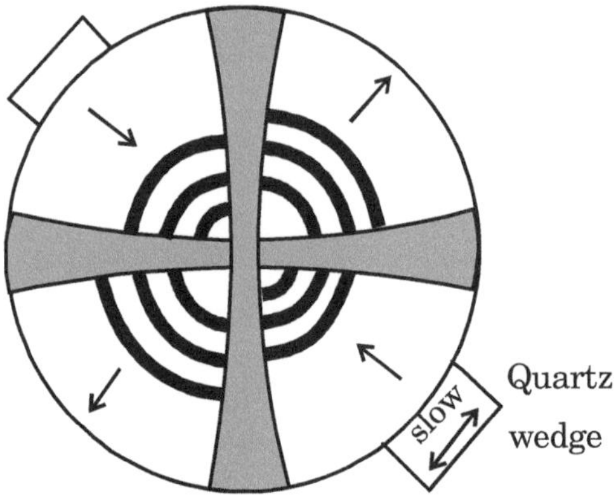

(*a*) uniaxial positive (*b*) biaxial negative
(*c*) uniaxial negative (*d*) biaxial positive

39. The standard thermodynamic data for enstatite ($Mg_2Si_2O_6$), quartz (SiO_2) and (SiO_2) and forsterite (Mg_2SiO_4) is given in the table below. The Gibb's free energy of the reaction $Mg_2SiO_4 + SiO_2 = Mg_2Si_2O_6$ at 600 K and 1 bar is __________ J.

(Assume $C_p = 0$ for all minerals in the reaction)

Mineral	$\Delta H°_{f,298}$ (kJ)	$S°(JK^{-1})$
Enstatite	–3090.47	132.5
Quartz	–910.83	41.5
Forsterite	–2172.2	95.1

40. The modal abundance in an ultramafic rock and the partition coefficients of lutetium (Lu) in clinopyroxene, orthopyroxene, olivine and plagioclase are tabulated below. The bulk distribution coefficient of lutetium (D_{Lu}) in the ultramafic rock is ________

Mineral	Modal abudance (%)	Partition coefficient
Clinopyroxene	45	0.506
Orthopyroxene	40	0.42
Olivine	10	0.045
Plagioclase	05	0.019

41. Match the following classical ore deposit (Group-I) with their associated ore minerals (Group-II)

Group I	Group II
P. Subdury type deposit	1. Molybdenite
Q. Mississippi valley type deposit	2. Uraninite and chalcopyrite
R. Climax type deposit	3. Pentlandite
S. IOCG type deposit	4. Psilomelane
	5. Sphalerite and Galena

(*a*) P-4; Q-3; R-2; S-1 (*b*) P-3; Q-5; R-1; S-2
(*c*) P-5; Q-2; R-4; S-1 (*d*) P-3; Q-5; R-2; S-4

42. Which one of the following microfossils is commonly used in biostratigraphic correlation of Palaezoic marine strata?

(*a*) Angiosperm pollen (*b*) Diatoms
(*c*) Dinoflagellates (*d*) Chitinozoans

43. Given below are pairs of "living fossils". Which one of the following is a brachiopod-mollusc pair?

(*a*) Lingula, Nautilus
(*b*) Ginkgo, Metasequia
(*c*) Syntexis, Notiothauna
(*d*) Coelacanths, Sikhotealinia

44. Match the sedimentary rocks and their features listed in Group I with depositional environments listed in Group II.

Group I	Group II
P. Sandstone with herring-bone bedding	1. Eolian
Q. Chalk with coccolith	2. Glacial
R. Well sorted arenite with large cross bedding (5-10 m thick)	3. Sabhka
S. Poorly sorted sediments with faceted and striated pebbles	4. Tidal
	5. Pelagic

(*a*) P-2; Q-1; R-4; S-5 (*b*) P-4; Q-5; R-1; S-2
(*c*) P-4; Q-1; R-2; S-5 (*d*) P-5; Q-1; R-2; S-3

45. Arrange the following stratigraphic formations sequentially from older to younger.

(P) Jodhpur Sandstone
(Q) Cambay Shale
(R) Kajrahat Limestone
(S) Tipam Sandstone

(*a*) P, R, Q, S (*b*) R, Q, P, S
(*c*) P, S, R, Q (*d*) R, P, Q, S

46. 2 g air dried coal contains 0.2 g moisture. 0.3 g ash and 0.5 g volatile matter. The volatile matter content in the coal in dry minerals matter free (d.m.f) basis is __________%.

(mineral matter content = 1.1 × ash content)

47. The approximate temperature for 'oil window' ranges from

(*a*) 30°C to 50°C (*b*) 60°C to 160°C
(*c*) 180°C to 250°C (*d*) 260°C to 350°C

48. Which one of the following biopolymers is the major source of liquid hydrocarbons?

(*a*) Lignin (*b*) Proteins
(*c*) Lipids (*d*) Carbohydrates

49. The hydraulic conductivity (K) of an isotropic aquifer is 10 m/day. If the hydraulic head within the aquifer drops 4 m over a distance of 750 m, the groundwater flow velocity within the aquifer is _______ m/day.

(Up to third decimal place)

50. Drainage network of a watershed ordered as per the strahler method is given below. Maximum observed bifurcation ratio for the given network is _______

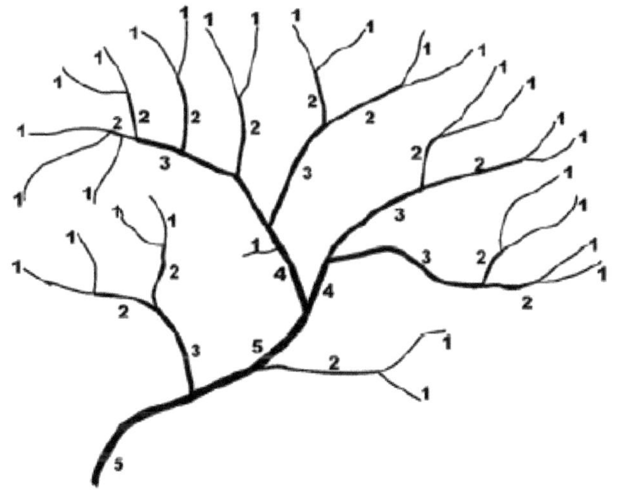

51. In a vertical aerial photo, the top and bottom of a tower built on a flat terrain is displayed by 2 mm. In the photograph, the distance between top of the tower and nadir point is 100 mm. The flying height of the aircraft was 3000 m above the ground. The estimated height of the tower is _____ m.

52. Brazilian test was conducted on a rock sample having radius of 27 mm and thickness of 22 mm. The failure load was 5 kN. The tensile strength of the rock is _________ N/m^2.

53. The average assay (a) and area of influence (A) of a placer gold deposit of uniform thickness sampled at four locations W, X, Y and Z are given below. The weighted average assay of the ore body is _____ g/t.

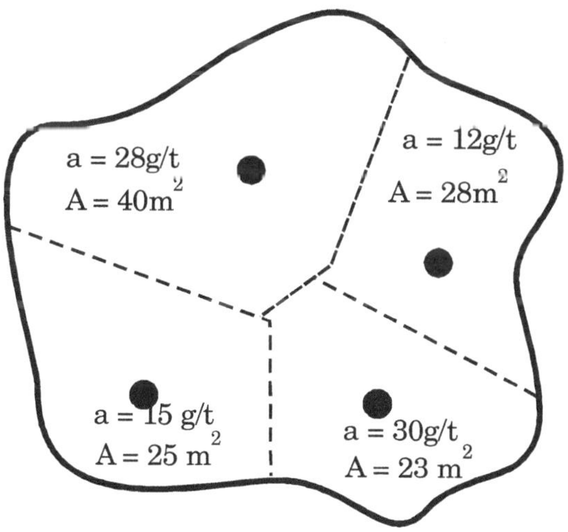

54. The minimum and maximum values of the digital number (DN) of a remote sensing image are 8 and 32 respectively. The digital data was linearly stretched between 0 and 255 by using min-max linear stretching method. The post stretched integer DN value of a pixel with an original DN value of 27 will be _________.

55. The length and width of concave and convex sides of a landslide is shown in the figure below. The Dilation Index of the landslide is ________.

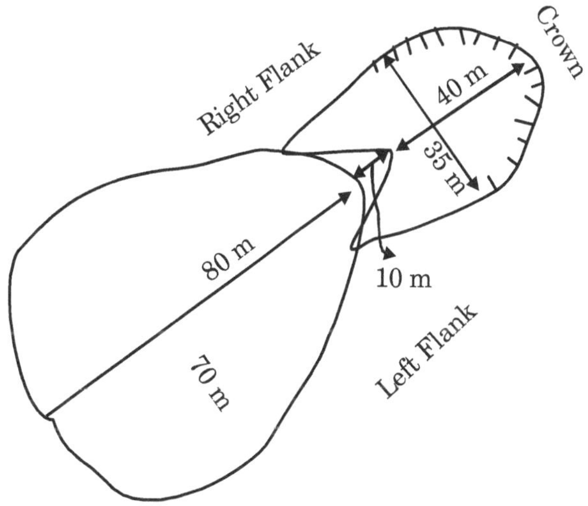

GEOPHYSICS

26. Which one of the following seismic phases is observable in the P-wave shadow zone?

(*a*) P (*b*) PmP

(*c*) PcS (*d*) PKiKP

27. Consider a geological body buried at the equator at a certain depth. If the same body were to be buried at the North pole at the same depth, how would the gravity and magnetic field responses measured over the body differ? Assume the same magnetic susceptibility and density contrasts.

(Consider only geomagnetic induction).

(*a*) Both gravity and magnetic field response do not change.

(*b*) Both gravity and magnetic field responses change significantly.

(*c*) Gravity field response changes significantly but magnetic field response does not change.

(*d*) Gravity field response does not change but magnetic field response changes significantly.

28. Given the Bouguer density of 2.8 g/cc, the Bouguer correction for a gravity station at an elevation of 30 m above the datum is ____ mGals.

(Use $\pi = 3.14$).

29. Given the following data for a resistivity sounding experiment over a two-layered half-space, the resistivity transform for the top layer is _____ Ωm.
(Data : resistivity of top layer $\rho_1 = 10\ \Omega m$, resistivity of half space $\rho_2 = \ \Omega m$, thickness of top layer $h_1 = 10$ m and current electrode spacing $\frac{AB}{2} = 5m$).

30. The ratio of centricity to the polar flattening of an ellipsoidal Earth with equatorial radius 'e' and polar radius 'p' can be expressed as

(*a*) $\frac{\sqrt{e^2+p^2}}{\sqrt{e-p}}$ (*b*) $\frac{\sqrt{e^2-p^2}}{\sqrt{e-p}}$

(*c*) $\frac{\sqrt{e+p}}{\sqrt{e-p}}$ (*d*) $\frac{\sqrt{e^2+p^2}}{\sqrt{e+p}}$

31. The vertical field intensity anomaly Δz due to a vertically polarized vertical dyke is given by

$$\Delta z = 2Mt\left(\frac{z_1}{z_1^2+x^2} - \frac{z_2}{z_2^2+x^2}\right),$$

where M is the magnitude of intensity of magnetization. All relevant parameters are provided in the figure below. The dyke has 1% magnetite (magnetic susceptibility of magnetic = 0.5 SI unit) distributed homogeneously. Then the magnitude of peak vertical field intensity over the dyke is _______ nT.

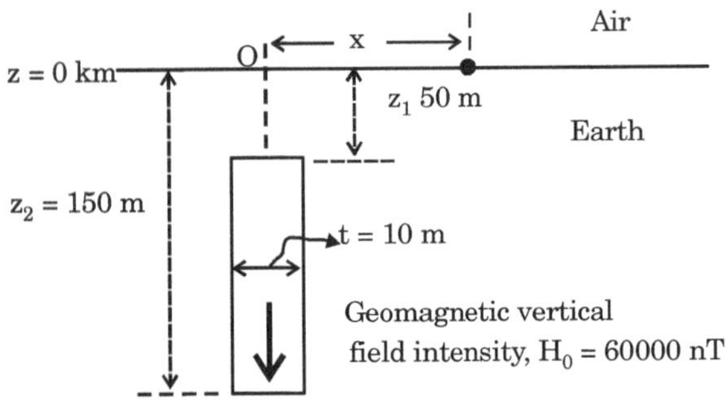

2-D dyke

32. In a magneto-telluric (MT) experiment over a homogeneous and isotropic half-space, the apparent resistivity is 50 Ωm for an electric field intensity of 12 m V/km and time period of 10 s. Then, the magnetic field strength is ______ nT.

33. The apparent resistivity for Wenner and Schlumberger configurations in an electrical sounding experiment is the same for a certain electrode spacing 'a' (Wenner configuration). Given the current electrode spacing of 18 m and the potential electrode spacing of 2 m for a Schlumberger configuration, the value of 'a' is ________m.

34. In a time-domain (T-D) induced polarization experiment with a steady voltage of 10 mV during the current flow interval, the voltage decay after the current cut-off is given by $v(t) = 4.0\ e^{-0.3t}$ mV. The chargeability after current cut-off between $t_1 = 1$ s and $t_2 = 4$ s is __________ ms.

35. Which one of the following statements is TRUE for near surface earthquake occurring in a homogeneous, isotropic Earth?

(*a*) Rayleigh wave are generated
(*b*) Love waves are generated.
(*c*) Shear waves are split.
(*d*) P waves undergo refraction.

36. A dynamic range of 60 dB in power corresponds to an increases in amplitude by a factor of______.

37. The slope of the Wadati plot obtained using the P and S arrival times of a local earthquake is 1.0 The corresponding Vp/Vs ratio of the subsurface medium is _________.

38. The beach ball figure given below depicts the focal mechanism of an earthquake. The shades and unshaded portions indicate compressional and dilatational quadrants, respectively. FP1 is the fault plane solution. The focal mechanism and FP1 represent

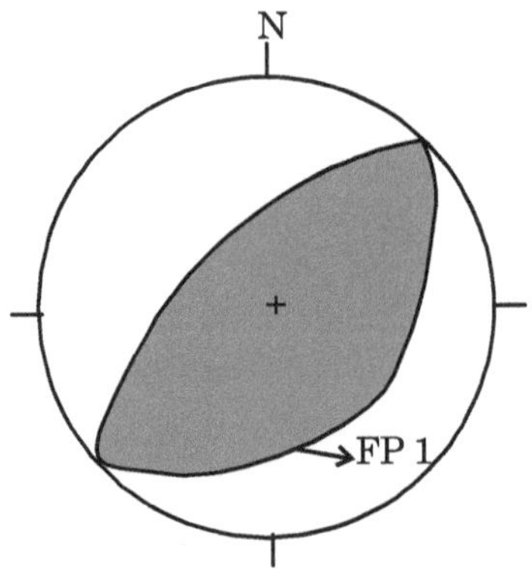

(*a*) a thrust fault with strike 45° and 30° with the tension axis in the compression quadrant.
(*b*) a normal fault with strike 45° and 30° with the tension axis in the compression quadrant.
(*c*) a thrust fault with strike 225° and 60° with the tension axis in the compression quadrant.
(*d*) a normal fault with strike 225° and 60° with the tension axis in the compression quadrant.

39. The characteristic log response of a thick coal seam are

(*a*) low transit time, low resistivity and high gamma ray count.
(*b*) low transit time, high resistivity and low gamma ray count.
(*c*) high transit time, high resistivity and low gamma ray count.
(*d*) high transit time, low resistivity and high gamma ray count.

40. The SP response of a thick, clean sandstone bed is –54V. Given the mud filtrate resistivity to be 0.45Ωm at a formation temperature (T_f) of 130°F and the coefficient, K = 77.29, the formation water resistivity is ________Ωm.

41. Which one of the following log responses is TRUE for a porous and permeable sandstone bed, when the resistivity of the mud filtrate used in equal to the resistivity of the formation water?

(*a*) A large negative SP is observed.

(*b*) A large positive SP is observed.

(*c*) LLs and LLm logs show appreciably large separation.

(*d*) LLm and LLd logs overlap with each other.

42. The number of half-lives $\left(T_{\frac{1}{2}}\right)$ required for a certain amount of radioactive isotope in a rock to reduce to 3% of its original amount is _______.

43. VLF fields can be measured over continental distance (r) because.

(*a*) the magnetic field decreases at the rate $\frac{1}{r}$ and the output power at the transmitting station is 1 to 10 kW.

(*b*) the magnetic field decreases at the rate $\frac{1}{r^3}$ and the output power at the transmitting station is 1 to 10 kW.

(*c*) the magnetic field decreases at the rate $\frac{1}{r}$ and the output power at the transmitting station is 100 to 1000 kW.

(*d*) the magnetic field decreases at the rate $\frac{1}{r^2}$ and the output power at the transmitting station is 100 to 1000 kW.

44. convolution of two box car functions of different widths yields a

(a) step function

(b) trapezoidal function

(c) box car function

(d) sinc function

45. Assuming the Z-transform to be defined with Z as the unit delay operator, the pole of the infinite sequence $\left[1, \frac{1}{2}, \frac{1}{4}, \frac{1}{8}, \ldots\ldots\right]$ is at Z = ________.

46. Normal movement (NMO) correction was applied to seismic data in the common midpoint (CMP) domain. The frequency distortion due to "NMO stretch" is highest for

(a) larger offsets of deeper reflections.

(b) smaller offsets of shallower reflections.

(c) larger offsets of shallower reflections.

(d) smaller offsets of deeper reflections.

47. Consider a hypothetical zero-offset seismic reflection survey acquired over a reflector whose dip is 30°. The velocity of the medium above the reflector is 2 km/s and the trace spacing is 25 m. The maximum unaliased frequency in the data is ________ Hz.

48. In statistical wavelet deconvalution, the reflectivity series is assumed to be a random sequence. Then, the autocorrelation of the wavelet is

(a) a scaled version of the autocorrelation of the seismic trace.

(b) a random sequence.

(c) zero.

(d) dirac-delta function.

49. A vector field u is expressed by its Helmholtz decomposition as $u = \nabla\phi + \nabla \times \Psi$, with $\phi = \frac{1}{2}$ $(x^2 - y^2 + z^2)$ and $zy^2 + xz\,j + x^2\,k$. The magnitude of the divergence of the vector field u at (1, 1, 1) is ________.

50. In the figure shown below, a ray corresponding to a P-wave is incident on the interface between layer 1 and layer 2 at an angle of 30°. The P-wave velocity is 1 km/s, 1.2 km/s and 1.5 km/s in layer 1, layer 2 and the half space, respectively. The emergence angle of the ray into the half space is ________ degrees.

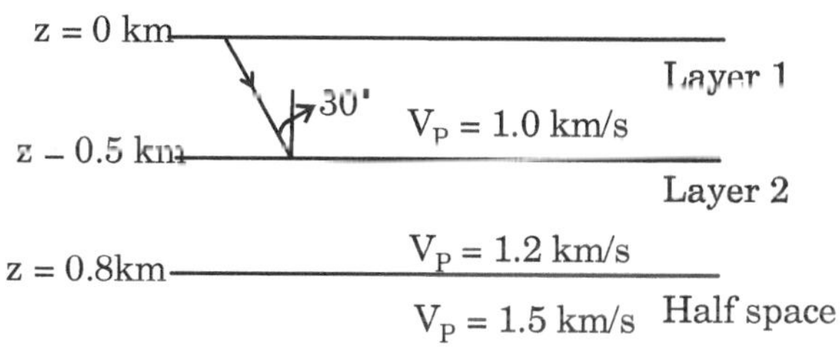

51. How do the P wave velocity (V_P), S-wave velocity (V_S), and Poisson's ratio (σ) change from water saturated sandstone to a gas saturated sandstone?

(a) V_P increases, V_S decreases and σ increases.

(b) V_P decreases, V_S remains the same and σ decreases.

(c) V_P decreases, V_S increases and σ decreases.

(d) V_P, V_S and σ all remain constant.

52. Consider a Vertical Seismic Profiling (VSP) data acquisition experiment as shown in the figure below. The subsurface consists of a horizontal layer of 2 km thickness underlain by a semi-infinite half-space. The P-wave velocities (V_p) in the first layer and the half-space are 2.0 km/s and 2.5 km/s, respectively. The vertical well has a string of receivers (denoted by inverted triangles) spaced 19 mm apart, with the shallowest receiver at a depth of 0.5 km and the deepest receiver at a depth of 1.5 km. The source (denoted by star) is placed 0.5 km from the well head. The traveltime of the primary reflection event at the deepest receiver is ________s.

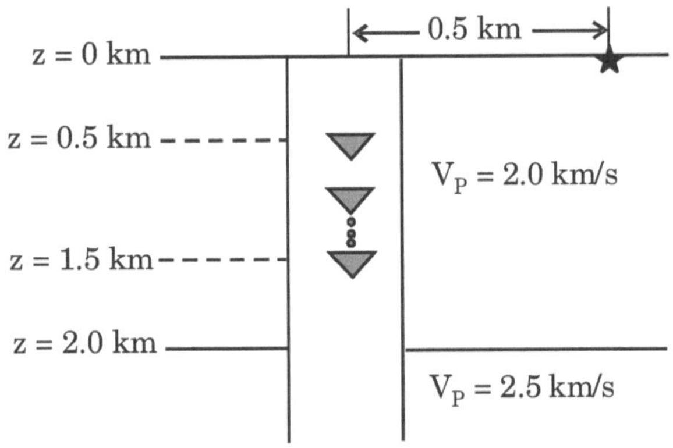

53. Which one of the following sets of vectors $\{v_1, v_2, v_3\}$ is linearly dependent?

(a) $v_1 = (0, -1, 3)$, $v_2 = (2, 0, 1)$, $v_3 = (-2, -1, 3)$
(b) $v_1 = (2, -2, 0)$, $v_2 = (0, 1, -1)$, $v_3 = (0, 4, 2)$
(c) $v_1 = (2, 6, 2)$, $v_2 = (2, 0, -2)$, $v_3 = (0, 4, 2)$
(d) $v_1 = (1, 4, 7)$, $v_2 = (2, 5, 8)$, $v_3 = (3, 6, 9)$

54. The condition number for the matrix $A = \begin{bmatrix} 2 & 1 \\ 0 & 3 \end{bmatrix}$ is ________.

55. Match the items listed in Group I with their respective analytical expressions in Group II.

Group I	**Group II**
P. Wave equation	1. $\|\nabla u\|^2 = 1$
Q. Heat conduction equation	2. $\frac{\partial^2 u}{\partial t^2} - \nabla^2 u = 0$
R. Eikonal equation	3. $\nabla^2 u = -4\pi\sigma$
S. Poisson's equation	4. $\frac{\partial u}{\partial t} - \nabla^2 u = 0$
	5. $\frac{\partial u}{\partial t} + u.\nabla u = 0$

(*a*) P-2; Q-3; R-4; S-1 (*b*) P-2; Q-4; R-1; S-3
(*c*) P-4; Q-2; R-5; S-3 (*d*) P-4; Q-3; R-1; S-5

GENERAL APTITUDE (GA)

1. The ways in which this game can be played ______ potentially infinite.

(a) is (b) is being
(c) are (d) are being

2. If you choose plan P, you will have to ______ plan Q, as these two are mutually ______.

(a) forgo, exclusive (b) forget, inclusive
(c) accept, exhaustive (d) adopt, intrusive

3. If a and b are integers and a – b is even, which of the following must always be even?

(a) ab (b) $a^2 + b^2 + 1$
(c) $a^2 + b + 1$ (d) ab – b

4. A couple has 2 children. The probability that both children are boys if the older one is a boy is

(a) $\frac{1}{4}$ (b) $\frac{1}{3}$
(c) $\frac{1}{2}$ (d) 1

5. P looks at Q while Q looks at R. P is married, R is not. The number of pairs of people in which a married person is looking at an unmarried person is

(a) 0 (b) 1
(c) 2 (d) Cannot be determined

6. "If you are looking for a history of India, or for an account of the rise and fall of the British Raj, or for the reason of the cleaving of the subcontinent into two mutually antagonistic parts and the effects this mutilation will have in the respective sections, and ultimately on Asia, you will not find it in these pages; for though I have spent a lifetime in the country, I lived too near the seat of events, and was too intimately associated with the actors, to get the perspective needed for the impartial recording of these matters."

Which of the following is closest in meaning to 'cleaving'?

(a) deteriorating (b) arguing
(c) departing (d) splitting

7. X bullocks and Y tractors take 8 days to plough a field. If we halve the number of bullocks and double the number of tractors, it takes 5 days to plough the same field, How many days will it take X bullocks alone to plough the field?

(a) 30 (b) 35
(c) 40 (d) 45

8. There are 4 women P, Q, R, S and 5 men V,W, X, Y, Z in a group. We are required to form pairs each consisting of one woman and one man. P is not to be paired with Z, and Y must necessarily be paired with someone. In how many ways can 4 such pairs be formed?

(a) 74

(b) 76

(c) 78

(d) 80

9. All people in certain island are either 'Knights' or Knaves' and each person knows every other person's identity. Kinghts NEVER lie, and knaves ALWAYS lie.

P says " Both of us are knights". Q says "None of us are knaves".

Which one of the following can be logically inferred from the above

(a) Both P and Q are knights

(b) P is knight; Q is a knave

(c) Both P and Q are knaves

(d) The identities of P, Q cannot be determined

10. In the graph below, the concentration of a particular pollutant in a lake is plotted over (alternate) days of a month in winter (average temperature 10°C) and a month in summer (average temperature 30 C)

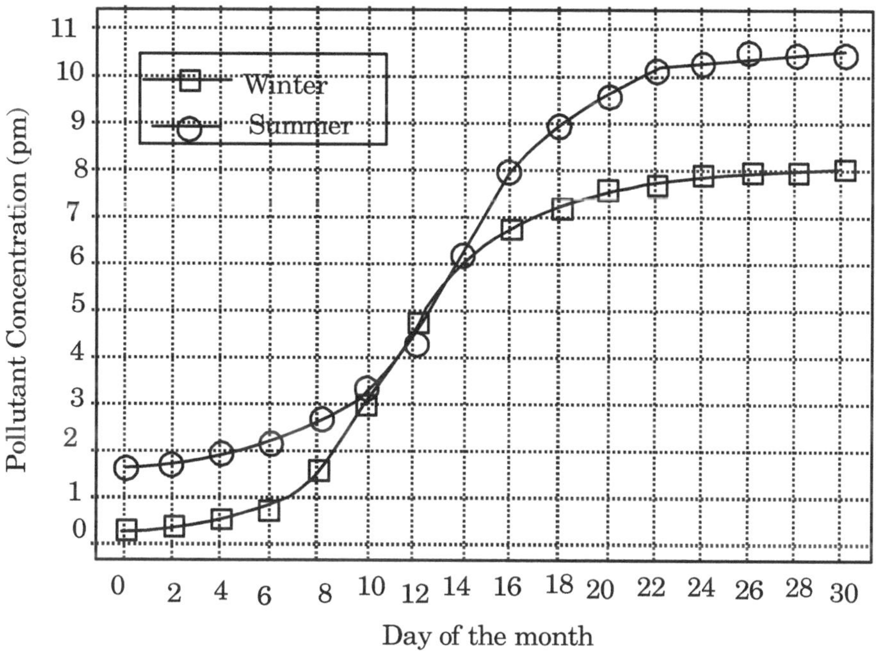

Consider the following statements based on the data shown above:

i. Over the given months, the difference between the maximum and the minimum pollutant concentrations is the same in both winter and summer.

ii. There are at least four days in the summer month such that the pollutant concentrations on those days are within 1 ppm of the pollutant concentrations on the corresponding days in the winter month.

Which one of the following options is correct?

(*a*) Only i

(*b*) Only ii

(*c*) Both i and ii

(*d*) Neither i nor ii

ANSWERS

PART A (Common Part)

1. (*d*)	**2.** (*b*)	**3.** (*a*)	**4.** (*d*)	**5.** (*a*)	**6.** (*a*)	**7.** (*d*)	**8.** (*a*)	**9.** (*)	**10.** (*d*)
11. (*c*)	**12.** (*b*)	**13.** (*c*)	**14.** (*c*)	**15.** (*b*)	**16.** (*c*)	**17.** (*b*)	**18.** (*b*)	**19.** (*d*)	**20.** (*c*)
21. (*c*)	**22.** (*)	**23.** (*)	**24.** (*c*)	**25.** (*a*)					

PART-B (Geology)

26. (*a*)	**27.** (*c*)	**28.** (*c*)	**29.** (*)	**30.** (*)	**31.** (*)	**32.** (*b*)	**33.** (*d*)	**34.** (*b*)	**35.** (*)
36. (*)	**37.** (*)	**38.** (*c*)	**39.** (*)	**40.** (*)	**41.** (*b*)	**42.** (*d*)	**43.** (*a*)	**44.** (*b*)	**45.** (*d*)
46. (*)	**47.** (*b*)	**48.** (*c*)	**49.** (*)	**50.** (*)	**51.** (*)	**52.** (*)	**53.** (*)	**54.** (*)	**55.** (*)

(Geophysics)

26. (*d*)	**27.** (*d*)	**28.** (*)	**29.** (*)	**30.** (*c*)	**31.** (*)	**32.** (*)	**33.** (*)	**34.** (*)	**35.** (*a*)
36. (*)	**37.** (*)	**38.** (*a*)	**39.** (*c*)	**40.** (*)	**41.** (*c*)	**42.** (*)	**43.** (*c*)	**44.** (*b*)	**45.** (*)
46. (*c*)	**47.** (*)	**48.** (*a*)	**49.** (*)	**50.** (*)	**51.** (*b*)	**52.** (*)	**53.** (*d*)	**54.** (*)	**55.** (*b*)

(General Aptitude)

1. (*c*)	**2.** (*a*)	**3.** (*d*)	**4.** (*c*)	**5.** (*b*)	**6.** (*d*)	**7.** (*a*)	**8.** (*c*)	**9.** (*d*)	**10.** (*b*)

EXPLANATIONS

PART A (COMMON PART)

1. Hotspots are volcanic regions thought to be fed by underlying mantle that is anomalously hot compared with the surrounding mantle. Their position on the Earth's surface is independent of tectonic plate boundaries. There are two hypotheses that attempt to explain their origins. One suggests that hotspots are due to mantle plumes that rise as thermal diapirs from the core–mantle boundary. The other hypothesis is that lithospheric extension permits the passive rising of melt from shallow depths. Some Continental hotspots are Afar, Iceland, Yellowstone etc.

2. From the figure in the question,

Let $\sigma_1 > \sigma_2$

At Point 3

Max shear stress, $\tau_{max} = \dfrac{\sigma_1 - \sigma_2}{2}$

At Point 2

Max stress, $\sigma_{mean} = \dfrac{\sigma_1 + \sigma_2}{2}$

3. In the given diagram, the extensional forces are in the same direction as indicated by the velocity vectors. These type of forces develops extensional or normal faults.

- Compressional forces leads to development of reverse faults.
- Shear forces leads to development of strike slip faults.

4. Most of the bituminous coal of India belongs to Barakar formation of Permian Age.

5. The time equivalent of the time-stratigraphic term 'Series' is Epoch.

6.

Stratigraphic units of India	**Age**
Barakar Formation	Permian
Warkalli Formation	Miocene
Bagh Beds	Cretaceous
Bhander Limestone	Proterozoic

7. **The Universal Transverse Mercator (UTM)** conformal projection uses a 2-dimensional Cartesian coordinate system to give locations on the surface of the Earth. Like the traditional method of latitude and longitude, it is a horizontal position representation, i.e. it is used to identify locations on the Earth independently of vertical position. Cylindrical map projection has co-ordinate lines with horizontal parallels crossing meridians at right angles. All meridians are equally spaced and the scale is consistent along each parallel.

8. Generalised groundwater flow equation is given as,

$$\frac{\partial\left(K_x \frac{\partial h}{\partial x}\right)}{\partial x}+\frac{\partial\left(K_y \frac{\partial h}{\partial y}\right)}{\partial y}+\frac{\partial\left(K_z \frac{\partial h}{\partial z}\right)}{\partial z}=S_s \frac{\partial h}{\partial t}$$

For homogeneous and isotropic aquifer

$$\frac{\partial^2 h}{\partial x^2}+\frac{\partial^2 h}{\partial y^2}+\frac{\partial^2 h}{\partial z^2}=\frac{S_s}{K}\frac{\partial h}{\partial t}$$

where, $K = K_x = K_y = K_z$

For confined aquifer of thickness b, $S = S_s b$ and $T = Kb$

Therefore, $$\frac{\partial^2 h}{\partial x^2}+\frac{\partial^2 h}{\partial y^2}+\frac{\partial^2 h}{\partial z^2}=\frac{S}{T}\frac{\partial h}{\partial t}$$

Now, For steady stat condition,

$$\frac{\partial^2 h}{\partial x^2}+\frac{\partial^2 h}{\partial y^2}+\frac{\partial^2 h}{\partial z^2}=0=\nabla^2 h=0$$

9. Given,

Initial weight = 4800 g

Aggregate weight = 3504 g

Now, Abrasion value = $\dfrac{\text{Loss in weight}}{\text{Initial weight}}$

$$=\frac{4800-3504}{4800}=0.27$$

$\therefore$ Abrasion value (%) = 0.27 × 100

= 27%

10. Brightness temperature or radiance temperature is the temperature a black body in thermal equilibrium with its surroundings would have to be to duplicate the observed intensity of a grey body object at a frequency. Brightness temperature is found by inverting the Plank's function, as

$$T_b=\frac{C_2}{\lambda \ln\left(1+\frac{C_1}{I_\lambda}\right)}$$

where, $C_1 = 1.1911\times10^8\ \text{Wm}^{-2}\text{S}^{-1}\mu\text{m}^4$

$C_2 = 1.4388\times10^4\ \text{K}\mu\text{m}$

T_b is the brightness temperature

λ is the wavelength

I_λ is the measured intensity

$\therefore$ Brightness temperature is the function of surface temperature and emissivity.

11. Quartz has poor cleavage in all directions.

12. From the given figure in the question,

Intercept at a axis = 2 units

Intercept at b axis = 1.5 units

Intercept at c axis = 3 units

Miller indicates is given as $\left(\frac{1}{2},\frac{1}{1.5},\frac{1}{3}\right)$

Now, Multiplied by 6

$$\left(\frac{6}{2},\frac{6}{1.5},\frac{6}{3}\right)=(3,4,2)=(342)$$

13. Granite is usually found in the central cores of Major Mountain ranges consist of intrusive igneous rocks. When exposed by erosion, these cores (called batholiths) may occupy huge areas of the Earth's surface. Intrusive igneous rocks are formed from magma that cools and solidifies within the crust of a planet, surrounded by pre-existing rock, the magma cools slowly and, as a result, these rocks are coarse-grained.

Basalt is a common extrusive igneous rock and forms lava flows, lava sheets and lava plateaus. Some kinds of basalt solidify to form long polygonal columns. Extrusive igneous rocks, also known as volcanic rocks, are formed at the crust's surface as a result of the partial melting of rocks within the mantle and crust.

Gneiss is a high-grade metamorphic rock, meaning that it has been subjected to higher temperatures and pressures than schist. It is formed by the metamorphosis of granite, or sedimentary rock. Gneiss displays distinct foliation, representing alternating layers composed of different minerals.

Sandstone is a clastic sedimentary rock composed of sand-size grains of mineral, rock, or organic material. It also contains a cementing material that binds the sand grains together and may contain a matrix of silt- or clay-size particles that occupy the spaces between the sand grains.

14. Southwest Indian Ridge: It is located along the floor of southwest Indian Ocean and southeast Atlantic Ocean. It is characterized by ultraslow spreading rates nearly 15 mm/yr. The SWIR opened during breakup of Gondwana during late Cretaceous.

15. Isogonic lines are lines on the Earth's surface along which the declination has the same constant value, and lines along which the declination is zero are called agonic lines. The lowercase Greek letter ´ (delta) is frequently used as the symbol for magnetic declination.

16.

Geophysical terms	Units
Transit time	Microsecond per feet
Conductivity	Siemens
Gravity anomaly	mGal
Magnetic field intensity	Nano Tesla

17. The Maxwell's equation based on Ampere's law is $\vec{\nabla} \times \vec{H} = \vec{J} + \frac{\partial \vec{D}}{\partial t}$

18. Normal gravity formula is given as

$$g_t = 987031.846\left(1 + 0.005278895\sin^2\phi\right.$$
$$\left.+0.000023462\sin^4\phi\right) mGal$$

where, ϕ is the geodetic latitude.

19. In the common midpoint (CMP) domain, the moveout (traveltime v/s offset) curve for any primary reflection event is best approximated by a hyperbola.

20. **Assertion (a):** Magnetic stripes are observed around mid-oceanic ridge regions

Reason (r): The earth's magnetic field undergoes reversals of polarity.

Both (a) and (r) are true and (r) is one of the correct reasons for (a)

21. A sesmic gap refers to a segment of an active belt where a historical great earthquake has not occurred.

22. Given,

Distance from epicentre to seismogram = 100 km

Velocity of P wave, V_P = 6 km/s

Velocity of S wave, V_S = 3.5 km/s

Therefore, Travel time for P wave, $t_P = \frac{100}{6}$ sec.

Travel time for S wave, $t_S = \frac{100}{3.5}$ sec.

Travel time difference $\Delta t = t_S - t_P$

$$= \frac{100}{3.5} - \frac{100}{6} = 11.8 \text{ sec}$$

23. 12-22 % increased in P wave velocities across Mohorovicic discontinuity from lower crust to upper mantle beneath a craton is found.

24. Laterolog 8 has the largest depth of investigation among the other logging tools.

25. Terrestrial naturally occurring radioactive material is potassium 40 (K-40). The long half-life of K-40 (1.25 billion years) means that it still exists in measurable quantities today. It beta decays, mostly to calcium-40, and forms 0.012% of natural potassium which is otherwise made up of stable K-39 and K-41. Potassium is the seventh most abundant element in the Earth's crust, and K-40 averages 850 Bq/kg there. It is found in many foodstuffs (bananas for example), and indeed fills an important dietary requirement, ending up in our bones.

PART-B (GEOLOGY)

26. Stylolites or styolite are serrated surfaces within a rock mass at which mineral material has been removed by pressure dissolution, in a process that decreases the total volume of rock. Insoluble minerals, such as clays, pyrite and oxides, as well as insoluble organic matter, remain within the stylolites and make them visible. Stylolites usually form parallel to bedding, because of overburden pressure.

27. The outcrop of a flat topography will be found in the updip direction. Therefore, if we drill a vertical exploratory hole it will always intersect the mention coal seam in the south of the outcrop at an elevation less than 1400 m.

28. Pseudotachylite is a cohesive glassy or very fine-grained rock that occurs as veins and often contains inclusions of wall-rock fragments. Pseudotachylite is typically dark in color; and is glassy in appearance. In most cases, researchers search for and describe good evidence that the pseudotachylite formed by frictional melting of the wall rocks during rapid fault movement associated with a seismic event. This has caused them to be termed "fossil earthquakes".

29. Given,

Angle between the hinge line and the median line change, $\phi = 45°$

Shear strain, $\psi = \tan\phi$

$\therefore \psi = \tan 45^o = 1$

30. Given,

The empirical probability distribution of gold (Au) grades showing a unimodal distribution with

Mode = 2 g/t

Median = 3 g/t

Mean = 5 g/t

We see that,

Mean > Median > Mode

Therefore,

The probability distribution is positively skewed.

31. Given,

Attitude of the limb of a non-plunging fold is 070°, 40° S.

As given, after rotation of the limb about its fold axis in the clockwise direction by 30° the dip of the limb becomes 70° S.

Pole of this limb will be plotted 90° away from maximum dip. As per question plunge of the pole limb is 20°.

32. The Bulk Silicate Earth (BSE) is best approximated by the average mantle and continental crust composition.

33. The stable mineral assemblage in metamorphism of a rock with politic bulk composition under granulite facies is garnet + cordierite + K - feldspar + sillimanite

34. P – T path 2 represent crustal thickening in a collisional tectonic setting.

In the collisional setting, first pressure increases rapidly when collision starts whereas temperature remains stationary, after that when two collisional plates intacts, melting of subducting plate starts and temperature rises. After this, pressure falls rapidly whereas temperature falls slowly with the cooling of magma.

35. Given,

Height, h = 7 km = 7×10^3 m

$\rho = 3100 \text{ kg/m}^3$

$g = 9.8 \text{ m/s}^2$

Now, Pressure, $P = \rho g h$

$$= 3100 \times 9.8 \times 7 \times 10^3 = 2126.6 \times 10^5 \ Pa$$

Also, $10^5 \, Pa = 1 \, bar$

$\therefore P = 2126.6 \, bar \approx 2.13 \, bar$

36. Given,

C_1 = Initial melt has 50 % of for sterite liquid and 50 % of fayalite liquid.

At 1500°C, weight in percentage of solid, C_S = 60%

At 1500°C, weight in percentage of liquid, C_l = 30%

Now, According to lever rule,

Fraction of liquid at 1500°C, = $f_s = \dfrac{C_s - C_o}{C_s - C_l}$

$$f_s = \frac{60-50}{60-30} = \frac{10}{30} \times 100 = 33.33 \ \%$$

37. Given,

lattice parameter, $a = 5.463 \ \dot{A}$

and Radius of $F^- = 1.71 \ \dot{A} \left(R_{F^-}\right)$

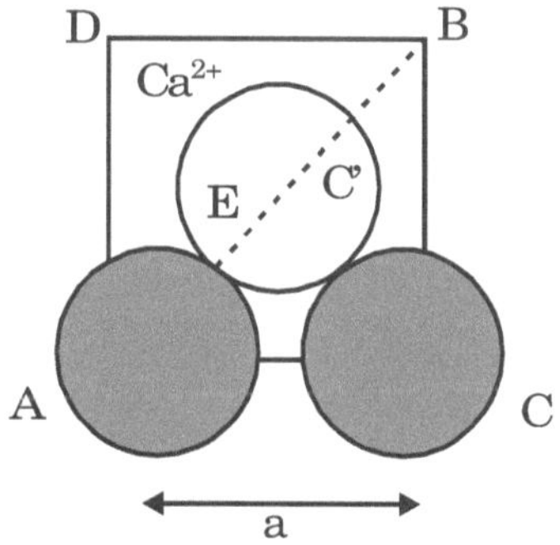

$AB = a\sqrt{2} = 5.463 \times 1.414 = 7.72$

$AC' = \dfrac{AB}{2} = \dfrac{7.72}{2} = 3.86 \ \dot{A}$

Therefore, Radius of Ca^{2+} is given as,

$R_{Ca^{2+}} = \left(AC' - AE\right) = 3.86 - 1.71 = 2.15 \ \dot{A}$

38. As per the diagram in the question, the plate used is quartz retardation plate. Retardation is shown to occur opposite to the slow direction of the retardation plate. Therefore, it is the uniaxial negative mineral.

39. Given, For Reaction,

$Mg_2SiO_4 + SiO_2 = Mg_2Si_2O_6$

Assume $C_P = 0$

$\Delta H_{enstatite} = -3090.47 \ kJ$ at T = 600 K and P = 1 bar

$\Delta H_{Quartz} = -910.83 \ kJ$

$\Delta H_{forsterite} = -2172.2 \ kJ$

Therefore,

Resultant, H = {–3090.47 – (–910.83 – 2172.2)}

= –7.44 kJ

Also,

Resultant, S = {132.5 – (41.5 + 95.1)} = –4.1 JK^{-1}

Now, $G = H - TS$

$\Rightarrow G = -7440 - \left(0.600 \times 4.1\right) = -4980 \ J$

40. As per table in the question,

Bulk distribution coefficient,

$$K_d = \sum \begin{pmatrix} \text{Model abundance of minerals} \\ \times \text{Partition coefficent} \end{pmatrix}$$

As per given question,

K_d = (0.45 × 0.506) + (0.42 × 0.42) + (0.10 × 0.045) + (0.05 × 0.019) = 0.4012

41.

Classical ore deposits	Associated ore minerals
Sudbury type deposit	Pentlandite
Mississippi valley type deposit	Sphalerite and Galena
Climax type deposit	Molybdenite
IOCG type deposit	Uraninite and chalcopyrite

42. **Chitinozoans** are a taxon of flask-shaped, organic walled marine microfossils produced by an as yet unknown animal. Common from the Ordovician to Devonian periods (i.e. the mid-Paleozoic), the millimetre-scale organisms are abundant in almost all types of marine sediment across the globe. This wide distribution, and their rapid pace of evolution, makes them valuable biostratigraphic markers.

43. Brachiopods live only in the sea, and most species avoid locations with strong currents or waves. The larvae of articulate species settle in quickly and form dense populations in well-defined areas while the larvae of inarticulate species swim for up to a month and have wide ranges. Brachiopods now live mainly in cold water and low light. Fish and crustaceans seem to find brachiopod flesh distasteful and seldom attack them. Among brachiopods, only the lingulids have been fished commercially, on a very small scale. The pair for brachiopod- mollusc pair with Lingula, Nautilus.

44. The depositional environment of Sandstone with herring- bone cross bedding has a Tidal depositional environment.

The depositional environment of Chalk with coccolith has a Pelagic depositional environment.

The depositional environment of Well sorted arenite with large cross bedding (5- 10 m thick) has a Eolian depositional environment.

The depositional environment of Poorly sorted sediments with faceted and striated pebbles has a Glacial depositional environment.

45. Sequentially from older to younger

Kajrahat Limestone → Jodhpur Sandstone → Cambay Shale → Tipam Sandstone

46. Given,

Weight of coal = 2 g

Moisture = 0.2 g

Ash = 0.3 g

Volatile matter = 0.5 g

Mineral matter content = 1.1 × ash content

= 1.1 × 0.3 = 0.33 g

$V_{d.m.f.}$ = weight of coal – Moisture – Mineral matter

= 2 – 0.2 – 0.33 = 1.47

$$\therefore V_{d.m.f}(\%) = \frac{0.5}{1.47} \times 100 = 34.01\,\%$$

47. Kerogen is insoluble in normal organic solvents because of the high molecular weight of its component compounds. The soluble portion is known as bitumen. When heated to the right temperatures in the Earth's crust, oil window 60–160 °C, gas window c. 150–200 °C, both depending on how quickly the source rock is heated some types of kerogen release crude oil or natural gas, collectively known as hydrocarbons.

48. Lipids covers all organism produced substances that are practically insoluble in water. This contains fatty substances such as vegetable oil, waxes and animal fats. These are main source of petroleum.

49. Given,

$K = 10$ m/day

Head loss $(h_1 - h_2) = 4$ m

Distance, $l = 750$ m

Groundwater flow velocity, q is given as

$$q = \left[K\frac{h_1 - h_2}{l}\right] = \frac{10 \times 4}{750} = \frac{40}{750} = 0.0533 \text{ m/day}$$

50. As per given figure,

Number of Ist order stream = 27

Number of IInd order stream = 13

Number of IIIrd order stream = 5

Number of IVth order stream = 2

Number of Vth order stream = 2

Therefore, Bifurcation ratio

$$= \frac{\text{Number of II}^{nd}\text{ order stream}}{\text{Number of III}^{rd}\text{ order stream}} = \frac{13}{5} = 2.6$$

51. Given,

Displacement of tower on photograph, d = 2 mm

Distance between top of the tower and nadir = 100 m

Height of the aircraft, H = 3000 m

Now, For vertical aerial photograph, the equation is

$$\frac{h}{H} = \frac{d}{r}$$

$$\Rightarrow h = \frac{H \times d}{r} = \frac{3000 \times 2}{100} = 60 \text{ m}$$

52. Given,

Radius of sample, $r = 27$

Thickness of sample, $t = 22$ m

Failure load, $P = 5\ KN = 5000\ N$

Now,

The Tensile strength, σ_t is

$$\sigma_t = \left(\frac{0.636P}{Dt}\right) = \frac{0.636 \times 5000}{54 \times 22} = 2.67 \text{ N/mm}^2$$

Therefore, $D = 2r = 2 \times 27 = 54$ mm

53. Given,

Array value and area of influence at four points as

At W, $a = 15$ g/t, A = 25 m^2

At X, $a = 30$ g/t, A = 23 m^2

At Y, $a = 12$ g/t, A = 28 m^2

At Z, $a = 28$ g/t, A = 40 m^2

∴ Weighted average array

$$= \frac{\sum aA}{\sum A}$$

$$= \frac{(30 \times 23 + 12 \times 28 + 15 \times 25 + 28 \times 40)}{(23 + 28 + 25 + 40)}$$

$$= \frac{2521}{116} = 21.7 \text{ g/t}$$

54. Given,

$DN_{min} = 8$

$DN_{max} = 32$

$DN = 27$

As per formula

$$DN_{strech} = 255 \times \frac{DN - DN_{\min}}{DN_{\max} - DN_{\min}}$$

$$DN_{strech} = 255 \times \frac{27 - 8}{32 - 8}$$

$$= \frac{4845}{24} = 201.88$$

55. Dilation in the length of landslide $= \frac{80}{40} = 2$

Dilation in the width of landslide $= \frac{70}{35} = 2$

Therefore,

Dilation = 2

(GEOPHYSICS)

26. PKiKP is the seismic phases that reflects at the boundary between outer core and inner core to rach in the shadow zone of p-wave, i.e., in between 103° to 143°.

27. Gravity field response is irrespective of the location of burial, it only depends on the geometry of the body, density contrast and depth to the body, Therefore, gravity response does not change from equator to pole for the same body at the same burial depth.

Bodies having same magnetic susceptibility but are at different locations on Earth shows, different magnetic field responses as the geomagnetic field induction varies considerably over the Earth;s surface. Therefore, the angle of magnetization and hence the field response.

28. Given,

Bouguer density, $\rho_B = 2.8$ g/cc

Elevation, $h = 30$ m

Now, The Bouguer correction is given as

$$\Delta g_B = 2\pi\rho_B Gh$$

where, G is gravitational constant

$$\therefore \Delta g_B = 2 \times 3.14 \times 2.8 \times 10^3 \times 6.67 \times 10^{-11} \times 30$$

$$= 0.00003518558 \text{ m/s}^2 = 3.518 \text{ mGal}$$

29. Given,

Resistivity of top layer, $\rho_1 = 10\ \Omega m$

Resistivity of half-space, $\rho_2 = 100\ \Omega m$

Thickness of top layer, $h_1 = 10\ m$

Current electrode spacing AB/2 = 5 m

For a two layer case, Resistivity transform is defined as

$$T(\lambda) = \rho_1 \left(\frac{1 + k_1 e^{-2\lambda h_1}}{1 - k_1 e^{-2\lambda h_1}}\right)$$

$$\text{where, } k_1 = \frac{\rho_2 - \rho_1}{\rho_2 + \rho_1} \text{ and } \lambda = \frac{1}{AB/2}$$

$$\therefore k_1 = \frac{100 - 10}{100 + 10} = \frac{9}{11} = 0.82 \text{ and } \lambda = \frac{1}{5} = 0.2$$

Hence,

$$T(\lambda) = \left\{\frac{1 + 0.82 \times e^{-2 \times 0.2 \times 10}}{1 - 0.82 \times e^{-2 \times 0.2 \times 10}}\right\} \times 10 = 10.33\ \Omega m$$

30. Given,

Equatorial radius = e

and Polar radius = p

Therefore, Eccentricity = $\sqrt{1-\frac{b^2}{a^2}} = \sqrt{1-\frac{p^2}{e^2}}$

Polar flattening = $\sqrt{\frac{e-p}{e}} = \sqrt{1-\frac{p}{e}}$

The ratio between eccentricity and polar flattening is

$$= \frac{\sqrt{1-\frac{p^2}{e^2}}}{1-\frac{p}{e}} = \frac{\sqrt{\left(1-\frac{p}{e}\right)\left(1+\frac{p}{e}\right)}}{\sqrt{\left(1-\frac{p}{e}\right)^2}} = \frac{\sqrt{\left(1+\frac{p}{e}\right)}}{\sqrt{\left(1-\frac{p}{e}\right)}} = \sqrt{\frac{e+p}{e-p}}$$

31. Given,

The vertical magnetic field anomaly is given as

$$\Delta z = 2Mt\left(\frac{z_1}{z_1^2+x^2} - \frac{z_2}{z_2^2+x^2}\right)$$

$\because$ Δz is maximum at the top of the body, i.e., $x = 0$

Thus, $\Delta z_0 = 2Mt\left(\frac{1}{z_1} - \frac{1}{z_2}\right)$

Now, $M = KH$ where, K is magnetic susceptibility

Also, given,

$K = 0.5,\ H = 60000\ nT$

$M = 0.5 \times 60000$

$= 30000\ nT$

Since, only 1% magnetic is present, thus M becomes

$$M = 30000 \times \frac{1}{100} = 300\ nT$$

As $z_1 = 50\ m,\ z_2 = 150\ m,\ t = 10\ m$

Thus, $\Delta z_0 = 2 \times 300 \times 10\left[\frac{1}{50} - \frac{1}{150}\right] = 80\ nT$

32. Given,

$\rho_a = 50\ \Omega m$

$f = 0.1\ Hz$

$E = 12\ mV/km$

The relation between apparent resistivity, magnetic field and electric field intensity is given as

$$\rho_a = \frac{0.2}{f}\left(\frac{E}{B}\right)^2$$

$$\Rightarrow B = \sqrt{\frac{0.2 \times E^2}{f \times \rho_a}} = \sqrt{\frac{0.2 \times 12^2}{0.1 \times 50}} = 2.4\ nT$$

33. Given,

The electrode spacing, L, as

$2L = 18$

$\Rightarrow L = 9\ m$

The potential electrode spacing, l

$2l = 2$

$\Rightarrow l = 1\ m$

For Schlumberger Array

$$\rho_s = \frac{\pi\left(L^2 - l^2\right)}{2l}\left(\frac{V}{I}\right)$$

$$\therefore \rho_s = \frac{\pi\left(9^2 - 1^2\right)}{2 \times 1}\left(\frac{V}{I}\right) = 40\pi\left(\frac{V}{I}\right)$$

For Wenner Array,

$$\rho_w = 2\pi a\left(\frac{V}{I}\right)$$

Now, As per question,

$$40\pi\left(\frac{V}{I}\right) = 2\pi a\left(\frac{V}{I}\right)$$

$\Rightarrow a = 20\ m$

34. Given,

$v(t) = 4e^{-0.3t}$

$V_o = 10\ mV$

$t_1 = 1\ \text{sec},\ t_2 = 4\ \text{sec}$

Now, Chargeability is defined as

$$M = \frac{1}{V_o}\int_{t_1}^{t_2} v(t)\,dt$$

$$\Rightarrow M = \frac{1}{10}\int_1^4 4e^{-0.3t} = \frac{-4}{10} \times \frac{1}{0.3}\left[e^{-0.3t}\right]_1^4$$

$$= (-1.33)\left[e^{-1.2} - e^{-0.3}\right] = 0.5846$$

35. For a near surface earthquake occurring in a homogenous, isotropic Earth, Rayleigh waves are generated. For heterogeneous Earth, Love waves are generated.

36. Given, Dynamic range = 60

Also, as per formula

$$\text{Dynamic range} = 20\log_{10}\left(\frac{A_{max}}{A_{min}}\right)$$

$$\Rightarrow 60 = 20\log_{10}\left(\frac{A_{max}}{A_{min}}\right)$$

$$\Rightarrow \log_{10}\left(\frac{A_{max}}{A_{min}}\right) = \frac{60}{20} = 3$$

$$\Rightarrow \left(\frac{A_{max}}{A_{min}}\right) = 10^3 = 1000$$

37. The Wadati Diagram gives the relation between $(t_S - t_P)$ and t_P where, t_S and t_P are arrival time for S and P- wave respectively,

Now,

For travelling a certain distance D by P and S-wave.

$$t_P = \frac{D}{\alpha}, \; t_S = \frac{D}{\beta}$$

where,

α is P – wave velocity

β is S – wave velocity

Therefore, $t_S - t_P = D\left(\frac{1}{\beta} - \frac{1}{\alpha}\right) = \frac{D}{\alpha}\left(\frac{\alpha}{\beta} - 1\right)$

$$\Rightarrow (t_S - t_P) = t_P\left(\frac{\alpha}{\beta} - 1\right) \quad \ldots (i)$$

The Wadati Diagram gives the plot between $t_S - t_P$ and t_P. Therefore, from equation (i), the slope is $\left(\frac{\alpha}{\beta} - 1\right)$

Now, Given that, slope = 1

$$\Rightarrow \frac{\alpha}{\beta} - 1 = 1$$

$$\Rightarrow \frac{\alpha}{\beta} = 2 \text{ or } \frac{V_P}{V_S} = 2$$

38. As per the beach ball in the figure which depicts as the focal mechanism of an earthquake. The shaded and unshaded portions indicate compressional and dilatational quadrants, respectively. FP1 is the fault plane solution. The focal mechanism represent a thrust fault with strike 45° and FP1 represents a dip 30° with the tension axis in the compression quadrant.

39. The characteristic log response of a thick coal seam is high transit time, high resistivity and low gamma ray count.

40. Given,

$SP = -54\ mV$

$K = 77.29$

Resistivity of mud filtrate, $R_{mf} = 0.95$ Wm

Now, As per formula,

$$SP = -K\log_{10}\left(\frac{R_{mf}}{R_w}\right)$$

$$\Rightarrow -54 = -77.29\log_{10}\left(\frac{0.95}{R_w}\right)$$

$$\Rightarrow \frac{54}{77.29} = \log_{10}\left(\frac{0.95}{R_w}\right)$$

$$\Rightarrow R_w = \frac{0.45}{4.99651} = 0.09006\ \Omega m$$

41. For a porous and permeable sandstone bed, when the resistivity of the mud filtrate used is equal to the resistivity of the formation water the LLs and LLm logs show appreciably large separation.

42. Given,

$$\frac{N}{N_o} = 0.03$$

where, N is number of atoms after n half-lives

N_0 is number of atom at the initial times

Now, as per formula,

$$\frac{N}{N_o} = \left(\frac{1}{2}\right)^n$$

$$\Rightarrow 0.03 = \frac{1}{2^n}$$

$$\Rightarrow n\ln 2 = \ln\left(\frac{1}{0.03}\right)$$

$$\Rightarrow n \times 0.693 = -\ln(0.03)$$

Neglecting the negative sign

$$\Rightarrow n = 5.05996$$

43. VLF fields can be measured over continental distances (r) because the magnetic field decreases at the rate $\frac{1}{r}$ and the output power at the transmitting station is 100 to 1000 kW.

44. Convolution of two box car function of different width gives trapezoidal function while of convolution of two boxcar function of same widths gives triangular function.

45. Given, The sequence is $\left[1, \frac{1}{2}, \frac{1}{9}, \frac{1}{8}, ...\right]$

The filter designed with this operator is

$$\left[1+\frac{z}{2}+\frac{z^2}{4}+\frac{z^3}{8}+.....\right]=\frac{1}{1-\frac{z}{2}}=\frac{2}{2-z}$$

For finding out the pole, substitute the denominator equal to zero.

$\therefore z-2=0$

$\Rightarrow z=2$

46. Normal moveout (NMO) correction was applied to seismic data in the common midpoint (CMP) domain. For shallower reflections, the frequency distortion due to NMO stretch is highest for larger offsets.

47. Given,

$\theta = 30^o$

$V = 2$ km/s

$\delta x = 25$ m

Now, The relation between the velocity, trace spacing, dip and unbiased frequency for zero-offset seismic reflection survey is given as

$$\delta x = \frac{V}{4f\sin\theta}$$

$$\therefore f = \frac{V}{4\delta x\sin\theta} = \frac{2\times 2\times 10^3}{4\times 25} = 40\ Hz$$

48. In statistical wavelet deconvolution, the reflectivity series is assumed to be a random sequence. Then, the autocorrelation of the wavelet is a scaled version of the autocorrelation of the seismic trace.

49. Given, Helmholtz decomposition

$u = \nabla\phi + \nabla\times\psi$

with $\phi = \frac{1}{2}\left(x^2 - y^2 + z^2\right)$

and $\psi = zy^2 i + xzj + x^2 k$

$\therefore \nabla.u = \nabla.(\nabla\phi) + \nabla.(\nabla\times\psi)$

As $\nabla(\nabla\times\psi) = 0$

Therefore, $\nabla.u = \nabla.(\nabla\phi)$

$$= \nabla\left\{\hat{i}\frac{\partial}{\partial x}+\hat{j}\frac{\partial}{\partial y}+\hat{k}\frac{\partial}{\partial z}\right\}\left\{\frac{1}{2}\left(x^2-y^2+z^2\right)\right\}$$

$$= \nabla\left[\frac{1}{2}\left\{2x\hat{i}-2y\hat{j}+z\hat{k}\right\}\right]$$

$$\nabla.u = \nabla\left\{x\hat{i}-y\hat{j}+z\hat{k}\right\}$$

$$= \left\{\hat{i}\frac{\partial}{\partial x}+\hat{j}\frac{\partial}{\partial y}+\hat{k}\frac{\partial}{\partial z}\right\}.\left\{x\hat{i}-y\hat{j}+z\hat{k}\right\}$$

$$= (x-y+z)$$

$$[\nabla.u]_{(1,1,1)} = (1-1+1) = 1$$

50. As per figure, Using Snell's law, for layer 1 and layer 2,

$$\frac{\sin\theta_1}{\sin\theta_2} = \frac{V_1}{V_2}$$

$$\Rightarrow \frac{\sin 30}{\sin\theta_2} = \frac{1}{1.2}$$

$$\Rightarrow \sin\theta_2 = 0.6$$

For second layer and half space,

$$\frac{\sin\theta_2}{\sin\alpha} = \frac{1.2}{1.5}$$

$$\Rightarrow \sin\alpha = \frac{\sin\theta_2\times 1.5}{1.2} = \frac{0.6\times 1.5}{1.2}$$

$$\Rightarrow \sin\alpha = 0.75$$

$$\Rightarrow \alpha = \sin^{-1}(0.75) = 48.59^o$$

51. For change from a water saturated sandstone to a gas saturated sandstone, the P- wave velocity (V_P), decreases with decrease in Poisson's ratio (σ) keeping S wave (V_S) the same.

The relationship between V_P, V_S, σ is given as

$$\sigma = \frac{1}{2}\frac{V_P^2 - 2V_S^2}{V_P^2 - V_S^2}$$

52.

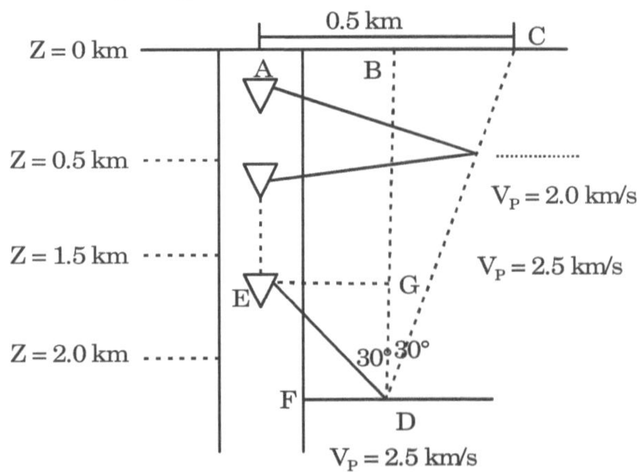

As per figure,

$AE = 1.5$ km

$$CD = \sqrt{(BD)^2 + (BC)^2} = \sqrt{2^2 + 0.25^2} = 2.015 \text{ km}$$

$$DE = \sqrt{(DG)^2 + (EG)^2} = \sqrt{0.5^2 + 0.25^2} = 0.55901 \text{ km}$$

$\therefore$ Total distance travelled by the seismic signal to reach the deepest geophone is

2.0155 + 0.55901 = 2.57951 km.

Now, Given speed is = 2 km/s

$$\therefore \text{ Travel time, } t_p = \frac{2.57451}{2} = 1.2872 \text{ sec.}$$

53. As per condition,

Linearly and non-linearly dependent vectors is given as

det (vectors) = 0 is Linearly dependent

det (vectors) ≠ 0 is Non-linearly dependent

Now, Given,

$v_1 = [1,4,7]$

$v_2 = [2,5,8]$

$v_3 = [3,6,9]$

$$\therefore \text{Let } A = \begin{bmatrix} 1 & 2 & 3 \\ 4 & 5 & 6 \\ 7 & 8 & 9 \end{bmatrix}$$

$$\det(A) = \begin{bmatrix} 1 & 2 & 3 \\ 4 & 5 & 6 \\ 7 & 8 & 9 \end{bmatrix} = 0$$

All other options have non-zero determinant.

54. Given,

$$A - \begin{bmatrix} 2 & 1 \\ 0 & 3 \end{bmatrix}$$

The eigen values of the given matrix are,

$[A - \lambda I] = 0$

$$\begin{bmatrix} 2-\lambda & 1 \\ 0 & 3-\lambda \end{bmatrix} = 0$$

$\Rightarrow (2-\lambda)(3-\lambda) = 0$

$\Rightarrow \lambda = 2,3$

As we know,

$$\text{Condition Number} = \frac{\lambda_{max}}{\lambda_{min}} = \frac{3}{2} = 1.5$$

55. (b)

Equations	Analytical expressions
Wave equation	$\frac{\partial^2 u}{\partial t^2} - \nabla^2 u = 0$
Heat conduction equation	$\frac{\partial u}{\partial t} - \nabla^2 u = 0$
Eikonal equation	$\lvert\nabla u\rvert^2 = 1$
Poisson's equation	$\nabla^2 u = -4\pi\sigma$

(GENERAL APTITUDE SECTION)

1. The ways in which this game can be played is potentially infinite.

2. If you choose plan P, you will have to forgo plan Q, as these two are mutually exclusive.

3. Given, a-b = even

Case I

a = odd

b = odd

Case II

a = even

b = even

Option A, ab

In Case I: ab = odd, In Case II : ab = even

Option B, $a^2 + b^2 + 1$

In Case I: $(\text{odd})^2 + (\text{odd})^2 + 1 = \text{even}$

In Case II: $(\text{even})^2 + (\text{even})^2 + 1 = \text{odd}$

Option C: $a^2 + b + 1$

In Case I: $(\text{odd})^2 + (\text{odd}) + 1 = \text{even}$

In Case II: $(\text{even})^2 + (\text{even}) + 1 = \text{odd}$

Option D: $ab - b$

In Case I: $(\text{odd})(\text{odd}) - \text{odd} = \text{even}$

In Case II: $(\text{even})(\text{even}) - \text{even} = \text{even}$

4. Given,

Total number of possible outcomes = 2

Number of outcome which consists that both children are boys if the older one is a boy = 1

Probability that both children are boys = $\frac{1}{2}$

5. **CASE 1:** When Q is married

QR is the pair.

CASE 2: When Q is unmarried

PQ is the pair.

Only one of the above case is possible. Therefore, number of pairs is 1.

6. Cleaving = splitting, separating

7. Given,

The number of Bullocks = X

The number of Tractors = Y

Also, Let, 1 bullock's 1 day work = X

and 1 tractor's 1 day work = Y

Therefore, Combined work is $X + Y = \frac{1}{8}$ ... (i)

Now, After having the number of bullocks and doubling the number of tractors, we get,

$$\frac{X}{2} + 2Y = \frac{1}{5} \quad \text{... (ii)}$$

From equation (i) and (ii), we get

$$X = \frac{1}{30}$$

Therefore, *X* bullocks will complete alone the work in 30 days.

8. Given, P, Q, R, S, are women

and V, W, X, Y, Z are men

Probability that P is not paired with Z,

$P_1 = 4 \times 4 \times 3 \times 2 = 96$

Probability that P is not paired with Z and also Y is not paired with anyone

$P_2 = 3 \times 3 \times 2 \times 1 = 18$

Probability that P is not paired with Z and also Y is necessary paired $P_1 - P_2 = 96 - 18 = 78$

9. As per question,

There can be more than one possibilities. Therefore, identities of P, Q cannot be determined.

10. Difference in pollutant concentration

In summer: 10.5 – 1.5 = 9.0

In winter: 8.0 – 0.25 = 7.75

SOLVED PAPER - 2016

GENERAL APTITUDE (GA)

Q. 1 – Q. 5 carry one mark each.

1. The volume of a sphere of diameter 1 unit is ________ than the volume of a cube of side 1 unit.

(*a*) least (*b*) less

(*c*) lesser (*d*) low

2. The unruly crowd demanded that the accused be ____________ without trial.

(*a*) hanged (*b*) hanging

(*c*) hankering (*d*) hung

3. Choose the statement(s) where the underlined word is used correctly:

(i) A prone is a dried plum.

(ii) He was lying prone on the floor.

(iii) People who eat a lot of fat are prone to heart disease.

(*a*) (i) and (iii) only (*b*) (iii) only

(*c*) (i) and (ii) only (*d*) (ii) and (iii) only

4. Fact: If it rains, then the field is wet.

Read the following statements:

(i) It rains

(ii) The field is not wet

(iii) The field is wet

(iv) It did not rain

Which one of the options given below is NOT logically possible, based on the given fact?

(*a*) If (iii), then (iv)

(*b*) If (i), then (iii)

(*c*) If (i), then (ii)

(*d*) If (ii), then (iv)

5. A window is made up of a square portion and an equilateral triangle portion above it. The base of the triangular portion coincides with the upper side of the square. If the perimeter of the window is 6 m, the area of the window in m^2 is _________.

(*a*) 1.43

(*b*) 2.06

(*c*) 2.68

(*d*) 2.88

Q. 6 – Q. 10 carry two marks each.

6. Students taking an exam are divided into two groups, P and Q such that each group has the same number of students. The performance of each of the students in a test was evaluated out of 200 marks. It was observed that the mean of group P was 105, while that of group Q was 85. The standard deviation of group P was 25, while that of group Q was 5. Assuming that the marks were distributed on a normal distribution, which of the following statements will have the highest probability of being TRUE?

(*a*) No student in group Q scored less marks than any student in group P.

(*b*) No student in group P scored less marks than any student in group Q.

(*c*) Most students of group Q scored marks in a narrower range than students in group P.

(*d*) The median of the marks of group P is 100.

7. A smart city integrates all modes of transport, uses clean energy and promotes sustainable use of resources. It also uses technology to ensure safety and security of the city, something which critics argue, will lead to a surveillance state.

Which of the following can be logically inferred from the above paragraph?

(i) All smart cities encourage the formation of surveillance states.

(ii) Surveillance is an integral part of a smart city.

(iii) Sustainability and surveillance go hand in hand in a smart city.

(iv) There is a perception that smart cities promote surveillance.

(*a*) (i) and (iv) only (*b*) (ii) and (iii) only

(*c*) (iv) only (*d*) (i) only

8. Find the missing sequence in the letter series.

B, FH, LNP, _ _ _ _.

(*a*) SUWY (*b*) TUVW

(*c*) TVXZ (*d*) TWXZ

9. The binary operation □ is defined as a □ b = ab + (a + b), where a and b are any two real numbers. The value of the identity element of this operation, defined as the number x such that a □ x = a, for any a, is _____.

(*a*) 0 (*b*) 1

(*c*) 2 (*d*) 10

10. Which of the following curves represents the function $y = \ln\left(\left|e^{\lfloor|\sin(|x|)|\rfloor}\right|\right)$ for $|x| < 2\pi$? Here, x represents the abscissa and y represents the ordinate.

(*a*)

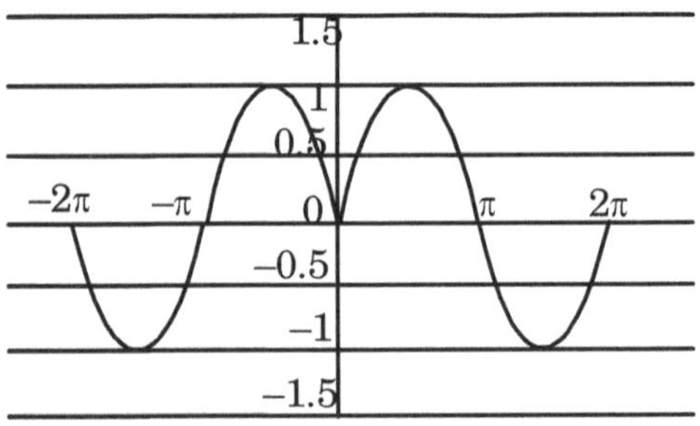

(*b*)

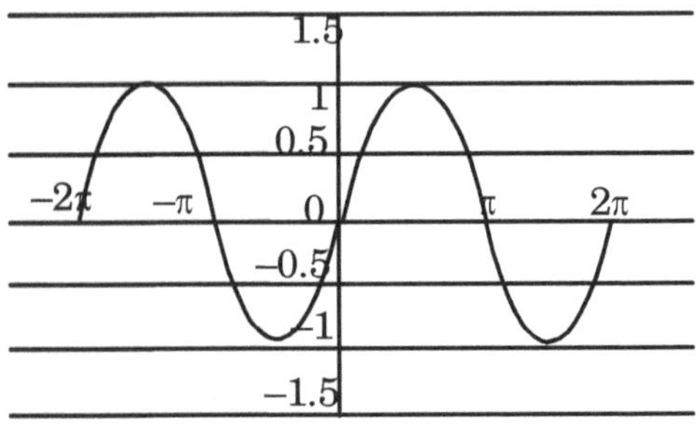

(*c*)

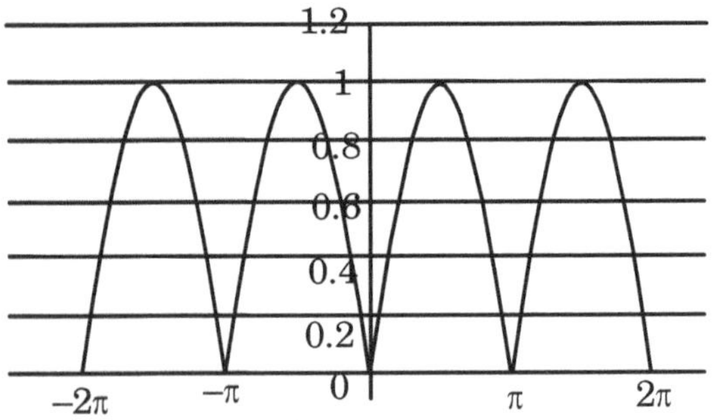

(*d*)

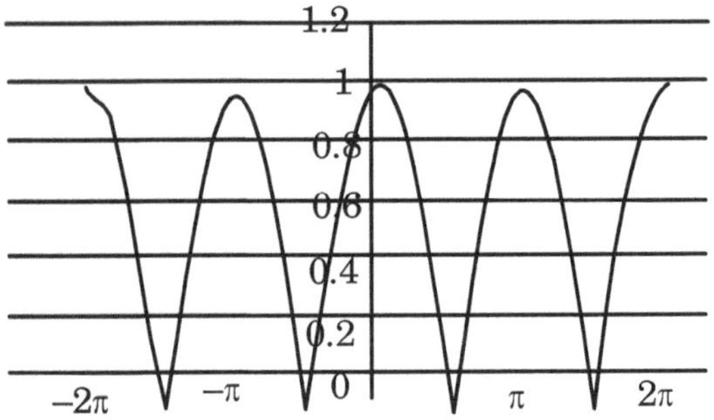

PART-A (Common Part)

Q. 1 – Q. 25 carry one mark each.

1. The first continental red beds appeared in the ____________ Eon.

(*a*) Proterozoic (*b*) Archaean

(*c*) Hadean (*d*) Phanerozoic

2. Which one of the following is a chro-nostratigraphic unit?

(*a*) Eon (*b*) Period

(*c*) Era (*d*) System

3. _____ is a well-sorted sandstone containing up to 75% quartz, with rock fragments in excess of feldspar.

(*a*) Arkose (*b*) Lithic arenite

(*c*) Quartz arenite (*d*) Feldspathic arenite

4. International Geomagnetic Reference Field (IGRF) is used in processing regional magnetic data

(*a*) to remove the secular variation of the geomagnetic field.

(*b*) to remove the diurnal variation of the geomagnetic field.

(*c*) to remove the latitudinal variation of the geomagnetic field.

(*d*) to remove the terrain effect.

5. Which one of the following layers of the Earth has the largest volume?

(*a*) Upper Mantle (*b*) Lower Mantle

(*c*) Outer core (*d*) Inner Core

6. The S-wave shadow zone of the Earth ranges from ________.

(*a*) 103° to 180° (*b*) 103° to 160°

(*c*) 103° to 153° (*d*) 103° to 143°

7. According to Airy's model, gravity anomalies for fully isostatically compensated topography are characterized by

(*a*) negative Bouguer anomaly and positive free-air anomaly.

(*b*) positive Bouguer anomaly and negative free-air anomaly.

(*c*) zero Bouguer anomaly and negative free-air anomaly.

(*d*) positive Bouguer anomaly and zero free-air anomaly.

8. Match the metals (listed in Group I) with the localities of their deposits (listed in Group II).

Group I	**Group II**
P. Iron	1. Boula
Q. Zinc	2. Gadag
R. Gold	3. Bellary
S. Chromium	4. Agucha

(*a*) P-1; Q-2; R-3; S-4 (*b*) P-4; Q-3; R-1; S-2

(*c*) P-3; Q-1; R-2; S-4 (*d*) P-3; Q-4; R-2; S-1

9. In a region, given the palaeomagnetic inclination (I_R), the palaeolatitude (λ_R) can be calculatedusing the formula ____________.

(*a*) $\cos I_R = \sin \lambda_R$ (*b*) $\tan I_R = \tan \lambda_R$

(*c*) $\tan I_R = 2 \tan \lambda_R$ (*d*) $\sin I_R = 2\cos \lambda_R$

10. Which one of the following parent-daughter systems has the longest half life?

(*a*) $^{147}Sm \rightarrow {}^{143}Nd$ (*b*) $^{40}K \rightarrow {}^{40}Ar$

(*c*) $^{87}Rb \rightarrow {}^{87}Sr$ (*d*) $^{187}Os \rightarrow {}^{187}Re$

11. For a soil, Liquidity Index = (Natural Water Content – X) / Plasticity Index.

Here, X is ___________ .

(*a*) Shrinkage Limit (*b*) Plastic Limit

(*c*) Liquid Limit (*d*) Activity

12. Match the following features (listed in Group I) with the different agents of erosion (listed in Group II).

Group I	Group II
P. Earth pillar	1. River
Q. Fjord	2. Wind
R. Pot hole	3. Glacier
S. Yardang	4. Rain

(*a*) P-2; Q-4; R-1; S-3 (*b*) P-2; Q-3; R-4; S-1

(*c*) P-4; Q-3; R-1; S-2 (*d*) P-3; Q-1; R-4; S-2

13. Match the parameters listed in Group I with the units listed in Group II.

Group I	Group II
P. Hydraulic conductivity	1. Newton sec./m^2
Q. Permeability	2. m/sec.
R. Viscosity	3. m
S. Hydraulic head	4. m^2

(*a*) P-2; Q-4; R-1; S-3 (*b*) P-1; Q-2; R-4; S-3

(*c*) P-2; Q-4; R-3; S-1 (*d*) P-4; Q-2; R-1; S-3

14. In digital remote sensing, land-water contrast is best identified in the ______wavelength band.

(a) ultraviolet (b) near IR

(c) middle IR (d) thermal IR

15. Which one of the following rocks has the highest magnetic susceptibility value?

(*a*) Quartzite (*b*) Limestone

(*c*) Gabbro (*d*) Shale

16. In which one of the following electromagnetic methods is the rate of change of secondary field recorded?

(*a*) Very Low Frequency method

(*b*) Time domain EM method

(*c*) Magnetotelluric method

(*d*) TURAM method

17. A Wenner array with 60 m spacing between current electrodes is placed over an in-homogeneous ground. If the measured potential difference and current flow in subsurface are 10 mV and 5 mA, respectively, the apparent resistivity will be _________ Ωm. (Use π = 3.14)

18. Which one of the following geophysical methods is most suitable for the exploration of a horizontally stratified graphite deposit at a depth of 50 m?

(*a*) Gravity (*b*) Magnetic

(*c*) Radiometric (*d*) Electromagnetic

19. Which one of the following logging techniques is most suitable to detect a shale layer sandwiched between two sandstone layers?

(*a*) Neutron-Gamma (*b*) Gamma-Gamma

(*c*) Natural Gamma (*d*) Sonic

20. The following schematic diagram is a plan view of three oceanic plates forming a stable triple junction on a flat earth. Plate A subducts below Plate C normal to the plate boundary, while the contact between Plates A and B is a transform fault, as indicated. The boundary between Plates B and C is a _________.

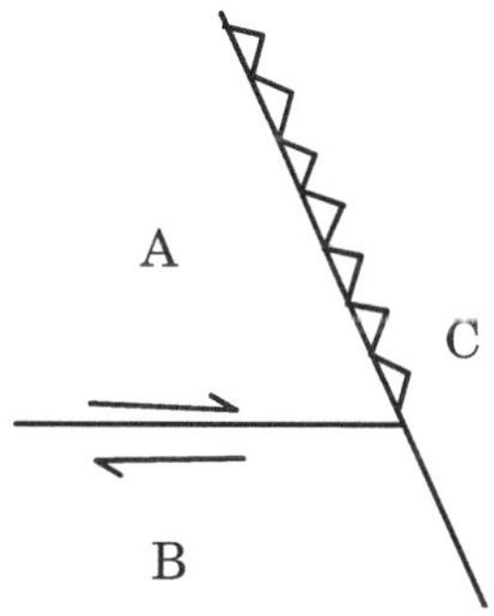

(*a*) mid-oceanic ridge

(*b*) subduction zone

(*c*) sinistral transform fault

(*d*) dextral transform fault

21. In Gondwanaland reconstructions, much of the present west coast of India is placed adjacent to ____.

(*a*) South America (*b*) Madagascar

(*c*) Antarctica (*d*) Australia

22. Two vertically dipping limbs of a fold have perpendicular strikes. The fold can be classified as ___________ .

(*a*) an antiformal fold (*b*) a synformal fold

(*c*) a vertical fold (*d*) a recumbent fold

23. Match the crystal forms (listed in Group I) with their corresponding number of faces (listed in Group II).

Group I	Group II
P. Cube	1. Two
Q. Tetrahedron	2. Four
R. Pinacoid	3. Six
S. Dodecahedron	4. Twelve

(*a*) P-4; Q-2; R-3; S-1 (*b*) P-3; Q-2; R-1; S-4

(*c*) P-3; Q-4; R-1; S-2 (*d*) P-1; Q-3; R-4; S-2

24. Match the rocks in Group I with their essential mineral assemblages in Group II.

Group I	Group II
P. Granodiorite	1. Hornblende-plagioclase
Q. Harzburgite	2. Plagioclase-quartz
R. Gabbro	3. Olivine-orthopyroxene
S. Diorite	4. Clinopyroxene-plagioclase

(*a*) P-2; Q-3; R-4; S-1 (*b*) P-3; Q-4; R-1; S-2
(*c*) P-4; Q-1; R-3; S-2 (*d*) P-1; Q-3; R-2; S-4

25. Which one of the following mineral assemblages is stable under eclogite facies conditions?

(*a*) Garnet-orthopyroxene-clinopyroxene-plagioclase
(*b*) Garnet-clinopyroxene-plagioclase-kyanite
(*c*) Garnet-orthopyroxene-hornblende-plagioclase
(*d*) Garnet-clinopyroxene-kyanite-quartz

PART-B
GEOLOGY

Q. 26 to Q. 55 carry two marks each.

26. Select the CORRECT statement from the following options.

(*a*) Hogback is an isolated tableland with sides that are usually steep.
(*b*) Crevasses are deposits of glacial origin.
(*c*) Loess comprises pebbles of rocks or minerals with some plane faces formed by wind abrasion.
(*d*) Loamy soil is a mixture of sand and clay.

27. Match the following patterns (listed in Group I) with their appropriate Cephalopod sutures (listed in Group II). Arrow gives the direction of aperture.

Group I	Group II
P. 	1. Ceratitic
Q. 	2. Nautilitic
R. 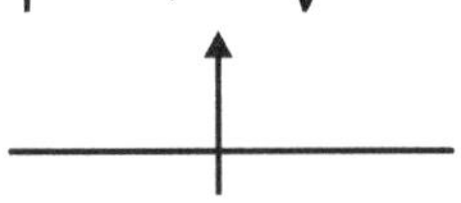	3. Goniatitic
S. 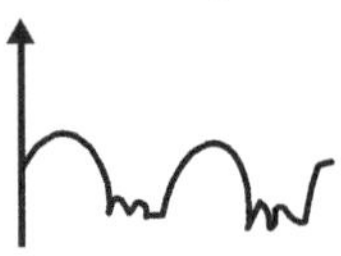	4. Orthoceratitic

(*a*) P-2; Q-3; R-4; S-1 (*b*) P-2; Q-1; R-4; S-3
(*c*) P-4; Q-3; R-1; S-2 (*d*) P-3; Q-1; R-4; S-2

28. Match the following test composition (listed in Group I) with the microfossil taxa (listed in Group II)

Group I	Group II
P. Organic-walled	1. Radiolaria
Q. Siliceous	2. Conodont
R. Phosphatic	3. Foraminifera
S. Calcareous	4. Acritarch

(*a*) P-4; Q-3; R-1; S-2 (*b*) P-2; Q-1; R-4; S-3
(*c*) P-4; Q-1; R-2; S-3 (*d*) P-3; Q-4; R-1; S-2

29. Which one of the following statements is CORRECT?

(*a*) Movement of the shoreline seaward is transgression.
(*b*) No movement of the shoreline is transgression.
(*c*) Movement of the shoreline seaward as a result of sea-level fall is forced regression.
(*d*) Movement of the shoreline landward is regression.

30. Mud-supported limestone containing greater than 10% allochems is called ____________.

(*a*) Packstone (*b*) Wackestone
(*c*) Grainstone (*d*) Mudstone

31. At a depth of 500 m, the determined in-situ stresses in a rock mass are as follows: maximum horizontal stress = 20 MPa, minimum horizontal stress = 8 MPa, vertical stress = 13.5 MPa.
Assume principal stress directions are vertical and horizontal. If this compressive stress field leads to faulting, the plausible fault would be a

(*a*) normal fault (*b*) reverse fault
(*c*) strike-slip fault (*d*) detachment fault

32. The following figure is a litholog showing various fossils found in the rock-strata. Identify the biozone (Note: The lines denote partial ranges of the fossils given in the figure).

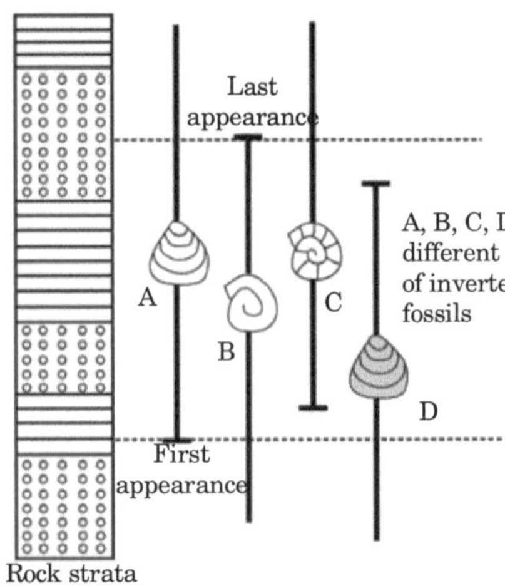

(*a*) Assemblage Zone
(*b*) Taxon Range Zone
(*c*) Consecutive Range Zone
(*d*) Acme Zone

33. Which one of the following stratigraphic successions is in the correct chronological order (from older to younger)?

(*a*) Iron Ore Group, Older Metamorphic Group, Kolhan Group

(*b*) Chitradurga Group, Sargur Group, Bababudan Group

(*c*) Jharol Group, Alwar Group, Ajabgarh Group

(*d*) Chitravati Group, Papaghni Group, Kurnool Group

34. Water content and total porosity of a soil are given as 10% and 25%, respectively. Specific gravity of soil particles is 2.5. The volume of water that should be added to 100 m^3 of this soil for full saturation is ______________m^3.

35. In a zone of superposed folding, poles to bedding show a great circle distribution. For such a case, the fold axes related to the first generation of folding will

(*a*) also be distributed along the same great circle girdle.

(*b*) be distributed on a great circle girdle orthogonal to the bedding plane girdle.

(*c*) show a cluster around the pole to the bedding plane girdle.

(*d*) show a small circle distribution around the pole to the bedding plane girdle.

36. For horizontal flow in a saturated aquifer, the product of hydraulic conductivity and thickness is equal to _____

(*a*) specific yield

(*b*) transmissivity

(*c*) coefficient of storage

(*d*) seepage force

37. If a rectangle is deformed into a parallelogram of equal area by simple shear deformation (with shear strain γ) parallel to the abscissa, the displacement matrix is ______________.

(*a*) $\begin{pmatrix} \gamma & 0 \\ 1 & 0 \end{pmatrix}$ (*b*) $\begin{pmatrix} 0 & 1 \\ \gamma & 0 \end{pmatrix}$

(*c*) $\begin{pmatrix} 0 & \gamma \\ 1 & 0 \end{pmatrix}$ (*d*) $\begin{pmatrix} 1 & \gamma \\ 0 & 1 \end{pmatrix}$

38. If tangent Young's modulus (at 50% of the uniaxial compressive strength) and modulus ratio of a rock are given as 60 GPa and 500, respectively, the uniaxial compressive strength of the rock is ______ MPa.

39. In a rock sample, the values of ($^{87}Sr/^{86}Sr$) present and ($^{87}Rb/^{86}Sr$) present are 0.7125 and 0.2, respectively. The decay constant (λ) of ^{87}Rb is 1.42×10^{-11} year^{-1}, and time before present (t) is 1000 million years. The value of the initial ratio ($^{87}Sr/^{86}Sr$) 0 is _______.

40. The ΔG^0 of a reaction $2\,Fe_3O_4 + 0.5\,O_2 = 3\,Fe_2O3$ at 300°C and 500 bars is ? 40.657 kilo calories. The value of the logarithm of oxygen ($\log fo_2$) at that temperature and pressure is ___________.

41. Match the types of mineralization in Group-I with their appropriate tectonic settings in Group-II. (VMS stands for volcanogenic massive sulfide)

Group I	Group II
P. Cyprus-type VMS	1. Island Arc
Q. Kuroko-type VMS	2. Continental Arc
R. Porphyry copper	3. Intraplate
S. Diamond in Kimberlite	4. Mid Oceanic Ridge

(*a*) P-1; Q-2; R-3; S-4 (*b*) P-4; Q-1; R-2; S-3

(*c*) P-4; Q-2; R-3; S-1 (*d*) P-2; Q-1; R-4; S-3

42. Clay minerals and Fe-oxide minerals, products of hydrothermal alteration and supergene oxidation, are good indicators of mineralization. Choose the CORRECT Thematic Mapper (TM) band ratio images for detection of these minerals.

(*a*) band ratio $\frac{5}{7}$ for clay and $\frac{3}{1}$ for Fe-oxide minerals

(*b*) band ratio $\frac{3}{1}$ for clay and $\frac{5}{7}$ for Fe-oxide minerals

(*c*) band ratio $\frac{3}{7}$ for clay and $\frac{5}{1}$ for Fe-oxide minerals

(*d*) band ratio $\frac{5}{1}$ for clay and $\frac{3}{7}$ for Fe-oxide minerals

43. The age range of reservoir rock in Cambay oil field is ______________.

(*a*) 34 – 15 million years

(*b*) 56 – 34 million years

(*c*) 65 – 56 million years

(*d*) 100 – 65 million years

44. Which one of the following statements is CORRECT in all respects for the amphibole glaucophane, $Na_2Mg_3Al_2Si_8O_{22}(OH)_2$?

(*a*) Na is in the M4-site, Al is in octahedral coordination and Si is in tetrahedral coordination.

(*b*) Na is in the A-site, both Al and Si are in tetrahedral coordination.

(*c*) Na is in the M4-site, Al is partly in octahedral and partly in tetrahedral coordination, Si is in tetrahedral coordination.

(*d*) Na is in the A-site, both Al and Si are in octahedral coordination.

45. Choose the CORRECT modern analog of Besshi type VMS (volcanogenic massive sulfide) deposits (all these are ocean floor rift zones).

(*a*) 21°N East Pacific Rise (EPR)

(*b*) Guaymas Basin

(*c*) Lau Basin

(*d*) Trans Atlantic Geotraverse (TAG)

46. Which one of the following options is arranged in the CORRECT increasing order of Vicker's micro-hardness?

(*a*) galena < chalcopyrite < sphalerite < magnetite

(*b*) sphalerite < galena < magnetite < chalcopyrite

(*c*) galena < magnetite < chalcopyrite < sphalerite

(*d*) sphalerite < magnetite < chalcopyrite < galena

47. The $\left(\frac{^{18}O}{^{16}O}\right)$ of a quartz sample yields a value of 0.0019. The value of $\delta^{18}O$ of the quartz sample is ________. (Use the value of the ratio in VSMOW as 0.002005.)

48. The ionic strength of a solution having 0.5 molal NaCl and 0.25 molal $CaCl_2$ is ________ molal.

49. During which stage of coalification is most of the methane gas generated?

(*a*) Lignite (*b*) Peat

(*c*) Bituminous (*d*) Anthracite

50. The figure shows the liquidus phase relations in the forsterite-anorthite-silica system at 1 bar pressure. From the options below, identify the CORRECT reaction that takes place at the isobaric invariant point P.

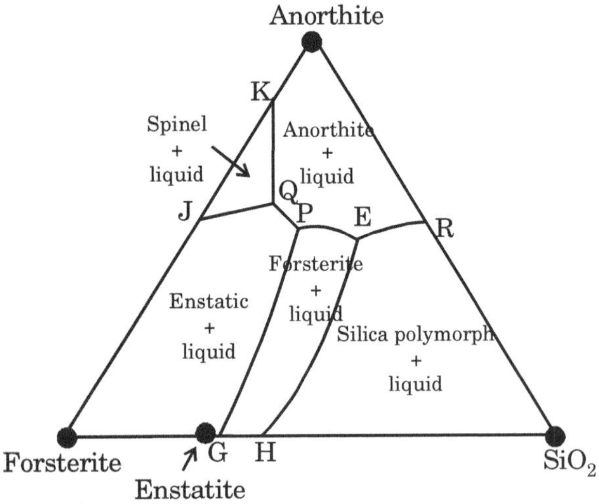

(*a*) Liquid (at P) = Forsterite + Anorthite + Enstatite

(*b*) Liquid (at P) + Forsterite = Anorthite + Enstatite

(*c*) Liquid (at P) + Forsterite + Anorthite = Enstatite

(*d*) Liquid (at P) = Forsterite + Anorthite + Silica polymorph

51. A garnet peridotite contains 2400 ppm of nickel. After 20% partial melting, a basaltic melt is generated, leaving a residue comprising 60% olivine, 30% orthopyroxene and 10% clinopyroxene. Given the K D^{Ni} (olivine) = 10, K^{Ni} (orthopyroxene) = 4 and K D^{Ni} (clinopyroxene) = 2, the nickel concentration in the melt, assuming equilibrium batch melting, is ________ ppm.

52. Which one of the following mineral assemblages is stable in a pelitic rock in the greenschist facies?

(*a*) Albite-epidote-actinolite-chlorite-quartz

(*b*) Muscovite-biotite-garnet-quartz

(*c*) Tremolite-talc-calcite-quartz

(*d*) Muscovite-biotite-garnet-sillimanite-quartz

53. Match the co-existing mineral pairs in Group I with the diagnostic metamorphic conditions they are associated with in Group II.

Group I	**Group II**
P. Talc-phengite	1. Ultrahigh temperature
Q. Cordierite-andalusite	2. Very low temperature
R. Spinel-quartz	3. Ultrahigh pressure
S. Laumontite-wairakite	4. Low pressure, high temperature

(*a*) P-2; Q-3; R-1; S-4 (*b*) P-3; Q-4; R-1; S-2

(*c*) P-4; Q-1; R-2; S-3 (*d*) P-3; Q-2; R-4; S-1

54. Out of the following symmetry elements, which one is present in all classes of the cubic system?

(*a*) Four axes of 3-fold symmetry

(*b*) Three axes of 4-fold symmetry

(*c*) Six axes of 2-fold symmetry

(*d*) Three mirror planes

55. Match the minerals in Group-I with their optical properties in Group-II.

Group I	**Group II**
P. Calcite	1. Uniaxial negative, low birefringence, high relief
Q. Nepheline	2. Uniaxial negative, high birefringence, moderately high relief
R. Apatite	3. Uniaxial positive, low birefringence, low relief
S. Quartz	4. Uniaxial negative, low birefringence, low relief

(*a*) P-4; Q-2; R-1; S-3

(*b*) P-3; Q-2; R-4; S-1

(*c*) P-2; Q-4; R-1; S-3

(*d*) P-1; Q-3; R-2; S-4

GEOPHYSICS

Q. 26 – Q. 55 carry two marks each.

26. Depth migration is applied to a stacked seismic section. Compared to the stacked section, dipping events in the migrated section

(*a*) have a steeper slope and move updip.

(*b*) remain unchanged.

(*c*) have a gentler slope and move downdip.

(*d*) have a steeper slope and move downdip.

27. A monochromatic elastic wave of frequency 20 Hz propagates in a medium with average velocity 3 km/s. For zero offset reflection from horizontal reflectors, the thickness of the vertical first Fresnel zone is ________ m.

28. The following figure shows a seismic reflection experiment above a reflector that dips 45°. The P-wave velocity in the medium is constant and equal to 2 km/s. The source is kept at location 'S' and the receiver is kept at location 'G'. The midpoint between S and G is denoted by 'M' and the depth to the reflector from 'M' is 1 km. The traveltime of the primary reflected arrival recorded at the receiver is equal to____ seconds.

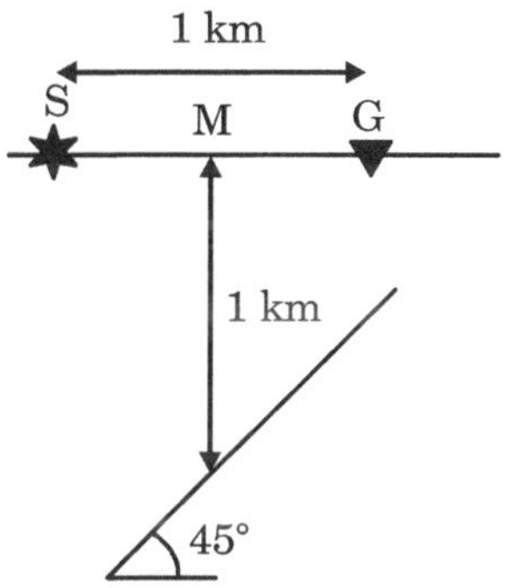

29. Given a seismic wavelet w = { 6, – 4, –2 } and reflectivity series r = { 0, 1, 0 }, the corresponding seismic trace is ___________.

(*a*) {0, 4, 0, 0, 0} (*b*) {0, 2, 4, 6, 0}

(*c*) {0, 6, 0, 0, 0} (*d*) {0, 6, –4, –2, 0}

30. The time period of the signal

$s(t) = \sin\left(\frac{\pi}{3}t\right) + \cos\left(\frac{\pi}{2}t\right)$ is ______ seconds.

31. Assertion (a) : The inverse of a minimum phase wavelet is causal and stable.

Reason (r) : The Z-transform of a minimum phase wavelet has all its zeros outside the unit circle.

(*a*) (a) is true but (r) is false

(*b*) (a) is false but (r) is true

(*c*) Both (a) and (r) are true and (r) is the correct reason for (a)

(*d*) {Both (a) and (r) are true and (r) is not the correct reason for (a)

32. The value of free-air correction (assuming sea level as datum plane) at an elevation of 150 m is _________ mGal.

33. A spherical cavity of radius 8 m has its centre 15 m below the surface. If the cavity is full of sediments of density 1.5×10^3 kg/m^3 and is in a rock body of density 2.4×10^3 kg/m^3, the maximum value of its gravity anomaly is __________ mGal.

34. Match the items (listed in Group I) with the corresponding corrections applied for reduction of marine gravity data (listed in Group II).

Group I	**Group II**
P. Effect of rotating homogeneous ellipsoidal Earth	1. Drift correction temperature
Q. Effect of deficit mass from mean sea level to average depth to ocean floor	2. Latitude correction
R. Effect of relative motion of ship with respect to revolving Earth	3. Bouguer correction
S. Effect of elastic gravimeter spring system and Earth tides	4. Eotvos correction

(*a*) P-4; Q-3; R-1; S-2 (*b*) P-2; Q-3; R-4; S-1

(*c*) P-4; Q-1; R-2; S-3 (*d*) P-3; Q-1; R-4; S-2

35. Which one of the following Natural Remanent Magnetization (NRM) gives a primary, stable magnetization for igneous rocks?

(*a*) Depositional Remanent Magnetization (DRM)

(*b*) Thermo Remanent Magnetization (TRM)

(*c*) Chemical Remanent Magnetization (CRM)

(*d*) Isothermal Remanent Magnetization (IRM)

36. The following figure shows the total magnetic field intensity anomaly above a spherical body polarized by the present day geomagnetic field. From among the options below, identify the region in which such an anomaly could be observed.

(*a*) Equator (*b*) Latitude 27°

(*c*) North pole (*d*) South pole

37. Which one of the following is the ray path for the P-wave that converts to S-wave while passing through the solid inner core?

(*a*) PKiKP (*b*) PKIKP

(*c*) pPcP (*d*) PKJKP

38. Which one of the following statements is CORRECT for the stress drop ($\Delta\sigma$) of an earthquake?

(*a*) Large slip on a small fault will cause more stress drop.

(*b*) Small slip on a large fault will cause more stress drop.

(*c*) Stress drop is inversely proportional to the slip of the fault.

(*d*) Stress is directly proportional to the rupture dimension.

39. The energy released by an earthquake of magnitude 7 is ________ times the energy released by an earthquake of magnitude 4 (use Kanamori's formula).

40. In resistivity logging using a 'Normal device', the distance between electrodes A and M is 0.40 m. If 20 mA current generates 10 mV potential, the apparent resistivity of the layer between the electrodes is ________ Ωm. (Use $\pi = 3.14$)

41. A cylindrical sandstone core sample of diameter 0.02 m and length 0.04 m is fully saturated with brine solution of resistivity 0.5Ωm. The resistance of the saturated sample measured in the laboratory is 500Ω . The formation factor of the sample is ________. (Use $\pi = 3.14$).

42. A Schlumberger array with current electrode separation 50 m and potential electrode separation 5 m is placed over an inhomogeneous medium. If the measured potential difference is 50 mV and the computed apparent resistivity is 100 Ω m, then the magnitude of current passing through the subsurface is ________ mA. (Use $\pi = 3.14$)

43. Two horizontal layers have resistivities and thicknesses of 10 Ωm, 5m and 50 Ωm, 10m, respectively. If the two layers are reduced to a single layer, then the coefficient of electrical anisotropy will be ________.

44. The five-layer Schlumberger resistivity sounding curve given below represents ________.

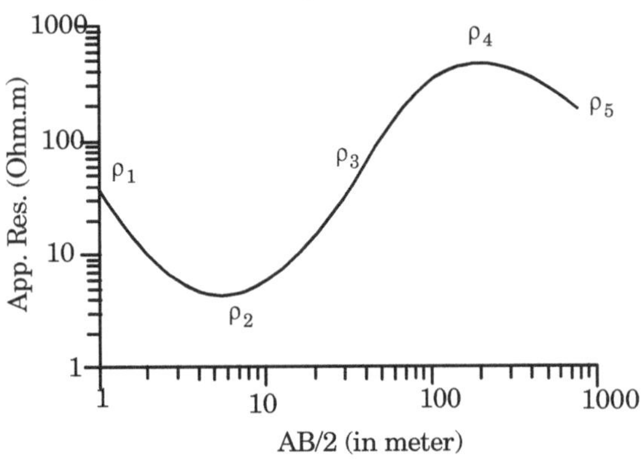

(*a*) HAQ-type (*b*) HKQ-type

(*c*) HKH-type (*d*) HAK-type

45. How are the numerical values of the real and imaginary components of the impedance tensor (Z) in Magnetotelluric (MT) method related over a homogeneous half-space?

(*a*) Imaginary component is one third of the real component.

(*b*) Imaginary component is half of the real component.

(*c*) Imaginary component is equal to the real component.

(*d*) Imaginary component is twice that of the real component.

46. The strike of a 2-D geological structure is in Y-direction. From the following options, choose the field components required to compute the apparent resistivity in E-Polarization mode for plane wave electromagnetic signals.

(*a*) Ex and Hx (*b*) Ex and Hy

(*c*) Ey and Hy (*d*) Ey and Hx

47. Dip angle electromagnetic methods are suitable to delineate

(*a*) both vertical and horizontal conductors.

(*b*) horizontal conductors only.

(*c*) vertical and dipping conductors.

(*d*) horizontal and dipping conductors.

48. Which one of the following equations is CORRECT for a time invariant field?

(*a*) $\nabla \times H = 0$ (*b*) $\nabla \times H = \dfrac{\partial D}{\partial t}$

(*c*) $\nabla \times H = J + \dfrac{\partial D}{\partial t}$ (*d*) $\nabla \times H = J$

49. The solution to the Laplace equation $\nabla^2 V = 0$ in a spherical coordinate system with spherical symmetry is ________.

(*a*) $V = -\dfrac{A}{r^2} + B$ (*b*) $V = -\dfrac{A}{r} + B$

(*c*) $V = -A \ln(r) + B$ (*d*) $V = -Ar + B$

50. If J is the Jacobian matrix in a geophysical inverse problem, then the addition of the regularization parameter, λ , as ($J^T J + \lambda I$), in finding the inverse leads to

(*a*) unstable solution with increased parameter resolution

(*b*) stable solution with increased parameter resolution

(*c*) unstable solution with decreased parameters resolution

(*d*) stable solution with decreased parameter resolution

51. The Singular Value Decomposition of a square nonsingular matrix J is given by $J = U\lambda V^T$. The inverse of matrix J will be

(*a*) $J^{-1} = U\lambda^{-1}V^T$ (*b*) $J^{-1} = V\lambda^{-1}U^T$

(*c*) $J^{-1} = U^T\lambda^{-1}V^T$ (*d*) $J^{-1} = U\lambda^{-1}V$

52. The fraction of a radioactive nuclide remaining after 10 half-lives is closest to

(*a*) 0.1 (*b*) 0.01

(*c*) 0.001 (*d*) 0.0001

53. The correct relationship between the residual amount P of the parent radionuclide and amount D of the daughter product in a radioactive decay is

(*a*) $D = P\left(e^{\lambda t} - 1\right)$ (*b*) $D = P(1 - e\lambda t)$

(*c*) $D = \dfrac{P}{\left(e^{\lambda t} - 1\right)}$ (*d*) $D = \dfrac{P}{\left(1 - e^{\lambda t}\right)}$

54. Which one of the following resistivity sounding curves exhibits both 'Equivalence' and 'Suppression' type ambiguities in interpretation of data?

(*a*) HA-type

(*b*) AH-type

(*c*) HK-type

(*d*) KH-type

55. For land seismic data acquisition, the following figure is a schematic plot of arrival times of seismic waves recorded at several detectors placed along the x-axis. The shot is placed at the origin (x = 0).

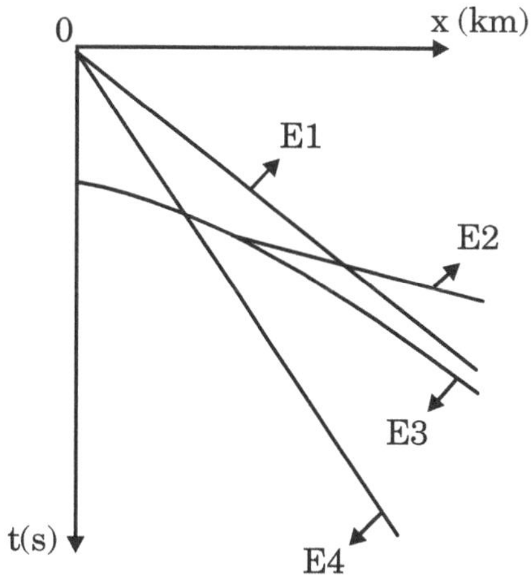

Match the events labeled in the figure (listed in Group I) with their corresponding types (listed in Group II)

Group I	Group II
P. E1	1. Ground roll
Q. E2	2. Direct arrival
R. E3	3. Refracted energy
S. E4	4. Primary reflection

(*a*) P-3; Q-1; R-2; S-4 (*b*) P-2; Q-3; R-4; S-1

(*c*) P-1; Q-4; R-3; S-2 (*d*) P-4; Q-2; R-1; S-3

ANSWERS

(General Aptitude)

1. (*b*) **2.** (*a*) **3.** (*d*) **4.** (*c*) **5.** (*b*) **6.** (*c*) **7.** (*c*) **8.** (*c*) **9.** (*a*) **10.** (*c*)

PART A (Common Part)

1. (*a*) **2.** (*d*) **3.** (*b*) **4.** (*c*) **5.** (*b*) **6.** (*a*) **7.** (*a*) **8.** (*d*) **9.** (*c*) **10.** (*a*)
11. (*b*) **12.** (*c*) **13.** (*a*) **14.** (*b*) **15.** (*c*) **16.** (*b*) **17.** (*) **18.** (*d*) **19.** (*c*) **20.** (*b,d*)
21. (*b*) **22.** (*c*) **23.** (*b*) **24.** (*a*) **25.** (*d*)

PART-B (Geology)

26. (*d*) **27.** (*a*) **28.** (*c*) **29.** (*c*) **30.** (*b*) **31.** (*c*) **32.** (*a*) **33.** (*c*) **34.** (*) **35.** (*c*)
36. (*b*) **37.** (*d*) **38.** (*) **39.** (*) **40.** (*) **41.** (*b*) **42.** (*a*) **43.** (*b*) **44.** (*a*) **45.** (*b*)
46. (*a*) **47.** (*) **48.** (*) **49.** (*c*) **50.** (*b*) **51.** (*) **52.** (*b*) **53.** (*b*) **54.** (*a*) **55.** (*c*)

(Geophysics)

26. (*a*) **27.** (*) **28.** (*) **29.** (*d*) **30.** (*) **31.** (*c*) **32.** (*) **33.** (*) **34.** (*b*) **35.** (*b*)
36. (*a*) **37.** (*d*) **38.** (*a*) **39.** (*) **40.** (*) **41.** (*) **42.** (*) **43.** (*) **44.** (*d*) **45.** (*c*)
46. (*d*) **47.** (*c*) **48.** (*d*) **49.** (*b*) **50.** (*d*) **51.** (*b*) **52.** (*c*) **53.** (*a*) **54.** (*a*) **55.** (*b*)

EXPLANATIONS

(GENERAL APTITUDE SECTION)

1. The volume of a sphere of diameter 1 unit is less than the volume of a cube of side 1unit.
2. The unruly crowd demanded that the accused be hanged without trial.
3. Prone means :
   - likely or liable to suffer from, which is option (iii)
   - lying flat, especially face downwards. which is option (ii)

   And a prune is a dried plum of any cultivar. Prune means a plum preserved by drying and having a black, wrinkled appearance. Therefore, statement (i) is wrong.

   Hence correct answer is option (d).
4. Option (b) and (d) are wrong due to the fact that question asks about which of the given option NOT logically possible .

   Option (b) is given fact .

   In Option (d), statement (ii) is direct result of statement (iv)

   Option (a), field may be wet but that does not mean there is a rain . So this logically possible.

   Option (c), it is logically not possible, if it rains then field must be wet. Thus option (c) is only correct option.
5. Perimeter is 6 so length of side is $\frac{6}{5} = 1.2$ m

   Therefore, area of square is 1.2 × 1.2 = 1.44

   Now, Area of equilateral triangle

   $$= \frac{\sqrt{3}}{4} \times 1.2 \times 1.2 = 0.62352$$

   Thus, the total area is 0.2352 + 1.44 = 2.06352.
6. Group Q students have less standard deviation than group P , means most students in group Q got less marks than group P but Not all students in group Q got less marks than group P . Therefore, Option A and B are Not correct. Also, Mean, Median and Mode of Normal Distribution is same, thus Option (d) is also not correct. Only option (c) is correct.
7. "It also uses technology to ensure safety and security of the city, something which critics argue, will lead to a surveillance state." Critics argue because of perception that smart city promotes surveillance that makes statement (iv) correct.

   There is nothing mention in passage about encouragement about formation of surveillance states so that makes statement (i) false.

   And, "will lead to a surveillance state tis makes " this line makes statement (ii) false.

   and there is nothing mention about " both Sustainability and surveillance" in passage so statement (iii) is wrong too.

   Hence only statement (iv) is correct which is option (c).
8. TVXZ is correct leaving one alphabet between immediately is gate of 3 alphabet between the next series no.
9. Given, $a \times b = ab + (a + b)$

   The operation when defined an identity element is given as

   $$a \times x = a$$
   $$= ax + (a + x) = a$$
   $$= ax + x = 0 = (a + 1)x = 0$$

   So, either $x = 0$ or $a + 1 = 0$

   Thus, the number x such that $a \times x = a$ for any a, is zero.
10. Given, $y = \ln(|e^{[|\sin(|x|)|]}|)$ for $|x| < 2\pi$

    As the mod is present in the function, the amplitude of the curve will always be +ve and as the sine term is present, it resembles to that of positive amplitude peak sine curve.

PART A (COMMON PART)

1. Proterozoic

   Red beds – These sedimentary rocks, which typically consist of sandstone, siltstone, and shale, are predominantly red in color due to the presence of ferric oxides. They appear red in color because of the content of Ferric oxide (hematite) in it. Occurrence of red beds indicate oxidizing environment. The first appeared in Proterozoic in continental areas.

2.

Lithostratigraphic units	Chronostratigraphic units	Geochronologic units	Biostrtigraphic units
Super group	Eonthem	Eon	Biozones
Group	Erathem	Era	Assemblage zone
Formation	System	Period	Abundance zone
Member	Series	Epoch	Interval zone
Bed	Stage	Age	Lineage zone

3. Lithic arenite:

Lithic sandstones, or lithic arenites, or litharenites, are sandstones with a significant (>5%) component of lithic fragments, though quartz and feldspar are usually present as well, along with some clayey matrix. Lithic sandstones can have a speckled (salt and pepper) or gray color, and are usually associated with one specific type of lithic fragment (i.e., igneous, sedimentary, or metamorphic).

Tectonically, lithic sandstones often form in a wide variety sedimentary depositional environments (including fluvial, deltaic, and alluvial sediments) associated with active margins. This tectonic setting provides the source of the lithic fragments, through either arc volcanism, thin-skinned faulting, continental collisions, unroofing, or subduction rollback.

4. To remove the latitudinal variation Geomagnetic Field;

The International geomagnetic reference field (IGRF) provides the global model of magnetic field.

The IGRF also gives the rate of change of each of the Gauss coefficients (its secular variation), which permits correlation of the current values between update years.

5.

Earth's layers	Volume in (%)	Mass in (%)
Crust	1	0.5
Upper Mantle	29	67
Lower Mantle	55	
Outer Core	14	32
Inner Core	1	

6. Shadow zone or seismic zone: A seismic shadow zone in the earth surface is the area where seismic gausses are not detected by seismographs.

- P wave shadow zone – 103° – 143° (From the epicenter)
- S wave shadow zone = 103° – 180° (From the epicenter)

7. Fully isostatically compensated topography are characterized by negative Bouguer anomaly and positive free air anomaly.

8. Bellary is a district in Karnataka state, India. Bellary district has 25% of India's Iron ore reserves. The annual production of Iron ore is anywhere between 2.75 and 4.5 million tonnes, and manganese ore between 0.13 million tonnes to 0.30 million tonnes (1991).

Rampura Agucha is a zinc and lead mine located on a massive sulfide deposit in the Bhilwara district of Rajasthan, India. Rampura Agucha is located 220 km from Jaipur. It is north of Bhilwara, and northwest of Shahpura. Rampura Agucha is 17 km southeast of Bijainagar on NH 79. The mine is owned by Hindustan Zinc Limited (HZL), and has the world's largest deposits of zinc and lead.

Gadag district is rich gold zone and are indicated in channel samples in Nabhapur old working (shallow pits, vertical shafts) area; gold is also confirmed in old workings (two clusters) of Sankatodak-Doni Tanda area.

Chromite deposits of Pre Cambrian (Iron Ore Group and Eastern Ghats) and Tertiary age are distributed in shield and tectonically mobile areas in India. Out of the 11 major chromite deposits distributed in 9 states of India, In Orissa, the two major deposits i. e. Sukinda Ultramafic Belt and Boula Nuasahi Igneous Complex hold around 98% of the total Indian reserve.

9. Given

I_R = palaeomagnetic indiaction

λ_R = palaeolatitude

Formula used to calculate

$\tan I_R = 2 \tan \lambda_R$

10.

Option	Parent-daughter system	Half-life (Ga)
A	$^{147}Sm \rightarrow {}^{143}Nd$	106
B	$^{40}K \rightarrow {}^{40}Ar$	1.25
C	$^{87}Rb \rightarrow {}^{87}Sr$	48.8
E	$^{187}Os \rightarrow {}^{187}Re$	41.6

11. Liquidity Index

$$= \frac{\text{Natural water content - Plastic Limit}}{\text{Plasticity Index}}$$

The Atterberg limits are a basic measure of the critical water contents of a fine-grained soil: its shrinkage limit, plastic limit, and liquid limit.

- The shrinkage limit (SL) is the water content where further loss of moisture will not result in any more volume reduction. The test to determine the shrinkage limit is ASTM International D4943. The shrinkage limit is much less commonly used than the liquid and plastic limits.
- The plastic limit (PL) is determined by rolling out a thread of the fine portion of a soil on a flat, non-porous surface. The procedure is defined in ASTM Standard D 4318. If the soil is at a moisture content where its behavior is plastic, this thread will retain its shape down to a very narrow diameter. The sample can then be remolded and the test repeated. As the moisture content falls due to evaporation, the thread will begin to break apart at larger diameters.

- The liquid limit (LL) is conceptually defined as the water content at which the behavior of a clayey soil changes from plastic to liquid. However, the transition from plastic to liquid behavior is gradual over a range of water contents, and the shear strength of the soil is not actually zero at the liquid limit.

12. **Earth pillar -** It is an erosional feature made by rain. It is formed when pillar like portion of the soil is left while surrounding portion is removal.

    Fjord - Drowned portion of the glacier in the ocean is known as fjord where glacier meets to the ocean.

    Potholes - Holes formed on the river valley due to swirling or eddy action of water.

    Yardang - Wind sculptured hills are known as yarding.

13. **Hydraulic conductivity** represented as K, is a property of vascular plants, soils and rocks, that describes the ease with which a fluid (usually water) can move through pore spaces or fractures. By definition, hydraulic conductivity is the ratio of velocity to hydraulic gradient indicating permeability of porous media. Hydraulic conductivity has units with dimensions of length per time (e.g., m/s, ft/day and (gal/day)/ft^2).

    Permeability in fluid mechanics and the earth sciences (commonly symbolized as κ, or k) is a measure of the ability of a porous material (often, a rock or an unconsolidated material) to allow fluids to pass through it. The SI unit for permeability is m^2.

    The **viscosity** of a fluid is the measure of its resistance to gradual deformation by shear stress or tensile stress. The unit of viscosity is given as Pa.s or Ns/m^2.

    Hydraulic head or piezometric head is a specific measurement of liquid pressure above a geodetic datum. The unit has dimension of length (e.g., m, cm)

14. Generally reflect high in the visible spectrum, however, clearer water has less reflectance than turbid water. In the Near IR water increasingly absorbs the light making it darker. This is dependent upon water depth and wavelength. Increasing amounts of dissolved inorganic materials in water bodies tend to shift the peak of visible reflectance toward the red region from the green region (clearer water) of the spectrum.

15. Gabbro – It is coarse grained plutonic rock having basic composition. It contains Fe-Mg in its composition which contribute to its high value of magnetic susceptibility.

16. Very low Frequency method – Measures the angle between the primary and secondary fields.

    Time Domain EM method – Measures rate of change of secondary field.

    Magnetotelluric method – Measures the components of electric and magnetic fields

    TURAM method – It is a phase measuring system

17. Given,

    Spacing between current electrodes = 60 m

    $\Delta v = 10\ mv$

    I = 5 mA

    a = 20 m

    Therefore, the apparent resistivity obtained for Wenner array configuration is given by:

    $$\rho_a = 2\pi a \times \frac{\Delta V}{\Delta I}$$

    $$= 2 \times 3.14 \times 20 \times \frac{10}{5} = 251.2\ \Omega\,\text{m}$$

18. Electromagnetic method is the most suitable method as because of the large resistivity contract between horizontally stratified graphite deposit and the surrounding rocks.

19. Natural Gamma, self-potential, caliper logging techniques are the most suitable technique to detect a shale layer sandwiched between two sandstone layers.

20. **(b,d)** Boundary between B and C can be both substitution zone and dextral transform fault.

21. In Gondwanaland reconstructions, much of the present west coast of India is placed adjacent to Madagascar.

22. Two vertically dipping limbs of a fold have perpendicular strikes. The fold is classified as a vetical fold.

23.

Crystal forms	Number of faces
Cube	6
Tetrahedron	4
Pinacoid	2
Dodechaedron	12

24. Granodiorite is a phaneritic-textured intrusive igneous rock similar to granite, but containing more plagioclase feldspar than orthoclase feldspar. According to the QAPF diagram, granodiorite has a greater than 20% quartz by volume, and between 65% to 90% of the feldspar is plagioclase. A greater amount of plagioclase would designate the rock as tonalite.

Harzburgite, an ultramafic, igneous rock, is a variety of peridotite consisting mostly of the two minerals, olivine and low-calcium (Ca) pyroxene (enstatite); it is named for occurrences in the Harz Mountains of Germany. It commonly contains a few percent chromium-rich spinel as an accessory mineral. Garnet-bearing harzburgite is much less common, found most commonly as xenoliths in kimberlite.

Gabbro is dense, greenish or dark-colored and contains pyroxene, plagioclase, and minor amounts of amphibole and olivine. The pyroxene content is mostly clinopyroxene, generally augite, but small amounts of orthopyroxene may also be present. If the amount of orthopyroxene is more than 95% of the total pyroxene content (5% or less clinopyroxene content), then the rock is termed norite.

Diorite is an intrusive igneous rock composed principally of the silicate minerals plagioclase feldspar (typically andesine), biotite, hornblende, and/or pyroxene. The chemical composition of diorite is intermediate, between that of mafic gabbro and felsic granite. Diorite is usually grey to dark-grey in color, but it can also be black or bluish-grey, and frequently has a greenish cast.

25. Garnet-clinopyroxene-kyanite-quartz

Ecologite facies is free of plagioclase feldspar.

PART-B (GEOLOGY)

26. Hogback: A hogback is a long, narrow ridge or a series of hills with a narrow crest and steep slopes of nearly equal inclination on both flanks. Typically, the term is restricted to a ridge created by the differential erosion of outcropping, steeply dipping (greater than 30–40°), homoclinal, and typically sedimentary strata.

Crevasse: A crevasse is a deep crack, or fracture, found in an ice sheet or glacier, as opposed to a crevice that forms in rock. Crevasses form as a result of the movement and resulting stress associated with the shear stress generated when two semi-rigid pieces above a plastic substrate have different rates of movement.

Loess: Loess is a clastic, predominantly silt-sized sediment that is formed by the accumulation of wind-blown dust. Loess or similar deposits cover 10% of the Earth's land area.

Loamy soil: Loam is soil composed mostly of sand, silt, and a smaller amount of clay. By weight, its mineral composition is about 40–40–20% concentration of sand-silt-clay, respectively

27. The patterns with their appropriate Cephalopod sutures.

Orthoceratitic (Nautilus)

Agoniatitic (Agoniatites)

Goniatitic (Goniatites)

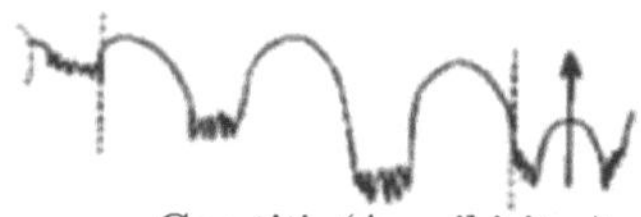

Ceratitic (Anasibirites)

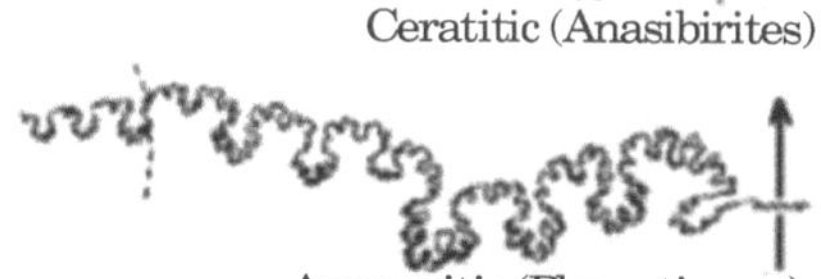

Ammonitic (Placenticeros)

28. Acritarchs were originally defined as non-acid soluble organic-walled microfossils consisting of a central cavity, and whose biological affinity cannot be determined with certainty. Most commonly they are composed of thermally altered acid insoluble carbon compounds (kerogen).

Radiolarians are planktonic protists that occur primarily in open marine, deep-water settings. They are useful time indicators and are found in rocks of Cambrian to Holocene age. They may be the only common microfossils in abyssal environments, commonly forming radiolarian oozes. Radiolarian chert, the product of silica diagenesis, is fairly widespread in the geologic record. Radiolarians are common in some marine source rocks.

Phosphatic microfossils, notably conodonts, are composed of crystallites of calcium phosphate (apatite) embedded in an organic matrix. There is one type of stratigraphically significant phosphatic microfossils (conodonts); but fish teeth, of less practical utility, are found in some marine strata.

Calcareous foraminifera are a group of unicellular organisms (protists) that secrete a rigid calcite or aragonite shell (or test). Fossils of these forms are found in sediments of brackish to marine origin from Silurian to Holocene in age. Most are benthic (bottom dwelling), but a significant group in the late Mesozoic and Cenozoic are planktonic (floating) forms.

29. Movement of the shoreline seaward as a result of sea-level fall is forced regression.

30.

Allocthonous limestones: Original components not organically bound during deposition					
Less than 10% gains > 2 mm				More than 10% gains > 2 mm	
Contains lime mud (<30 mm)			No lime mud	Matrix supported	Grain (>2 mm) supported
Mud supported		Grain supported			
>10% gains0.03-2.0 mm	<10% grains0.03-2.0 mm				
Mudstone	Wackestone	Packstone	Grainstone	Floatstone	Rudstone

31. Given

At depth, h = 500 m

$\sigma_{H_{max}}$ = 20 MPa

$\sigma_{H_{min}}$ = 8 MPa

σ_V = 13.5 MPa

If this compressive stress field leads to faulting, the plausible fault would be a strike-slip fault.

For strike-slip fault, maximum and minimum stresses are horizontal. Intermediate stress is vertical.

32. As per the figure of a lithology showing various fossils found in the rock strata. The Assemblage zone is the biozone. As a body of rock characterized by a unique association of three or more taxa. It may be based on single or more taxon.

33. The stratigraphic successions from older to younger is given as

Jharol Group → Alwar Group → Ajabgarh Group

34. Given,

Density of the soil particle, ρ_{soil} = 2.5 g/cc

Let, the total volume of soil be 100 m^3

Therefore, the mass of the soil particle in 75 $m^3$of volume is

$$m_{75} = \rho_{soil} \times V_{75} = 2500 \times 75 = 187.5 \times 10^3 \text{ kg}$$

Now, considering water content is 10%

Therefore, the mass of water content is

$187.5 \times 10^3 \times 0.1 = 18.75 \times 10^3$

We know that density of water is 1000 kg/m^3

Thus, the volume of water is

$$\frac{18.75 \times 10^3}{1000} m^3 = 18.75 \ m^3$$

For full saturation, the volume of water to be added is $(100 - 75 + 18.75)\ m^3 = 6.25\ m^3$

35. In a zone of superposed folding, poles to bedding show a great circle distribution. For such a case, the fold axes related to the first generation of folding will show a cluster around the pole to the bedding plane girdle.

36. For horizontal flow in a saturated aquifer, the product of hydraulic conductivity and thickness is equal to transmissivity.

37. $\begin{bmatrix} 1 & \gamma \\ 0 & 1 \end{bmatrix}$ → Deformation matrix for simple shear

$\begin{bmatrix} 0 & 0 \\ 0 & \gamma \end{bmatrix}$ → Pure shear

38. Given,

Tangent Young's Modulus = 60 GPa = 6000 MPa

Modulus ratio = 500

Uniaxial compresive strength

$$= \frac{\text{Tangent Young's Modulus}}{\text{Modulus ratio}} = \frac{60000}{500} = 20$$

$\therefore$ C = 120 MPa

39. $\left({}^{87}Sr / {}^{86}Sr\right)_{present} = 0.7125$

$\left({}^{87}Rb / {}^{86}Sr\right) = 0.2$

$\lambda(\text{decay constant}) = 1.42 \times 10^{-11} yr^{-1}$

$t = 1000$ million years $= 10^9$ years

$$\therefore \left(\frac{{}^{87}Sr}{{}^{86}Sr}\right)_{present} = \left(\frac{{}^{87}Sr}{{}^{86}Sr}\right)_0 + \left(\frac{{}^{87}Rb}{{}^{86}Sr}\right)\left(e^{\lambda t} - 1\right)$$

$$\Rightarrow \left(\frac{{}^{87}Sr}{{}^{86}Sr}\right)_0 = \left(\frac{{}^{87}Sr}{{}^{86}Sr}\right)_{present} - \left(\frac{{}^{87}Rb}{{}^{86}Sr}\right)\left(e^{\lambda t} - 1\right)$$

$$\Rightarrow \left(\frac{{}^{87}Sr}{{}^{86}Sr}\right)_0 = 0.7125 - 0.2\left(e^{1.42 \times 10^{-11} \times 10^9} - 1\right)$$

$$= 0.7125 - 0.2\left(e^{0.0142} - 1\right)$$

$$\therefore \left(\frac{{}^{87}Sr}{{}^{86}Sr}\right)_0 = 0.7097$$

40. Given, The reaction is

$\Delta G^o = -40.657$ kcal

$\Rightarrow \Delta G^o = -40.657 \times 4184 = 170108.9\ J$

$T = 300^o C = 300 + 273 = 537\ K$

Therefore, Equilibrium constant,

$$k = \frac{[Fe_2O_3]^3}{[Fe_3O_4][PO_2]^{0.5}}$$

$[Fe_2O_3]$ and $[Fe_3O_4]$ are 1, as they are soil.

$$k = \frac{1}{[PO_2]^{0.5}}$$

Now,

$\Delta G^o = -RT \ln k$

$\Delta G^o = 2.303RT \log k$

$$-170108.9 = -2.303 \times 8.314 \times 573 \times \log \frac{1}{[PO_2]^{0.5}}$$

$$[R = 8.314\ J\ mole^{-1} K^{-1}]$$

$$\Rightarrow \log \frac{1}{[PO_2]^{0.5}} = \frac{170108.9}{2.303 \times 8.314 \times 573} = 15.505$$

$$\Rightarrow 0.5 \log(PO_2) = -15.503$$

$$\Rightarrow \log(PO_2) = -15.503 \times 2 = -31.01$$

41. Submarine mafic-volcanic rocks and their altered equivalents, typically in brecciated rocks commonly associated with pillow lavas, which have good buffering capacity, host Cyprus-type deposits.

Host-rocks for Kuroko-type deposits range from basalt to rhyolite, which have high and low buffering capacities, respectively.Many deposits are associated with subaqueous dacitic-domes that have intermediate buffering capacity. Host rocks are commonly brecciated and are typically moderately to highly alter. Associated volcaniclastic or hemipelagic sedimentary rocks that overly submarine volcanic sequences host some deposits.

Besshi-type deposits are typically hosted by turbiditic to hemipelagic graywacke interbedded with or intruded by basalt.

42. Band ratio for clay is 5/7

and band ratio for Fe-oxides mineral is 3/1

43. The Cambay basin is a rift basin forming the inland extension of the large offshore west coast basin and located on the west-north-west margin platform of the Indian Craton, covers an area of 56,000 Sq. Km. between latitudes 21° & 25° N and longitudes 71°30' & 79°30'E. The age range of reservoir rock in Cambay oil field is 56 34 million years.

44. For the amphibole glaucophane,

$$Na_2Mg_3Al_2Si_8O_{22}(OH)_2$$

Na is in the M4-site, *Al* is in octahedral coordination and Si is in tetrahedral coordination.

45. Volcanic-associated massive sulfide deposits (VMS) are predominantly stratiform accumulations of sulfide minerals that precipitate from hydrothermal fluids at or below the sea floor, in a wide range of ancient and modern geo-logical settings. They occur within volcano-sedimentary stratigraphic successions, and are commonly coeval and coincident with volcanic rocks. Modern analog of Besshi type VMS (volcanogenic massive sulfide) deposits (all these are ocean floor rift zones) is Guaymas Basin.

46. Increasing order of Vicker's micro-hardness

galena < chalcopyrite < sphalerite < magnetite

47. Given,

$$({}^{18}O/{}^{16}O)_{sample} = 0.0019$$

$$({}^{18}O/{}^{16}O)_{VSMOW} = 0.002005$$

As per formula

$$\delta^{18}O = \left[\frac{({}^{18}O/{}^{16}O)_{sample}}{({}^{18}O/{}^{16}O)_{VSMOW}} - 1\right] \times 10^3$$

$$\Rightarrow \delta^{18}O = \left[\frac{0.0019}{0.002005} - 1\right] \times 10^3$$

$$= -0.0524 \times 10^3 = -52.4\ \%$$

48. Given,

$$NaCl = 0.5 \text{ molal} = Na^+ + Cl^-$$

$$CaCl_2 = 0.25 \text{ molal} = Ca^{2+} + 2Cl^-$$

As per formula the ionic strength, *I* is given as,

$$I = \frac{1}{2}\sum_{i=1}^{n} C_i Z_i^2$$

where, C_i = molar concentration of ion *i*

Z_i = change number of ion *i*

Therefore,

$$I = \frac{1}{2}\left[0.5(+1)^2 + 0.5(-1)^2 + 0.25(+2)^2 + 0.25 \times 2(-2)^2\right]$$

$$\Rightarrow I = \frac{1}{2}[2.5] = 1.25$$

49. Methane gas is generated during the formation of coal through 'coalification' process of vegetal matter. This can broadly be divided into biochemical and physico-chemical stages of coalification incorporating five successive steps-

- Peatification (anaerobic degradation of organic materials in the peat swamp);
- Humification (formation of dark coloured humic substances by anaerobic degradation);
- Bituminization (generation of hydrocarbons with increase in temperature and pressure);
- Debituminization (thermal degradation of matter and generated hydrocarbons); and
- Graphitization (formation of graphite).

50. As per figure, the reaction that takes place at the isobaric invariant point P is

Liquid (at P) + Forsterite = Anorthite + Enstatite

51. Given,

Concentration of nickel, $C_0 = 2400$ ppm

Degree of melting, $f = 20\% = 0.2$

Bulk distribution coefficient, $D_i = SwikO$

$D_i = (0.6 \times 10 + 0.3 \times 4 + 0.1 \times 2) = 7.4$

Now, as per formula of batch melting, C_L

$$\frac{C_L}{C_0} = \frac{1}{D_i(1-f)+f}$$

$$\Rightarrow C_L = \frac{C_0}{D_i(1-f)+f}$$

$$\Rightarrow C_L = \frac{2400}{7.4(1-0.2)+0.2} = 392.15$$

52. The equilibrium mineral assemblage of rocks subjected to greenschist facies conditions depends on primary rock composition.

- **Basalt:** chlorite + actinolite + albite +/– epidote
- **Ultramafic:** chlorite + serpentine +/– talc +/ – tremolite +/– diopside +/– brucite
- **Pelites:** quartz +/– albite +/– k-feldspar +/- chlorite, muscovite, garnet, pyrophyllite +/- graphite
- **Calc-silicates:** calcite +/– dolomite +/– quartz +/– micas, scapolite, wollastonite, etc.

53.
- The rock with Talc-phengite (± chloritoid ± chlorite) assemblage looks silvery white in the field and so is called 'micascisti argentei' in the western Alps; it has been interpreted as metasomatic derivatives from granite along shear zones during HP and ultrahigh-pressure (UHP) conditions.
- Metapelitic rocks from the Marble Hall Fragment, enclosed in the granites of the magmatic Bushveld Complex, record a two stage, low pressure, high temperature metamorphism. An early paragenesis containing chiastolitic andalusite, cordierite, biotite and quartz ± garnet crystallized in most rocks and equilibrated at 550–600° C, 0.2GPa.
- Petrological studies and thermodynamic modeling of the spinel + quartz-bearing assemblage shows that these rocks experienced extreme metamorphism at Ultrahigh Temperature conditions.
- The rate and mechanism of a key diagenetic reaction, laumontite-wairakite + water was experimented with different temperature ranges where at very low temperature nucleation of wairakite occurred on the smallest laumontite fragments in the starting material, whereas at higher temperatures wairakite and other phases occur.

54. All classes of the cubic system have four axes of 3-fold symmetry.

55. **Calcite** is a uniaxial hexagonal-rhombohedral negative mineral with moderate refractive index, but extreme birefringence. It is so birefringent that it appears to have both negative and positive relief, depending on orientation.

Nepheline is a colorless uniaxial hexagonal-rhombohedral negative mineral with extremely low birefringence. They have low relief. They are only seen in lavas.

Apatite is a colorless uniaxial hexagonal-rhombohedral negative mineral with extremely low birefringence and high relief. Usually as tiny elongate crystals with round or hexagonal outline.

Quartz is a uniaxial hexagonal-rhombohedral positive mineral with extremely low birefringence. It is easy to determine on account of its lack of alteration, absence of cleavage or twinning. It is also one of the most common rock-forming minerals.

(GEOPHYSICS)

26. When depth migration is applied to stacked seismic section, then the migration moves in the direction of updip and have steeper slope compared to the stacked section.

27. Given,

Frequency of elastic wave, $f = 20$ Hz

Velocity of elastic wave, $v = 3000$ m/s

As per formula, $v = f\lambda$

where λ is the wavelength

$$\therefore \lambda = \frac{v}{f} = \frac{3000}{20} = 150 \text{ m}$$

As we know,

For zero offset reflection from horizontal reflectors, the thickness of the vertical first Fresnel zone is $\frac{\lambda}{4}$ m.

Therefore, we get $t_f = \frac{150}{4} = 37.5$ m

28. Given,

Angle of dip of reflector, $\theta = 45°$

Velocity of P wave, $V_P = 2000$ m/s

Source – receiver distance, $x = 1000$ m

Therefore, the time recorded at the receiver is the dip move out time given as,

$$T_d = \frac{2x\sin\theta}{V_P}$$

$$\Rightarrow T_d = \frac{2 \times 1000 \times \sin(45)}{2000} = 0.707s$$

29. Given,

Seismic wavelet, $w = \{6, -4, -2\}$

Reflectivity series, $r = \{0, 1, 0\}$

Therefore,

The seismic trace is the convolution of these two i.e., $y = w \times r$

Now, By Folding method, we get

$y =$

w/r	0	1	0
6	0	6	0
–4	0	–4	0
–2	0	–2	0

$y = \{0, 6, -4, -2, 0\}$

30. As we know,

Periodicity of both sine and cosine curve is 2π. Therefore, substituting their corresponding values to 2π, we get,

$$\frac{\pi}{3}t = 2\pi \quad \text{or} \quad \frac{\pi}{2}t = 2\pi$$

$$t = 6 \quad \text{or} \quad t = 4$$

Thus, the L.C.M. of 6 and 4 gives the time period, i.e., 12 seconds.

31. **Assertion (a):** The inverse of a minimum phase wavelet is causal and stable.

Reason (r): The Z-transform of a minimum phase wavelet has all its zeros outside the unit circle.

Both (a) and (r) are true and (r) is the correct reason for (a)

32. Given,

Elevation, $h = 150$ m

Therefore, the free air correction is 0.3086 hmGal

Value of free air = 0.3086 × 150 mgal

= 46.29 mgal

33. Given,

Radius of Sperical Cavity, $R = 8$ m

Depth, $d = 15$ m

Density of sediments, $\rho_s = 1.5 \times 10^3$ kg/m^3

Density of rock body, $\rho_{rb} = 2.4 \times 10^3$ kg/m^3

∴ Density anomaly

$\Delta\rho = \rho_s - \rho_{rb} = (1.5 - 2.4) \times 10^3 = -0.9 \times 10^3$ kg/m^3

Therefore, the maximum value of gravity anomaly produced is given by

$$\Delta g_{max} = \frac{4\pi G \Delta\rho R^3}{3z^2}$$

$$\Rightarrow \Delta g_{max} = \frac{4 \times \pi \times 6.67 \times 10^{-11} \times -0.9 \times 10^3 \times 8^3}{3 \times 15^2}$$

$$\Rightarrow \Delta g_{max} = -0.05719 \ mgal$$

34. **Drift Corrections:** Observed gravity changes as a function of time at a given location, you could measure this with the gravimeter in the lab. The changes are due to tidal effects, instrument drift, and in some cases real changes (e.g. motions on faults, swelling magma chambers).

Latitude correction: Correction from observed gravity that accounts for earth's elliptical shape and rotation. the gravity value that would be observed if earth were a perfect (no geologic or topographic complexities), rotating ellipsoid is referred to as the normal gravity. gravity increases with increasing latitude. correction is added as we move toward the equator. correction is applied only for relitive movement in the n-s direction. correction for a givenlatitude is linear over about 1 km.

The Bouguer correction is a firstorder correction to account for the excess mass underlying observation points located at elevations higher than the elevation datum (sea level or the geoid). Conversely, it accounts for a mass deficiency at observation points located below the elevation datum.

Eotvos correction: The Eotvos effect is the change in perceived gravitational force caused by the change in centrifugal acceleration resulting from eastbound or westbound velocity. When moving eastbound, the object's angular velocity is increased (in addition to the earth's rotation), and thus the centrifugal force also increases, causing a perceived reduction in gravitational force.

35. Thermo Remanent Magnetization (TRM) gives a primary, stable magnetization for igneous rocks while rest varies with time are also depend on various perturbation effects

36. From the given figure it clearly depicts that in the Equator shows the total magnetic field intensity anomaly above a spherical body polarized by the present day geomagnetic field.

37. For a solid inner core, the ray path for the P-wave that converts to S-wave which have the script 'I' in PKIKP, changes 'J'. Therefore, the resultant PKJKP.

38. Stress-drop during an earthquake is given as

$$\Delta\sigma \sim \mu\varepsilon \sim c\mu\frac{\bar{D}}{A^{1/2}}$$

where, μ = shear modulus for an elastic solid

ε= strain developed

c = content of order 1

$\bar{D}$ = average displacement on fault

A = average fault that serptuses during the earthquake

Therefore, as per formula, large slip on a small fault will cause more stress drop.

39. According to kanamori's formula

The energy released in an earthquake is given as,

$\log_{10} E = 4.8 + 1.5M_s$

where, E is in Joules.

For $M_S = 7$

$\log_{10} E_7 = 4.8 + 1.5 \times 7 = 15.3$

For $M_S = 4$

$\log_{10} E_4 = 4.8 + 1.5 \times 4 = 10.8$

Now, substracting we get,

$\log_{10} E_7 - \log_{10} E_4 = 15.3 - 10.8 = 4.5$

$$\Rightarrow \log_{10}\left(\frac{E_7}{E_4}\right) = 4.5$$

$$\Rightarrow \frac{E_7}{E_4} = 10^{4.5} = 31622.77\ J$$

40. Given,

The distance between electrodes A and M is,

d = 0.40 m

Current generated, $I = 20\ mA$

Voltage induced, $\Delta V = 10\ mV$

Therefore, the apparent resistivity produced by normal device configuration is given by,

$$\rho_d = \frac{4\pi d\Delta V}{I}$$

$$\Rightarrow \rho_d = \frac{4 \times 3.14 \times 0.40 \times 10}{20} = 2.512\ \Omega m$$

41. Given,

Diameter of core sample, d = 0.02 m

Length of core sample, l = 0.04 m

Resistance of saturated sample, $R = 500\ \Omega$

Resistivity of brine solution, $\rho_w = 0.5\ \Omega m$

Therefore, the total resistivity of core sample fully saturated with brine solution is

$$\rho_0 = \frac{R \times A}{l} \quad \left[\text{where } A = \frac{\pi d^2}{4}\right]$$

$$\Rightarrow \rho_0 = \frac{R \times \pi d^2}{4l} = \frac{500 \times \pi \times (0.02)^2}{4 \times 0.04} = 3.925\ \Omega m$$

Now, by using Archie's first equation

$$\rho_0 = F\rho_w$$

$$\Rightarrow F = \frac{\rho_0}{\rho_w} = \frac{3.925}{0.5} = 7.85$$

42. Given,

$L = 50$ m

$a = 5$ m

$\rho_a = 100\ \Omega m$

$V = 50$ mV

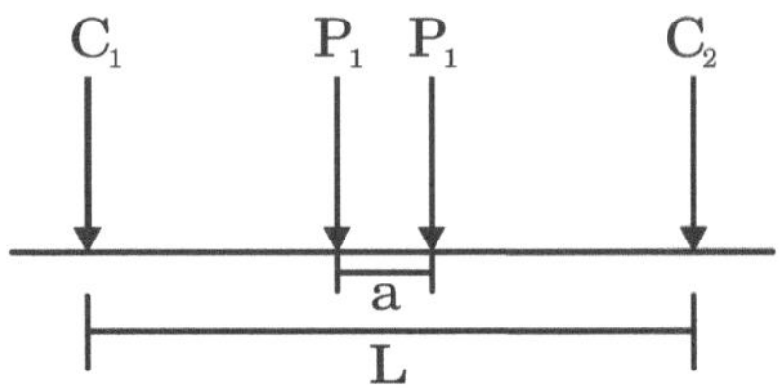

Fig. Schlumberger Arrangement

As per given arrangement of electrodes in the Schlumberger arrangement, the apparent resistivity obtained is,

$$\rho_a = \frac{\pi(L^2 - a^2)V}{4aI}$$

$$\Rightarrow I = \frac{\pi(L^2 - a^2)V}{4a\rho_a}$$

$$\Rightarrow I = \frac{\pi\left((50)^2 - (5)^2\right) \times 50}{4 \times 5 \times 100} = 194.28\ mA$$

43. Given,

For layer 1

$\rho_1 = 10\ \Omega m,\ z_1 = 5\ m$

For layer 2

$\rho_2 = 50\ \Omega m,\ z_2 = 10\ m$

Now, as per definition of coefficient of anisotropy

$$\lambda = \sqrt{\frac{\rho_v \text{(Vertical resistivity)}}{\rho_h \text{(Horizontal resistivity)}}}$$

$$\text{Also, } \rho_v = \left(\frac{T \text{(Transverse resistance)}}{Z_e \text{(Effective thickness)}}\right)$$

$$\rho_h = \left(\frac{Z_e \text{(Effective thickness)}}{S \text{(Longitudinal conductance)}}\right)$$

$$\text{Again, } T = \rho_1 Z_1 + \rho_2 Z_2 + \ldots\ldots + \rho_n Z_n = \sum_{i=1}^{n} \rho_i Z_i$$

$$\text{and } S = \frac{Z_1}{\rho_1} + \frac{Z_2}{\rho_2} + \ldots\ldots + \frac{Z_n}{\rho_n} = \sum_{i=1}^{n} \frac{Z_i}{\rho_i}$$

Now, as per question

$$T = \rho_1 Z_1 + \rho_2 Z_2 = \{(10 \times 5) + (50 \times 10)\} = 550\ \Omega$$

$$\text{and } S = \frac{Z_1}{\rho_1} + \frac{Z_2}{\rho_2} = \frac{5}{10} + \frac{10}{50} = 0.7\ \Omega^{-1}$$

$$Z_e = 5 + 10 = 15\ m$$

$$\rho_v = \frac{T}{Z_e} = \frac{550}{15} = 36.67\ \Omega$$

$$\rho_h = \frac{Z_e}{s} = \frac{15}{0.7} = 21.42\ \Omega$$

Therefore,

$$\lambda = \sqrt{\frac{\rho_v}{\rho_h}} = \sqrt{\frac{36.67}{21.42}} = 1.308$$

44. Any combination of three layer resistivity values gives four different type of curves which are:

- A-type ($r_1 < r_2 < r_3$)
- Q-type ($r_1 > r_2 > r_3$)
- K-type ($r_1 < r_2 > r_3$)
- H-type ($r_1 < r_2 < r_3$)

Therefore, the given resistivity curve represents HAK type curve in which three successive layers are taken at a time for defining each stage of the curve.

As, $(\rho_1 > \rho_2 < \rho_3)$ represents H-type

$(\rho_2 < \rho_3 < \rho_4)$ represents A-type

$(\rho_3 < \rho_4 > \rho_5)$ represents K-type

45. The numerical values of the real and imaginary components of the impedance tensor (Z) in Magnetotelluric (MT) method related over a homogeneous half-space are equal and gives the phase of 45° while the heterogeneous space are not equal.

46. For E-polarization and B-polarization in magneto telluric, the different field component along the three perpendicular axes are depicted as

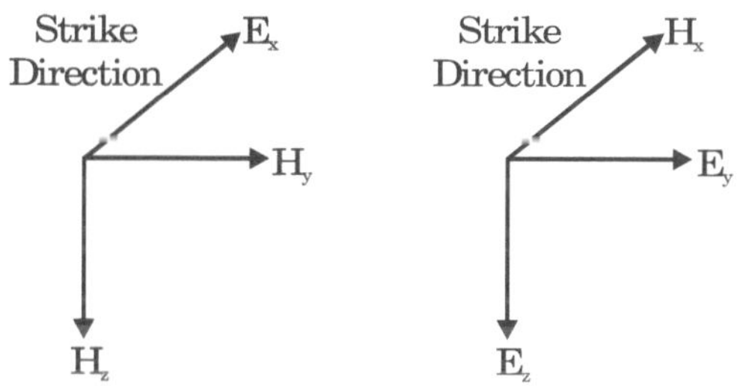

E-Polarization B-Polarization

As per question, the strike direction is in the y direction. Therefore, for E-polarization model the field components are H_x, E_y and H_z.

47. Dip angle electromagnetic methods are suitable to delineate vertical and dipping conductors but it does not give any value in case of horizontal conductors. Moreover, if a number of transverse lines are taken over a dipping conductor, then dip angle methods also helps in finding out its strike direction.

48. The maxwell's equation for time varying field are :-

$$\nabla . D = \rho$$

$$\nabla . B = 0$$

$$\nabla \times E = \frac{\partial B}{\partial t}$$

$$\nabla \times H = J + \frac{\partial D}{\partial t}$$

For invariant field are :-

$$\nabla . D = \rho$$

$$\nabla . B = 0$$

$$\nabla \times E = 0$$

$$\nabla \times H = J$$

49. The laplacian operator in spherical coordinate system is given by,

$$\nabla^2 = \frac{1}{r^2}\frac{\partial}{\partial r}\left(r^2\frac{\partial}{\partial r}\right) + \frac{1}{r^2 \sin^2\phi}\frac{\partial^2}{r\theta^2} + \frac{1}{r^2 \sin\theta}\frac{\partial}{\partial\theta}\left(\sin\phi\frac{\partial}{\partial\phi}\right)$$

Considering the spherical symmetry and taking only r terms, the laplacian operator for potential V is

$$\nabla^2 V = \frac{1}{r^2}\frac{\partial}{\partial r}\left(r^2\frac{\partial V}{\partial r}\right)$$

As per question, $\nabla^2 V = 0$

Therefore,

$$\frac{1}{r^2}\frac{\partial}{\partial r}\left(r^2\frac{\partial V}{\partial r}\right) = 0$$

$$\Rightarrow \frac{\partial}{\partial r}\left(r^2\frac{\partial V}{\partial r}\right) = 0$$

$$\Rightarrow \left(r^2\frac{\partial V}{\partial r}\right) = A$$

Now, integrating both sides

$$\Rightarrow \int\frac{\partial V}{\partial r} = \int\frac{A}{r^2}$$

$$\Rightarrow \int\partial V = \int\frac{A}{r^2}\partial r$$

$$\Rightarrow V = \frac{-A}{r} + B$$

[where A and B are integrating constants]

50. Given,

J is the Jacobian matrix in a geophysical inverse problem,

Addition of a regularization parameter λ as $(J^T J + \lambda I)$

The inverse leads to a stable solution also the parameter resolution decreases.

51. Given,

Singular Value Decomposition of a square nonsingular matrix J is

$$J = U\lambda V^T$$

Therefore, the inverse of it reverses the order of the individual component

i.e. $J^{-1} = V\lambda^{-1}U^T$

52. Given,

$t_{1/2} = 10$

Now, as per formula relating the fraction of nuclide with the original nuclide with half life

$$\frac{N}{N_0} = \left(\frac{1}{2}\right)^{t/t_{\frac{1}{2}}}$$

After $t = t_{1/2}$

$$\frac{N}{N_0} = \left(\frac{1}{2}\right)^{10t_{\frac{1}{2}}/t_{\frac{1}{2}}} = \frac{1}{2^{10}}$$

$$\Rightarrow N = \frac{1}{1029}N_0$$

$$\Rightarrow N = 0.001N_0$$

53. Let, the parent radionuclide be P_0 and the residual be P.

Therefore, as per the definition of radioactive decay

$$P = P_0e^{-\lambda t}$$

The daughter radionuclide is

$$D = P_0 - P$$

$$\Rightarrow D = Pe^{-\lambda t} - P$$

$$\Rightarrow D = P\left(e^{-\lambda t} - 1\right)$$

54. Both K and H type curve exhibit 'Equivalence' type ambiguity. Both A and Q type curve exhibit 'Suppression' type ambiguity.

Therefore, a possible combination of these resistivity sounding curves exhibits both 'Equivalence' and 'Suppression' type ambiguities in interpretation of data is HA, KQ, AK and QH.

55. A seismic wave travelling through an isotropic homogeneous medium will propagate at a constant velocity. Therefore, the time t required for a seismic wave to travel from source to receiver in a homogeneous earth layer with velocity v is simply given by the formula

$$t = \frac{d}{v}$$

where d is the distance travelled in the layer.

Travel times of visible arrivals are related to the distance between source and receiver (x), thickness of the layer (h) and the wave velocities in the upper layer and basement (v_1 and v_2). Let us denote the arrival times at point x for the direct, reflected and refracted waves as t_{dir}, t_{refl}, t_{refr} respectively. These times are given by the following formulas.

$$t_{dir} = \frac{x}{v_1}$$

$$t_{refl} = \frac{\sqrt{x^2 + 4h^2}}{v_1}$$

$$t_{refr} = \frac{x}{v_2} + \frac{2h\sqrt{v_2^2 - v_1^2}}{v_1 v_2}$$

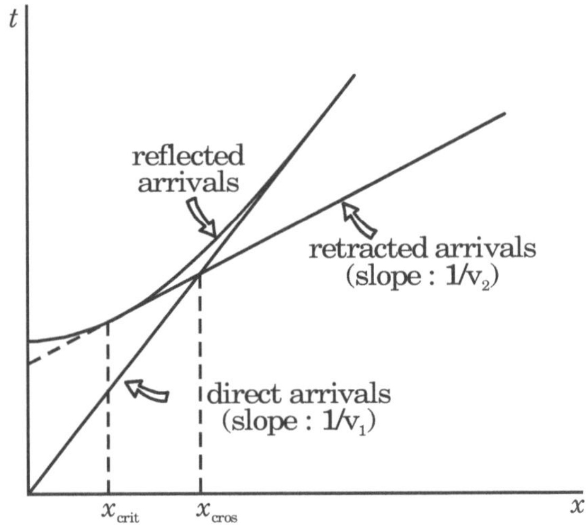

Therefore, the exact match is P-2; Q-3; R-4; S-1.

SOLVED PAPER - 2015

GENERAL APTITUDE (GA)

Q. 1 – Q. 5 carry one mark each.

1. Choose the appropriate word/phrase, out of the four options given below, to complete the followign sentence:

Apparent lifelessness _____ dormant life.

(*a*) harbours (*b*) leads to

(*c*) supports (*d*) affects

2. Fill in the blank with the correct idiom/phrase.

That boy from the town was a ____ in the sleepy village.

(*a*) dog out of herd (*b*) sheep from the heap

(*c*) fish out of water (*d*) bird from the flock

3. Choose the statement where underlined word is used correctly.

(*a*) What the teacher eludes to different authors, he is being elusive.

(*b*) When the thief keeps eluding the police, he is being elusive.

(*c*) Matters that are difficult to understand, identify or remember are allusive.

(*d*) Mirages can be allusive, but a better way to express them is illusory.

4. Tanya is older than Eric.

Cliff is older than Tanya.

Eric is older than Cliff.

If the first two statements are true, then the third statement is:

(*a*) True (*b*) False

(*c*) Uncertain (*d*) Data insufficient

5. Five teams have to compete in a league, with every team playing every other team exactly once, before going to the next round. How many matches will have to be held to complete the league round of matches?

(*a*) 20 (*b*) 10

(*c*) 8 (*d*) 5

Q. 6 – Q. 10 carry two marks each.

6. Select the appropriate option in place of underlined part of the sentence.

Increased productivity necessary reflects greater efforts made by the employees.

(*a*) Increase in productivity necessary

(*b*) Increase productivity is necessary

(*c*) Increase in productivity necessarily

(*d*) No improvement required

7. Given below are two statements followed by two conclusions. Assuming these statements to be true, decide which one logically follows.

Statements: I. No manager is a leader.

II. All leaders are executives.

Conclusions: I. No manager is an executive.

II. No executive is a manager.

(*a*) Only conclusion I follows.

(*b*) Only conclusion II follows.

(*c*) Neither conclusion I nor II follows.

(*d*) Both conclusions I and II follows.

8. In the given figure angle Q is a right angle, PS : QS = 3 : 1, RT : QT = 5 : 2 and PU : UR = 1 : 1. If area of triangle QTS is 20 cm^2, then the area of triangle PQR in cm^2 is _____.

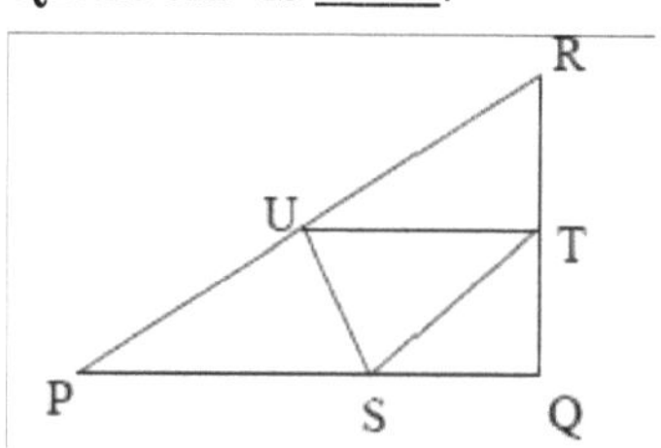

9. Right triangle PQR is to be constructed in the xy-plane so that the right angle is at P and line PR is parallel to the x-axis. The x and y coordinates of P, Q and R are to be integers that satisfy the inequalities : $-4 \le x \le 5$ and $6 \le y \le 16$. How many different triangles could be constructed with these properties ?

(*a*) 110 (*b*) 1100

(*c*) 9900 (*d*) 10000

10. A coin is tossed thrice. Let X be the event that head occurs in each of the first two tosses. Let Y be the event that a tail occurs on the third toss. Let Z be the event that two tails occur inthree tosses. Based on the above information, which one of the following statements is TRUE?

(*a*) X and Y are not independent

(*b*) Y and Z are dependent

(*c*) Y and Z are independent

(*d*) X and Z are independent

PART-A (Common Part)

Q. 1 – Q. 25 carry one mark each.

1. The shape of the earth is best described as

(*a*) spheroid (*b*) prolate ellipsoid

(*c*) ellipsoid (*d*) oblate spheroid

2. Which one amongst the following is the CORRECT attitude of a bed?

(*a*) 221°, 95° (*b*) N45°W, 40°SE

(*c*) 090°/ 20°W (*d*) 089°, 75°S

3. Hawaiian Island chain is the result of

(*a*) collision of two oceanic plates

(*b*) intraplate hot spot activity

(*c*) divergence of two oceanic plates

(*d*) interplate hot spot activity

4. In which one of the following configurations the electrodes are uniformly spaced?

(*a*) Schlumberger array

(*b*) Pole-dipole array

(*c*) Wenner array

(*d*) Pole-pole array

5. In Triclinic crystal system, the three crystallographic axes a, b, c are of

(*a*) equal lengths with angle between b and c as 90°

(*b*) equal lengths with angle between a and c ≠ 90°

(*c*) unequal lengths with angle between a and c ≠ 90°

(*d*) unequal lengths with angle between b and c as 90°

6. A landform that results from free fall of rocks is called

(*a*) talus slope (*b*) eskers

(*c*) alluvial fan (*d*) debris flow

7. Which one of the following figures correctly depicts the geomagnetic declination (D) and inclination (I) angles ? (X: Geographic North; Y: Geographic East; Z: Vertical direction; H: Geomagnetic North; F: Total Field direction)

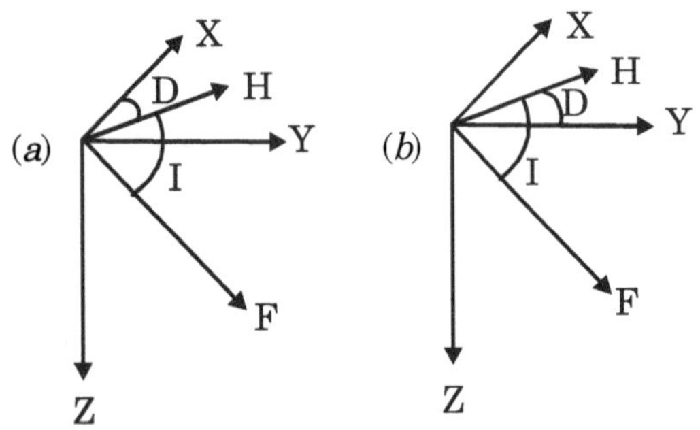

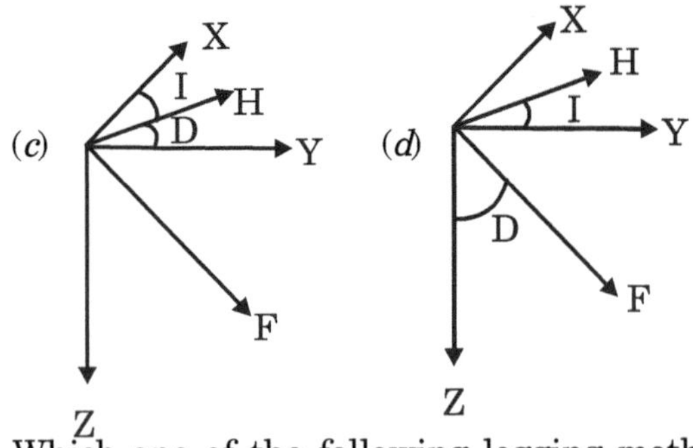

8. Which one of the following logging methods is NOT used to determine porosity?

(*a*) Sonic (*b*) SP

(*c*) Neutron (*d*) Gamma-gamma

9. PcP and ScS phases are reflected from

(*a*) crust - mantle boundary

(*b*) core - mantle boundary

(*c*) inner core - outer core boundary

(*d*) lithosphere - asthenosphere boundary

10. Identify the CORRECT sequence of the electromagnetic waves in their increasing frequency

(*a*) radio wave, micro-wave, infrared, visible, ultra violet, X-ray

(*b*) radio wave, infrared, micro-wave, visible, ultra violet, X-ray

(*c*) micro-wave, radio wave, infrared, visible, X-ray, ultra violet

(*d*) infrared, visible, micro-wave, radio wave, X-ray, ultra violet

11. Considering the Airy isostatic compensation for a mountain having elevation of 2.0 km above the mean sea level at a point P, the thickness of its root below P would be ________km. (consider densities of crustal rocks and upper mantle as 2.7 gcm^{-3} and 3.3 gcm^{-3} respectively).

12. The reflection coefficient at the interface separating sandstone (V_p = 2000 ms^{-1}; ρ = 1.5 gcm^{-3}) underlain by shale (V_p = 2500 ms-1; ρ = 2.0 gcm^{-3}) is ______.

13. Gardner's formula relates the seismic P-wave velocity (V_P) to

(a) density (b) porosity

(c) permeability (d) lithology

14. Which one of the following sedimentary basins is related to extension?

(a) foredeep (b) half-graben

(c) piggyback (d) fore-arc

15. In a seismic section, paraconformity is marked by

(*a*) onlap

(*b*) downlap

(*c*) erosional truncation

(*d*) concordance

16. Match the names listed in Group I with its attributes listed in Group II.

Group I	Group II
P. Carlsberg Ridge	1. Aseismic
Q. Ninetyeast Ridge	2. Subduction
R. Pranhita-Godavari basin	3. Spreading
S. Makran Coast	4. Transform
	5. Rift

(*a*) P-5; Q-3; R-1; S-4 (*b*) P-3; Q-1; R-5; S-2
(*c*) P-3; Q-4; R-1; S-2 (*d*) P-1; Q-3; R-5; S-4

17. In India, bituminous coal occurs at
(a) Panandhro (b) Palana
(c) Neyveli (d) Jharia

18. On the Earth, all conditions being same, the time period of a simple pendulum will be maximum at the
(*a*) Poles
(*b*) Tropic of Cancer
(*c*) Tropic of Capricorn
(*d*) Equator

19. The two most abundant elements in the Earth are
(*a*) oxygen and iron (*b*) iron and magnesium
(*c*) oxygen and silicon (*d*) iron and silicon

20. The pair of curves that depicts the radioactive decay and growth of a parent-daughter pair in the following figure is (N – Number of nuclides, Time in multiples of half-life).

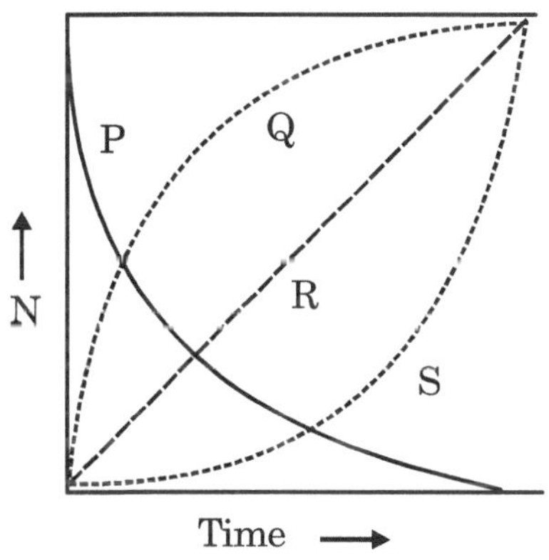

(*a*) P, Q (*b*) P, R
(*c*) P, S (*d*) S, Q

21. A drainage basin with an area of 2.0×10^6 m^2 receives continuous rainfall for 48 hours at a uniform rate of 3 mmh^{-1}. The volume of precipitation is ___________ m^3 of water.

22. The main source of error in computing the orientation of planar features from drill cores is
(*a*) rotation of the core during extraction
(*b*) cylindrical shape of the core
(*c*) non-vertical orientation of the drill axis
(*d*) staining during drilling operations

23. Which combination of sorting and roundness of sand grains results in highest permeability?
(*a*) well sorted, poorly rounded
(*b*) well sorted, well rounded
(*c*) poorly sorted, poorly rounded
(*d*) poorly sorted, well rounded

24. Amongst the different gases in the atmosphere, which one of the following pairs DOES NOT contribute to heating of the atmosphere?
(*a*) CO_2 , H_2 O
(*b*) N 2 , O_2
(*c*) H_2 O, CH_4
(*d*) H_2 O, O_3

25. The data of which one of the following active electromagnetic techniques can be used to correct static shift effect in magnetotelluric apparent resistivity data?
(*a*) Slingram
(*b*) Turam
(*c*) VLF
(*d*) TEM

PART-B
GEOLOGY

Q. 26 to Q. 55 carry two marks each.

26. Which one of the following statements describing aspects of partial melting behavior of a binary eutectic system is NOT TRUE?
(*a*) Melting is complete at temperature just above the liquidus temperature.
(*b*) Two solid phases and one liquid phase co-exist at eutectic temperature.
(*c*) The lowest temperature at which partial melting occurs is independent of the chemical composition.
(*d*) The composition of the first liquid to form depends on the composition of the sample.

27. Find the CORRECT statement amongst the following.
(*a*) Delthyrium is a triangular cavity in cephalopod
(*b*) Madreporite is a skeletal part of Brachiopoda
(*c*) Pleuron is a part of thorax in Trilobite
(*d*) Endocone is the jaw of an Ammonoid

28. Based on the figure below that shows typical distribution / partition coefficients (K D = mineral/ liquid) for REEs between various minerals and basaltic melt, which one of the following statements is NOT true?

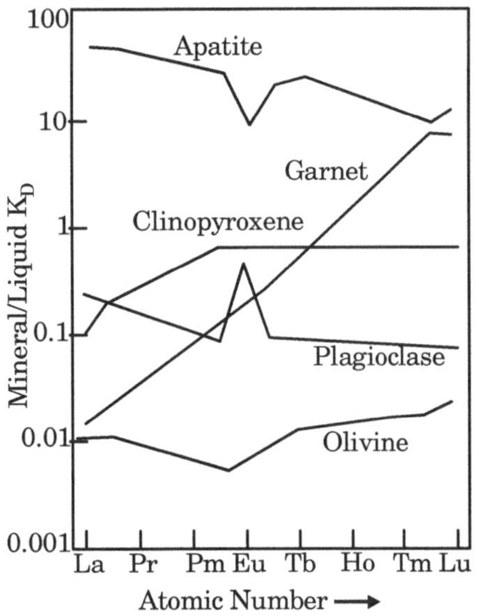

(*a*) REEs are compatible only in apatite.

(*b*) Heavy REEs are compatible whereas Light REEs are incompatible in garnet.

(*c*) REEs are incompatible only in apatite.

(*d*) REEs are incompatible in olivine.

29. Which one of the following is NOT a set of polymorphous minerals?

(*a*) calcite, aragonite, vaterite

(*b*) quartz, coesite, tridymite

(*c*) graphite, anthracite, diamond

(*d*) kyanite, sillimanite, andalusite

30. Chemical analysis reveals that basalts contain much more aluminum (Al_2O_3~15%) in comparison to peridotites (Al_2O_3 ~4%). This is because they contain

(*a*) very little olivine

(*b*) higher proportion of pyroxene

(*c*) feldspars as dominant mineral

(*d*) no quartz

31. A sandstone bed whose attitude is 090°, 30° is exposed on a flat surface. The true thickness of the bed is 100 m. The width of the outcrop of the sandstone bed along a N-S traverse on the ground is ______ m.

32. Assertion (a): The $\frac{^{18}O}{^{16}O}$ ratio in natural systems can be used as a thermometer.

Reason (r): The fractionation of $\frac{^{18}O}{^{16}O}$ depends on temperature.

(*a*) Both (a) and (r) are True and (r) is the correct reason for (a).

(*b*) Both (a) and (r) are not True.

(*c*) (a) is True but (r) is not True

(*d*) Both (a) and (r) are True but (r) is not the correct reason for (a).

33. Based on the schematic figure below, match the boreholes B1, B2, B3 and B4 listed in Group I with their features listed in Group II.

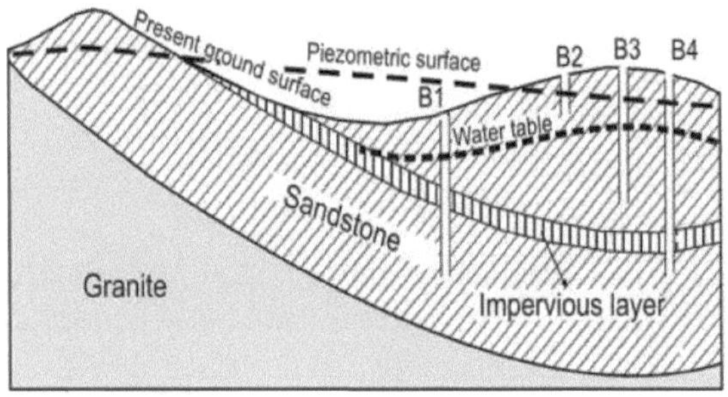

Group I	Group II
P. Borehole B1	1. well in unconfined aquifer
Q. Borehole B2	2. artesian well with water not flowing to surface
R. Borehole B3	3. artesian well with water flowing to surface
S. Borehole B4	4. dry well

(*a*) P-1; Q-3; R-2; S-4

(*b*) P-2; Q-4; R-1; S-3

(*c*) P-3; Q-4; R-1; S-2

(*d*) P-3; Q-1; R-4; S-2

34. If the total volume of water in the Earth's atmosphere, estimated to be about 1.29×10^4 km³, were to completely precipitate and uniformly cover the Earth's surface, estimated to be 5.1×10^8 km², the height of the resulting water column would be ____________ cm.

35. Samples of copper ores are drawn from locations X_1, X_2 and X_3 as shown in figure below. The values of (% Cu) at sampling locations are given in brackets. The estimated grade at point X_0 using inverse distances weighting is ______%.

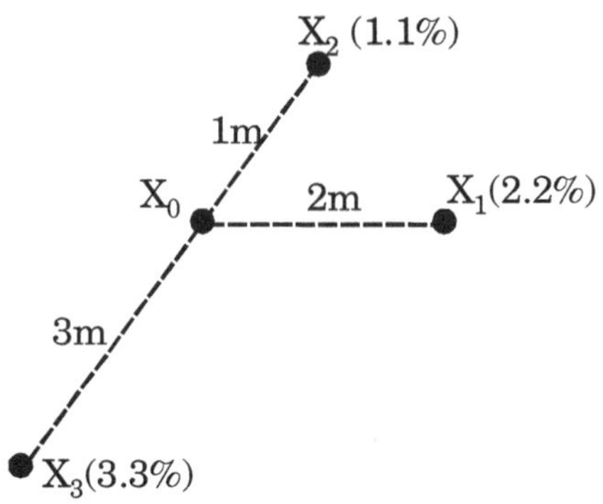

36. Match the point group (HM symbol) in Group I with its corresponding general form in Group II

	Group I	Group II
P.	$\bar{6}2m$	1. Ditrigonal Dipyramid
Q.	3/m	2. Tetragonal Scalenohedron
R.	422	3. Trigonal Dipyramid
S.	$\bar{4}2m$	4. Tetragonal Trapezohedron
		5. Hexagonal Dipyramid

(*a*) P-5; Q-1; R-2; S-4 (*b*) P-1; Q-3; R-4; S-2
(*c*) P-1; Q-3; R-2; S-5 (*d*) P-3; Q-5; R-2; S-4

37. Identify the CORRECT pair of minerals both of which show optical properties as shown in figures X (optic axis figure) and Y (with increasing free working distance between objective and stage). CB – Canada Balsam

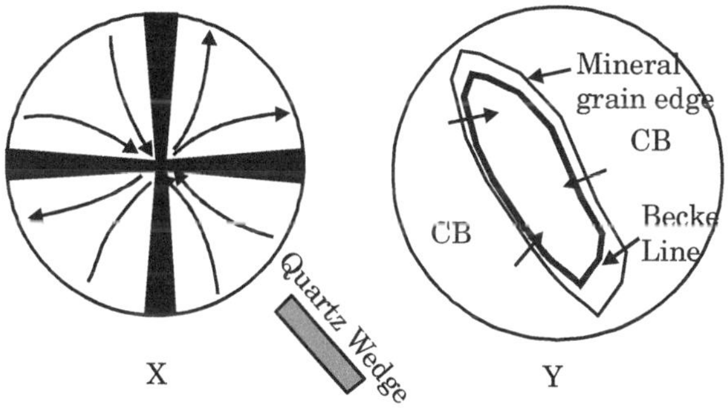

(*a*) Quartz, Stishovite (*b*) Cordierite, Chlorite
(*c*) Apatite, Tourmaline (*d*) Nosean, Halite

38. From the figure given below depicting a recovered core of a total length of 200 cm, the RQD (Rock Quality Designation) is________%.

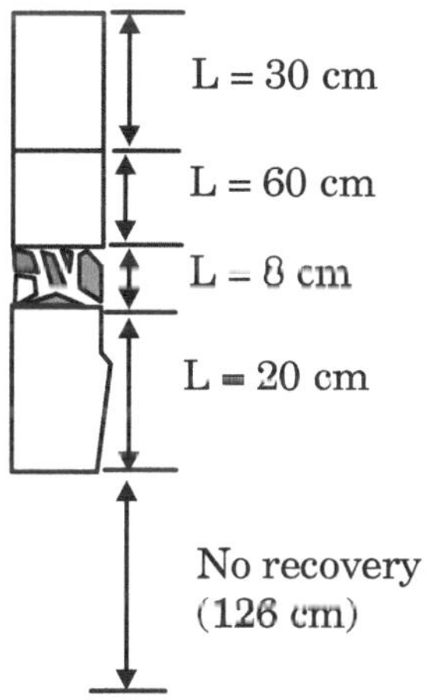

39. Interlimb angle and shape of a fold is best studied in a

(*a*) section parallel to the plunge of the fold axis
(*b*) section parallel to the axial plane of the fold
(*c*) section parallel to dip of bedding in the fold
(*d*) section whose pole is the fold axis

40. The cross-section below shows a thrust fault with an associated fault-related fold. For the hanging wall, which one of the combinations of (P), (Q) and (R) is correct?

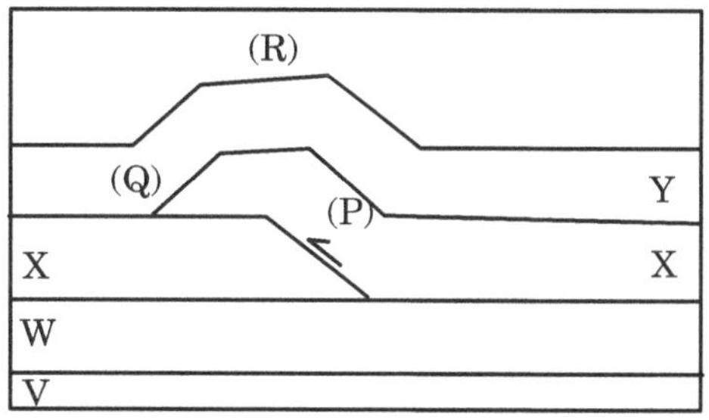

(*a*) Ramp (P), Flat (Q), Fault Bend Fold (R)
(*b*) Ramp (P), Flat (Q), Fault Propagation Fold (R)
(*c*) Flat (P), Ramp (Q), Fault Bend Fold (R)
(*d*) Flat (P), Ramp (Q), Fault Propagation Fold(R)

41. Euler Poles defined for plate motions on a spherical earth are

(*a*) parallel to associated transform faults
(*b*) perpendicular to associated transform faults
(*c*) not related to associated transform faults
(*d*) oblique to associated transform faults

42. Which one of the following sedimentary structures CANNOT be identified in vertical sections?

(*a*) Convolute lamination
(*b*) Gutter cast
(*c*) Dish structures
(*d*) Skip marks

43. A predominantly siliciclastic Mesozoic stratigraphic unit in mainland Kutch containing *Trigonia* and abundant plant fossils including *Ptillophyllum* is

(*a*) Baisakhi Formation
(*b*) Chari Formation
(*c*) Pachcham Formation
(*d*) Umia Formation

44. Match the texture in Group I with its corresponding description in Group II.

Group I	Group II
P. Cumulus texture	1. triple point junction
Q. Exsolution texture	2. banding and crustification in open spaces
R. Caries texture	3. protuberances of replacing mineral with replaced host
S. Cockade texture	4. spindles or lamellae of one mineral in another
	5. aggregates of minerals with non-penetrative mineral boundaries

(*a*) P-5; Q-4; R-3; S-2 (*b*) P-4; Q-5; R-3; S-1
(*c*) P-5; Q-4; R-2; S-3 (*d*) P-4; Q-3; R-2; S-5

45. Choose the CORRECT statement regarding coal.

(*a*) Sapropelic coal is a potential source rock of oil.

(*b*) Vitrinite reflectance value (Ro %) shoud be > 1 for a lignite sample.

(*c*) H/C content of the vitrinite maceral groups is more than that of liptinite maceral groups.

(*d*) In Ranigunj field coal seams alternate with limestone beds.

46. Match the stratigraphic units in Group I with the economic deposits in Group II.

Group I	Group II
P. Bailadila Group	1. Mn
Q. Nallamalai Group	2. Phosphorite
R. Udaipur Group	3. BIF
S. Sausar Group	4. Pb-Zn
	5. Pyrite

(*a*) P-3; Q-4; R-2; S-1 (*b*) P-4; Q-2; R-3; S-5

(*c*) P-2; Q-3; R-4; S-5 (*d*) P-3; Q-4; R-1; S-2

47. Match the igneous bodies in Group I with the cratons where they occur in Group II.

Group I	Group II
P. Untala Granite	1. Singbhum craton
Q. Singbhum craton	2. Aravalli craton
R. Chamundi Granite	3. Bastar craton
S. Bijli Rhyolite	4. Dharwar craton
	5. Bundelkhand craton

(*a*) P-2; Q-1; R-5; S-3 (*b*) P-2; Q-1; R-4; S-3

(*c*) P-3; Q-4; R-1; S-5 (*d*) P-1; Q-3; R-1; S-5

48. The reflectance spectrum of solar energy by the hydrous molecules in plant leaves is best represented in an optical spectrometer in the wavelength range of

(*a*) Near Infrared (0.7 - 1.3 m)

(*b*) Short Infrared (1.3 - 3.0 m)

(*c*) Mid Infrared (3 - 8 m)

(*d*) Long Infrared (8 - 15 m)

49. Match the type of mantled porphyroclasts in Group I with the corresponding figure in Group II.

Group I	Group II
P. δ type	1. 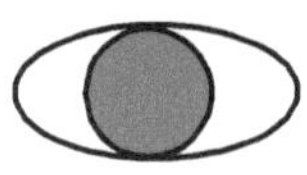
Q. σ type	2. 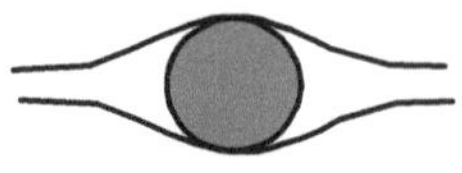
R. θ type	3. 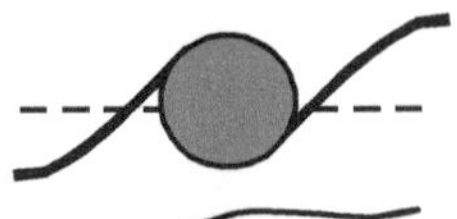
S. ϕ type	4. 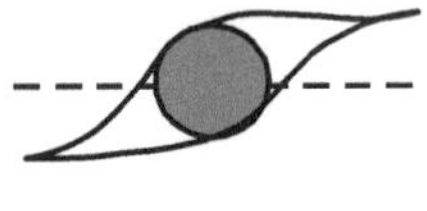

(*a*) P-1; Q-3; R-2; S-4 (*b*) P-3; Q-4; R-1; S-2

(*c*) P-3; Q-1; R-2; S-4 (*d*) P-2; Q-1; R-4; S-3

50. Choose the CORRECT symmetry operations that can create all possible two dimensional planar point groups.

(*a*) translation, rotation, screw, glide

(*b*) translation, reflection, rotation, glide

(*c*) screw, reflection, rotation, glide

(*d*) translation, reflection, screw, glide

51. In the folded and faulted sequence of beds given in the map below, the fault F-F (dipping 30 NE) is which type of fault?

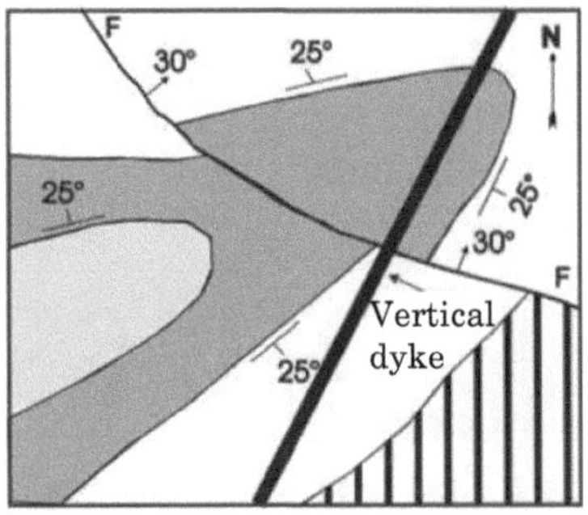

(*a*) sinistral strike-slip

(*b*) reverse

(*c*) normal

(*d*) dextral strike-slip

52. Which one of the following sets of isotopic ratios contains ONLY those that change with time?

(*a*) $^{87}Sr/^{86}Sr$, $^{143}Nd/^{144}Nd$, $^{207}Pb/^{206}Pb$, $^{147}Sm/^{144}Nd$

(*b*) $^{88}Sr/^{86}Sr$, $^{145}Nd/^{144}Nd$, $^{238}U/^{204}Pb$, $^{207}Pb/^{204}Pb$

(*c*) $^{84}Sr/^{86}Sr$, $^{143}Nd/^{144}Nd$, $^{208}Pb/^{204}Pb$, $^{85}Rb/^{87}Sr$

(*d*) $^{145}Nd/^{144}Nd$, $^{86}Sr/^{84}Sr$, $^{147}Sm/^{144}Nd$, $^{208}Pb/^{86}Sr$

53. Sediments derived exclusively from the Deccan basalt are deposited on a high-energy beach and are lithified under shallow burial conditions. The sedimentary rock formed would be a/an

(*a*) arkose (*b*) greywacke

(*c*) lithic arenite (*d*) quartz arenite

54. Choose the CORRECT mineral assemblages in mafic rocks that indicate eclogite facies metamorphism.

(*a*) orthopyroxene + plagioclase + garnet

(*b*) glaucophane + omphacite + lawsonite ± garnet

(*c*) ugrandite garnet + omphacite + plagioclase

(*d*) pyralspite garnet + omphacite ± kyanite

55. The maximum velocity of the Indian Plate is observed in

(*a*) Maldives (*b*) Bangalore

(*c*) Delhi (*d*) Srinagar

GEOPHYSICS

Q. 26 – Q. 55 carry two marks each.

26. Which type of VES curve is obtained for a three-layered earth model consisting of wet shale (top layer), poorly water saturated sandstone (middle layer) and impermeable granite (bottom layer)?

(*a*) K (*b*) Q

(*c*) H (*d*) A

27. In the estimation of magnetotelluric transfer function, the time-independent conservation of current at conductivity discontinuities will result in

(*a*) phase rotation

(*b*) static-shift

(*c*) null tipper

(*d*) equal bi-modal apparent resistivity values

58. In any given signal, removal of all periods shorter than Nyquist period is achieved by

(*a*) high-pass filtering (*b*) band-pass filtering

(*c*) low-pass filtering (*d*) band-reject filtering

29. The magnetic flux density, $\vec{B}$ and the magnetic vector potential, $\vec{A}$ are related by

(*a*) $\vec{B} = \nabla . \vec{A}$ (*b*) $\vec{B} = \nabla \times \vec{A}$

(*c*) $\vec{A} = \nabla \vec{B}$ (*d*) $\vec{A} = \nabla \times \vec{B}$

30. The frequency range (in Hz) that defines dead-band in magnetotelluric source signal is

(*a*) 0.1 – 10 (*b*) 10 – 100

(*c*) 100 – 1000 (*d*) 1000 – 10000

31. The maximum foldage obtained from a 48-channel common-depth-point (CDP) reflection survey with the geophone and shot point spacing of 50 m and 100 m respectively, is ______.

32. The deviation in the geographical locations of the magnetic poles from the geomagnetic poles of the Earth's magnetic field is due to the

(*a*) orientation of dipole axis

(*b*) external magnetic field

(*c*) non-dipole component

(*d*) ionospheric currents

33. The analytic signal for the function f(t)= sin ωt is

(*a*) –cos ωt (*b*) – sin ωt

(*c*) $e^{i\omega t}$ (*d*) $-e^{i\omega t}$

34. The minimum frequency at which a signal comprising of 30 Hz, 50 Hz and 70 Hz frequencies should be sampled to avoid aliasing is ______ Hz.

35. **Assertion (a) :** The Gutenberg-Richter frequency-magnitude relation of earthquakes globally suggests that subduction zones in general are characterized by lower b-values (b-value is slope of frequency-magnitude relation) when compared to the mid-oceanic ridges.

Reason (r) : Earthquakes in the subduction zones occur at deeper focal depths also, whereas, earthquakes along mid-oceanic ridges occur at shallow focal depths.

(*a*) (a) is false but (r) is true

(*b*) Both (a) and (r) are true; and (r) is correct reason for (a)

(*c*) Both (a) and (r) are true; and (r) is not a reason for (a)

(*d*) Both (a) and (r) are false

36. The masses and radioactive heat generation values respectively for different parts of the Earth are tabulated as given below.

Region	Mass × 10^{21} kg	Radioactive heat generation × 108 (m Wkg^{-1})
Upper continental crust	8	96.4
Lower continental crust	8	40.00
Oceanic crust	7	18.60
Mantle	4080	0.26
Core	1880	0

Deduce which one of the following statements is NOT correct from the given data

(*a*) Core does not contain any radioactive isotope

(*b*) Lower continental crust is depleted in heat producing elements related to upper continental crust

(*c*) Mantle produces the highest radiogenic heat

(*d*) Upper continental crust produces the highest radiogenic heat

37. Which ONE of the following statements is CORRECT with regard to the application of reduction-to-pole (RTP) technique on the total field magnetic anomaly map of any region?

(*a*) RTP is an efficient tool in the areas close to the equator (below ±20° Lat.)

(*b*) RTP assumes mainly induced magnetization for the source bodies

(*c*) RTP cannot be applied at higher latitudes (above ±60° Lat.)

(*d*) RTP completely eliminates the sources of remnant magnetization.

38. After migration, an anticline observed on an unmigrated seismic section becomes

(*a*) broader (*b*) tighter

(*c*) unaltered (*d*) flat

39. A clean, thick and hydrocarbon bearing sandstone bed can be identified through a combination of

(*a*) low SP and high resistivity

(*b*) large SP and high resistivity

(*c*) low transit time and high resistivity

(*d*) large SP and low resistivity

40. In a consolidated sandstone formation, the interval transit times of the formation, matrix and fluid are 70 s, 55 s and 190 s respectively. The porosity of the formation is ________.

41. Which one of the following statements is NOT CORRECT?

(*a*) A well-conditioned matrix has a condition number close to 1.

(*b*) An ill-conditioned matrix has a large condition number

(*c*) The inverse of a well-conditioned matrix can be computed with good accuracy.

(*d*) A matrix that is not invertible has a condition number close to 1.

42. Match the type of inverse problem in Group I with its solution in Group II.

Group I	Group II
P. Over determined	1. $m = [G^TG + K^2I]^{-1} G^Td$
Q. Under determined	2. $m = [G^TG]^{-1} G^Td$
R. Mixed determined	3. $m = G[G^TG]^{-1} G^Td$
S. Even determined	4. $m = G^T[GG^T]^{-1} d$
	5. $m = G^{-1} d$ (N = M rank of G = N)

(*a*) P-2; Q-4; R-1; S-5 (*b*) P-2; Q-3; R-1; S-5

(*c*) P-2; Q-1; R-3; S-4 (*d*) P-3; Q-5; R-2; S-1

43. In frequency domain IP, which one of the following frequency ranges (in Hz) is used to measure apparent resistivity at DC and AC limits?

(*a*) 0.01 – 01 (*b*) 0.1 – 1

(*c*) 0.1 – 10 (*d*) 10 – 100

44. The expression for electrical potential, V, at a distance r from a subsurface point source of current in a homogeneous medium is given by

(*a*) $V = \frac{2\pi r\rho}{I}$ (*b*) $V = \frac{\rho I}{4\pi r}$

(*c*) $V = \frac{2\pi r I}{\rho}$ (*d*) $V = \frac{r\rho}{4\pi I}$

45. The Bouguer anomaly obtained after applying all necessary corrections is due to

(*a*) topographic undulations above the datum

(*b*) increase in densities of crustal rocks with depth

(*c*) lateral density variations

(*d*) vertical density contrast across Moho

46. In a 3-D seismic survey, the bin size for the maximum frequency (f_{max}) of 80 Hz at the target having a reflector dip of 15° and interval velocity of 3600 ms^{-1} is________.

47. A spherical body with its centre located at a depth of 1040 m gives a symmetric residual gravity anomaly high with Δg max = 5.2 mGal. If the same anomaly were to be obtained over a 2-D horizontal cylinder, the depth to the centre of the horizontal cylinder (in m) is________.

48. Analysis of data from a 3-component broadband seismological station yields seismic velocities, V p = 7.0 km/s and V_s = 3.87 km/s for the lower crust. The resulting Poisson's ratio of the lower crustal rocks (rounded to two decimal places) is

(*a*) 0.24 (*b*) 0.26

(*c*) 0.28 (*d*) 0.30

49. Match the geometry of multiple reflections shown in Group I with their corresponding names in Group II.

Group I **Group II**

P. Q. R. S.

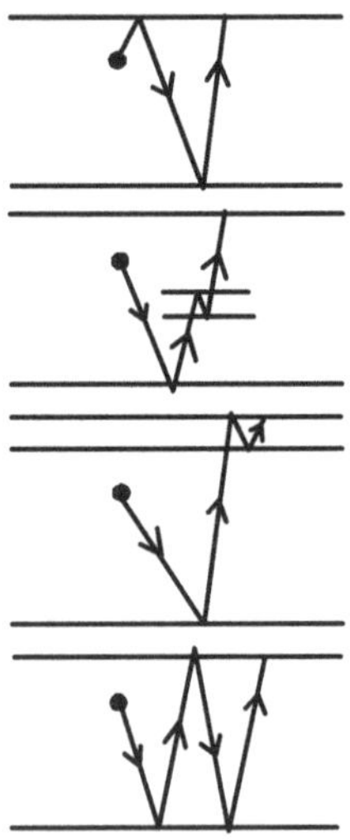

1. peg-leg multiple
2. simple multiple
3. near-surface multiple
4. ghost multiple

(*a*) P-1; Q-4; R-2; S-3 (*b*) P-4; Q-1; R-3; S-2

(*c*) P-2; Q-4; R-1; S-3 (*d*) P-3; Q-1; R-4; S-2

50. TheKönigsberger ratio, Q_n, related to magnetization of rocks is very low (Q_n <<1) for

(*a*) sandstone

(*b*) continental shield rocks

(*c*) oceanic basalt

(*d*) continental volcanic rocks

51. In free-space, the integral from of Faraday's law is expressed as

(*a*) $\oint \vec{H}.\,dl = \varepsilon \int_s \frac{\partial \vec{E}}{\partial t}\,ds$

(*b*) $\oint \vec{E}.\,dl = -\int_s \frac{\partial \vec{B}}{\partial t}\,ds$

(*c*) $\oint \vec{E}.\,ds = 0$

(*d*) $\oint \vec{E}.\,ds = 0$

52. Four point charges, $Q_1 = 40$ nC, $Q_2 = 50$ nC, $Q_3 = 20$ nC, $Q_4 = -60$ nC, are enclosed by a Gaussian surface, S. The next flux crossing S is ______ nC.

(*a*) 1-10 (*b*) 15-25

(*c*) 70-100 (*d*) 800-1000

53. The highest frequency range (in Hz) of an inducing electromagnetic wave that can penetrate up to a depth of 178 m in a medium having a resistivity of 10 Ω -m is (Consider permeability of the medium, = 1).

54. For the given near offset reflection geometry, the RMS velocity (in km/s) to the bottom of the second layer is ________.

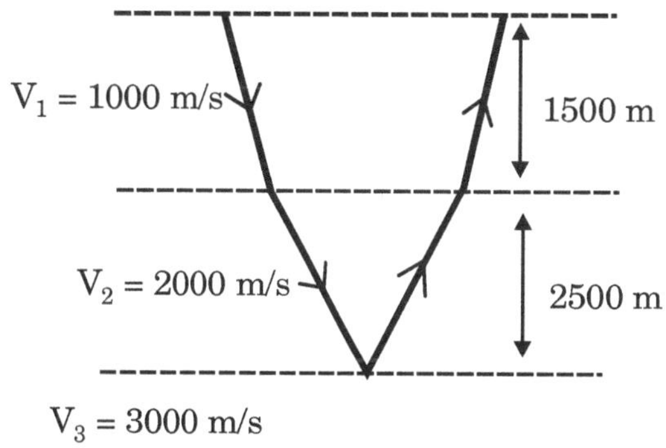

55. In seismic exploration the dynamite source is generally considered to be a wavelet of

(*a*) zero phase

(*b*) minimum phase

(*c*) mixed phase

(*d*) maximum phase

ANSWERS

(General Aptitude)

1. (*a*)	**2.** (*c*)	**3.** (*b*)	**4.** (*b*)	**5.** (*b*)	**6.** (*c*)	**7.** (*c*)	**8.** (*)	**9.** (*c*)	**10.** (*b*)

PART A (Common Part)

1. (*d*)	**2.** (*d*)	**3.** (*b*)	**4.** (*c*)	**5.** (*a*)	**6.** (*a*)	**7.** (*a*)	**8.** (*b*)	**9.** (*b*)	**10.** (*a*)
11. (*)	**12.** (*)	**13.** (*a*)	**14.** (*b*)	**15.** (*d*)	**16.** (*b*)	**17.** (*d*)	**18.** (*d*)	**19.** (*a*)	**20.** (*a*)
21. (*)	**22.** (*a*)	**23.** (*b*)	**24.** (*b*)	**25.** (*d*)					

PART-B (Geology)

26. (*d*)	**27.** (*c*)	**28.** (*c*)	**29.** (*c*)	**30.** (*c*)	**31.** (*)	**32.** (*a*)	**33.** (*c*)	**34.** (*)	**35.** (*)
36. (*b*)	**37.** (*c*)	**38.** (*)	**39.** (*d*)	**40.** (*c*)	**41.** (*b*)	**42.** (*d*)	**43.** (*d*)	**44.** (*a*)	**45.** (*a*)
46. (*a*)	**47.** (*b*)	**48.** (*b*)	**49.** (*b*)	**50.** (*b*)	**51.** (*b*)	**52.** (*a*)	**53.** (*c*)	**54.** (*d*)	**55.** (*a*)

(Geophysics)

26. (*d*)	**27.** (*b*)	**28.** (*c*)	**29.** (*b*)	**30.** (*a*)	**31.** (*a*)	**32.** (*c*)	**33.** (*d*)	**34.** (*)	**35.** (*c*)
36. (*d*)	**37.** (*b*)	**38.** (*b*)	**39.** (*a*)	**40.** (*)	**41.** (*d*)	**42.** (*a*)	**43.** (*c*)	**44.** (*b*)	**45.** (*c*)
46. (*)	**47.** (*)	**48.** (*c*)	**49.** (*b*)	**50.** (*b*)	**51.** (*b*)	**52.** (*)	**53.** (*c*)	**54.** (*)	**55.** (*b*)

EXPLANATIONS

(GENERAL APTITUDE SECTION)

1. Apparent lifelessness harbours dormant life.

   Harbours- To give shelter.

2. The boy from the town was a fish out of water in the sleepy village.

   Fish out of water is an idiom used to refer to a person who is in unfamiliar, and often uncomfortable, surroundings.

3. **Elusive** - difficult to find, catch or achieve.

   Allusive – using or containing suggestion rather than explicit mention.

4. CLIFF<TANYA<ERIC

   It is clear from question, third statement is false.

5. Number of combination is given by

   $${}^{5}C_2 = \frac{n(n-1)}{2} = \frac{5\times 4}{2} = 10$$

6. Increase in productivity necessarily reflects greater efforts made by the employees.

7. Every leader is executive and no manager is leader so manager can be other than leader which is also executive so (I) is false and (II) is also false because some executive which is not leader can be manager. Therefore, neither conclusion I nor II follows.

8. Given, $\frac{RT}{QT} = \frac{5x}{2x}$

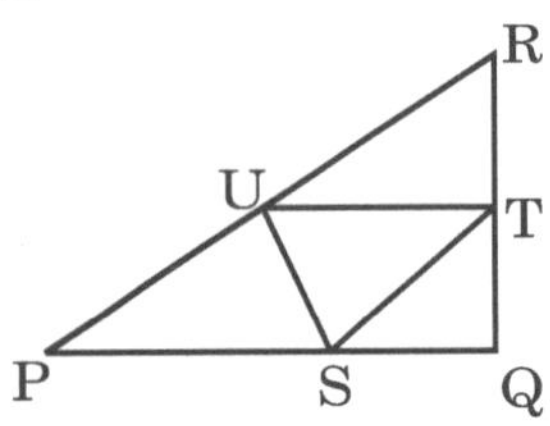

   $\Rightarrow RQ = 7x$

   $\frac{PS}{QS} = \frac{3y}{1y}$

   $\Rightarrow PQ = 4y$

   Area of the triangle $QTS = \frac{1}{2}\times QS\times QT$

   $= \frac{1}{2}\times 1y\times 2x = xy = 20\text{ cm}^2$

   Area of the triangle $PQR = \frac{1}{2}\times PQ\times RQ$

   $= \frac{1}{2}\times 4y\times 7x = 14xy = 14\times 20 = 280\text{ cm}^2$

9. Since, PR is parallel to x-axis and P is right angled therefore, PQ is parallel to y-axis.

   Total number of x-values available is 10

   Total number of y-values available is 11

   At point P

   Coordinate of P can have any value of x and y, hence it can be chosen in = 10 × 11 = 110 ways

   At point Q

   PQ is parallel to y-axis, the value of x-coordinate is already fixed due to point P, hence Q can be chosen in = 10 ways.

   At point R

   PR is parallel to x-axis its y-coordinate is already fixed due to point P, hence point p can be chosen in = 9 ways (not 10 ways as x-coordinate is already occupied by P)

   Total number of ways are given by

   = 110 × 9 × 10 = 9900.

10. X and Y are independent if,

    $P(X\cap Y) = P(X)P(Y)$

    Sample space is 2 × 2 × 2 = 8

    $Y = \{HHT, TTT, HTT, THT\}$

    $P(Y) = \frac{4}{8}$

    $Z = \{HTT, THT, TTH\}$

    $P(Z) = \frac{3}{8}$

    $Y\cap Z = \{HTT, THT\}$

    $P(Y\cap Z) = \frac{2}{8}$

    To check if Y and Z are independent

    $P(Y)P(Z) = \frac{3}{16}$

    $P(Y\cap Z) = \frac{2}{8}$

    Hence, we have

    $P(Y)P(Z) \neq P(Y\cap Z)$

    ∴ Y and Z are dependent.

PART A (COMMON PART)

1. Due to the combined effects of gravity and rotation, the figure of the Earth is not quite a sphere, but instead is slightly flattened in the direction of its axis of rotation. For that an oblate spheroid instead of a sphere often approximates reason, in cartography the Earth.

2. The correct representation of the attitude of bed is Strike direction, dipping amount and dipping direction. It is always noted that there is a 90° difference between the strike direction and dip direction. Thus, the best option is 89°, 75°S.

3. The Hawaiian island were formed by such a hot spot occurring in the middle of the Pacific plate. The Hawaiian Emperor seamount chain is a well known example of a large segment and island chain created by hot spot volcanism. While the hot spot itself is fixed, the plate is moving, so as the plate moved over the hot spot, the string of islands that make up the Hawaiian island chain were formed.

4. The Wenner array consists of four collinear, equally spaced electrodes. The outer two electrodes are typically the current (source) electrodes and the inner two electrodes are the potential (receiver) electrodes. The array spacing expands about the array midpoint while maintaining an equivalent spacing between each electrode.

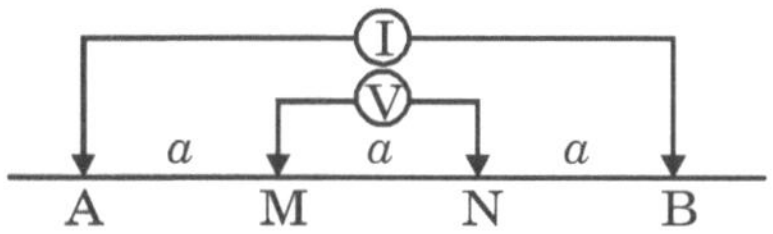

$\rho_A = 2\pi a \frac{V}{I}$

5. In Triclinic crystal system, the three crystallographic axes a, b, c are of unequal lengths with angle between a and $c \neq 90°$.

6. Talus slope is a type in which rock debris piles upto a characteristic angle of repose. When new debris is added to the slope, thereby locally increasing the angle, the slope adjust by movement of the debris to reestablish the angle.

7. **Inclination:** The magnetic vector dips below the horizontal at the angle.

   Declination: It is the angle between the magnetic meridian and the geographic meridian.

8. Self-potential (SP) log is NOT used to determine porosity.

   It is used for detection of permeable beds, determination of Rw, the indication of shaliness of formation, Correlation.

9. The reflected phases PcP and ScS are reflected from the core mantle boundary where 'c' stands for core.

10. The correct order of increasing frequency of different wave in a EM spectrum is Radiowave $(10^2 - 10^8$ Hz$)$ < Microwave $(10^8 - 10^{11}$Hz$)$ < Infrared $(10^{11} - 10^{14}$ Hz$)$ < Visible $(10^{14} - 10^{15}$ Hz$)$ < Ultraviolet $(10^{15} - 10^{18}$ Hz$)$ < X-rays $(10^{18} - 10^{21}$ Hz$)$

11. Given, Crustal rock density, $\rho_c = 2.7$ g/cm^3

    Upper mantle density, $\rho_m = 3.3$ g/cm^3

    Elevation of mountain, $h = 2$ km

    Root depth of mountain, r is given as,

    $$r = \frac{\rho_c}{\rho_m - \rho_c} \times h = \frac{2.7}{3.3 - 2.7} \times 2 = 9 \text{ km}$$

12. Given, For SST

    $V_{P_{SST}} = 2000$ m/s

    $\rho_{SST} = 1.5$ g/cm^3

    For shale

    $V_{P_{shale}} = 2500$ m/s

    $\rho_{shale} = 2.0$ g/cm^3

    The reflection coefficient at the interface of SST and shale is

    $$R = \frac{(V_P \times \rho)_{shale} - (V_P \times \rho)_{SST}}{(V_P \times \rho)_{shale} + (V_P \times \rho)_{SST}}$$

    $$= \frac{2500 \times 2 - 2000 \times 1.5}{2500 \times 2 + 2000 \times 1.5} = 0.25$$

13. Gardner's formula is an empirical equation that relates P-wave velocity to bulk density. Mathematically given as,

    $\rho = \alpha V_P^{\beta}$

    where, ρ is bulk density in g/cm^3

    V_P is P-wave velocity

    α, β is empirically derived constant that depends on the geology.

14. **Half Graben Basin:** Extensional tectonism produce half graben block system whose facies mosaics are influenced by tectonically induced slopes resulting from hanging wall down tilting and footwall uplift.

15. An unconformity is a buried erosional or non-depositional surface separating two rock masses or strata of different ages, indicating that sediment deposition was not continuous. In seismic section, parallel beds are marked by concordant lines which move parallel to the bedding planes.

16.

Names	Attributes
Carlsberg Ridge	Spreading
Ninety- east Ridge	Aseismic
Pranhita- Godavari basin	Rift
Makran Coast	Subduction

17. In India Bituminous coal occurs at Jharia coal field which lie in the Damodar River valley and cover about 110 square miles and is suitable for coke.

18. The time period of simple pendulum given as,

    $T = 2\pi\sqrt{\frac{L}{g}}$

    where, L is the length of pendulum,

    g is the acceleration due to gravity

    At, equator, the value of g is minimum w.r.t to pole. Thus, the time period will be maximum.

19. The most abundant element in the Earth is oxygen found 46.1% in Earth crust and iron found 5.63% in Earth Crust and form the basin of Earth core along with nickel.

20. Curve P denotes the decaying rate of the parent nucleus while curve B leads to growth odf daughter nucleus.

21. Given, Area of Drainage basin = 2×10^6 m^2

Rate of rainfall is 3 mm/h = 3×10^{-3} m/h

Rainfall last for 48 hours, thus the water column made by rainfall for 48 hours is

$3 \times 10^{-3} \times 48 = 144 \times 10^{-3}$ m^3

Therefore, Volume of precipitation

$= 2 \times 10^6 \times 144 \times 10^{-3} = 288000$ m^3

22. The main source of error in computing the orientation of planar features from drill cores is rotation of the core during extraction.

23. Highest permeability in sand rock can be achieved if the sand grains are well sorted and well rounded.

24. Besides N_2 and O_2, all other gases are greenhouse and contribute to hearing of atmosphere.

25. Time-domain electromagnetic data can be used as a static shift correction for magnetotelluric data because the technique does not rely on direct electrical measurements to obtain the apparent resistivity profile with depth.

PART-B (GEOLOGY)

26. The crystallization partial melting both are independent of the composition of sample and melt as all the lowest temperature point in binary system, all the phases crystallize together and the temperature remains constant until all the melt is exhausted.

27. Pleuron is the segmented parts of thorax in trilobite.

28. REEs are incompatible only in apatite is NOT true as REEs are compatible in apatite, only 'Eu' is relatively incompatible in apatite.

29. Anthracite does not have the purely Carbon composition but Graphite and diamond are polymorph having same Carbon composition.

30. Basalts have more feldspars than the peridotites. Therefore, they are abundant in aluminium.

31. $\sin 30 = \frac{100}{x} \Rightarrow x = \frac{100}{\sin 30} = 200\ m$

32. **Assertion (a):** The $^{18}O/^{16}O$ ratio in natural systems can be used as a thermometer.

Reason (r): The fractionation of $^{18}O/^{16}O$ depends on temperature.

Both (a) and (r) are True and (r) is the correct reason for (a).

33. As per figure in the question,

Borehole B1-artesian well with water flowing surface.

Borehole B2- dry well

Borehole B3-well in unconfined aquifer

Borehole B4- artesian well with water not flowing to surface.

34. Let thickness be x km, then

Area = 5.1×10^8 km^2

Volume = 1.29×10^4 km^3

Area × Thickness = volume

$5.1 \times 10^8 \times x = 1.29 \times 10^4$

$$\Rightarrow x = \frac{1.29 \times 10^4}{5.1 \times 10^8} = 0.259 \times 10^{-4} \text{ km}$$

$\Rightarrow x = 2.529$ km

$\Rightarrow x = 5.29$ cm

35. For inverse distance weighted method

$$Z(x_0) = \frac{\sum W_i / Z_i}{\sum 1/Z_i}$$

where, $Z(x)$ is value of unknown point

W_i is grade at known points

Z_i is distances of respective grades from unknown points

$$Z(x_0) = \frac{1.1/1 + 2.2/2 + 3.3/3}{1/1 + 1/2 + 1/3} = \frac{(1.1+1.1+1.1) \times 6}{(6+3+2)}$$

$$= \frac{19.8}{11} = 1.8\ \%$$

36.

HM symbol	Form
$\bar{6}\,2m$	**Ditrigonal Dipyramid**
$3/m$	**Trigonal Dipyramid**
422	**Tetragonal Trapezohedron**
$\bar{4}\,2m$	**Tetragonal Scalenohedron**

37. As per figures in the question. Figure X i.e., optic axis figure is the Apatite mineral and figure Y represents Tourmaline.

38. $$RQD = \frac{\ell_{\text{sum of 10}}}{\ell_{\text{total core length}}} \times 100$$

where, RQD is Rock quality designation

$\ell_{\text{sum of 10}}$ is the sum of the core sticks longer than 10 cm measured along the centre line of the core

$\ell_{\text{total core length}}$ is total of the core length

$$RQD = \frac{30+16+20}{200} \times 100 = 33\ \%$$

39. Interlimb angle and shape of a fold is best studied in the profile section, i.e., section whose pole is the fold axis or section perpendicular to the fold axis.

40. Thrust faults particularly those involved in thickening style of deformation have a so called ramp geometry. Thrust mostly propagate along zones of weakness within a sedimentary sequence such as mudstone or salt layers. These parts of the thrusts are called flats. If the effectiveness of the decollement becomes reduced, the thrust will bend to cut up the section to a higher stratigraphic level until it reaches another effective decollement where it can continue as bedding parallel flat. The part of the thrust linking the two flats is known as ramp and from 15 – 30° to the bedding.

41. Euler poles defined for plate motions of a spherical earth are always perpendicular to the associated transform faults.

42. **Skip mark:** A type of tool mark formed by the intersection at a low angle of an object with a muddy sediment surface, so that the object skips across the surface, producing a linear series of depressions. Skip marks are characterized by their even spacing and crescent shaped marks that left on the bed. Skip marks run parallel to the palaeo-flow and cannot be identified in vertical section.

43. A predominantly siliciclastic Mesozoic stratigraphic unit in mainland Kutch containing Trigonia and abundant plant fossils including Ptillophyllum is Umia Formation.

44. Cumulus texture is aggregates of minerals with not penetrative mineral boundaries.

Exsolution is spindle or lamellae of one mineral in another.

Caries texture is protuberances of replacing mineral with replaced host.

Cockade texture is banding and crustification in texture open spaces.

45. Sapropelic coal is a potential source rock of oil. Sapropelic coal, hydrogen-rich coal, including cannel coal and boghead coal (see torbanite), derived from sapropels (loose deposits of sedimentary rock rich in hydrocarbons) and characterized by a dull black, sometimes waxy lustre. Sapropelic coals are rich in liptinites (microscopic organic matter derived from waxy or resinous plant parts) and have high yields of volatile matter.

46. Bailadila group in Madhya Pradesh has the best quality of iron content in BIF in the world.

Nallamalai group of Cuddapah basin contains Pb-Zn deposits. It is in Andhra Pradesh.

Udaipur group of Rajesthan contains phosphorite deposits

Sausar group of Singhbhum has Mn deposits.

47.

Igneous bodies	Craton
Utala Granite	Aravalli craton
Dalma Volcanics	Singbhum craton
Chamundi Granite	Dharwar craton
Bijli Rhyolite	Bastar craton

48. Hydrous molecules generally absorbs visible spectrum short infrared and are reflected by the hydrous molecules of plants.

49. The symbols are given according to their shape.

The exact match is P-3; Q-4; R-1; S-2

These porphyroclasts are formed by the deformation

50. **Translation:** An operations that generate a pattern at regular time intervals.

Reflection: Operation when the reflection of a 2-D object occurs across the plane.

Glide: It is a two-step operation, Reflection followed by translation.

51. It is reverse fault as the Fault FF caused the shortening of the footwall side and broadening of the hanging wall side.

52. The sets of isotopic ratios contains only those that change with time is

$$^{87}Sr/^{86}Sr,\ ^{143}Nd/^{144}Nd,\ ^{207}Pb/^{206}Pb,\ ^{147}Sm/^{144}Nd$$

53. A sandstone containing mainly lithic fragments, which is known as lithic arenite.

54. Pyralspite garnet + omphacite + kyanite are the index mineral of ecologite facies.

55. The maximum velocity of the Indian Plate is observed in Maldives

(GEOPHYSICS)

26. Shale is more conducting than sandstone therefore, giving relatively less resistivity than sandstone. Moreover, wet shale also results in lower resistivity than saturated sandstone, while impermeable granite has relatively highest resistivity.

$$\rho_{\text{wet shale}} < \rho_{\text{water saturated SST}} < \rho_{\text{impermeable granite}}$$

The type of curve is A-type i.e., Ascending type.

27. Static-shift is defined as vertical displacements of apparent resistivity curves, between adjacent sites or between the two curves at one site, without other differences in either the shapes of the curves or the phases. The implication is that the offset is a result of conductivity feature at surfaces or any conductivity discontinuities.

28. Removal of all periods shorter than Nyquist period is the removal of all frequencies higher than Nyquist frequency. Therefore, we have to remove higher frequency component and hence we need low pass filter.

29. The relation between magnetic flux density $\vec{B}$ and the magnetic vector potential $\vec{A}$ is given as $\vec{B} = \vec{\nabla} \times \vec{A}$

30. The frequency range that defines dead band in magnetotelluric source signal is (0.1 – 10) Hz, which generally corresponds to low amplitude signal and is attributable to inductive source mechanism.

31. Given,

Number of channels = 48

Receiver spacing = 50

Shot spacing = 100 m

Now, As per definition

$$\text{Fold} = \frac{1}{2} \times \text{Number of channels} \times \frac{\text{Receiver spacing}}{\text{Shot spacing}}$$

$$= \frac{1}{2} \times 48 \times \frac{50}{100} = 12 \text{ fold}$$

32. The part of the field of internal origin, obtained by subtracting the field of the inclined geocentric dipole from the total field, is collectively called the non-dipole field. A map of the non-dipole field consists of a system of irregularly sized, long wavelength magnetic anomalies.

33. Analytic signal is a complex valued function that has no negative frequency components. The real and imaginary parts of an analytic signal are real valued function related to each other by the Hilbert transform.

If S is signal, then its analytic signal is

$$S_a(t) = S(t) + iH[S(t)]$$

where, $S_a(t)$ is analytic signal of $S(t)$

$$H[S(t)] = \sin\left(wt - \frac{\pi}{2}\right) = -\cos wt$$

$$\Rightarrow S_a(t) = S(t) + iH[S(t)]$$

$$= (\sin wt - i\cos wt)$$

$$= (i\sin wt - i^2 \cos wt)/i$$

$$= -i(\cos wt + i\sin wt)$$

$$\Rightarrow S_a(t) = -ie^{iwt}$$

34. The signal given consists of 30 Hz, 50 Hz and 70 Hz frequencies of which 70 Hz is the maximum frequency. Therefore, in order to avoid aliasing, we have the highest frequency i.e., the Nyquist frequency which is twice of the maximum frequency i.e., 140 Hz.

35. Assertion (a): The Gutenberg-Richter frequency-magnitude relation of earthquakes globally suggests that subduction zones in general are characterized by lower b-values (b-value is slope of frequency-magnitude relation) when compared to the mid-oceanic ridges.

Reason (r): Earthquakes in the subduction zones occur at deeper focal depths also, whereas, earthquakes along mid-oceanic ridges occur at shallow focal depths.

Both the Assertion and Reason are independently true, one dealing with the frequency of earthquake occurring while other deals with the depth at which the earthquakes occurs.

36. As per the given data in the question, the mantle doesn't produce the highest radiogenic heat.

37. Reduction to the pole (RTP): Removing the dependence of magnetic data on the magnetic inclination, i.e., converting data that have been recorded in the inclined Earth's magnetic field to what they would have looked like if the magnetic field had been vertical. Reduction to the pole removes anomaly asymmetry caused by inclination and locates anomalies above the causative bodies, assuming that the remanent magnetism is small compared to the induced magnetism. It is difficult to do at low magnetic inclinations, in which case reduction to the equator is preferred.

38. After migration, anticline structure is tighter while the syncline structure is broader as migration moves in updip direction.

39. Low self-potential (SP) and high resistivity value on the log is an indication of clean, thick hydrocarbon bearing sandstone.

40. Given,

Transit time of formation, $\Delta t_{log} = 70\mu s$

Transit time of the matrix, $\Delta t_{ma} = 55\mu s$

Transit time of the fluid, $\Delta t_f = 190$ s

Now, As per formula of sonic porosity

$$\phi_s = \frac{\Delta t_{log} - \Delta t_{ma}}{\Delta t_f - \Delta t_{ma}} = \frac{70 - 55}{190 - 55} = \frac{15}{135} = 0.11$$

41. As per the condition of a matrix. For a matrix A, the condition number is the product of the norm of A and the norm of A inverse. Condition number depends on the underlying norm. However, regardless of the norm, it is always greater or equal to 1.

42.

Inverse problem	Solution
Overdetermined	$m = \left[G^T G\right]^{-1} G^T d$
Underdetermined	$m = G^T \left[GG^T\right]^{-1} d$
Mixed determined	$m = \left[G^T G + K^2 I\right]^{-1} G^T d$
Even determined	$m = G^{-1} d$ $(N = M, rank\ of\ G = N)$

43. In frequency domain IP, the apparent resistivity measured at DC limit is $f \approx 0.05\text{-}0.5$ Hz and at AC limit is $F \approx 1\text{-}10$ Hz.

44. For a subsurface point source of current in homogenous medium, the area enclosed by it is $4\pi r^2$.

The electric field of lines is given as

$$E = \rho J = \rho \frac{I}{4\pi r^2}$$

where, J is the current density = $\frac{\text{Current}}{\text{Area}}$

Now, Electric Potential is given as,

$$E = \frac{-dV}{dr} = \rho \frac{I}{4\pi r^2}$$

$$\Rightarrow dV = -\rho \frac{I}{4\pi r^2} dr$$

Integrating both sides

$$\Rightarrow \int_0^V dV = \frac{\rho I}{4\pi} \int_0^r \frac{dr}{r^2}$$

$$\Rightarrow V = \frac{\rho I}{4\pi r}$$

45. The gravity anomalies obtained after applying all necessary corrections is always due to lateral density variation.

46. Given, Interval Velocity, V_{in} = 3600 m/s

Amount of reflector dip, θ = 15°

Maximum frequency, f_{max} = 80 Hz

Now, As per definition of Bin size,

$$B = \frac{V_{in}}{4 f_{\max} \sin\theta}$$

$$= \frac{3600}{4 \times 80 \times \sin 15^o}$$

$$= 43.46$$

47. The depth to the center of a spherical body from its gravity anomaly is given as,

$Z = 0.652 \times W$

where, W is Half-width/Half Height width for spherical body

For a two dimensional horizontal body, the depth to the centre of the body is given as

$Z = 0.5 \times W'$

where, W' is Half Height Width for cylindrical body

Now, as per question,

For a spherical body

Z = 1040 m

$$\therefore W = \frac{1040}{0.552}$$

$$= 1595.09 \text{ m}$$

For the two dimensional horizontal body with same maximum gravity, anomaly is given as

$Z = 0.5 \times W$

$= 0.5 \times 1595.09$

$= 795.5$ m

48. Given,

V_P = 7.0 km/s

V_S = 3.87 km/s

As per definition of Poisson's ratio in terms of velocities is

$$\sigma = \frac{1}{2}\left[\frac{\left(\frac{V_P}{V_S}\right)^2 - 2}{\left(\frac{V_P}{V_S}\right)^2 - 1}\right]$$

$$\therefore \sigma = \frac{1}{2}\left[\frac{\left(\frac{7.0}{3.87}\right)^2 - 2}{\left(\frac{7.0}{3.87}\right)^2 - 1}\right]$$

$$= \frac{1}{2} \times \left(\frac{1.2717}{2.2717}\right) = 0.279 \approx 0.28$$

49.

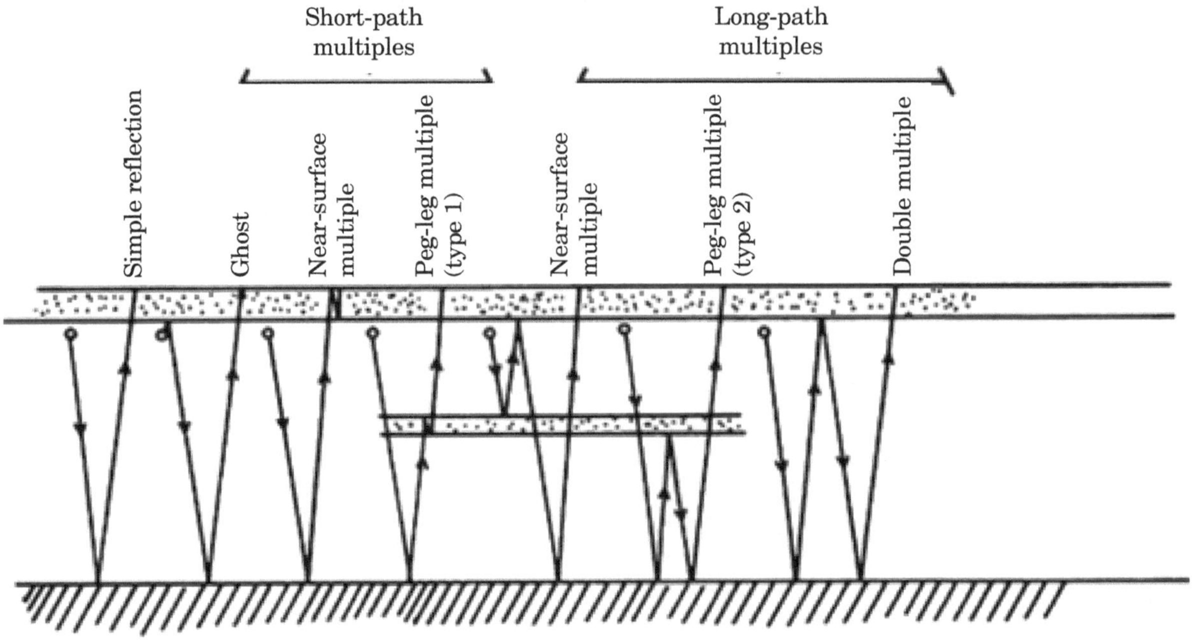

50. Koenigsberger Ratio Q_n is defined as the ratio in a rock of remanent magnetization to the induced magnetization in the Earth's field. It is used as a measure of stability to indicate rock's capability of maintaining a stable remanence.

For continental shield rock which is of granitic composition and consist of sediments or metasediments, induced magnetization is dominant which leads to very low value of Q_n.

51. The integral form of Faraday's law of electromagnetic induction relates the line integral of the electric field to the surface integral of magnetic flux changes through a closed surface area,

$$\vec{E}dl = -\int_S \left(\frac{\partial \vec{B}}{\partial t}\right)$$

where, –ve sign gives the direction of the electromotive force and is found by Lenz's law.

52. The net flux crossing the Gaussian surface S, enclosing four charges Q_1, Q_2, Q_3 and Q_4 is the sum of all four charges.

Therefore, Net Flux = $Q_1 + Q_2 + Q_3 - Q_4$

$= 40 + 50 + 20 - 60 = 50\ nc$

53. Given, $Z = 178$ m

$\rho = 10\ \Omega m$

Now, The skin depth is given as,

$$Z = 503\sqrt{\frac{\rho}{f}}$$

$$\Rightarrow f = \frac{503^2 \rho}{Z^2}$$

where, f is the frequency of inducing *em* waves

$$\therefore f = \frac{503^2 \times 10}{178^2} = 79.8\ Hz$$

54. Given,

$V_1 = 1000$ m/s

$V_2 = 2000$ m/s

$V_3 = 3000$ m/s

$h_1 = 1500$ m

$h_2 = 2500$ m

$$t_1 = \frac{h_1}{V_1} = \frac{1500}{1000} = 1.5 \text{ sec}$$

$$t_2 = \frac{h_2}{V_2} = \frac{2500}{2000} = 1.25 \text{ sec}$$

$$\therefore V_{rms} = \sqrt{\frac{V_1^2 t_1 + V_2^2 t_2 + V_3^2 t_3 + ...}{t_1 + t_2 + t_3 + ...}}$$

$$\Rightarrow V_{rms} = \sqrt{\frac{1000^2 \times 1.5 + 2000^2 \times 2.5}{1.5 + 2.5}} = 153 \text{ km/sec.}$$

55. Minimum Phase Wavelet: The minimum phase wavelet has a short time duration and a concentration of energy at the start of the wavelet. It is zero before time zero (causal). An ideal seismic source would be a spike (maximum amplitude at every frequency), but the best practical one would be minimum phase. It is quite common to convert a given wavelet source wavelet into it's minimum phase equivalent since several processing stages (e.g. predictive deconvolution) work best by assuming that the input data is minimum phase.

GENERAL APTITUDE (GA)

Q. 1 – Q. 5 carry one mark each.

1. Choose the most appropriate word from the options given below to complete the following sentence.

A person suffering from Alzheimer's disease short-term memory loss.

(*a*) experienced (*b*) has experienced
(*c*) is experiencing (*d*) experiences

2. Choose the most appropriate word from the options given below to complete the following sentence.

___________ is the key to their happiness; they are satisfied with what they have.

(*a*) Contentment (*b*) Ambition
(*c*) Perseverance (*d*) Hunger

3. Which of the following options is the closest in meaning to the sentence below?

"As a woman, I have no country."

(*a*) Women have no country.
(*b*) Women are not citizens of any country.
(*c*) Women's solidarity knows no national boundaries.
(*d*) Women of all countries have equal legal rights

4. In any given year, the probability of an earthquake greater than Magnitude 6 occurring in the Garhwal Himalayas is 0.04. The average time between successive occurrences of such earthquakes is ____ years.

5. The population of a new city is 5 million and is growing at 20% annually. How many years would it take double at this growth rate?

(*a*) 3-4 years (*b*) 4-5 years
(*c*) 5-6 years (*d*) 6-7 years

Q. 6 – Q. 10 carry two marks each.

6. In a group of four children, Som is younger to Riaz. Shiv is elder to Ansu. Ansu is youngest in the group. Which of the following statements is/are required to find the eldest child in the group?

Statements

1. Shiv is younger to Riaz.
2. Shiv is elder to Som.

(*a*) Statement 1by itself determines the eldest child.
(*b*) Statement 2 by itself determines the eldest child.
(*c*) Statements 1 and 2 are both required to determine the eldest child.
(*d*) Statements 1 and 2 are not sufficient to determine the eldest child.

7. Moving into a world of big data will require us to change our thinking about the merits of exactitude. To apply the conventional mindset of measurement to the digital, connected world of the twenty-first century is to miss a crucial point. As mentioned earlier, the obsession with exactness is an artefact of the information-deprived analog era. When data was sparse, every data point was critical, and thus great care was taken to avoid letting any point bias the analysis. From "BIG DATA" Viktor Mayer-Schonberger and Kenneth Cukier The main point of the paragraph is:

(*a*) The twenty-first century is a digital world
(*b*) Big data is obsessed with exactness
(*c*) Exactitude is not critical in dealing with big data
(*d*) Sparse data leads to a bias in the analysis

8. The total exports and revenues from the exports of a country are given in the two pie charts below. The pie chart for exports shows the quantity of each item as a percentage of the total quantity of exports. The pie chart for the revenues shows the percentage of the total revenue generated through export of each item. The total quantity of exports of all the items is 5 lakh tonnes and the total revenues are 250 crore rupees. What is the ratio of the revenue generated through export of Item 1 per kilogram to the revenue generated through export of Item 4 per kilogram?

Exports

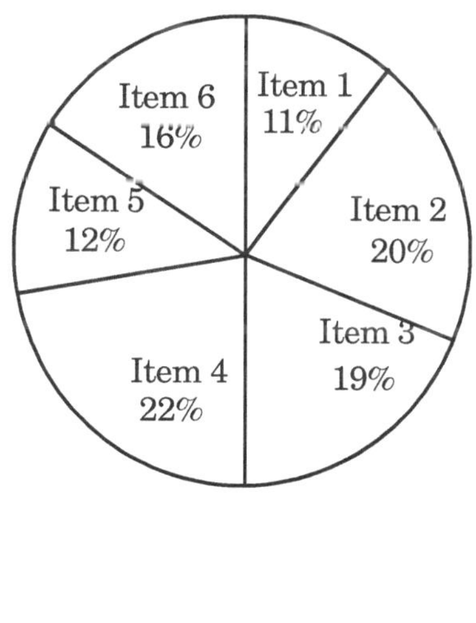

Revenues

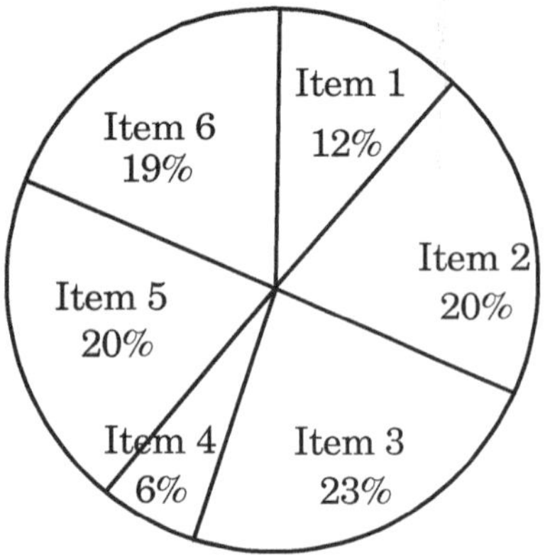

(a) 1 : 2 (b) 2 : 1

(c) 1 : 4 (d) 4 : 1

9. X is 1 km northeast of Y. Y is 1 km southeast of Z. W is 1 km west of Z. P is 1 km south of W. Q is 1 km east of P. What is the distance between X and Q in km?

(a) 12 (b) $\sqrt{2}$

(c) $\sqrt{3}$ (d) 2

10. 10% of the population in a town is HIV^+. A new diagnostic kit for HIV detection is available; this kit correctly identifies HIV^+ individuals 95% of the time, and HIV^- individuals 89% of the time. A particular patient is tested using this kit and is found to be positive. The probability that the individual is actually positive is ______

PART-A (Common Part)

Q. 1 – Q. 25 carry one mark each.

1. Which one of the following planets has the highest bulk density?

(a) Jupiter (b) Venus

(c) Quartz (d) Muscovite

2. Mid-Oceanic ridges mark __________ plate margins and can be traced by belts of ______ focus earthquakes.

(a) constructive, shallow

(b) destructive, shallow

(c) constructive, deep

(d) destructive, deep

3. From the surface to the Earth's interior, the velocity of P-wave decreases and the material density increases at the boundary between

(a) Outer core and inner core

(b) Mantle and outer core

(c) Crust and mantle

(d) Upper crust and lower crust

4. The following gamma ray (GR) log data are recorded in a borehole:

GR log value against a formation = 30 API units,

Maximum GR log value = 45 API units,

Minimum GR log value = 20 API units.

What is the fraction of shale in the formation?

(a) 0.33 (b) 0.40

(c) 0.66 (d) 0.75

5. Cirques are formed by

(a) glaciers (b) rivers

(c) lakes (d) oceans

6. During which of the following geological eras did birds and mammals first appear on the Earth?

(a) Cenozoic (b) Mesozoic.

(c) Paleozoic (d) Proterozoic

7. Select the copper ore minerals from the following:

(P) Chalcopyrite (Q) Pyrite

(R) Pyrrhotite (S) Bornite

(T) Sphalerite (U) Chalcocite

(a) P, S, U (b) P, Q, R

(c) S, T, U (d) Q, R, U

8. The reflection coefficient at the interface between two layers of resistivities 9Ωm and 1Ωm respectively is

(a) 0.6 (b) 0.7

(c) 0.8 (d) 0.9

9. In electromagnetic (EM) sounding, the depth of investigation ________ with increasing frequency.

(a) increases

(b) decreases

(c) remains unchanged

(d) varies randomly

10. The International Gravity Formula predicts the theoretical gravity value at a given point assuming a

(a) non-rotating homogeneous spherical earth model

(b) decreases rotating inhomogeneous spherical earth model

(c) rotating homogeneous oblate spheroidal earth model

(d) rotating inhomogeneous oblate spheroidal earth model

11. The diurnal variation of geomagnetic elements is due to a system of electric currents flowing in the

(a) ionosphere

(b) Earth's outer core

(c) inter-planetary medium

(d) oceans

12. Match the mineral deposits (listed in Group I) with the most appropriate geophysical exploration methods (listed in Group II)

Group I	Group II
P. Mineralized conductive veins	1. Gravity
Q. Disseminated sulphides	2. Magnetic
R. Massive barytes	3. Induced Polarization
S. Kimberlite pipes	4. Resistivity profiling
	5. Low frequency Magnetotellurics

(a) P-4; Q-3; R-1; S-5
(b) P-2; Q-1; R-4; S-5
(c) P-5; Q-1; R-4; S-3
(d) P-4; Q-3; R-1; S-2

13. In seismic refraction surveys, the critical distance
(*a*) is always less than the crossover distance
(*b*) is always more than the crossover distance
(*c*) is always equal to the crossover distance
(*d*) cannot be compared with the crossover distance

14. As compared to large earthquakes, small earthquakes are
(a) more frequent and caused by short fault slip and long rupture lengths
(b) more frequent and caused by long fault slip and short rupture lengths
(c) less frequent and caused by short fault slip and short rupture lengths
(d) more frequent and caused by short fault slip and short rupture lengths

15. Match the type of well logs (listed in Group I) with the characteristics of measurement (listed in Group II).

Group I	Group II
P. Dipmeter	1. Hydrogen concentration in pores
Q. Neutron	2. Velocity of compressional waves
R. SP	3. Correlation of resistivity changes
S. Sonic	4. Natural radioactivity
	5. Natural electric potential

(*a*) P – 3; Q – 1; R – 5; S – 2
(*b*) P – 4; Q – 1; R – 5; S – 3
(*c*) P – 3; Q – 4; R – 5; S – 2
(*d*) P – 3; Q – 1; R – 4; S – 2

16. For earthquakes of magnitudes 6 and 7, the seismic wave amplitudes are A 6 and A 7 and the radiated energies are E 6 and E 7 respectively. Which one of the following is true?

(*a*) $A_7 \approx \left(\frac{7}{6}\right)A_6$ and $E_7 \approx 10E_6$

(*b*) $A_7 \approx 10A_6$ and $E_7 \approx 100E_6$

(*c*) $A_7 \approx 10A_6$ and $E_7 \approx \left(\frac{7}{6}\right)E_6$

(*d*) $A_7 \approx 10A_6$ and $E_7 \approx 32E_6$

17. Structure contours of a bedding plane at 100 m interval are spaced in such a manner that the horizontal equivalent is also 100m. The dip of the bedding plane is
(a) 30° (b) 45°
(c) 60° (d) 90°

18. Horizontal slickensides are observed on the surface of a vertical fault. What is the type of fault?
(*a*) Normal fault (*b*) Reverse fault
(*c*) Strike-slip fault (*d*) Oblique fault

19. Match the mineral habits (listed in Group I) with the minerals (listed in Group II)

Group I	Group II
P. Acicular	1. Kyanite
Q. Fibrous	2. Beryl
R. Bladed	3. Sillimanite
S. Columnar	4. Chrysotil
	5. Olivine

(*a*) P-3; Q-2; R-5; S-1
(*b*) P-4; Q-5; R-1; S-2
(*c*) P-2; Q-3; R-4; S-1
(*d*) P-3; Q-4; R-1, S-2

20. The correct chronological order (older to younger) of the following volcanic events is
(P) Rajmahal volcanism
(Q) Deccan volcanism
(R) Panjal volcanism
(S) Malani volcanism
(*a*) P, Q, R, S (*b*) S, R, Q, P
(*c*) S, R, P, Q (*d*) S, Q, R, P

21. A clastic rock dominantly composed of feldspar grains is
(*a*) shale (*b*) arenite
(*c*) greywacke (*d*) arkose

22. A metamorphic rock consists of pyroxene, plagioclase and quartz, and exhibits hornfelsic texture.

The rock has undergone________ metamorphism.

(*a*) regional (*b*) contact
(*c*) cataclastic (*d*) impact

23. An igneous body with a flat top and a concave-upward base is known as a

(*a*) laccolith (*b*) lopolith
(*c*) sill (*d*) stock

24. The velocity discontinuity between the upper crust and the lower crust is known as __________ discontinuity.

(*a*) Lehmann (*b*) Gütenber
(*c*) Mohorovicic (*d*) Conrad

25. Match the items listed in Group I with those in Group II

Group I	Group II
P. Isopachs	1. Contours of equal slope
Q. Isotherms	2. Contours of equal thickness
R. Isochrons	3. Contours of equal temperature
S. Isotans	4. Contours of equal core thickness
	5. Contours of equal age

(*a*) P-2; Q-3; R-1; S-5 (*b*) P-2; Q-3; R-5; S-1
(*c*) P-1; Q-3; R-2; S-4 (*d*) P-5; Q-4; R-3; S-1

PART-B
GEOLOGY

Q. 26 – Q. 55 carry two marks each.

26. Stylolitic foliation developed during diagenetic processes is typically

Group I	Group II
P. Interference colour	1. Property of a single grain seen under microscope in polarized light
Q. Twinkling	2. Property of a single grain seen under microscope under crossed nicols
R. Pleochroism	3. Property seen when several grains are viewed collectively under microscope in polarized light
S. Play of colours	4. Property of a mineral seen in hand specimen

(*a*) P-2; Q-3; R-1; S-4 (*b*) P-2; Q-3; R-4; S-1
(*c*) P-3; Q-4; R-1; S-2 (*d*) P-1; Q-4; R-2; S-3

27. Which one of the following represents a closed crystallographic form?

(*a*) Hexagonal prism
(*b*) Hexagonal dipyramid
(*c*) Tetragonal pyramid
(*d*) Ditetragonal prism

28. In the figure given below a, b and c are the crystallographic axes of a crystal. The Miller Index of the crystal face PQR is:

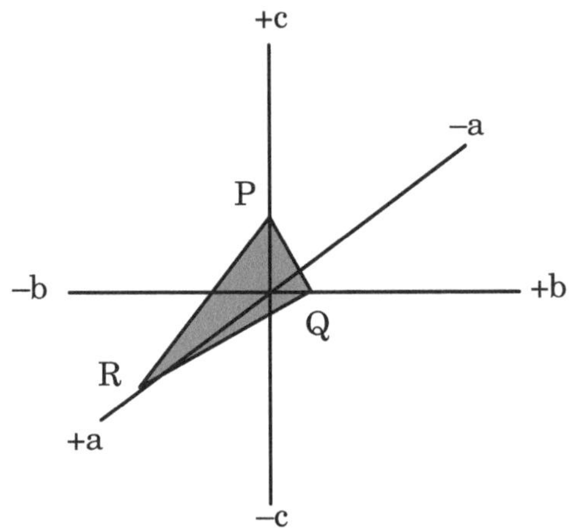

(*a*) (421) (*b*) (124)
(*c*) (142) (*d*) (214)

29. Match the alkaline rocks listed in Group I with their characteristics listed in Group II

Group I	Group II
P. Basanite	1. Volcanic rock lacking feldspar
Q. Nephelinite	2. Ultrapotasic volcanic rock
R. Shonshonite	3. Feldspathoid-bearing basalt
S. Lamproite	4. K-rich basalt

(*a*) P-4; Q-1; R-3; S-3
(*b*) P-1; Q-2; R-3; S-4
(*c*) P-3; Q-1; R-4; S-2
(*d*) P-2; Q-1; R-4; S-3

30. In a metamorphic terrain, crenulations at the hinge zone of a fold along with the development of axial plane foliation is an evidence of

(*a*) one phase of deformation
(*b*) at least two phases of deformation
(*c*) no deformation
(*d*) extensional regime of the deformation

31. A phase-diagram with a specified bulk-composition is known as

(*a*) isograd diagram
(*b*) AFM diagram
(*c*) pseudosection
(*d*) ACF diagram

32. The uniaxial interference figure of a mineral given below shows the changes in the position of color bands when a mica plate is inserted in the accessory slot of the microscope as shown. The changes in the interference figure are due to

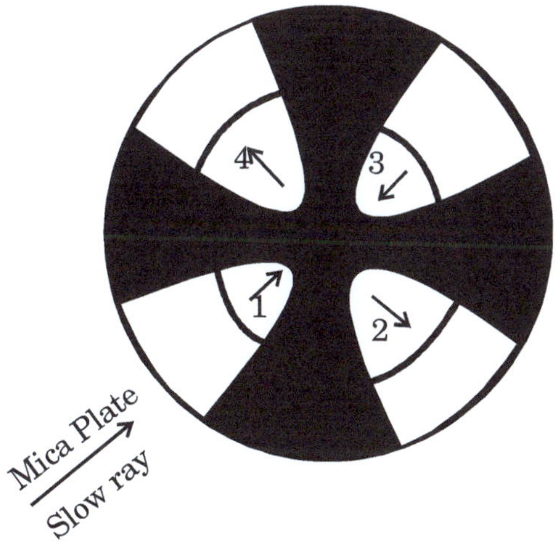

(*a*) increase in retardation along the quadrants 1 and 3

(*b*) increase in retardation along the quadrants 2 and 4

(*c*) decrease in retardation along the quadrants 1 and 3

(*d*) increase in retardation in all quadrants

33. The relative enrichment factors (? values) of sulphur isotopes of two sulphide minerals A and B in equilibrium with H 2 S at the same P-T-X conditions are +5.9 ‰and –11.2 ‰respectively. If A and B are in equilibrium under the same P-T-X conditions and d 34 S value of A is +6.8 ‰ then the d 34 S value of B is

(*a*) –10.3 % (*b*) +10.3 %

(*c*) –9.3 % (*d*) +9.3 %

34. If $Fe^{2+} \longrightarrow Fe^{3+} + c$, $E^0 = +0.77$ volt , Eh = 0.6 volt, $K = \frac{[Fe^{3+}]}{[Fe^{2+}]}$ and the basic equation to be used is $Eh = E^0 + \frac{0.059}{n} \log K$, then the value of $\frac{Fe^{2+}}{Fe^{3+}}$ ratio in the solution is ________.

35. In an ore mine exposing stratified sulfide ore with sulfide bands having thickness between 10 and 100 cm, which one of the following sampling methods is the most appropriate?

(*a*) Chip sampling

(*b*) Channel sampling

(*c*) Bulk sampling

(*d*) Grab sampling

36. From the given Eh-pH diagram, which one of the following pairs can be inferred to be a di-sequilibrium assemblage

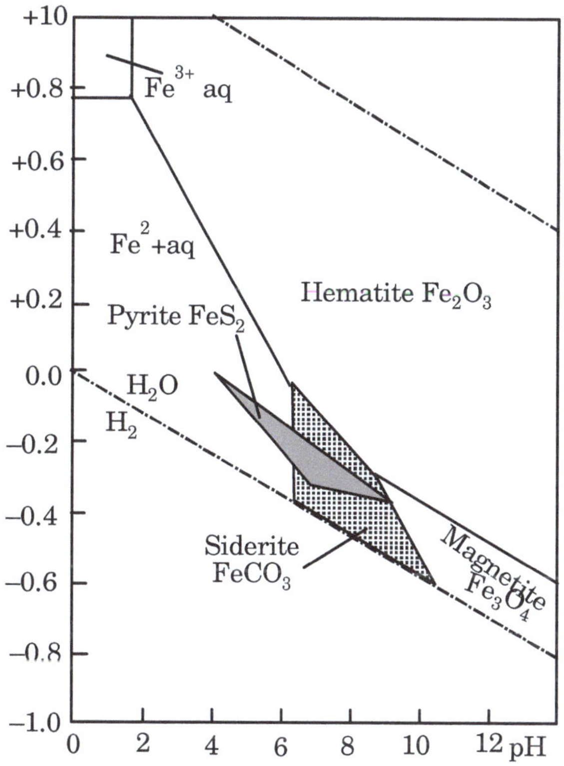

(*a*) Hematite-magnetite

(*b*) Magnetite-pyrite

(*c*) Pyrite-siderite

(*d*) Hematite-pyrite

37. Metal content (in metric tonnes) of an ore having specific gravity and assay values of 2.86 and 1.49 % respectively in a mining block 40 m long, 30 m wide and with an average thickness of 2.13 m is ________.

38. From the list of planktic foraminifera below, the pair having a supplementary sutural aperture is

(P) Globigerina (Q) Globorotalia

(R) Globigerinoides (S) Orbulina

(*a*) P, Q (*b*) Q, R

(*c*) P, R (*d*) R, S

39. Match the morphological features (listed in Group I) with the corresponding fossils (listed in Group II)

Group I	Group II
P. Callus	1. Graptolite
Q. Cusp	2. Gastropod
R. Sicula	3. Conodont
S. Calyx	4. Foraminifer
	5. Trilobite
	6. Coral

(*a*) P-2; Q-3; R-1; S-6 (*b*) P-5; Q-3; R-1; S-2
(*c*) P-3; Q-1; R-4; S-2 (*d*) P-2; Q-3; R-4; S-6

40. Which one of the following marine environments is indicated by the assemblage of benthic foraminifera

(*a*) Abyssal (*b*) Bathyal
(*c*) Shelf (*d*) Hadal

41. The correct chronological order (older to younger) of the following geological units is

(P) Talchir Tillite
(Q) Muth Quartzite
(R) Umia Ammonites Bed
(S) Umaria Marine Bed

(*a*) P-R-S-Q (*b*) Q-P-S-R
(*c*) R-Q-P-S (*d*) P-Q-R-S

42. The best match of terms in Group I with those in Group II is

Group I	**Group II**
P. Alkali reaction	1. Tunnelling in hard rocks
Q. Arching	2. Earth dam
R. Rip rap	3. Concrete aggregate
S. Clay core	4. Surface slope protection
	5. Concrete gravity dam

(*a*) P-4; Q-5; R-1; S-3 (*b*) P-5; Q-4; R-2; S-3
(*c*) P-3; Q-1; R-4; S-2 (*d*) P-1; Q-3; R-4; S-2

43. Knick points indicate changes in the

(*a*) attitude of beds (*b*) strike of a fault
(*c*) attitude of joints (*d*) stream gradient

44. A confined sandy aquifer has a thickness of 10 m and transmissivity of 0.75 m^2 per day. Its hydraulic conductivity is __________m/day.

45. A geological reconnaissance survey is being carried out using remote sensing multispectral data. Which set of the two band data of the following is most appropriate for mapping limonite bearing zones?

(*a*) Near infrared band and Thermal infrared band image data
(*b*) Blue band and Red band image data
(*c*) Shortwave infrared band and Thermal infrared image data
(*d*) Thermal infrared band and X-band radar image data

46. The maximum amount of hydrogen (dry mineral matter free basis) in bituminous-anthracite is

(*a*) less than 10% (*b*) 10-15%
(*c*) 15-20% (*d*) 20-25%

47. The standard free energy change (in kJ) at 25°C of the dissolution of anhydrite at equilibrium in the equation $CaSO_4 \rightleftharpoons Ca^{2+} + SO_4^{2-}$, given K = 3.4×10^{-5} and R = 8.314 J/mol/K, is

(*a*) 43.7
(*b*) 37.4
(*c*) 30.2
(*d*) 25.5

48.

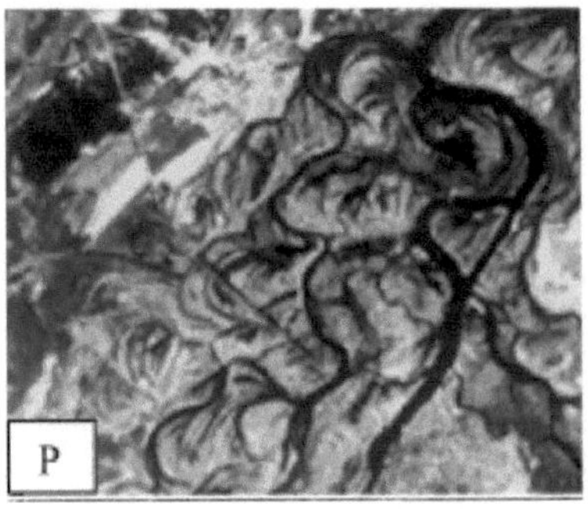

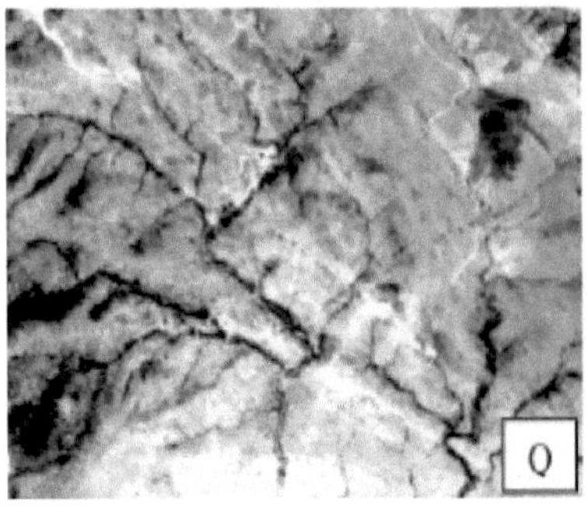

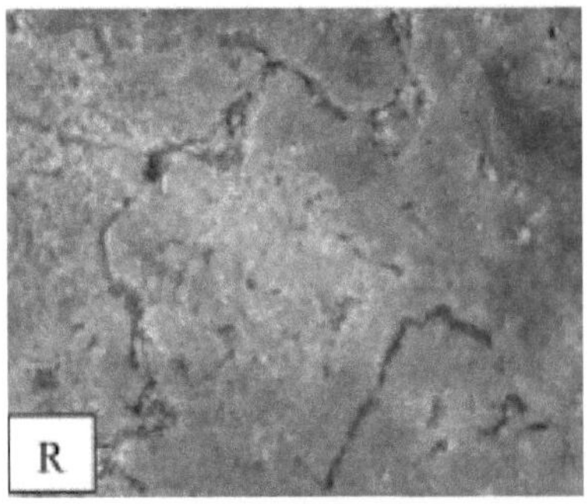

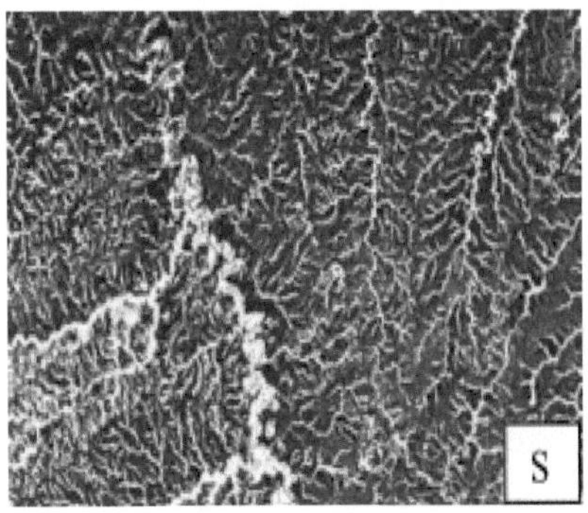

Drainage patterns observed in four areas are shown in black-and-white panchromatic images P, Q, R and S. Field work in these areas has indicated presence of the following lithology/ geological unit.

1. Fractured quartzite
2. Shale
3. Limestone
4. Alluvial plain

The correct match of the drainage patterns with the lithology/geological unit is

(*a*) P-1; Q-2; R-4; S-3

(*b*) P-4; Q-1; R-3; S-2

(*c*) P-4; Q-1; R-2; S-3

(*d*) P-2; Q-1; R-3; S-4

49.

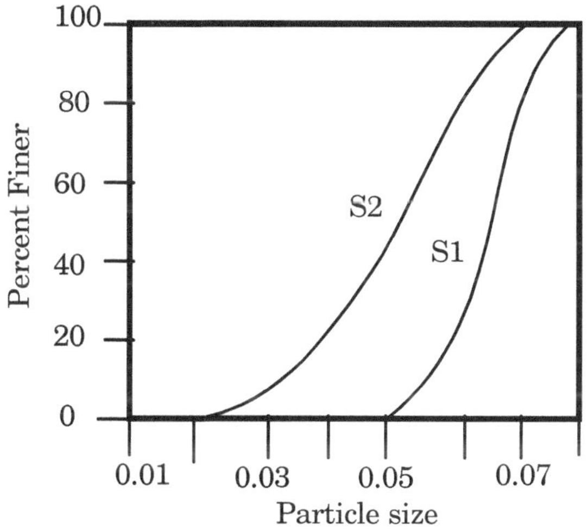

The given figure shows the grain size distribution of two soil samples S1 and S2. The uniformity coefficient is defined as $\frac{d_{60}}{d_{10}}$, where d_{60} and d_{10} represent particle sizes corresponding to 60 and 10 percent finer respectively. Determine the correctness or otherwise of the Assertion (a) and Reason (r).

Assertion (a): S1 has a higher value of uniformity coefficient than S2.

Reason (r): S1 has less variation in grain-size than S2.

(*a*) Both (a) and (r) are true, and (r) is the correct reason for (a).

(*b*) Both (a) and (r) are false.

(*c*) (a) is false but (r) is true, (r) being not the correct reason for (a).

(*d*) (a) is true but (r) is false.

50. The geological map given below shows beds in a normal stratigraphic order. Which one of the following statements is true in respect of features near locations P and Q?

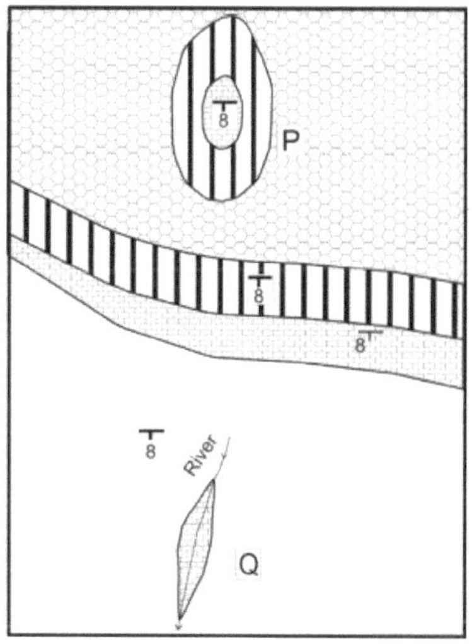

(*a*) P is an anticline and Q is a syncline

(*b*) Q is an anticline and P is a syncline

(*c*) P is an outlier and Q is an inlier

(*d*) Q is an outlier and P is an inlier

51. Four aqueous-vapor fluid inclusions P, Q, R and S are petrographically identical at room temperature, and contain approximately 90 % liquid and 10 % vapor. The freezing temperatures of the fluid inclusions are: P = –5.3°C, Q = –16.6°C, R = –21.2°C, S = –8.7°C. With respect to P, Q, R and S, the correct statement is

(*a*) salinity of "P" is highest but density is lowest

(*b*) both salinity and density of "Q" are lowest

(*c*) both salinity and density of "R" are highest

(*d*) both salinity and density of "S" are lowest

52. Which one of the following is the youngest marine formation in the Himalaya?

(*a*) Dagshahi Formation

(*b*) Subathu Formation

(*c*) Kasauli Formation

(*d*) Karewa Formation

53. Which one of the following environments is represented by molasse facies?

(*a*) Atectonic

(*b*) Pre-tectonic

(*c*) Syn-tectonic

(*d*) Post-tectonic

54. In the given ternary (Fo = forsterite; Di = diopside; An = anorthite) eutectic diagram, the point A represents the composition of magma. What will be the sequence of crystallization during cooling of this magma?

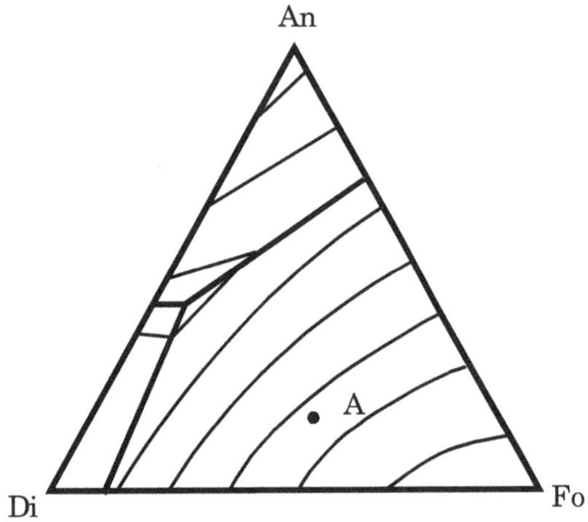

(*a*) olivine and olivine + plagioclase

(*b*) olivine and olivine + pyroxene

(*c*) olivine, olivine + plagioclase and olivine + plagioclase + pyroxene

(*d*) olivine, olivine + pyroxene and olivine + pyroxene + plagioclase

55. Which one of the following is the best suited mining method for a low-dipping, tabular-shaped, hard and compact ore body with 2 to 2.5 m thickness sandwiched between hard and compact roof and floor rock?

(*a*) Cut and fill method

(*b*) Shrinkage stope method

(*c*) Open stope method

(*d*) Caving method

GEOPHYSICS

Q. 26 – Q. 55 carry two marks each.

26. A gaseous hydrocarbon-bearing zone can be best identified by a combined analysis of

(*a*) Density and Self potential(SP) logs

(*b*) Density and Neutron logs

(*c*) Sonic and Neutron logs

(*d*) Natural gamma ray (GR) and Neutron logs

27. In general, geophysical inverse problems dealing with real data obtained from field measurements are

(*a*) grossly over determined

(*b*) even determined

(*c*) over determined

(*d*) grossly underdetermined

28. In vector calculus, Stoke's theorem relates

(*a*) line-integral to volume integral

(*b*) surface integral to volume integral

(*c*) scalar product integral to norm

(*d*) line integral to surface integral

29. The radial dependence of the solution of the Laplace equation in cylindrical coordinates is expressed in terms of

(*a*) Bessel function

(*b*) Legendre polynomial

(*c*) Exponential function

(*d*) Hermite polynomial

30. For an electrostatic field, the Maxwell's equations reduce to

(*a*) Wave equation

(*b*) Diffusion equation

(*c*) Helmholtz equation

(*d*) Poisson equation

31. Which one of the following functions is used as a source-term to obtain the Green's function of a boundary value problem?

(*a*) Heaviside unit step function

(*b*) Exponential function

(*c*) Rectangular function

(*d*) Dirac delta function

32. The heat flow through a unit area of the Earth's surface is given by the product of

(*a*) vertical thermal gradient and thermal conductivity

(*b*) horizontal thermal gradient and thermal conductivity

(*c*) vertical thermal gradient and thermal diffusivity

(*d*) horizontal thermal gradient and thermal diffusivity

33. The S-wave velocity of a medium having a Poisson's ratio and a P-wave velocity of 0.5 and 3 km/s respectively is ________km/s.

34. The PKiKP phase denotes the passage of a seismic wave in the Earth as

(*a*) P in mantle, S in outer core, reflected as P from inner-outer core boundary, S in outer core, P in mantle and crust

(*b*) P in crust, P in mantle, reflected as P from core-mantle boundary, P in mantle, P in crust

(*c*) P in mantle, P in outer core, P in inner core, P in outer core, P in mantle and crust

(*d*) P in mantle, P in outer core, reflected as P from inner-outer core boundary, P in outer core, P in mantle and crust

35. Match the items of Group I with those in Group II

Group I	Group II
P. Proton precession magnetometer	1. Induction in a pair of high permeable cores
Q. Alkali-vapor magnetometer	2. SQUID
R. Fluxgate magnetometer	3. Radio-spectroscopy
S. Superconducting magnetometer	4. Nuclear magnetic resonance

(*a*) P-2; Q-3; R-4; S-1 (*b*) P-4; Q-3; R-1; S-2
(*c*) P-4; Q-1; R-3; S-2 (*d*) P-4; Q-2; R-1; S-3

36. Konigsberger ratio refers to
(*a*) anisotropy of magnetic susceptibility
(*b*) ratio of remnant magnetization and induced magnetization
(*c*) ratio of longitudinal and transverse electrical resistivities
(*d*) ratio of P and S wave velocities

37. The Poisson's relation linking the gravity and magnetic potentials assumes the same anomaly source with
(*a*) inhomogeneous density and intensity of magnetization
(*b*) uniform density contrast and inhomogeneous intensity of magnetization
(*c*) uniform density contrast and homogeneous intensity of magnetization
(*d*) inhomogeneous density and homogeneous intensity of magnetization

38. Compute the coefficient of anisotropy from the following parameters estimated from a Vertical Electric Sounding (VES) survey.
Resistivity of first layer, $\rho_1 = 15\ \Omega$-m
Resistivity of second layer, $\rho_2 = 4\ \Omega$-m
Resistivity of lower half space, $\rho_3 = 50\ \Omega$-m
Thickness of first layer, $h_1 = 3$m
Thickness of second layer, $h_2 = 16$m
(*a*) 1.43 (*b*) 1.28
(*c*) 1.19 (*d*) 1.13

39. The convolution of two finite length sequences $x_n = [1, 0, -2]$ and $y_n = [1, -1]$ is
(*a*) [-1, 1, 2, -2]
(*b*) [1, -1, -2, 2]
(*c*) [1, 0, -2, 2]
(*d*) [1, -2, -1, 2]

40. Arrange the following electrode configurations in the ascending order of their depth of investigation
(P) Dipole-Dipole (Q) Schlumberger
(R) Wenner (S) Pole-Pole
(*a*) R – S – Q – P (*b*) P – Q – S – R
(*c*) R – Q – P – S (*d*) R – Q – S – P

41. Which one of the following transforms relates the real and imaginary components of harmonic electromagnetic (EM) field?
(*a*) Fourier transform (*b*) Laplace transform
(*c*) Hilbert transform (*d*) Wavelet transform

42. Which one of the following geophysical methods is most suitable for exploration of possible hydrocarbon-bearing sediments underlying the Deccan Traps?
(*a*) Seismic (*b*) Magnetotellurics
(*c*) DC resistivity (*d*) Airborne EM

43. A collection of traces having a common mid-point is called a CMP gather. The number of traces in an n-fold survey in a CMP gather is
(*a*) n – 1 (*b*) n + 1
(*c*) n (*d*) $\frac{n}{2}$

44. In seismic prospecting, migration is the process of moving data elements from
(a) midpoint locations to subsurface locations
(b) subsurface locations to midpoint locations
(c) midpoint locations to surface locations
(d) subsurface locations to surface locations

45. An 80 Hz seismic signal is sampled at a rate of 100 samples/s. What will be its aliased period (in seconds) in the sampled signal?
(*a*) 30 (*b*) 10
(*c*) 0.1 (*d*) 0.05

46. The Fourier transform and integral of the Dirac delta function respectively are
(a) 1 and 1
(b) 0 and 0
(c) 0 and 1
(d) 1 and ∞

47. A signal $x_n = [2, 1]$ is input to a system whose impulse response is $h_n = [8, 4, 2, 1]$. The z-transform of the output is
(a) $16 + 16\,z^{-1} + 3\,z^{-2} + 4\,z^{-3} + z^{-4}$
(b) $10 + 5\,z^{-1} + 2\,z^{-2} + 4\,z^{-3} + z^{-4}$
(c) $16 + 16\,z^{-1} + 8\,z^{-2} + 4\,z^{-3} + z^{-4}$
(d) $16 + 16\,z^{-1} + 8\,z^{-2} + 2\,z^{-3} + z^{-4}$

48. Calculate the formation water saturation, S_w from the following well log data:

Resistivity of completely saturated formation, R_o = 1.8 Ω-m

True resistivity of formation, R_t = 25 Ω-m

(a) 31% (b) 29%

(c) 27% (d) 25%

49. Consider the four systems of algebraic equations (listed in Group I).

The systems (Q), (R) and (S) are obtained from (P) by restricting the accuracy of data or coefficients or both respectively, to two decimal places.

Match these systems to their characteristics (listed in Group II)

Group I	Group II
P. $x+1.0000y = 2.0000$ $x+1.0001y = 2.0001$	1. instability
Q. $x+1.0000y = 2.00$ $x+1.0001y = 2.00$	2. inconsistency
R. $x+1.00y = 2.0000$ $x+1.00y = 2.0001$	3. non-uniqueness
S. $x+1.00y = 2.00$ $x+1.00y = 2.00$	4. exact

(a) P-1; Q-4; R-3; S-2 (b) P-4; Q-1; R-2; S-3

(c) P-4; Q-1; R-3; S-2 (d) P-1; Q-4; R-2; S-3

50. The eigenvalue (Λ) and eigenvector (U) matrices for singular value decomposition of the matrix $\begin{pmatrix} 2 & 1 \\ 1 & 2 \end{pmatrix}$ respectively are

(a) $\Lambda = \begin{pmatrix} 3 & 0 \\ 0 & 1 \end{pmatrix}$ and $U = \frac{1}{\sqrt{2}}\begin{pmatrix} 1 & -1 \\ 1 & 1 \end{pmatrix}$

(b) $\Lambda = \begin{pmatrix} 3 & 0 \\ 0 & 1 \end{pmatrix}$ and $U = \frac{1}{\sqrt{2}}\begin{pmatrix} 1 & -1 \\ 1 & -1 \end{pmatrix}$

(c) $\Lambda = \begin{pmatrix} 2 & 0 \\ 0 & 2 \end{pmatrix}$ and $U = \frac{1}{\sqrt{2}}\begin{pmatrix} 1 & -1 \\ 1 & 1 \end{pmatrix}$

(d) $\Lambda = \begin{pmatrix} 2 & 0 \\ 0 & 2 \end{pmatrix}$ and $U = \frac{1}{\sqrt{2}}\begin{pmatrix} 1 & 1 \\ 1 & 1 \end{pmatrix}$

51. The amplitude spectrum of a band pass filter, A_B, can be obtained by a combination of spectra of a low pass filter, A_L, and that of a high pass filter, A_H, as

(a) $A_B = A_L \times A_H$ (b) $A_B = A_L + A_H$

(c) $A_B = A_L - A_H$ (d) $A_B = \frac{A_L}{A_H}$

52. Compute the maximum value of gravity anomaly in Gal over a buried sphere from the following data:

Radius of a sphere = 5 m

Depth to centre of sphere =11 m

Density contrast = 0.1 gm/cc

$G = 6.673 \times 10^{-8}$ dyne-cm^2/gm^2

(a) 2887.58 (b) 288.76

(c) 28.88 (d) 2.89

53. Given the potential field anomaly data at the datum level z = 0, match the spatial frequency expressions (listed in Group I) with the corresponding operations (listed in Group II).

(k is wave number)

Group I	Group II
P. exp (–zk)	1. Second vertical derivative at the datum level
Q. k exp (–zk)	2. Analytic continuation into upper half-space
R. k^2	3. Analytic continuation into lower half-space
S. k exp (zk)	4. First vertical derivative of upward continued values
	5. First vertical derivative of downward continued values

(a) P-1; Q-3; R-2; S-5

(b) P-2; Q-1; R-4; S-3

(c) P-2; Q-4; R-1; S-5

(d) P-3; Q-1; R-5; S-2

54. Assertion (a): An efficient marine seismic survey should use an implosive source.

Reason (r): The performance of a marine seismic source is rated by high pulse-to-bubble ratio.

(*a*) Both (a) and (r) are true and (r) is the correct reason for (a)

(*b*) Both (a) and (r) are true but (r) is not the correct reason for (a)

(*c*) (a) is true but (r) is false

(*d*) (a) is false but (r) is true

55. The electric field intensity vector (E) and the displacement vector (D) are given by $E = 2\hat{i} + 2\hat{j} + 4\hat{k}$ and $D = \hat{i} + \hat{j} + \hat{k}$. The energy of the field is

(*a*) 2

(*b*) 4

(*c*) 6

(*d*) 8

ANSWERS

General Aptitude (GA)

1. (*d*)	**2.** (*a*)	**3.** (*c*)	**4.** (*)	**5.** (*a*)	**6.** (*a*)	**7.** (*c*)	**8.** (*d*)	**9.** (*c*)	**10.** (*)

PART A (Common Part)

1. (*b*)	**2.** (*a*)	**3.** (*b*)	**4.** (*b*)	**5.** (*a*)	**6.** (*b*)	**7.** (*a*)	**8.** (*c*)	**9.** (*b*)	**10.** (*c*)
11. (*a*)	**12.** (*d*)	**13.** (*a*)	**14.** (*d*)	**15.** (*a*)	**16.** (*d*)	**17.** (*b*)	**18.** (*c*)	**19.** (*d*)	**20.** (*c*)
21. (*d*)	**22.** (*b*)	**23.** (*b*)	**24.** (*d*)	**25.** (*b*)					

PART-B (Geology)

26. (*a*)	**27.** (*b*)	**28.** (*b*)	**29.** (*c*)	**30.** (*b*)	**31.** (*c*)	**32.** (*a*)	**33.** (*a*)	**34.** (*)	**35.** (*b*)
36. (*b*)	**37.** (*)	**38.** (*d*)	**39.** (*a*)	**40.** (*c*)	**41.** (*b*)	**42.** (*c*)	**43.** (*d*)	**44.** (*)	**45.** (*b*)
46. (*a*)	**47.** (*d*)	**48.** (*b*)	**49.** (*c*)	**50.** (*c*)	**51.** (*c*)	**52.** (*b*)	**53.** (*d*)	**54.** (*d*)	**55.** (*c*)

(Geophysics)

26. (*b*)	**27.** (*d*)	**28.** (*d*)	**29.** (*a*)	**30.** (*d*)	**31.** (*d*)	**32.** (*a*)	**33.** (*)	**34.** (*d*)	**35.** (*b*)
36. (*b*)	**37.** (*c*)	**38.** (*d*)	**39.** (*b*)	**40.** (*c*)	**41.** (*c*)	**42.** (*b*)	**43.** (*c*)	**44.** (*a*)	**45.** (*d*)
46. (*a*)	**47.** (*c*)	**48.** (*c*)	**49.** (*b*)	**50.** (*a*)	**51.** (*a*)	**52.** (*d*)	**53.** (*c*)	**54.** (*a*)	**55.** (*b*)

EXPLANATIONS

GENERAL APTITUDE (GA)

1. A person suffering from Alzheimer's disease experiences short-term memory loss.
2. Contentment is the key to their happiness; they are satisfied with what they have.
3. Virginia Woolf quote this famous word "As a women, I have no country. As woman, I want no country. As a woman, my country is the whole world."
4. Probability of an earthquake greater than magnitude 6 is 0.04.

   This means 4 out of 100 years will face an earthquake greater than magnitude 6. So average time between successive earthquakes will be

   $$\frac{100}{4} = 25 \text{ years.}$$

5. Initial population $P = 5$ m

   After 1st year $P = 5 \times 12 = 6$ m

   Now 2nd year Current $P = 6$ m

   Now after inc $= 6 \times 12 = 7.2$ m

   After 3rd year $= 7.2 \times 12 = 8.64$ m

   After 4th year $= 8.64 \times 12 = 10.368$ m

6. Given,

   Som is younger to Riaz.

   Shiv is elder to Ansu.

   Ansu is youngest.

   Shiv is younger to Riaz, Som is also younger to Riaz, Ansu is the youngest. Therefore, Riaz would be the eldest.

7. The first sentence of the given paragraph clearly explains that the main point of the paragraph is option c, i.e., Exactitude is not critical in dealing with big data
8. Total exports = 5 lakh tonnes

   Total revenue = 250 Crores

   Item _1 total export = 5 lakh × 0.11

   = 55,000 tonnes = 55,000,00 kg

   Item _2 total revenue = 250 × 0.12

   $= 30$ crores $= 30 \times 10^7$

   $$\text{Item \_1 total revenue}/kg = \frac{30 \times 10^7}{5500000} = \frac{60}{11}$$

   Item _2 total export = 5 lakh × 0.22

   = 1,10,000 tonnes = 1,10,000,00 kg

   Item _2 total revenue = 250 × 0.06

   $= 15$ crores $= 15 \times 10^7$

   $$\text{Item \_2 total revenue}/kg = \frac{15 \times 10^7}{11000000} = \frac{15}{11}$$

   Item _1 revenue : Item _2 revenue

   $$= \frac{60}{11} : \frac{15}{11} = 4 : 1$$

9.

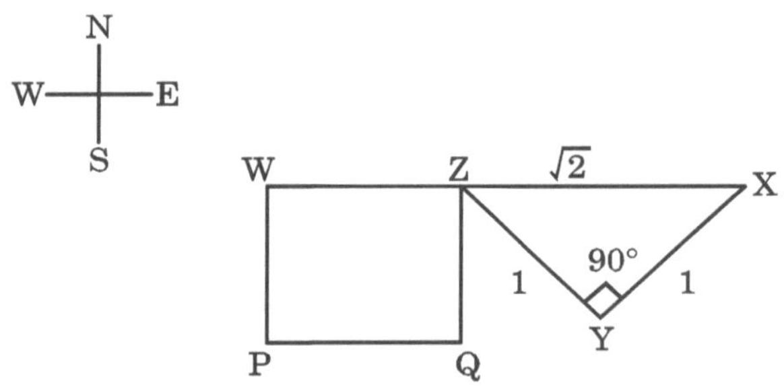

Distance between XQ is $\sqrt{1^2+\left(\sqrt{2}\right)^2}=\sqrt{3}$.

10.

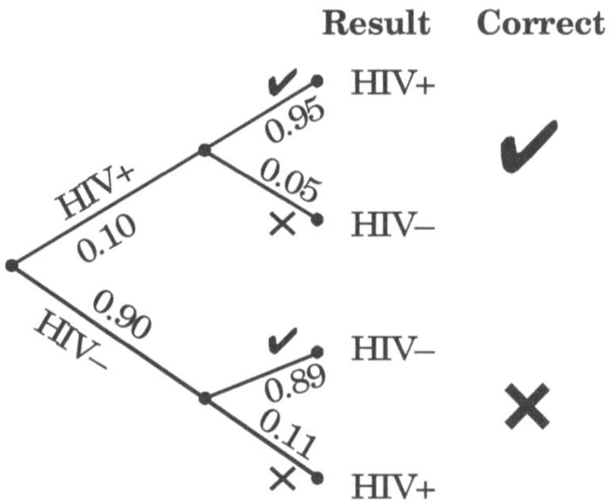

$$\text{Probability} = \frac{0.10\times0.95}{0.10\times0.95+0.90\times0.11} = 0.4896$$

PART A (COMMON PART)

1. The bulk density of different planets of the solar systems are:

Planets	Bulk density (kg/m^3)
Mercury	5427
Venus	5243
Earth	5515
Mars	3933
Jupiter	1326
Saturn	687
Uranus	1270
Neptune	1638

2. **Mid-oceanic Ridges** – Constructive plate margins and produces shallow focus earthquakes.

Subduction Zone – Destructive plate margins and produces deep focus earthquakes.

3. P- wave velocity decreases sharp from 13.5 km/s in the lower mantle to 6.5-8.5 km/s in the outer core while the density increases from 4200 kg/m^3 in the mantle to 7600 kg/m^3 in the outer core to 8000 kg/m^3 in the inner core.

4. Given,

$GR_{log} = 30$

$GR_{max} = 45$

$GR_{min} = 20$

Now, the volume of shale content can be calculated direct from the formula

$$V_{sh} = \frac{GR_{log}-GR_{min}}{GR_{max}-GR_{min}}$$

$$= \frac{30-20}{45-20} = \frac{10}{25} = 0.40$$

5. A cirque is an amphitheatre-like valley formed by glacial erosion. Alternative names for this landform are corrie and cwm. A cirque may also be a similarly shaped landform arising from fluvial erosion. Glacial cirques are found amongst mountain ranges throughout the world; 'classic' cirques are typically about one kilometer long and one kilometer wide. Situated high on a mountainside near the firn line, they are typically partially surrounded on three sides by steep cliffs.

6. Birds and mammals first appear on the Earth in Mesozoic eras.

7. The different copper ore containing minerals are:

Chalcopyrite – $CuFeS_2$

Bornite – Cu_5FeS_4

Chalcocite – Cu_2S

8. Given,

$\rho_1 = 9\ \Omega m$

$\rho_2 = 1\ \Omega m$

Therefore, Reflection coefficient,

$$R = \frac{\rho_1-\rho_2}{\rho_1+\rho_2} = \frac{9-1}{9+1} = \frac{8}{10} = 0.8$$

9. **Depth of investigation:** It is the depth upto which a given geophysical method or tool can extract the useful information within the subsurface.

10. The international Gravity formula for the prediction of theoretical gravity is

$$g_\phi = g_0\left(1+k_1\sin^2\phi - k_2\sin^2\phi\right)$$

where, g_ϕ is predicted value of gravity at latitude ϕ

g_0 is value of gravity at the equator

k_1, k_2 is dependent upon the shape and speed of rotation of Earth

Values of g_0, k_1 and k_2 are taken prior to rotating homogeneous oblate spheroidal earth model

11. The ionized molecule in the ionosphere release swarms of electrons that form powerful, horizontal, ring like electrical currents. As the Earth rotates beneath the ionosphere, the observed intensity of the geomagnetic field fluctuates with a range of amplitude of about 10 – 30 nT at the Earth's surface and period of one day leads to diurnal variations.

12.

Mineral Deposit	Geophysical exploration
Mineralized conductive veins	Resistivity profiling
Disseminated sulphides	Induced Polarization
Massive barytes	Gravity
Kimberlite pipes	Magnetic

13. Critical Distance is the distance traversed by a ray from the shot-point after reflection at a critical angle from the first interface to the surface.

Crossover Distance is the surface distance from the shot-point upto the point on the surface where refracted rays crosses the distance traversed by direct rays.

14. Smaller earthquake rupture smaller portions of the fault. Thus the area of the rupture is an indicator of the earthquake size. Small earthquakes have slips that are less than a centimeter, large earthquakes move the rocks about 10-20 meters.

15.

Well logs	Characteristics of measurements
Dipmeter	Correlation of resistivity change
Neutron	Hydrogen concentration in pores
SP	Natural electric potential
Sonic	Velocity of compressional waves

16. Surface wave magnitude of an earthquake is given as

$$M_s = \log_{10}\left(\frac{A_s}{T}\right) + 1.66\log_{10}(\Delta) + 3.3$$

where,

A_s is surface amplitude

T is period of the wave

D is epicenter distance in degree

For magnitude = 6,

$$M_6 = \log_{10}\left(\frac{A_6}{T}\right) + 1.66\log_{10}(\Delta) + 3.3$$

For magnitude = 7,

$$M_7 = \log_{10}\left(\frac{A_7}{T}\right) + 1.66\log_{10}(\Delta) + 3.3$$

Now, Substracting M_7 from M_6

$$M_7 - M_6 = \log_{10}\left(\frac{A_7}{T}\right) - \log_{10}\left(\frac{A_6}{T}\right)$$

$$\Rightarrow 7 - 6 = \log_{10}\left(\frac{A_7}{T} \times \frac{T}{A_6}\right) = \log_{10}\left(\frac{A_7}{A_6}\right)$$

$$\Rightarrow 1 = \log_{10}\left(\frac{A_7}{A_6}\right)$$

$$\Rightarrow A_7 = 10A_6$$

Now, Energy released during an Earthquake is given as

$$\log_{10} E = 4.8 + 1.5M_S$$

For magnitude = 6

$$\log_{10} E_6 = 4.8 + 1.5M_6$$

For magnitude = 7

$$\log_{10} E_7 = 4.8 + 1.5M_7$$

Subtracting E_7 from E_6, we get

$$\log_{10} E_7 - \log_{10} E_6 = 1.5(M_7 - M_6)$$

$$\log_{10}\left(\frac{E_7}{E_6}\right) = 1.5(7-6) = 1.5$$

$$\Rightarrow \left(\frac{E_7}{E_6}\right) = 10^{1.5} = 31.62$$

$$\Rightarrow E_7 = 32E_6$$

17. Structure Contours are the curves that connects points of equal height above a datum level that are contained within a structure. For a dip of 45°, the structure contour intervals and its horizontal equivalent are equal.

18. **Strike-slip** (also called transcurrent, wrench, or lateral) faults are similarly caused by horizontal compression, but they release their energy by rock displacement in a horizontal direction almost parallel to the compressional force. The fault plane is essentially vertical, and the relative slip is lateral along the plane. These faults are widespread. Many are found at the boundary between obliquely converging oceanic and continental tectonic plates.

19. **Sillimanite** is one of three aluminosilicate polymorphs, the other two being andalusite and kyanite. A common variety of sillimanite is known as fibrolite, so named because the mineral appears like a bunch of fibres twisted together when viewed in thin section or even by the naked eye. Both the fibrous and traditional forms of sillimanite are common in metamorphosed sedimentary rocks.

Chrysotile or white asbestos is the most commonly encountered form of asbestos, accounting for approximately 95% of the asbestos. It is a soft, fibrous silicate mineral in the serpentine subgroup of phyllosilicates; as such, it is distinct from other asbestiform minerals in the amphibole group.

Kyanite is a mineral found mainly in metamorphic rocks. It most often forms from the high-pressure alteration of clay minerals during the metamorphism of sedimentary rocks. It is found in the schists and gneisses of regionally metamorphosed areas and less often in quartzite or eclogite. Kyanite's typical habit is a bladed crystal, although it sometimes occurs as radiating masses of crystals. Kyanite is often associated with other metamorphic minerals such as garnet, staurolite, and corundum.

Beryl belongs to the hexagonal crystal system. Normally Beryl forms hexagonal columns but can also occur in massive habits. As a cyclosilicate beryl incorporates rings of silicate tetrahedral od Si_6O_{18} that are arranged in columns along the C axis and as parallel layers perpendicular to the C axis, forming channels along the C axis.

20. **Rajmahal Volcanism:** They are well developed in the Rajmahal hills of Jharkhand and West Bengal. The lava flows are associated with sedimentary beds. The age of volcanism is from Middle to Upper Jurassic age.

    Deccan Volcanism: It leads to lava flows of basic composition and covers the central and western parts of India. The age of this volcanism ranged from Upper Cretaceous to Lower Eocene.

    Panjal Volcanism: It leads to lava flows of basaltic composition and covers a part of Kashmir. The age of this volcanism ranges from Upper Carboniferous to Lower Permian age.

    Malani Volcanism: It includes acid volcanic rocks such as rhyolites and tuffs. They cover enormous area around Jodhpur in Rajesthan. They range from Lower Vindhyan to Upper Vindhyan age.

21. A clastic rock dominantly composed of feldspar grains is arkose which is a coarse grained sandstone containing notable amount of feldspar.

22. A metamorphic rock consists of pyroxene, plagioclase and quartz, and exhibits hornfelsic texture. The rock has undergone contact metamorphism. Also called as thermal metamorphism, and is caused due to local heating of rock by the intrusion of hot igneous body nearby. The zone of contact metamorphic rocks which occurs surrounding the intrusion is called aureole.

23. Lopolith is a large igneous intrusion which is lenticular in shape with a depressed central region. Lopoliths are generally concordant with the intruded strata with dike or funnel-shaped feeder bodies below the body. Its diameter is usually 10 to 20 times its thickness.

24. Conrad Discontinuity is the discontinuity, separating the continental crust into an upper crustal layer and lower crustal layer. It is poorly defined and is absent in some areas.

25. An **isopach map** illustrates thickness variations within a tabular unit, layer or stratum. Isopachs are contour lines of equal thickness over an area. Isopach maps are utilized in hydrographic survey, stratigraphy, sedimentology, structural geology, petroleum geology and volcanology.

    An **isotherm** is a line that connects points on a map that have the same temperature. Therefore, all points through which an isotherm passes have the same or equal temperatures at the time indicated.

    An **isochron** is a set of initial conditions for the system that all lead to the same long-term behaviour.

    An **isotans** is contours of equal slope.

PART-B (GEOLOGY)

26. **Interference colour:** Property of a single grain seen under microscope under crossed nicols.

    Twinkling: Property seen when several grains are viewed collectively under microscope in polarized light

    Pleochroism: Property of a single grain seen under microscope in polarized light

    Play of colours: Property of a mineral seen in hand specimen

27. **Closed Crystallographic form:** Closed form, enclose space without other form being present, example, scalenohedrons, dipyramids, cubes, tetrahedrons, octahedrons, etc.

28. Miller indices are the reciprocal of intercepts on crystallographic axes.

As per the figure,

Intercept at + a axis is 4 units

Intercept at + b axis is 1 units

Intercept at + c axis is 2 units

Therefore,

Miller indices is given by,

$$\left(\frac{1}{4}, \frac{1}{1}, \frac{1}{2}\right)$$

Whole digits multiplied by 4 gives the Miller Index (142).

29. Basanite is an igneous, volcanic (extrusive) rock with aphanitic to porphyritic texture. The mineral assembly is usually abundant feldspathoids (nepheline or leucite), plagioclase, and augite, together with olivine and lesser iron-titanium oxides such as ilmenite and magnetite-ulvospinel; minor alkali feldspar may be present, as illustrated by the position of the field for basanite in the QAPF diagram. Clinopyroxene (augite) and olivine are common as phenocrysts and in the matrix.

Nephelinite is also associated with the highly alkalic volcanism of the Ol Doinyo Lengai volcanic field in Tanzania. Nyiragongo, another African volcano known for its semipermanent lava lake activity, erupts lava made of melilite nephelinite. The unusual chemical makeup of this igneous rock may be a factor in the unusual fluidity of its lavas.

Shoshonitic rocks tend to be associated with calc-alkaline island-arc subduction volcanism, but the K-rich shoshonites are generally younger and above deeper, steeper parts or the Benioff zone.

Lamproite is an ultrapotassic mantle-derived volcanic or subvolcanic rock. It has low CaO, Al_2O_3, Na_2O, high K_2O/Al_2O_3, a relatively high MgO content and extreme enrichment in incompatible elements.

30. For one phase of deformation, hinge line is straight. Crenulated hinge shows at least two phases of deformation.

31. A pseudosection, also called an equilibrium phase diagram, is a type of phase diagram that shows the fields of stability of different equilibrium mineral assemblages for a single bulk-rock composition. Pseudosections are generally simpler and much easier to interpret than standard phase diagrams that show many reactions.

32. Increase in retardation occur along the quadrant where retardation plate as in the question the mica plate is inserted.

33. Let, two compounds A and B are in equilibrium with a standard deviation $\left(\frac{R_A}{R_{std}}\right)$ and $\left(\frac{R_B}{R_{std}}\right)$ be the relative proportion w.r.t. standards, then

$$\delta_A = \left(\frac{R_A}{R_{std}} - 1\right) \times 100 = 5.9\%$$

$$\delta_B = -11.2\% \qquad \text{[Given]}$$

Therefore,

$$100 \times 5.9 = \left(\frac{R_A}{R_{std}} - 1\right) \times 100$$

$$\Rightarrow 100 \times 5.9 = \left(\frac{6.8}{R_{std}} - 1\right) \times 100$$

Similarly,

$$100 \times (-11.2) = \left(\frac{R_B}{R_{std}} - 1\right) \times 100$$

When A and B are in equilibrium

$$5.9 - (6.8 - 1) = -11.2 - (R_B - 1) = -11.2$$

$$\Rightarrow 6.9 - 6.8 = -10.2 - R_B$$

$$\Rightarrow R_B = -10.2 + 6.8 - 6.9$$

$$\Rightarrow R_B = -10.3\ \%$$

34. Given,

$$Fe^{2+} \rightarrow Fe^{3+} + e$$

Also, E^0 = +0.77 volt = 0.6 volt

$$K = \left[\frac{Fe^{3+}}{Fe^{2+}}\right]$$

Equation used is

$$Eh = E^0 + \frac{0.059}{n} \log k$$

where, n is the number of electrons emitted.

Now, Putting n = 1, we get

$$0.6 = 0.77 + \frac{0.059}{1} \log\left(\frac{Fe^{3+}}{Fe^{2+}}\right)$$

$$\Rightarrow \log\left(\frac{Fe^{3+}}{Fe^{2+}}\right) = \frac{0.6 - 0.77 + 1}{0.059} = -2.8814$$

Taking antilog, we get,

$$\left(\frac{Fe^{3+}}{Fe^{2+}}\right) = e^{-2.8814} = 1.314 \times 10^{-3}$$

$$\Rightarrow \left(\frac{Fe^{2+}}{Fe^{3+}}\right) = \frac{1}{1.314 \times 10^{-3}} = 761.04$$

35. Chip Sampling: The method is less laborious and used as a regular method of known samples, is used for hard or uniform ores where it is difficult to cut channels. In this method the samples are collected by taking a small series of chips of rocks on a regular grid pattern from the working face in regular intervals. The blasted, broken material are sampled. The shape of grid is adopted to the morphology and structure of deposit. The main advantage of this sampling is its high productivity.

Channel Sampling: It is the most accepted method of sampling which best suited to bedded, banded and vein type of deposits, this method consists of cutting channels across the face of exposed ore and collecting resulting chips, fragments and dust from each channels to make a sample. In some cases, the channel may also be cut along a line making a small angle with thickness of deposit.

Bulk Sampling: This type sampling method is used in checking of the reliability of other types of samples and sometimes may be taken to determine a correction factor for use in a estimate based on samples of other types. The samples are taken by blasting down drift blocks or a section in a stope or otherwise obtaining a sample of several tons to several hundreds or even thousands of tons, either from trench, pit, channel or from the run-of-mine, where the entire lot is milled separately.

Grab Sampling: As the term indicates that grab sampling is not true sampling. A specimen picked up from ore or a mineral deposits or a portion of mineralized rock, which taken out of an ore body are called grab samples. The samples are taken and analyzed to obtain a preliminary idea about the nature and grade of whole deposit a, to know appreciate metal content.

36. Magnetite form in oxidizing condition whereas pyrite form in reducing conditions. Therefore, magnetite and pyrite can never be in equilibrium.

37. Given,

Length, $L = 40$ m

Width, $W = 30$ m

Thickness, $T = 2.13$ m

$\therefore$ Volume of block $= L \times W \times T$

$$= 40 \times 30 \times 2.13 = 2556\ m^3$$

Specific gravity, $\rho = 2.86$

Therefore,

Tonnage of ore = Volume × ρ

$$= 2556 \times 2.86 = 7310.16 \text{ tonnes}$$

$$\text{and Metal content} = \frac{\text{tonnage} \times \text{assay value}}{100}$$

$$= \frac{10092.14}{100} = 108.92 \text{ metric tonne}$$

38. Globigerina: Umbilical, extraumbilical, equatorinal, spiroumbilical or secondary aperture.

Globorotalia: Umbilical to extraumbilical aperture, no secondary aperture

Globigerinoides and Orbulina: Sutural aperture

39. Callus: Thickend margin of gastropod aperture is known as callus.

Cusp: Draped basal cavity in conodonts is known as cusp.

Sicula: In graptolites, the first thica from which all other buds develop is called sicula.

Calyx: The inner surface of corallite is known as calyx.

40. Benthic forminifera living in shelf environment: Quinqueloculina, Lenticulina, Ammonia, Elphidium etc.

41.

Geological Units	Age
Talchir Tillite	Upper carboniferous
Muth Quartzite	Silurian
Umia Ammonites Bed	Jurassic
Umaria Marine Bed	Permian

42. Alkali–aggregate reaction is a term mainly referring to a reaction, which occurs over time in concrete between the highly alkaline cement paste, and non-crystalline silicon dioxide, which is found in many common aggregates. This reaction can cause expansion of the altered aggregate, leading to spalling and loss of strength of the concrete.

Arching is a phenomenon that occurs when a yielding part of a soil mass transfers pressure to adjoining soil mass which is less yielding or rigid. The action is similar to one in a structural arch, which transfers the load to abutments. When a part of the soil mass yields, it has a tendency to move out of its original position. This tendency is resisted by the shearing resistance at the zone of contact between the yielding and non-yielding parts. Consequently, the pressure on the yielding part is reduced, whereas that on the non- yielding parts is increased. The soil thus arches over the yielding part and transfers the load to the non-yielding parts, which act as abutments.

Riprap slope protection is an erosion control measure consisting of geotextile fabric and stone riprap that is placed on an unvegetated slope to protect the soil from erosive forces.

43. Knickpoints reflect different conditions and processes on the river, often caused by previous erosion due to glaciation or variance in lithology.

44. Given,

Transmisivity = 0.75 m^2/day

Thickness = 10 m

Therefore, Hydraulic conductivity

$$= \frac{\text{Transmitivity}}{\text{Thickness}}$$

$$= \frac{0.75}{10}$$

= 0.075 m/day

45. Blue and red spectral bands are the best spectral reflectance for limonite mapping.

46. Bituminous anthracite have maximum amount of hydrogen < 10 % and lignite 10-20 %.

47. Given,

R = 8.314 J/mol/k

$K = 3.4 \times 10^{-5}$

T = 25°C = 25 + 273 = 298 K

Now,

$$\Delta G = RT \ln K$$

$$\Rightarrow \Delta G = 8.314 \times 298 \times \ln\left(3.4 \times 10^{-5}\right)$$

= 25492 Joule = 25.492 KJ

48.
- ➢ Fractured quartzite generally develops rectangular pattern.
- ➢ Shale generally develops dendritic pattern.
- ➢ Limestone develops appearing and disappearing type of drainage pattern.
- ➢ Alluvial plain develops generally braided and meandering pattern.

49. As per given figure in the question,

For S_1,

$d_{60} \approx 0.065$

$d_{10} \approx 0.055$

For S_2,

$d_{60} \approx 0.055$

$d_{10} \approx 0.035$

Therefore,

Uniformity coefficient

$$\left(\frac{d_{60}}{d_{10}}\right)_{S_2} = \frac{0.055}{0.035} = 1.57 \text{ (High)}$$

Uniformity coefficient

$$\left(\frac{d_{60}}{d_{10}}\right)_{S_1} = \frac{0.065}{0.055} = 1.18 \text{ (Low)}$$

As per question, the assertion (a) is false but (r) is true, (r) being not the correct reason for (a).

50. **Outlier-** Younger rocks surrounded by older rocks.

Inlier- Older rocks surrounded by younger rocks.

51. R has minimum freezing point, freezing point decreases with salinity increment. Also, density increases with increase in salinity.

52.

Formation	Age
Dagshai	Oligocene
Subathu	Eocene
Kasauli	Early Miocene
Karewa	Pliocene/Pliestocene

53. **Molasse facies:** A paralic sedimentary facies consisting, mainly of shale, subgreywacke sandstone and conglomerate. It is more clastic and sub- rhythmic than the preceeding flush and is generally post- tectonic.

54. First of all, F_o will crystallize from the magma represented by point 'a' because of high melting point of 'Fo'(olivine), then the olivine+ pyroxene will crystallize together. All the ternary eutectic point all the three phases (F_o + D_i + A_n) will crystallize together.

55. **Open Stope Method:** Useful where rock requires no artificial support (here given compact roof and floor rock) and thickness of the orebody is also low.

(GEOPHYSICS)

26. A gaseous hydrocarbon bearing zone leads to over estimation and underestimation of porosity of the formation when analyzed using porosity logging techniques like density and neutron logging technique.

Density log – If a gas is present in the formation, porosities can be overestimated. If the formation is gas bearing zone, a significant amount of gas is always left in the invaded zone. This gas will reduce the mean fluid density of the invaded zone, and will cause overestimation of the porosity.

Neutron log – This log is responsible to the amount of hydrogens in the formation and to a less extent upon elements. If hydrocarbon gas is present, it leads to much lower hydrogen index from its low density and its presence will give rise to underestimation of the porosity.

27. As the real data obtained from field measurement consists of more unknown data than the data itself for the general case, the geophysical inverse problem becomes grossly underdetermined because the equation Gm = d does not provide enough information to determine all the model parameters uniquely.

28. Stoke's Theorem: It states that the surface integral of the curl of a function over any surface bounded by a closed path is equal to the line integral of a particular vector function round the path.

$$\int_s \vec{\nabla}\times\vec{F}ds = \oint_c \vec{F}.dr$$

where,

F = vector function

ds = small surface area

dr = small line path

29. The general form of Laplace's equation is

$$\nabla^2 f = 0$$

where, ∇^2 is the Laplacian operator.

$$\frac{1}{r}\frac{\partial}{\partial r}\left(r\frac{\partial f}{\partial r}\right)+\frac{1}{r^2}\frac{\partial^2 f}{\partial\theta^2}+\frac{\partial^2 f}{\partial z^2}=0 \quad \ldots(i)$$

Solving this equation by separation of variable method, let,

$$f(r,\theta,Z)=R(r)T(\theta)Z(Z) \quad \ldots(ii)$$

Replacing this solution in (i) yields the intermediate result

$$TZ\frac{d^2R}{dr^2}+\frac{TZ}{r}\frac{dR}{dr}+\frac{RZ}{r^2}\frac{d^2Z}{rZ^2}=0$$

Dividing both sides by RTZ and shifting the term, containing Z on the right hand side, we get,

$$\frac{1}{R}\frac{d^2R}{dr^2}+\frac{1}{rR}\frac{dR}{dr}+\frac{1}{r^2T}\frac{d^2T}{d\theta^2}=\frac{-1}{Z}\frac{d^2Z}{dZ^2} \quad \ldots(iii)$$

Now, $\frac{1}{Z}\frac{d^2Z}{dZ^2}=1$

$$\Rightarrow \frac{d^2Z}{dZ^2}-1Z=0$$

The general solution of this equation is

$$Z(z)=a_1e^{lz}+a_2e^{-lz}$$

Once sorted the z dependence, we need to take care of r and θ. Equation (iii) gives

$$\frac{1}{R}\frac{d^2R}{dr^2}+\frac{1}{rR}\frac{dR}{dr}+\frac{1}{r^2T}\frac{d^2T}{d\theta^2}=-1^2$$

$$\frac{1}{R}\frac{d^2R}{dr^2}+\frac{r}{R}\frac{dR}{dr}+1^2r^2=-\frac{1}{T}\frac{d^2T}{d\theta^2}$$

Therefore, we are in a situation where the only way a solution can be found for the above equation is where both members are equal to a constant.

Let, the constant be a positive constant m^2. The equation for T becomes:

$$\frac{d^2T}{d\theta^2}+m^2T=0$$

the general solution is given as

$$T(\theta)=K_1\sin(m\theta)+K_2\cos(m\theta)$$

Taking the left part of equation (iii) with r dependencies,

$$\frac{r^2}{R}\frac{d^2R}{dr^2}+\frac{r}{R}\frac{dR}{dr}+1^2r^2-m^2=0$$

$$r^2\frac{d^2R}{dr^2}+r\frac{dR}{dr}+\left(1^2r^2-m^2\right)R=0$$

This equation is well known equation in mathematical physics called parametric Bessel's equation.

30. For an electrostatic field, Maxwell's equation reduce to Poisson's equation.

31. For most of the cases, Dirac delta function is used as a source terms. Therefore, it is also the case of Green's function.

32. The Heat flow equation is given as,

$$\Delta Q = KA\frac{T_2-T_1}{L}\Delta t$$

where,

K = Thermal conductivity

$\frac{T_2 - T_1}{L}$ = Temperature Gradient

A = Area of cross – section

Δt = Time of observation

ΔQ = Net amount of heat

Therefore, the heat flow through a unit area of the Earth's surface is the product of vertical thermal gradient and thermal conductivity.

33. Given,

Poisson ratio, $\sigma = 0.5$

Velocity of P wave, $V_P = 3$ km/s

As per given formula

$$\sigma = \frac{1}{2}\left(\frac{V_P^2 - 2V_S^2}{V_P^2 - V_S^2}\right)$$

$$\Rightarrow 0.5 = \frac{1}{2}\left(\frac{(3)^2 - 2V_S^2}{(3)^2 - V_S^2}\right)$$

$$\Rightarrow 0.5 \times 2 = \frac{9 - 2V_S^2}{9 - V_S^2}$$

$$\Rightarrow 9 - V_S^2 = 9 - 2V_S^2$$

$$\Rightarrow V_S^2 = 0$$

$$\Rightarrow V_S = 0$$

34. Labelling of seismic wave path of some important refracted and reflected P and S-wave phases.

- P_cP/S_cS – Seismic phases that are reflected at the outer core boundary, the letter 'c' is used.
- SKiKS/SKiKP- Reflections from the inner core are designated with letter 'i'.
- PP/SS – Seismic wave phases that refracted once from the crust.
- PKP/SKS – Seismic wave phases after encountering second refraction and emerges beyond the shadow zone ($103° < \Delta < 143°$). The letter 'K' stands for kern, the german word core.
- PKIKP/SKIKS – Seismic wave that travels through mantle, fluid core and inner core.

35. The **proton magnetometer**, also known as the proton precession magnetometer (PPM), uses the principle of Earth's field **nuclear magnetic resonance** (EFNMR) to measure very small variations in the Earth's magnetic field, allowing ferrous objects on land and at sea to be detected. It is used in land-based archaeology to map the positions of demolished walls and buildings, and at sea to locate wrecked ships, sometimes for recreational diving.

Alkali-metal atomic magnetometers are among the most sensitive technologies for detecting and characterizing magnetic fields, making them ideal for many applications of NMR. An atomic magnetometer consists of a glass cell containing a vapor of alkali-metal atoms (such as rubidium or cesium), which are optically pumped using a resonant laser beam, yielding polarization on the order of unity. The polarization state of the atoms is also probed using a laser, in order to measure their magnetic resonance frequency, which is in turn directly proportional to the local magnetic field strength.

A **fluxgate magnetometer** consists of a small, magnetically susceptible core wrapped by two coils of wire. An alternating electric current is passed through one coil, driving the core through an alternating cycle of magnetic saturation; i.e., magnetised, unmagnetised, inversely magnetised, unmagnetised, magnetised, and so forth.

SQUIDs, or superconducting quantum interference devices, measure extremely small changes in magnetic fields. They are very sensitive vector magnetometers, with noise levels as low as 3 fT $Hz^{-1/2}$ in commercial instruments and 0.4 fT $Hz^{-1/2}$ in experimental devices. Many liquid-helium-cooled commercial SQUIDs achieve a flat noise spectrum from near DC (less than 1 Hz) to tens of kilohertz, making such devices ideal for time-domain biomagnetic signal measurements. SERF atomic magnetometers demonstrated in laboratories so far reach competitive noise floor but in relatively small frequency ranges

36. The **Koenigsberger ratio** (Q ratio) is defined as the ratio in a rock of remanent magnetization to the induced magnetization in the Earth's field.

37. The Poisson's relation linking the gravity and magnetic potentials is given as

$$A = \left(\frac{M}{r\rho}\right) g_a$$

where,

M = Magnetic moment

ρ = Density

g_a = Component of g in the direction of a

This is pseudo relationship between the gravity and magnetic taking uniform density contrast and homogeneous intensity of magnetization.

38. For layer 1

$\rho_1 = 15\ \Omega m$, $h_1 = 3\ m$

For layer 2

$\rho_2 = 4\ \Omega m$, $h_2 = 16\ m$

Now, as per definition of coefficient of anisotropy

$$\lambda = \sqrt{\frac{\rho_v \text{(Vertical resistivity)}}{\rho_h \text{(Horizontal resistivity)}}}$$

Also, $\rho_v = \left(\frac{T\text{(Transverse resistance)}}{Z_e\text{(Effective thickness)}}\right)$

$$\rho_h = \left(\frac{Z_e\text{(Effective thickness)}}{S\text{(Longitudinal conductance)}}\right)$$

Again, $T = \rho_1 h_1 + \rho_2 h_2 + ... + \rho_n h_n = \sum_{i=1}^{n} \rho_i h_i$

and $S = \frac{h_1}{\rho_1} + \frac{h_2}{\rho_2} + ... + \frac{h_n}{\rho_n} = \sum_{i=1}^{n} \frac{h_i}{\rho_i}$

Now, as per question

$$T = \rho_1 h_1 + \rho_2 h_2 = \{(15 \times 3) + (4 \times 16)\} = 109\ \Omega$$

and $S = \frac{h_1}{\rho_1} + \frac{h_2}{\rho_2} = \frac{3}{15} + \frac{16}{4} = 4.2\ \Omega^{-1}$

$$h_e = 3 + 16 = 19\ m$$

$$\rho_v = \frac{T}{h_e} = \frac{109}{19} = 5.73\ \Omega$$

$$\rho_h = \frac{h_e}{s} = \frac{19}{4.2} = 4.52\ \Omega$$

Therefore, $\lambda = \sqrt{\frac{\rho_v}{\rho_h}} = \sqrt{\frac{5.73}{4.52}} = 1.125 \approx 1.13$

39. Given, $x_n = [1, 0, -2]$

$y_n = [1, -1]$

$\therefore$ Convolution $Z_n = x_n \times y_n = [1, 0, -2] \times [1, -1]$

Now, as per folding method we get,

x_n / y_n	1	−1
1	1	−1
0	0	0
−2	−2	2

Z_n = [1, −1, −2, 2]

40. The ascending order of the depth of investigation of different electrode configuration is Wenner < Schlumberger < Dipole-Dipole < Pole-Pole

41. In signal processing, Hilbert Transform introduces a 90° phase shift to the parent signal.

42. **Magnetotellurics** (MT) is an electromagnetic geophysical method for inferring the earth's subsurface electrical conductivity from measurements of natural geomagnetic and geoelectric field variation at the Earth's surface. Investigation depth ranges from 300 m below ground by recording higher frequencies down to 10,000 m or deeper with long-period soundings. This is the best geophysical methods suitable for exploration of possible hydrocarbon bearing sediments in underlying the deccan traps.

43. A collection of traces having a common mid-point is called a CMP gather. The number of traces in an n-fold survey in a CMP gather is 'n'.

44. From the definition of Migration, it brings back, the mid- point location to the subsurface location by collapsing diffraction. Therefore, enhancing the resolution for better visualization of the subsurface.

45. Given, The sampling rate is 100 samples/sec.

Therefore, the sampling frequency is 100 Hz

The seismic signal is 80 Hz and sampling frequency is 100 Hz

So, for 80 Hz signal, the aliased frequency is 100-80 = 20 Hz

Now, Aliased period = $\frac{1}{20}$ = 0.05 sec

46. The Fourier transform and Fourier Integral of Dirac delta function are 1 and 1 respectively.

47. Given,

$x_n = [2,1]$

$h_n = [8,4,2,1]$

The Z transform of x_n and h_n are:

$f(x) = (2 + Z^{-1})$

$g(h) = (8 + Z^{-1} + 2Z^{-2} + Z^{-3})$

$y(z) = f(x).g(h)$

$= (2 + Z^{-1}).(8 + Z^{-1} + 2Z^{-2} + Z^{-3})$

$= \{16 + 8Z^{-1} + 4Z^{-2} + 2Z^{-3} + 8Z^{-1} + 4Z^{-2} + 2Z^{-2} + Z^{-4}\}$

$= \{16 + 16Z^{-1} + 8Z^{-2} + 4Z^{-3} + Z^{-4}\}$

48. As per Archie's second law,

$$S_w = \sqrt{\frac{R_o}{Rt}}$$

Now, As per given question,

$$S_w = \sqrt{\frac{1.8}{25}} = 0.268 = 26.8\ \% \approx 27\ \%$$

49.

	Group-I	Group-II
P.	$x + 1.0000y = 2.0000$ $x + 1.0001y = 2.0001$	Exact
Q.	$x + 1.0000y = 2.00$ $x + 1.0001y = 2.000$	Instability
R.	$x + 1.00y = 2.0000$ $x + 1.00y = 2.0001$	Inconsistency
S.	$x + 1.00y = 2.00$ $x + 1.00y = 2.00$	Non-uniqueness

50. Given, $A = \begin{bmatrix} 2 & 1 \\ 1 & 2 \end{bmatrix}$

The SVD theorem states that,

$A_{n\times P} = U_{n\times n} \quad S_{n\times P} \quad V^T_{P\times p}$

where,

$U^TU = I_{n\times n}$

$V^TV = I_{P\times P}$

(U and V are orthogonal)

Now, $AA^T = \begin{bmatrix} 2 & 1 \\ 1 & 2 \end{bmatrix}\begin{bmatrix} 2 & 1 \\ 1 & 2 \end{bmatrix} = \begin{bmatrix} 5 & 4 \\ 4 & 5 \end{bmatrix} = K$

The eigen values of K can be determined by considering

$Kx = \lambda x$

where,

x is eigen vectors

λ is eigen values

$(2 - \lambda I)x = 0$

$$\begin{bmatrix} 5-\lambda & 4 \\ 4 & 5-\lambda \end{bmatrix} = 0$$

$\Rightarrow (5-\lambda)^2 - 16 = 0$

$\Rightarrow 25 - 10\lambda + \lambda^2 - 16 = 0$

$\Rightarrow \lambda^2 - 10\lambda + 9 = 0$

$\Rightarrow \lambda = 9, 1$

For $\lambda_1 - 9$

$$\begin{bmatrix} 5-9 & 4 \\ 4 & 5-9 \end{bmatrix}\begin{bmatrix} x_1 \\ x_2 \end{bmatrix} = 0$$

$$\Rightarrow \begin{bmatrix} -4 & 4 \\ 4 & -4 \end{bmatrix}\begin{bmatrix} x_1 \\ x_2 \end{bmatrix} = 0$$

$\Rightarrow -4x_1 + 4x_2 = 0$

$\therefore x_1 = x_2$

Let, $x_1 = c$ and $x_2 = c$, then

$$x = \begin{bmatrix} x_1 \\ x_2 \end{bmatrix} = \begin{bmatrix} c \\ c \end{bmatrix} = c\begin{bmatrix} 1 \\ 1 \end{bmatrix}$$

A possible value of $c = \frac{1}{\sqrt{2}}$

For $\lambda_2 = 1$

$$\begin{bmatrix} 5-1 & 4 \\ 4 & 5-1 \end{bmatrix}\begin{bmatrix} x_1 \\ x_2 \end{bmatrix} = 0$$

$$\Rightarrow \begin{bmatrix} 4 & 4 \\ 4 & 4 \end{bmatrix}\begin{bmatrix} x_1 \\ x_2 \end{bmatrix} = 0$$

$\Rightarrow 4x_1 + 4x_2 = 0$

$\therefore x_1 = -x_2$

Let, $x_1 = c$ and $x_2 = c$, then

$$x = \frac{1}{\sqrt{2}}\begin{bmatrix} -1 \\ 1 \end{bmatrix}$$

The eigen vectors of A^TA makes up the columns of V

$$A^TA = \begin{bmatrix} 2 & 1 \\ 1 & 2 \end{bmatrix}\begin{bmatrix} 2 & 1 \\ 1 & 2 \end{bmatrix} = \begin{bmatrix} 5 & 4 \\ 4 & 5 \end{bmatrix} = W$$

The eigen value matrix S is

$$S = \begin{bmatrix} \sqrt{9} & 0 \\ 0 & \sqrt{1} \end{bmatrix} = \begin{bmatrix} 3 & 0 \\ 0 & 1 \end{bmatrix}$$

and the eigen vector matrix is

$$U = \frac{1}{\sqrt{2}}\begin{bmatrix} 1 & -1 \\ 1 & 1 \end{bmatrix}$$

51. The amplitude spectrum of a band pass filter, AB, can be obtained by a combination of spectra of a low pass filter, A_L, and that of a high pass filter, A_H, as

$$A_B = A_L \times A_H$$

52. Given, $R = 5$ m

$\Delta\rho = 0.1$ gm/cc.

$z = 11$

$G = 6.673 \times 10^{-8}$ dyne-cm²/gm²

Now, As per using formula,

$$\Delta g_o = \frac{4}{3}\pi G\left(\frac{\Delta\rho R^3}{z^2}\right)$$

$$= \frac{4}{3}\pi \times 6.673 \times 10^{-8} \times \frac{0.1 \times 125}{121} = 2.89\mu\, Gal$$

53. **(c)**

Spatial frequency expressions	**Operations**
$\exp(-zk)$	Analytic continuation into lower half-space
$k\exp(-zk)$	First vertical derivation of upward continued values
k^2	Second vertical derivative at the datum level
$k\exp(zk)$	First vertical derivation of downward continued values

54. An efficient marine seismic survey should use an implosive source is correct and the response that the performance of a marine seismic source is rated by high pulse-to-bubble ratio is also true for the given reason.

55. Given,

Electric field intensity vector,

$$E = 2\hat{i} + 2\hat{j} + 4\hat{k}$$

and Displacement vector,

$$D = \hat{i} + \hat{j} + \hat{k}$$

Now, Energy of the field

$$= \frac{1}{2}E.D$$

$$= \frac{1}{2}\left\{2\hat{i} + 2\hat{j} + 4\hat{k}\right\}\left\{\hat{i} + \hat{j} + \hat{k}\right\} = \frac{1}{2} \times 8 = 4$$

SOLVED PAPER - 2013

PART-A (Common Part)

Q. 1 – Q. 5 carry one mark each.

1. The number of hydrous minerals in the Moh's scale of hardness is ________.

2. It takes approximately ________ minutes for sunlight to reach the Earth.

3. In a remotely sensed data of a planet, the presence of hydrous species can be inferred using _______ region of the electromagnetic spectrum?

(*a*) Radiowave (*b*) Gamma

(*c*) Infrared (*d*) Visible

4. Amongst the following, which one will have the highest P-wave velocity?

(*a*) Granite (*b*) Diamond

(*c*) Shale (*d*) Talc

5. Assuming the Earth to be a perfect sphere, its equatorial velocity is approximately _______ km/hr

6. Both strength and plasticity of a rock increase with the

(A) increase in temperature

(B) decrease in strain rate

(C) increase in confining pressure

(D) increase in pore fluid pressure

7. Amongst the following options, the acceptable value of the Poisson's ratio of a rock is

(*a*) 0.55 (*b*) 1.00

(*c*) 0.25 (*d*) -1.00

8. The acceleration due to gravity, 'y' is maximum at

(*a*) equator (*b*) poles

(*c*) mid-latitudes (*d*) sub-tropical regions

9. The most abundant mineral in the Earth's crust is

(*a*) quartz (*b*) K-feldspar

(*c*) biotite (*d*) garnet

10. Acoustic impedance is the ____________ of density and velocity.

(*a*) sum (*b*) difference

(*c*) product (*d*) ratio

11. Choose the diamagnetic mineral from the following.

(a) Calcite (b) Enstatite

(c) Pyrite (d) Ilmenite

12. Two bodies made up of same material with different dimensions have

(a) same resistances and resistivities

(b) same resistivities but different resistances

(c) same resistances but different resistivities

(d) different resistances and resistivities

13. The type of wave that arrives first at a station from an earthquake hypocenter is

(a) P-wave (b) S-wave

(c) Rayleigh wave (d) Love wave

14. Which one of the following is the correct statement?

(a) Accretionary wedge is part of the foreland basin

(b) Spreading ridge is a major zone of metamorphism

(c) Dehydration of subducting slab induces mantle melting

(d) Back arc basin represent a convergent regime

15. Match the following items of Group I with those of Group II.

Group I	Group II
P) Electrical Method	1) Density
Q) Magnetic Method	2) Velocity
R) Gravity Method	3) Resistivity
S) Seismic Method	4) Susceptibility
	5) Dielectric Permittivity

(*a*) P – 3 ; Q – 2 ; R – 5 ; S – 1

(*b*) P – 3 ; Q – 4 ; R – 1 ; S – 2

(*c*) P – 3 ; Q – 4 ; R – 2 ; S – 1

(*d*) P – 5 ; Q – 4 ; R – 3 ; S – 2

16. If a radioactive isotope has a decay constant of 1.55×10^{-10} year^{-1}, its half-life (in years) would be

(a) 4.57×10^{9} (b) 4.47×10^{9}

(c) 4.57×10^{10} (d) 4.47×10^{10}

17. Which of the following physical properties of rocks has the widest range of variation?
(a) Magnetic permeability
(b) Dielectric permittivity
(c) Seismic velocity
(d) Electrical resistivity

18. Which of the following is NOT an inverse square law?
(*a*) Newton's law of gravitation
(*b*) Coulomb's law of electrostatics
(*c*) Coulomb's law of magnetostatics
(*d*) Hooke's law

19. A type of unconformity characterized by the occurrence of sedimentary rocks on igneous/ metamorphic rocks is known as
(*a*) angular unconformity
(*b*) nonconformity
(*c*) paraconformity
(*d*) disconformity

20. For seismic S-wave velocity, , the rigidity modulus, , is proportional to
(*a*) $\sqrt{V}$ (*b*) V
(*c*) V^2 (*d*) V^3

21. An active trench is present in the vicinity of
(*a*) Andaman & Nicobar Islands
(*b*) Gulf of Cambay
(*c*) Lakshadweep
(*d*) Krishna-Godavari delta

22. In a homogeneous anisotropic medium, the physical property varies
(*a*) with position but not with direction
(*b*) with both position and direction
(*c*) with direction but not with position
(*d*) neither with position nor with direction

23. Which one of the following stable isotopic ratios is used for estimation of palaeo-temperature of seawater?
(a) $^{13}C/^{12}C$ (b) $^{18}O/^{16}O$
(c) $^{87}S/^{86}Sr$ (d) $^{15}N/^{14}N$

24. Match the items of Group I with those of Group II.

Group I	Group II
P. Coal	1. Gandhar
Q. Copper	2. Singareni
R. Oil	3. Khetri
S. Uranium	4. Jadugoda
	5. Degana

(a) P-4, Q-3, R-1, S-2
(b) P-2, Q-3, R-5, S-4
(c) P-1, Q-3, R-2, S-5
(d) P-2, Q-3, R-1, S-4

25. Which of the following logging techniques is best suited to estimate the shaliness of hydrocarbon reservoirs?
(*a*) Resistivity (*b*) Sonic
(*c*) Induction (*d*) Gamma ray

PART-B
GEOLOGY

Q. 26 to Q. 55 carry two marks each.

26. Which of the following statements is correct?
(*a*) Eolian sands do not exhibit cross bedding.
(*b*) Deep marine sands are well sorted.
(*c*) Glacier deposit may contain faceted pebble.
(*d*) Wave ripples do not form on shallow marine sands.

27. The test of organic-walled foraminifera is termed as
(*a*) Microgranular (*b*) Hyaline
(*c*) Porcellaneous (*d*) Tectinous

28. The void ratio (in percentage) of sandstone is 25. Its porosity in percentage is ________.

29. On a 1:10,000 scale map, the length of a fault trace on a horizontal plane is represented as 5 cm.
The same on a 1:25,000 scale vertical aerial photograph is ________ cm.

30. In high-grade metamorphism, biotite melting indicates
(*a*) rock cooling (*b*) rock hydration
(*c*) rock uplifting (*d*) rock dehydration

31. Match the dentition type in Group I with the bivalves in Group II.

Group I	Group II
P. Desmodont	1.Mytilus
Q. Dysodo	2. Cerastoderma
R. Isodont	3. Mya
S. Heterodont	4. Spondylus
	5. Nucula
	6. Arca

(*a*) P – 3, Q –1, R – 4, S – 2
(*b*) P – 1, Q –2, R – 6, S – 5
(*c*) P – 3, Q – 1, R – 5, S – 2
(*d*) P – 2, Q - 1, R – 4, S – 6

32. Which one of the following is the correct statement regarding hydrocarbon generation?

(*a*) H/C content of organic matter increases as it matures.

(*b*) O/C content of organic matter increases as it matures.

(*c*) Lignite does not form any hydrocarbon during maturation.

(*d*) Oil source rock is most abundant in Mesozoic.

33. In the stereographic projection, 1, 2 and 3 represent poles of three planes. Choose the correctcombination of statements from the following.

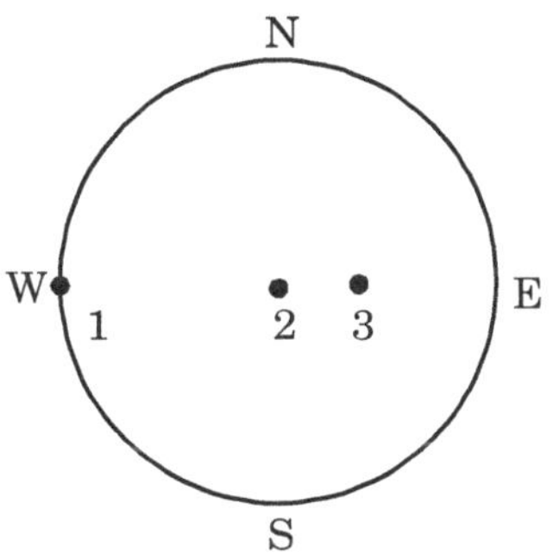

(*a*) The plane corresponding to 1 is horizontal and the plane corresponding to 2 is inclined.

(*b*) The plane corresponding to 1 is striking N-S and the plane corresponding to 2 is horizontal.

(*c*) The plane corresponding to 2 is vertical and the plane corresponding to 3 is striking E-W

(*d*) The plane corresponding to 2 is striking E-W and the plane corresponding to 3 is incline

34. Match the minerals in Group I with its corresponding industrial application in Group II.

Group I	Group II
P. Kaolinite	1. Pigment
Q. Rutile	2. Asbestos
R. Graphite	3. Cement
S. Serpentine	4. Lubricant
	5. Abrasive

(*a*) P – 1, Q – 3, R – 4, S – 2

(*b*) P – 3, Q – 1, R – 2, S – 4

(*c*) P – 3, Q – 1, R – 4, S – 2

(*d*) P – 1, Q – 5, R – 3, S – 2

35. Match the Hermann-Maugin symbol in Group I with its corresponding general form in Group II.

Group I	Group II
P. 6/m	1. Trigonal Dipyramid
Q. 3m	2. Ditrigonal Dipyramid
R. 6 m2	3. Dihexagonal Pyramid
S. 6	4. Ditrigonal Pyramid
	5. Hexagonal Dipyramid

(*a*) P – 5, Q – 4, R – 2, S – 1

(*b*)) P – 5, Q – 4, R – 1, S – 2

(*c*) P – 5, Q – 4, R – 1, S – 3

(*d*) P – 3, Q – 4, R – 2, S – 1

36. Which of the following is a type of dam?

(*a*) Anchor (*b*) Shotcrete

(*c*) Geogrid (*d*) Buttress

37. Match the items in Group I with those in Group II.

Group I	Group II
P. Kersantite	1. Hornblende-diopside-plagioclase lamprophyre
Q. Fenite	2. Basaltic trachyandesite
R. Mugearite	3. Volcanic nepheline syenite
S. Phonolite	4. Biotite-plagioclase lamprophyre
	5. Metasomatic rock associated with carbonatites

(*a*) P – 1, Q – 2, R – 4, S – 3

(*b*) P – 4, Q – 5, R – 2, S – 3

(*c*) P – 3, Q –1, R – 2, S – 4

(*d*) P – 4, Q – 5, R – 3, S – 2

38. A chondrite normalized REE pattern of quartzo-feldspathic gneiss shows a sharp positiveEu anomaly. This indicates presence of

(*a*) plagioclase in the sample.

(*b*) quartz in the sample.

(*c*) clinopyroxene in the sample.

(*d*) sillimanite in the sample.

39. Choose the correct expression from the following that explains the changing vertical position of a point on the land surface at any time (Surface Uplift – SU, Bedrock Uplift – BU, Deposition – D, Compaction – C, Erosion – E)

(*a*) SU = BU – D – C – E

(*b*) SU = BU – D + C – E

(*c*) SU = BU + D – C + E

(*d*) SU = BU + D – C – E

40. Match the following stratigraphic units listed in Group I with the Precambrian basins in Group II. Group II.

Group I	Group II
P. Badami Group	1. Vindhyan
Q. Kheinjua Formation	2 . Chhatisgarh
R.. Sullavai Group	3. . Kaladgi
S. Papaghni Group	4. Cuddapah
	5. Pranhita-Godavari

(*a*) P – 3, Q – 1, R – 5, S – 4

(*b*) P – 1, Q – 5, R – 4, S – 3

(*c*) P – 1, Q – 2, R – 3, S – 5

(*d*) P – 3, Q – 2, R – 5, S – 4

41. Mantle xenoliths are observed in

(*a*) Kimberlite (*b*) Granite

(*c*) Pegmatite (*d*) Granulite

42. Dimension of hydraulic conductivity is

(*a*) LT^{-2} (*b*) L^3T^{-1}

(*c*) ML^{-3} (*d*) LT^{-1}

43. Match the items in Group I with those in Group II.

Group I	**Group II**
P. Katrol Formation	1. Oligocene
Q. Barail Formation	2 . Cretaceous
R.. Ariyalur Formation	3. . Eocene
S. Sylhet Formation	4. Jurassic
	5. Paleocene
	6. Miocene

(*a*) P – 2, Q – 4, R – 5, S – 3

(*b*) P – 2, Q – 5, R –3, S – 1

(*c*) P – 4, Q – 2, R – 4, S – 5

(*d*) P – 4, Q – 1, R – 2, S – 3

44. The outcrop pattern of folded sedimentary strata on the map given below represents

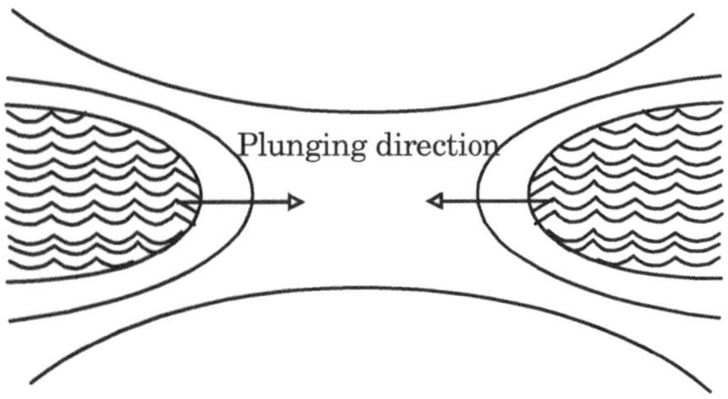

(*a*) culmination of antiform

(*b*) culmination of synform

(*c*) depression of antiform

(*d*) depression of synform

45. Match the economic deposits in Group I with the host rocks in Group II.

Group I	**Group II**
P. Malanjkhand copper	1. Granite
Q. Salem magnesite	2. Dolomite
R.. Zawar Pb-Zn	3. Graphitic Schist
S. Rampura-Agucha	4. Ultramafics
	5. Basalt
	6. Rhyollite

a) P – 1, Q – 4, R – 3, S – 2

(*b*) P – 2, Q –3, R – 5, S – 2

(*c*) P – 1, Q – 4, R – 2, S – 3

(*d*) P – 3, Q - 2, R – 6, S – 5

46.. The stereographic projection below shows the principal stress axes and fault planes. The projection represents a

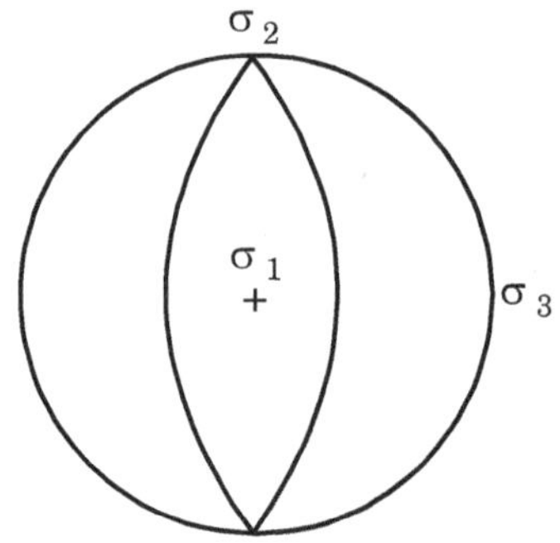

(*a*) normal fault (*b*) reverse fault

(*c*) dextral fault(*d*) sinistral fault

47. Select the correct the statement from the following.

(*a*) Incised channels form an account of aeolin action.

(*b*) Mesa structures are observed only in steeply dipping beds.

(*c*) Crevasse splay is commonly associated with meandering river.

(*d*) Coral reefs are abundant in Gulf of Cambay.

Common Data Questions

Common Data for Questions 48 and 49:

A, B, C, D, E, F and G are minerals in a sample of metamorphic rock. The micro-texture of the assemblage is given below. A, D and G are porphyroblasts, B and C are coronas, E and F are inclusions.

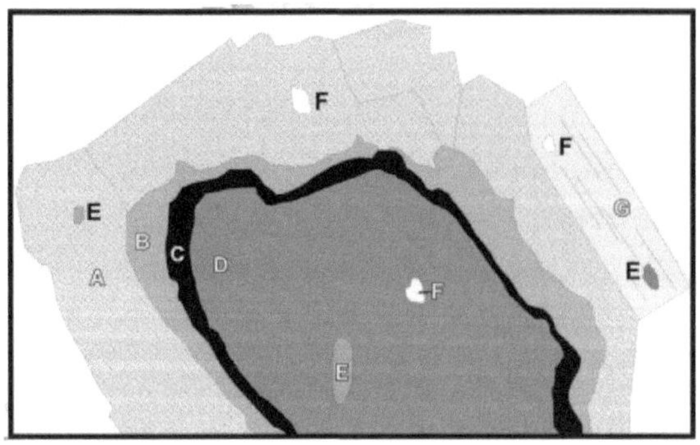

48. Select the appropriate metamorphic reaction from the following options.

(*a*) A + B = C + D (*b*) A + C = D + G

(*c*) A + D = B + C (*d*) E + D = C + A

49. Based on the micro-texture, select the oldest assemblage from the following.

(*a*) A-D (*b*) E-F

(*c*) B-C (*d*) A-G

Common Data for Questions 50 and 51:

The Mohr-Coulomb failure envelope (A-B) of a porous limestone is given below.

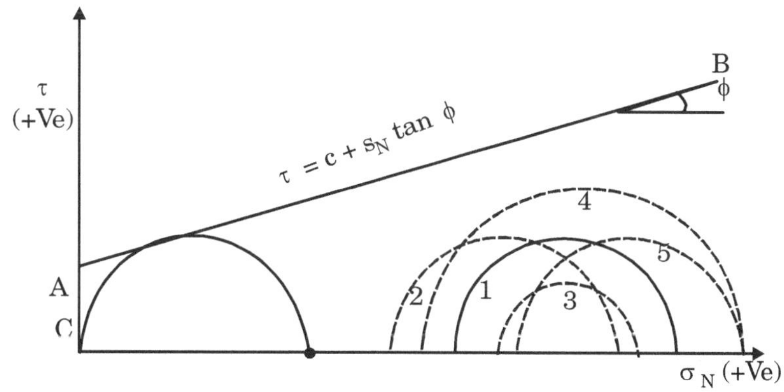

50. The point P represents

(*a*) uniaxial tensile strength.

(*b*) uniaxial compressive strength.

(*c*) indirect tensile strength.

(*d*) shear strength.

51. For a condition represented by the circle 1, if pore water pressure increases, the circle will change to

(*a*) circle 2 (*b*) circle 3

(*c*) circle 4 (*d*) circle 5

Linked Answer Questions

Statement for Linked Answer Questions 52 and 53:

Sedimentary structures are useful for determining the younging direction of a bed.

52. Which one of the following sedimentary structure represents the bottom of a bed?

(*a*) Current crescent (*b*) Desiccation crack

(*c*) Rain print (*d*) Load cast

53. Which sedimentary process is responsible for the generation of the structure identified above?

(*a*) Wave reworking

(*b*) Liquefaction of sediments

(*c*) Drying and desiccation

(*d*) Erosion of cohesive substrate

Statement for Linked Answer Questions 54 and 55:

The table below represents recalculated cation compositions data of minerals.

	I	II	III	IV
Si	3.000	3.000	1.910	2.000
Ti	0.000	0.003	0.003	0.000
Al	1.997	2.000	0.186	0.009
Fe	1.400	6.000	0.160	1.405
Mn	0.000	0.000	0.000	0.032
Mg	1.038	0.510	0.877	0.998
Ca	0.568	0.475	0.848	1.567
Na	0.000	0.024	0.021	0.000
Total	**8.003**	**12.012**	**4.005**	**6.011**

54. Select the correct garnet [$(Ca,Fe,Mg,Mn)_3 Al_2 Si_3 O_{12}$] and clinopyroxene [$Ca(FeMg)Si_2 O_6$] pair respectively.

(*a*) II and III (*b*) II and IV

(*c*) I and IV (*d*) I and III

55. Calculate the distribution coefficient [K_D] for the Fe-Mg system.

(*a*) 0.504 (*b*) 0.620

(*c*) 1.420 (*d*) 1.535

GEOPHYSICS

Q. 26 – Q. 55 carry two marks each.

26. A P-wave is reflected as both P- and S- waves from an interface at angles r_p and r_s respectively. The relationship between r_p and r_s is

(*a*) $r_p > r_s$ (*b*) $r_p = r_s$

(*c*) $r_p < r_s$ (*d*) r_p $2r_s$

27. Which of the following ways of measuring the size of an earthquake does not require instrumental recording?

(*a*) Richter magnitude (*b*) Moment

(*c*) Mw (*d*) Intensity

28. In what circumstances, the migrated reflection seismic section will be same as the unmigrated one?

(*a*) Inclined interfaces

(*b*) Undulating interfaces

(*c*) Horizontal interfaces

(*d*) Vertical interfaces

29. Which of the following methods is best suited to estimate the resistivity variations in the upper mantle?

(*a*) Deep electrical resistivity

(*b*) Ground Penetrating Radar

(*c*) Controlled Source Electromagnetics

(*d*) Magnetotellurics

30. Amongst the following 4-electrode configurations of the electrical resistivity method, which is best suited for archeological investigations?

(*a*) Schlumberger (*b*) Pole-Pole
(*c*) Wenner (*d*) Dipole-Dipole

31. A singular value of an $m \times n$ matrix, A, is defined as

(*a*) positive square root of eigenvalue of AA^T
(*b*) modulus of eigenvalue of A
(*c*) eigenvalue of A^TA
(*d*) square of eigenvalue of A

32. In an ill-posed geophysical inverse problem, stated as non-singular matrix equation, the magnitude of determinant of the coefficient matrix is

(*a*) large (*b*) zero
(*c*) near zero (*d*) very large

33. In a 4-layer subsurface model, which combination of A-, H-, K- and Q- type electrical resistivity sounding curves is **NOT** possible?

(*a*) HA (*b*) AK
(*c*) KQ (*d*) HQ

34. Which of the following characteristics of a Self Potential (SP) anomaly gives the approximate position of centre of the buried ore body?

(*a*) Position of maximum of the anomaly
(*b*) Position of minimum of the anomaly
(*c*) Position of zero crossing
(*d*) Position midpoint between maximum and minimum of the anomaly

35. Given a scalar function, $f(x, y) = xy$. The curl of gradient of $f(x, y)$ is

(*a*) $2x\hat{i}$ (*b*) $-2y\hat{j}$
(*c*) $0\hat{i}$ (*d*) $x\hat{i} + y\hat{j}$

36. Which of the following is NOT correct?

(*a*) In VLF-EM technique, the tilt-angle mode is best suited to locate conductive bodies
(*b*) Fraser filter is a difference filter
(*c*) Static shift affects MT impedance phase
(*d*) Tipper vector is derived from the three magnetic field components, Hx, Hy and Hz.

37. If L, B, F and T respectively stand for Latitude correction, Bouguer correction, Free- air correction and Terrain correction, then the order in which they will have to be applied for gravity data analysis is

(*a*) LFBT (*b*) LBTF
(*c*) FLBT (*d*) TBLF

38. Geomagnetic secular variations originate from the

(*a*) inner core (*b*) outer core
(*c*) crust (*d*) mantle

39. Removal of regional component from magnetic data is similar to

(*a*) band-pass filtering
(*b*) low-pass filtering
(*c*) high-pass filtering
(*d*) band-reject filtering

40. Which of the following is useful to estimate the depth to the centre of a spherical body from a gravity anomaly curve?

(*a*) Surface integration
(*b*) low-pass filteringVolume integration
(*c*) Twice the absolute maximum
(*d*) Half-width of the anomaly

41. Application of reduction-to-pole technique to a magnetic anomaly results in

(*a*) flattening the anomaly curve.
(*b*) transforming the asymmetry in the anomaly to symmetry.
(*c*) halving the amplitude.
(*d*) doubling the amplitude.

42. The Fourier transform of a comb function is

(*a*) delta function (*b*) comb function
(*c*) sync function (*d*) rectangular function

43. In Cartesian coordinate system, if the geological strike of a two-dimensional body is oriented along the x-direction, then the electromagnetic field components associated with TM mode of magnetotelluric method are

(*a*) Hx, Ey and Ez
(*b*) Ex, Hy and Ez
(*c*) Hx, Hy and Ez
(*d*) Ex, Hy and Hz

44. A seismic signal is recorded in the frequency band 100-250 Hz. While digitizing the signal, the sampling interval one should choose to avoid aliasing is __________ ms.

45. Wadati diagram is a plot of the difference in P- and S- wave arrival times against the arrival time of P-wave. It helps in estimating the

(*a*) velocity of P-wave.
(*b*) velocity of S-wave.
(*c*) time of occurrence of earthquake.
(*d*) hypocenter of earthquake.

46. Match the items of Group I with those of Group II

Group I	Group II
P) Caliper log	1) Permeability
Q) NMR log	2) Resistivity
R) Neutron log	3) Diameter
S) SP log	4) Velocity
	5) Porosity

(*a*) P – 3, Q – 4, R – 2, S – 5
(*b*) P – 3, Q – 1, R – 5, S – 2
(*c*) P – 4, Q – 2, R – 4, S – 3
(*d*) P – 1, Q – 3, R – 2, S – 4

47. The most common hydrocarbon indicator is
(*a*) flat spot (*b*) dim spot
(*c*) bright spot (*d*) velocity sag

Common Data Questions

Common Data for Questions 48 and 49:

A recursive filter y_n is given by $y_n = 2x_n - 1.x_{n-1} + y_{n-2}$.

48. The order of y_n is________.

49. The transfer function of y_n in z-domain is

(*a*) $\frac{1-1.5z}{2-z^2}$ (*b*) $\frac{1-z^2}{2-1.5z}$

(*c*) $\frac{2+z^2}{1+1.5z}$ (*d*) $\frac{2-1.5z}{1-z^2}$

Common Data for Questions 50 and 51:

In a linear inverse problem, the coefficient matrix,

$$A = \begin{bmatrix} 2.00 & 2.01 \\ 2.01 & 2.00 \end{bmatrix}$$

50. The eigenvalues of A are
(*a*) (4.01, -0.01) (*b*) (–4.01, –0.01)
(*c*) (4.01, 0.01) (*d*) (–4.01, 0.01)

51. If the elements of A are expressed up to first decimal place only, then the number of possible solution(s) of the resulting inverse problem is
(*a*) 1 (*b*) 2
(*c*) 3 (*d*) ∞

Linked Answer Questions

Statement for Linked Answer Questions 52 and 53:

In an electrical resistivity sounding survey a current of 20 mA is passed through the current electrodes separated by a distance of 50 m and a voltage of 3 V is measured across the potential electrodes, separated by 10 m

52. The above electrode configuration is known as
(*a*) Schlumberger (*b*) Wenner
(*c*) Pole-Dipole (*d*) Pole-Pole

53. The apparent resistivity (in Ω-m) for the above electrode configuration is close to
(*a*) 100 (*b*) 200
(*c*) 300 (*d*) 400

Statement for Linked Answer Questions 54 and 55:

An electromagnetic (EM) wave of frequency 25 Hz is impinging on a homogeneous half-space, having resistivity of 100 Ω-m.

54. The skin-depth of the wave is about
(*a*) 1 km (*b*) 1 m
(*c*) 500 km (*d*) 500 m

55. The velocity of the EM wave (in km/s) is close to
(*a*) 20 π (*b*) 30 π
(*c*) 40 π (*d*) 50 π

GENERA1 APTITUDE (GA)

Q. 56 – Q. 60 carry one mark each.

56. A number is as much greater than 75 as it is smaller than 117. The number is:
(*a*) 91 (*b*) 93
(*c*) 89 (*d*) 96

57. The professor ordered to the students to go out of the class.
I II III IV

Which of the above underlined parts of the sentence is grammatically incorrect?
(*a*) I (*b*) II
(*c*) III (*d*) IV

58. Which of the following options is the closest in meaning to the word given below:
Primeval (*a*) Modern
(*b*) Historic (*c*) Primitive
(*d*) Antique

59. Friendship, no matter how ________it is, has its limitations.
(*a*) cordial (*b*) intimate
(*c*) secret (*d*) pleasant

60. Select the pair that best expresses a relationship similar to that expressed in the pair:

Medicine: Health

(*a*) Science: Experiment
(*b*) Wealth: Peace
(*c*) Education: Knowledge
(*d*) Money: Happiness

Q. 61 to Q. 65 carry two marks each

61. X and Y are two positive real numbers such that $2X + \leq = 6$ and $X + 2Y \leq 8$. For which of thefollowing values of (X, Y) the function f(X, Y) = 3X + 6Y will give maximum value?

(*a*) $\left(\frac{4}{3}, \frac{10}{3}\right)$ (*b*) $\left(\frac{8}{3}, \frac{20}{3}\right)$

(*c*) $\left(\frac{8}{3}, \frac{10}{3}\right)$ (*d*) $\left(\frac{4}{3}, \frac{20}{3}\right)$

62. If $|4X - 7| = 5$ then the values of $2\ |X| - |-X|$ is:

(*a*) $2, \frac{1}{3}$ (*b*) $\frac{1}{2}, 3$

(*c*) $\frac{3}{2}, 9$ (*d*) $\frac{2}{3}, 9$

63. Following table provides figures (in rupees) on annual expenditure of a firm for two years - 2010 and 2011.

Category	2010	2011
Raw material	5200	6240
Power & fuel	7000	9450
Salary & wages	9000	12600
Plant & machinery	20000	25000
Advertising	15000	19500
Research & Development	22000	26400

In 2011, which of the following two categories have registered increase by same percentage?

(*a*) Raw material and Salary & wages

(*b*) Salary & wages and Advertising

(*c*) Power & fuel and Advertising

(*d*) Raw material and Research & Development

64. A firm is selling its product at Rs. 60 per unit. The total cost of production is Rs. 100 and firm is earning total profit of Rs. 500. Later, the total cost increased by 30%. By what percentage the price should be increased to maintained the same profit level.

(*a*) 5

(*b*) 10

(*c*) 15

(*d*) 30

65. Abhishek is elder to Savar.

Savar is younger to Anshul.

Which of the given conclusions is logically valid and is inferred from the above statements?

(*a*) Abhishek is elder to Anshul

(*b*) Anshul is elder to Abhishek

(*c*) Abhishek and Anshul are of the same age

(*d*) No conclusion follows

ANSWERS

PART A (Common Part)

1. (*)	**2.** (*)	**3.** (*c*)	**4.** (*b*)	**5.** (*)	**6.** (*c*)	**7.** (*c*)	**8.** (*b*)	**9.** (*a*)	**10.** (*c*)
11. (*a*)	**12.** (*b*)	**13.** (*a*)	**14.** (*c*)	**15.** (*b*)	**16.** (*b*)	**17.** (*d*)	**18.** (*d*)	**19.** (*b*)	**20.** (*c*)
21. (*a*)	**22.** (*c*)	**23.** (*b*)	**24.** (*d*)	**25.** (*d*)					

PART-B (Geology)

26. (*c*)	**27.** (*d*)	**28.** (*)	**29.** (*)	**30.** (*d*)	**31.** (*a*)	**32.** (*d*)	**33.** (*b*)	**34.** (*c*)	**35.** (*a*)
36. (*d*)	**37.** (*b*)	**38.** (*a*)	**39.** (*d*)	**40.** (*a*)	**41.** (*a*)	**42.** (*d*)	**43.** (*d*)	**44.** (*c*)	**45.** (*c*)
46. (*a*)	**47.** (*c*)	**48.** (*c*)	**49.** (*b*)	**50.** (*b*)	**51.** (*a*)	**52.** (*d*)	**53.** (*b*)	**54.** (*d*)	**55.** (*a,b,c,d*)

(Geophysics)

26. (*a*)	**27.** (*d*)	**28.** (*c*)	**29.** (*d*)	**30.** (*d*)	**31.** (*a*)	**32.** (*c*)	**33.** (*d*)	**34.** (*b*)	**35.** (*c*)
36. (*c*)	**37.** (*a*)	**38.** (*b*)	**39.** (*c*)	**40.** (*d*)	**41.** (*b*)	**42.** (*b*)	**43.** (*a*)	**44.** (*)	**45.** (*c*)
46. (*b*)	**47.** (*c*)	**48.** (*)	**49.** (*d*)	**50.** (*a*)	**51.** (*d*)	**52.** (*a*)	**53.** (*)	**54.** (*a*)	**55.** (*d*)

(General Aptitude)

56. (*d*)	**57.** (*b*)	**58.** (*c*)	**59.** (*b*)	**60.** (*c*)	**61.** (*a*)	**62.** (*b*)	**63.** (*d*)	**64.** (*a*)	**65.** (*d*)

EXPLANATIONS

PART A (COMMON PART)

1. The hydrous minerals in the Moh's scale of hardness are:

Mohs hardness	Mineral	Chemical formula
1	Talc	$Mg_3Si_4O_{10}(OH)_2$
2	Gypsum	$CaSO_4 \cdot 2H_2O$
5	Apatite	$Ca_5(PO_4)_3(OH^-,Cl^-,F^-)$
8	Topaz	$Al_2SiO_4(OH^-,F^-)_2$

The number of hydrous minerals in the Moh's scale of hardness is 4

2. Given, The distance between Earth and Sun is,

$d = 1.496 \times 10^8\ m$

Velocity of light reaching Earth is,

$V = 3 \times 10^8$ m/s

Therefore, Time taken by the light to reach earth

$$= \frac{d}{V} = \frac{1.496 \times 10^8}{3 \times 10^8} = 8.31 \text{ min}$$

3. Hydrous species consists of water which absorbs longer wavelength of visible and near infrared radiation and thus looks typically blue or blue-green due to stronger reflectance at these shorter wavelengths and darker if viewed at red or near infrared wavelengths.

4. The higher the density, the higher the P-wave velocity. As diamond is the highly dense or hardest mineral on the Earth surface, so they have the highest P-wave velocity.

5. Equatorial velocity is the velocity acquired by an observer who is on the equator and its related to the Earth rotational speed.

Now, As we know, Earth takes 24 hours to complete on rotation on its axis. Therefore, its rotational speed in one rotation per 24 hours = 0.041 rad/hr

Thus, the angular velocity of earth

$= 2\pi \times$ rotational speed $= 2\pi \times 0.041$

$= 0.261$ rad/hr

Using formula

$v = r\omega$

where,

v is linear velocity

r is the distance between axis point of mass

ω is the angular velocity

$\therefore$ Equatorial velocity $= r \times \omega$

$= 6400 \times 0.261$ km/hr $= 1674$ km/hr

6. An equal all sided pressure, such as lithostatic pressure is produced by overlying rocks in the crust of earth. Therefore, the greater the confining pressure, greater the strength and hence increases the plasticity of the rock.

7. The acceptable value of the Poisson's ratio of a rock is 0.25.

8. The acceleration due to gravity, 'g' is maximum at poles and minimum at equator.

9. On the Earth's surface, the most abundant minerals would be Quartz, Feldspars, Clay minerals, Ice, Chlorite, etc. In the Earth's crust, the most abundant minerals are Feldspars (about 40-60%) and Quartz (about 30-50%). The remaining 10% would be Micas, Pyroxenes, Amphiboles, Olivine, Ice, etc.

10. Acoustic Impedence,

$Z = \rho \times V$

where,

ρ is density

V is velocity

11. Calcite ($CaCO_3$) is diamagnetic mineral and is not affected by external magnetic field.

12. Resistivity is the property of material, i.e., inherent composition dependence while resistance depends upon the dimension of the material,

$$R = \rho \frac{l}{A}$$

where,

ρ is resistivity of the material

A is area of cross sectional of material

l is the length of material

13. P-waves travel faster than other seismic waves and hence are the first signal from an earthquake to arrive at any affected location or at a seismograph.

14. Dehydration of subducting slab induces mantle melting

15.

Detection method	Parameter
P) Electrical Method	Resistivity
Q) Magnetic Method	Susceptibility
R) Gravity Method	Density
S) Seismic Method	Velocity

16. Given,

Decay constant, $\lambda = 1.55 \times 10^{-10}$ year^{-1}

Half-life of Radioactive isotope is defined as

$$t_{1/2} = \frac{0.693}{\lambda} = \frac{0.693}{1.55 \times 10^{-10}} = 4.47 \times 10^9 \text{ year}$$

17. The electrical resistivity of rocks varies from 1-10^6 Ωm. Sedimentary rocks have the lowest resistivity while igneous and metamorphic rocks have the highest.

18. Hooke's law is defined as

Stress $\propto$ strain

Therefore, it clearly states that it is not an inverse square law.

19. When bedded sedimentary rocks overlie the non-bedded igneous or metamorphic mass the structure is called non- conformity.

20. Seismic S- wave velocity is defined as

$$\beta = \sqrt{\frac{\mu}{\rho}}$$

where, μ is rigidity modulus

ρ is density

$\therefore \beta^2 \propto \mu$

21. An active trench is present in the vicinity of Andaman and Nicobar Islands.

22. **Anisotropy:** Variation of physical property depending on the direction in which it is measured. Anisotropy involves directional variation in one point but heterogeneity involves from point to point.

23. The isotopic ratio of ^{18}O to ^{16}O, usually in form tests or ice cores. High values mean low temperatures. Confounded by ice volume - more ice means higher $\delta^{18}O$ values. Ocean water is mostly $H_2{}^{16}O$, with small amounts of $HD^{16}O$ and $H_2{}^{18}O$. In Standard Mean Ocean Water (SMOW) the ratio of D to H is 155.8 × 10^{-6} and $^{18}O/^{16}O$ is 2005 × 10^{-6}. Fractionation occurs during changes between condensed and vapour phases: the vapour pressure of heavier isotopes is lower, so vapour contains relatively more of the lighter isotopes and when the vapour condenses the precipitation preferentially contains heavier isotopes. The ratio of ^{18}O to ^{16}O oxygen isotopes has changed over the ages and these changes are proxy to changing climate that have been used in both ice cores from glaciers and ice caps and cores of deep sea sediments.

24. The Singareni Collieries Company Limited (SCCL) is a Government coal mining company jointly owned by the Government of Telangana and Government of India on a 51 : 49 equity basis. The **Singareni coal** reserves stretch across 350 Km of the Pranahita – Godavari Valley of Telangana with a proven geological reserves aggregating to whopping 8791 million tonnes.

Khetri is situated at the foothills of the Aravalli Range, which hosts copper mineralization, giving rise to an 80 km long metallogenetic province from Singhana in the north to Raghunathgarh in the south, popularly known as **Khetri Copper Belt**. The belt comprises of tightly folded Proterozoic metasediments that rest over basement gneisses and is a part of the North Delhi fold belt.

Gandhar Oil Refinery (India) Limited is a well-known name and an established player in Specialty Oils and Lubricants industry. Our range of speciality oils and lubricants include liquid paraffin, industrial oil and greases, transformer oils, automotive lubricants, petroleum jelly and rubber processing oils.

The **Jaduguda Mine** also known as Jadugoda or Jadugora is a uranium mine in Jaduguda village in the Purbi Singhbhum district of the Indian state of Jharkhand. It commenced operation in 1967 and was the first uranium mine in India. The deposits at this mine were discovered in 1951.

25. Gamma ray logging is a method of measuring naturally occurring gamma radiation to characterize the rock or sediment in a borehole or drill hole. It is a wireline logging method used in mining, mineral exploration, water-well drilling, for formation evaluation in oil and gas well drilling and for other related purposes.

PART-B (GEOLOGY)

26. A glacial feature is known as 'crag and tale' has faceted pebble.

27. Tectin is an organic matter which makes wall of organic walled foraminifera.

28. The relationship between porosity and void ratio are given as,

$$e = \frac{V_V}{V_s} = \frac{V_V}{V_T - V_V} = \frac{\phi}{1-\phi}$$

where,

ϕ is the porosity

e is the void ratio

V_v is the volume of voids

V_s is the volume of solids

V_T is the bulk volume

Also, $\phi = \frac{V_V}{V_T} = \frac{e}{1+e}$

Now, As per question,

Given, e = 25% = 0.25

$$\therefore \phi = \frac{0.25}{1+0.25} = 0.20 = 20\ \%$$

29. 1 : 10000 scale means 1 cm on map = 10000 cm in ground.

Given, Fault trace is 5 cm on the map according to 1 : 10000 scale, hence actual length on the ground is 5 × 10000 = 50000 cm

On the 1 : 25000 map scale, this length will be represented by $\frac{50000}{25000} = 2$ cm

30. Dehydration is the process of removal of water from the rock or any other material. Biotite compositions have water in its structure and hence melting of biotite indicates rock dehydration.

31.

Dentition Type	Bivalves
P. Desmodont	Mya
Q. Dysodont	Mytilus
R. Isodont	Spondylus
S. Heterodont	Cerastoderma

32. Oil source rock is most abundant in Mesozoic.

33. As per the figure in the given question,

The plane corresponding to 1 is striking N-S and the plane corresponding to 2 is horizontal.

34. Kaolinite is a clay mineral, part of the group of industrial minerals, with the chemical composition $Al_2Si_2O_5(OH)_4$. It is a layered silicate mineral, with one tetrahedral sheet of silica (SiO_4) linked through oxygen atoms to one octahedral sheet of alumina (AlO_6) octahedra. Rocks that are rich in kaolinite are known as kaolin or china clay. Kaolinite in its altered metakaolin form, as a pozzolan; when added to a concrete mix, metakaolin accelerates the hydration of Portland cement and takes part in the pozzolanic reaction with the portlandite formed in the hydration of the main cement minerals (e.g. alite).

In large enough quantities in beach sands, rutile forms an important constituent of heavy minerals and ore deposits. Miners extract and separate the valuable minerals – e.g., rutile, zircon, and ilmenite. The main uses for rutile are the manufacture of refractory ceramic, as a pigment, and for the production of titanium metal.

Graphite: Used in air compressors, food industry, railway track joints, brass instrument valves, piano actions, open gear, ball bearings, machine-shop works, etc. It is also very common for lubricating locks, since a liquid lubricant allows particles to get stuck in the lock worsening the problem. It is often used to lubricate the internal moving parts of firearms in sandy environments.

Serpentine asbestos has curly fibers made up of sheets of crystals. The single type of asbestos from the serpentine family, chrysotile, has historically accounted for more than 95 percent of all asbestos used around the world. As a result of asbestos-industry lobbying, some countries that have banned other types of asbestos still permit the "controlled use" of chrysotile.

35.

H-M symbol	crystallographic groups
6/m	Hexagonal Dipyramid
3m	Ditrigonal Pyramid
$\bar{6}m2$	Ditrigonal Dipyramid
$\bar{6}$	Trigonal Dipyramid

36. Buttress is dam with a solid, water light upstream side that is supported at intervals on the downstream side by a series of vertices.

37. **Kersantite:** A lamprophyre with plagioclase > K-feldspar and biotite as the dominant mafic mineral; no feldspathoid. A lamprophyre containing biotite and plagioclase (usually oligoclase or andesine), with or without clinopyroxene and olivine.

Fenite: The fenites are the metasomatic rocks and occupy about 85% of the total volume of the rocks exposed in the complex. Since, the fenites lie in close proximity to the intrusive mafic and carbonatites, they form a screen between unaltered quartzo- feldspathic gneiss and the intrusive rocks. The fenites include both light and dark coloured variety, the light coloured are the syentic fenites while melteigte represent the darker type.

Mugearite: Sodium-rich trachyandesite is called benmoreite. Basaltic trachyandesite is transitional to basalt and comes in two varieties, mugearite (sodium-rich) and shoshonite (potassium-rich).

Phonolite: Phonolite is a fine-grained equivalent of nepheline syenite. They are products of partial melting, are silica-undersaturated, and have feldspathoids in their normative mineralogy.

38. Plagioclase shows positive 'Eu' anomaly because Ca^{2+} is replaced by Eu^{2+} in its structure.

39. Surface uplift is defined by the bedrock uplift plus the thickness of sediment deposited. Compaction and erosion lowers the area. Thus, compaction and erosion must be substracted from the total thickness to get surface uplift.

40. The Proterozoic Kaladgi–Badami and Bhima basins are intracratonic basins occurring over the Archaean Dharwar craton. The Kaladgi–Badami Basin contains arenites, shales and carbonates with minor cherts and conglomerates deposited in continental, transitional and shallow-marine environments presumably during the late Palaeoproterozoic/Mesoproterozoic to Neoproterozoic. The lower part of the succession (Bagalkot Group) is deformed into east–west-trending elongated doubly plunging synclines and anticlines. The upper part of the succession (Badami Group) is undeformed and unconformably overlies the lower part. The evolution of the Kaladgi–Badami Basin was controlled by movements along east–west-trending normal faults under an extensional stress regime.

A well preserved and diversified microfossil assemblage is reported from a new locality, Newari, Son Valley area, Uttar Pradesh from the black bedded chert belonging to the Fawn Limestone Member of the Kheinjua Formation (~ 1200 Ma), Semri Group (Lower Vindhyans). In all, 28 species belonging to 18 genera representing both coccoid and filamentous forms are described. These are associated with microbial laminites.

The Pranhita-Godavari Basin in central eastern India is one of the Proterozoic "Pur•na" basins of cratonic India. The similarity in the maximum depositional age with previously published authigenic glauconite ages suggest that the origin of the Pranhita-Godvari Graben originated as a rift that formed at a high angle to the coeval evolving late Meosproterozoic Krishna Province as Enderby Land collided with the Dharwar craton of India. In contrast, detrital zircons from the Cycle III Sullavai Group red sandstones yielded a maximum depositional age of 970 ± 20 Ma and had age peaks of ~2550 Ma, ~1600 Ma and then a number of Mesoproterozoic detrital zircons terminating in three analyses at ~970 Ma.

The Mesoproterozoic Papaghni Group in the Cuddapah basin of southern Andhra Pradesh comprises mainly arenaceous, argillaceous and calcareous sediments. These sediments occur in sequences that are mappable on large scale (15000) and the sequences are idenified by unconfornities which are recognised by conglomerate/breccia beds in Vempalle Formation (Papaghni Group).

41. Kimberlite are intruded from the mantle. These are diamond bearing ultrapotassic rocks.

42. Unit of hydraulic conductivity is m/day or m/sec

Dimension of meter is [L]

Dimension of day or sec is [T]

Therefore, the dimension of hydraulic conductivity is $[LT^{-1}]$

43.

Formation	Age
P. Katrol Formation	Jurassic
Q. Barail Formation	Oligocene
R. Ariyalur Formation	Cretaceous
S. Sylhet Formation	Eocene

44. Since limbs are dipping away from each other. Hence, it is antiform. Also, since both folds are plunging in the same direction, depression of antiform is formed.

45. Malanjkhand Copper Project was established in 1982.Initial project has been set up by Hindustan Copper Ltd to exploit the copper ore through an open pit mine. Geological Survey of India took systematic geological exploration at this deposit during 1969. Mining lease of the ore was granted to HCL during 1973. With advancement of time this project was enhanced with viable operational developments.

Most of the magnesite deposits in South India are confined to the southern part of the Dharwar craton and are associated with the ultramafics emplaced into the older supracrustal rocks. Mineralisation of magnesite is observed at different places along the shear zone. Chalk hills, Salem, Tamil Nadu, host the major magnesite deposit in South India.

The Zawar Belt comprises a group of carbonate hosted deposits spread over a strike length of up to 20 km, within dolomites and phyllites of the Lower to Middle Proterozoic Aravalli Supergroup (2400 to 1700 Ma). The individual deposits, which include Zawar, Mochia and Balaria, are hosted by dolomites as disseminations, stringers and veinlets and together contain >40 Mt @ 4.5% Zn, 1.9% Pb.

Rampura Agucha is a zinc-lead sulfide deposit that is located in the Bhilwara belt which is part of the Aravalli-Delhi orogen. The deposit was originally a sedex deposit before experiencing a metamorphic event. There are a few sulphides and oxide minerals that form within the ore that are a particular interest, the major one being Sphalerite. Galena, pyrite, pyrrhotite, and marcasite commonly occur with the sphalerite along with some minor arsenopyrite and chalcopyrite. Gahnite and rutile are the most common oxide minerals that form within the ore, with rutile being the most abundant. Graphite is also a mineral that is commonly found within the ore and surrounding rock.

46. Since limbs are dipping away from each other. Hence, it is antiform. Also, since both folds are plunging in the same direction, depression of antiform is formed.

47. A crevasse splay is a sedimentary fluvial deposit which forms when a stream breaks its natural or artificial levees and deposits sediment on a floodplain. A breach that forms a crevasse splay deposits sediments in similar pattern to an alluvial fan deposit. Once the levee has been breached the water flows out of its channel. As the water spreads onto the flood plain sediments will start to fall out of suspension as the water loses energy. The resulting deposition can create graded deposits similar to those found in Bouma sequences. In some cases crevasse splays can cause a river to abandon its old river channel, a process known as avulsion. Breaches that form a crevasse splay deposits occur most commonly on the outside banks of meanders where the water has the highest energy.

48. As B and C are the coronas, they are formed by the alteration of prophyrobalsts A and D. i.e., A + D = B + C

49. Inclusion are always older than rocks which contains it.

50. Uniaxial compressive strength – Uniaxial compressive strength is the strength of a material to withstand when compressive stress is applied from one direction.

51. Increase in pore water pressure decreases the normal strength of the rock.

52. Load casts are bulges, lumps, and lobes that can form on the bedding planes that separate the layers of sedimentary rocks. The lumps "hang down" from the upper layer into the lower layer, and typically form with fairly equal spacing. These features form during soft-sediment deformation shortly after sediment burial, before the sediments lithify.

53. Liquefaction is the process in which the strength and stiffness of a soil is reduced by rapid loading or earthquake shaking.

54. The correct garnet [(Ca, Fe, Mg, Mn)$_3$Al$_2$Si$_3$O$_{12}$] and clinopyroxene [Ca(FeMg)Si$_2$O$_6$] pair respectively is I and III from the table.

55. All the coefficients are correct.

(GEOPHYSICS)

26. For an oblique incidence of P-wave on an interface of acoustic impudence contrast, the reflected and reflected P-waves follows the principles of reflection and refraction while the generated S-wave does not. The angle it makes to the normal is always smaller than those made by P-wave. This results due to the change in velocity of the incident P-wave and generated S-wave.

27. Intensity: It is a measure of earthquake size based on the extent of local damage it causes at the location of an observer, it does not need any instrumental recording.

28. Migration is the process of repositioning the reflector position by collapsing diffraction. For a horizontal reflection, the migrated reflection is similar to the unmigrated reflection. Migration is done for inclined reflectors, undulating reflectors, vertical reflectors etc.

29. Magnetotellurics (MT) is an electromagnetic geophysical method for inferring the earth's subsurface electrical conductivity from measurements of natural geomagnetic and geoelectric field variation at the Earth's surface. Investigation depth ranges from 300 m below ground by recording higher frequencies down to 10,000 m or deeper with long-period soundings.

30. When conducting geophysical surveys in archaeological exploration it must be kept in mind that a uniform coverage of the survey area is needed. Thus, the first step in field operations is the gridding of the total area to investigate. Any electrode arrangement should take advantage of the gridding already done. Therefore, not all the electrode configurations used in resistivity methods should be considered if field operations are to be optimized. Generally two dimensional grids, most of the time square or rectangular ones, are considered and this imposes a practical limitation to the array to be used. That is, in accordance with their geometry the Wenner, Square, Dipole Dipole, Tri electrode are favoured.

31. The properties for singular value of a matrix are:

I. The singular values $\sigma_1, \sigma_2, \ldots\ldots\ldots\ldots, \sigma_r$ of a $m \times n$ matrix A are the positive square root, $\sigma_1 = \sqrt{\lambda_i > c}$ of the non-zero eigenvalues of the associated Gram matrix $K = A^T A$. The corresponding eigen vectors of K are known as the singular vectors of A.

II. If $A = A^T$ is a symmetric matrix, its singular values are the absolute values of its non-zero eigen values, $\sigma_1 = |\lambda_i| > 0$, its singular vectors coincide with the associated non-null eigenvector.

32. In an ill-posed geophysical inverse problem, stated as non-singular matrix equation, the magnitude of determinant of the coefficient matrix is near zero.

33. Any combination of three layer resistivity values gives four different type of curves which are:

- A-type ($r_1 < r_2 < r_3$)
- Q-type ($r_1 > r_2 > r_3$)
- K-type ($r_1 < r_2 > r_3$)
- H-type ($r_1 < r_2 < r_3$)

Any combination of these type of curve will produce four layer, five layer theoretical model taking three layer at a time and leaving one layer each time as we proceed to the deeper parts.

Therefore, we see that for 4 layer, HQ-type curve doesn't exist.

34. The self-potential anomaly produced due to an orebody is negative. Therefore, as we go more closer to the body, the anomaly is negatively maximum which corresponds to the minimum position of the anomaly and hence the center of the body.

35. Given,

Scalar function $f(x, y) = xy$

Therefore,

Gradient of (x, y), grad$\{f(x, y)\}$

$$= \frac{\partial f(x,y)}{\partial z}\hat{i} + \frac{\partial f(x,y)}{\partial y}\hat{j}$$

$$= \left\{\frac{\partial}{\partial x}(xy)\hat{i} + \frac{\partial}{\partial y}(xy)\hat{j}\right\} = y\hat{i} + x\hat{j}$$

Therefore,

The curl gradient is $f(x, y) = \begin{vmatrix} \hat{i} & \hat{j} & \hat{k} \\ \frac{\partial}{\partial x} & \frac{\partial}{\partial y} & \frac{\partial}{\partial z} \\ y & x & 0 \end{vmatrix} = 0$

36. Static shift affects the apparent resistivity curve and does not affect impedence phase. Therefore, the calculation are made upon impedence phase and not apparent resistivity.

37. The correct sequence of gravity data correction are as follows :

1. Drift Correction
2. Latitudinal correction
3. Free-air correction
4. Bouguer correction
5. Terrain correction
6. Tidal correction
7. Eotvos correction

38. The Earth's magnetic field of internal origin is generated by a geodynamo due to the motion of iron alloys in its outer core that changes over time.

39. Regional anomaly is associated with the low frequency of a potential field data. Therefore, by using high pass filter, regional component can be removed and residual component can be preserved.

40. Half-width of the anomaly is easy and convenient for estimating the depth to the center of anomaly just by taking the half of the maximum of the anomaly and then calculating the depth using the relationship, this equation is for spherical body is

$$Z = 0.652 \times x_{1/2}$$

41. Removing the dependence of magnetic data on the magnetic inclination, i.e., converting data that have been recorded in the inclined Earth's magnetic field to what they would have looked like if the magnetic field had been vertical. Reduction to the pole removes anomaly asymmetry caused by inclination and locates anomalies above the causative bodies, assuming that the remanent magnetism is small compared to the induced magnetism. It is difficult to do at low magnetic inclinations, in which case reduction to the equator is preferred.

42. **Comb function:** It is an infinite series of delta functions spaced at the intervals of T.

It is defined as,

$$comb(t) = \sum_{n=-\infty}^{\infty} \delta(t - nT)$$

Fourier Transform of comb function is

$$COMB(j\omega) = \int_{\infty}^{\infty} comb(t) e^{-Jwt} dt$$

$$= \int_{\infty}^{\infty} \left[\sum_{n=-\infty}^{\infty} \delta(t - nT)\right] e^{-jwt} dt$$

$$= \sum_{n=-\infty}^{\infty} \int_{\infty}^{\infty} \delta(t - nT)\, e^{-jwt} dt = \sum_{n=-\infty}^{\infty} e^{-jwnT}$$

$$= \frac{2\pi}{T} \sum_{n=-\infty}^{\infty} \delta(w - Kw_o) = \frac{1}{T} \sum_{k=-\infty}^{\infty} \delta\left(f - \frac{K}{T}\right)$$

Hence, Fourier Transform of comb function is itself a comb function.

43. For E-polarization and B-polarization in magneto telluric, the different field component along the three perpendicular axes are depicted as

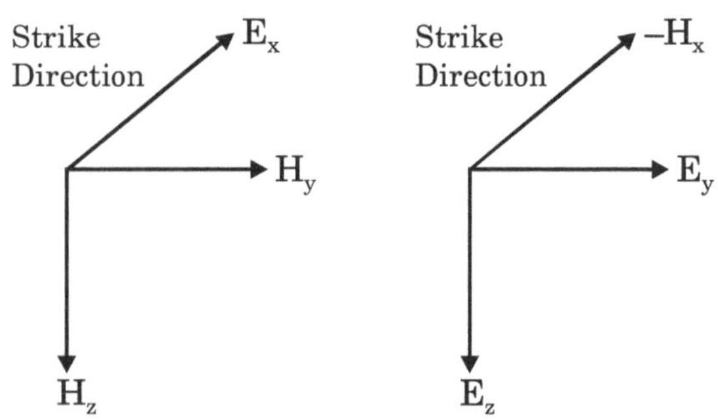

E-Polarization **B-Polarization**

As per question, the strike direction is in the y direction. Therefore, for E-polarization model the field components are H_x, E_y and H_Z.

44. As per question,

The recorded frequency band is 100-250 Hz

The highest frequency recorded is 250 Hz

Thus, the Nyquist frequency is 250 Hz

Therefore,

Sampling frequency, $f_s = 2 \times f_N = 500\ Hz$ and

Sampling interval $= \frac{1}{500}\ s = 2\ ms$

45. The origin time of an earthquake can be determined with a very simple graphical technique, called Wadati plot. The time separation of the P and S phase (ts-tp) is plotted against the arrival time of the P-wave. Since ts-tp = 0 at the hypocentre, a straight line fit on the Wadati diagram gives the origin time at the intercept with the P-arrival-time axis.

46. The Caliper Log is a tool for measuring the diameter and shape of a borehole. It uses a tool which has 2, 4, or more extendable arms. The arms can move in and out as the tool is withdraw from the borehole, and then movement is converted into an electrical signal by a potentiometer.

The ability to estimate formation permeability is one of the earliest benefits of nuclear magnetic resonance (NMR) logging and remains the most important application. This artcle provides an overview of permeability estimation techniques by use of NMR logging.

The most difficult nuclear logs to interpret are those that exploit neutron scattering to estimate porosity. The log targets the average hydrogen density of the volume investigation. If all the hydrogen in the formation is in the form of porosity-filling liquid, in particular water or oil, the hydrogen index will track the porosity.

Resistivity logging is an important branch of well logging. Essentially, it is the recording, in uncased (or, recently, even cased) sections of a borehole, of the resistivities (or their reciprocals, the conductivities) of the subsurface formations, generally along with the spontaneous potentials (SPs) generated in the borehole. This recording is of immediate value for geological correlation of the strata and detection and quantitative evaluation of possibly productive horizons.

47. **Bright spot:** A seismic amplitude anomaly or high amplitude that can indicate the presence of hydrocarbons. Bright spots result from large changes in acoustic impedance and tuning effect, such as when a gas sand underlies a shale, but can also be caused by phenomena other than the presence of hydrocarbons, such as a change in lithology. The term is often used synonymously with hydrocarbon indicator.

48. Given

A recursive filter y_n,

$y_n = 2x_n - 1.5x_{n-1} + y_{n-2}$

The order of y_n is 2

49. Given,

A recursive filter y_n,

$y_n = 2x_n - 1.5x_{n-1} + y_{n-2}$

Transforming this to Z-transform domain, we get,

$y_n = 2 - 1.5z + z^2 y_n$

$\Rightarrow y_n\left(1 - z^2\right) = 2 - 1.5z$

$\Rightarrow y_n = \left(\frac{2 - 1.5z}{1 - z^2}\right)$

50. Given,

$$A = \begin{bmatrix} 2.00 & 2.01 \\ 2.01 & 2.00 \end{bmatrix}$$

The eigen values are given as,

$|A - \lambda I| = 0$

$\therefore \begin{vmatrix} 2-\lambda & 2.01 \\ 2.01 & 2\ \ \lambda \end{vmatrix} = 0$

$(2-\lambda)(2-\lambda) - 2.01 \times 2.01 = 0$

$\Rightarrow (2-\lambda)^2 = 2.01^2$

$\Rightarrow 2 - \lambda = \pm 2.01$

$\Rightarrow \lambda = -0.01, 4.01$

51. When the elements of matrix A is expressed up to first decimal place only, the matrix is singular and hence, there exists infinite number of solution for the resulting inverse problem.

52. Consider the electrode configuration given in the question.

As potential electrode spacing is 1/5 of current electrode spacing, the configuration is Schlumberger sounding

53. Given,

Voltage, $V = 3V$

Distance, $d = 50\ m$

Current, $I = 20\ mA$

Measured across the potential electrodes,

$a = 10\ m$

The apparent resistivity due to Schlumberger sounding is given by

$$\rho_a = \frac{\pi}{4}\frac{V}{I}\frac{\left(d^2 - a^2\right)}{a}$$

$$\Rightarrow \rho_a = \frac{\pi}{4} \times \frac{3}{20} \times 10^3 \times \frac{50^2 - 10^2}{10} = 28274.33\ \Omega - m$$

54. Given,

Resistivity, $\rho = 100\ \Omega$-m

Frequency, $f = 25\ Hz$

Now, The skin depth is defined as

$$d = 503.8\sqrt{\frac{\rho}{f}} = \sqrt{\frac{100}{25}} = 1000\ m = 1\ km$$

55. The velocity of EM waves is defined by the relation

$$V = \frac{\omega}{k} = \frac{2\pi f}{k}$$

where, k is the wave number

and f is the frequency

ω is the angular frequency

Also, $k = \frac{1}{d}$

$\therefore k = 2\pi f d$

Now, Given,

$f = 25\ Hz$

$d = 1\ km$ [From above question]

(GENERAL APTITUDE SECTION)

56. Let, the number be x.

As per question

$x - 75 = 117 - x$

$\Rightarrow\ 2x = 192$

$\Rightarrow\ x = 96$

57. According to the question, in given sentence part II is a grammatical error. it should be 'ordered' instead of 'ordered to'.

The professor ordered the students to go out of the class.

58. Primitive, it is synonym for Primeval

59. Friendship, no matter how intimate it is, has its limitations.

Intimate means closely acquainted; familiar.

Statement says about limitations of friendship and our required word follows "no matter how" meaning it should be something which increases the friendship bond.

60. Medicine improves health; education improves knowledge.

61. $f(x, y) = 3x + 6y = 3(x + 2y)$

Maximum value of $x + 2y$ is given by equation $8(x + 2y \le 8)$

i.e., Maximum value of $f(x, y) = 3 \times 8 = 24$

$\therefore x = \frac{4}{3}$ and $y = \frac{10}{3}$

62. $|4X - 7| = 5$, since it is in absolute form the regular form of this equation is given as $|4X - 7| = 5$

$(4X - 7) = -5$

By solving the above equations we get the following answer

$X = \frac{1}{2}, X = 3$

Now, $2|X| - |-X| = 2|X| - |X| = |X|$.

63. Percentage increase in Raw material

$= \frac{6240 - 5200}{5200} = 20\%$

Percentage increase in Power & fuel

$= \frac{9450 - 7000}{7000} = 35\%$

Percentage increase in Salary & wages

$= \frac{12600 - 9000}{9000} = 40\%$

Percentage increase in Plant & machinery

$= \frac{25000 - 20000}{20000} = 25\%$

Percentage increase in Advertising

$= \frac{19500 - 15000}{15000} = 30\%$

Percentage increase in Research & Developement

$= \frac{26400 - 22000}{22000} = 20\%$

64. Let N units be made.

Selling price per item = Rs.60

Let X be the cost per unit

Given 500(as profit) = 60 – X + 60 – X + 60 – X + 60 – X + ... 60 – X

N(60 – X) = 500

$\Rightarrow$ 65N – NX = 500

Total cost is Rs. 100.

$\Rightarrow$ 60N – 100 = 500

$\Rightarrow$ N = 10

Now, the cost is increased by 30%.

Therefore,

the new cost is Rs. 130 and the extra 30 has to be equally divided among 10 units to maintain same profit level.

Thus, selling price should icnrease by 3 from 60

$\Rightarrow \frac{3}{60} \times 100 = 5\%$ increase.

65. No conclusion follows as we cannot derive any relationship between Abhishek and Anshul with the given data. If all the three are brothers, then Abhishek is elder to Anshul.

SOLVED PAPER - 2012

PART-A (Common Part)

Q.1 – Q.25 carry one mark each.

1. In Mohs' scale of hardness, how many minerals are of silicate composition?

(*a*) 4 (*b*) 5

(*c*) 6 (*d*) 7

2. Which one of the following river systems forms the largest fluvio-deltaic system in the world?

(*a*) Mississippi–Ohio

(*b*) Red–Mekong

(*c*) Ganga–Brahmaputra

(*d*) Yellow–Ba Hoi

3. Which one amongst the following rocks commonly has highest unconfined compressive strength?

(*a*) Coarse-grained sandstone

(*b*) Mica schist

(*c*) Fossiliferous limestone

(*d*) Massive basalt

4. Eparchean unconformity separates geological units of

(*a*) early Archaean from late Archaean

(*b*) Archaean from Proterozoic

(*c*) Archaean from Proterozoic

(*d*) Archaean from Phanerozoic

5. Point bar deposit is associated with

(*a*) braided river (*b*) estuary

(*c*) meandering river (*d*) beach

6. Polymetallic nodules on the ocean floor contain significant amounts of:

(*a*) Cu–Ni–Co (*b*) Pb–Zn–Ti

(*c*) Hg–Mo–Pt (*d*) U–Th–Nb

7. If the rake of net slip of an inclined fault is 90°, the fault is

(*a*) strike-slip fault (*b*) dip-slip fault

(*c*) oblique-slip fault (*d*) transcurrent fault

8. On a photo-scale of 1:40000, a square shaped open cast coal mine of 1 km 2 area would have an area of (in cm 2)

(*a*) 2.50 (*b*) 4.00

(*c*) 6.25 (d) 12.00

9. Bouguer correction is applied to correct for the gravity anomaly due to mass between station location and

(*a*) mean sea level

(*b*) local datum plane

(*c*) base of upper crust

(*d*) Mohorovicic discontinuity

10. Which one of the following can be estimated from SP log against a saline-water saturated sandstone formation encountered in a well?

(*a*) Resistivity of formation water

(*b*) Degree of water saturation

(*c*) Depth of invasion

(*d*) Permeability

11. During its orbital motion around the Sun, the Earth is nearest to the Sun on

(a) March 21 (*b*) July 4

(*c*) September 23 (*d*) January 3

12. Which one of the following can be best explored using electromagnetic method?

(*a*) Oil-bearing strata

(*b*) Coal-bearing strata

(*c*) Disseminated sulphide deposit

(*d*) Massive sulphide deposit

13. Name the planet in the solar system which has its "day" longer than its "year".

(*a*) Mercury (*b*) Venus

(*c*) Mars (*d*) Neptune

14. The most sensitive instrument for magnetic survey is

(*a*) magnetic field balance

(*b*) fluxgate magnetometer

(*c*) proton precession magnetometer

(*d*) optically pumped magnetometer

15. Which physical property of the medium governs the response of Ground Penetrating Radar (GPR)?

(*a*) Electrical conductivity

(*b*) Electromagnetic conductivity

(*c*) Seismic wave velocity

(*d*) Electrical permeability (dielectric permittivity)

16. Out of the following gases which one has the highest contribution towards the greenhouse effect on the Earth?

(*a*) CO_2 (*b*) CO
(*c*) CH_4 (*d*) H_2O

17. Depth range of the 'transition zone' associated with phase changes in the Earth's mantle is (in km)

(*a*) 35 to 150 (*b*) 150 to 410
(*c*) 410 to 660 (*d*) 660 to 800

18. Choose the correct pair of plutonic rock and its volcanic equivalen

(*a*) Gabbro–Trachyte (*b*) Syenite–Andesite
(*c*) Granite–Rhyolite (*d*) Granodiorite–Basalt

19. Which of the following is NOT a variety of silica (SiO_2)?

(*a*) Jasper (*b*) Coesite
(*c*) Stishovite (*d*) Flinkite

20. Which one of these is NOT a source of sufficient water supply but can transmit certain quantity of water on a regional scale due to leakage?

(*a*) Aquifer (*b*) Aquitard
(*c*) Aquiclude (*d*) Aquifuge

21. Identify the type of fault present in the given aerial photograph.

(*a*) Normal fault
(*b*) Reverse fault
(*c*) Left-lateral strike-slip fault
(*d*) Right-lateral strike-slip fault

22. The Jurassic stratigraphic succession of Kutch is characterized by which one of the following?

(*a*) Cephalopods (*b*) Trilobites
(*c*) Brachiopods (*d*) Graptolites

23. Which one of the following mineral constituents exhibits strong absorption in the UV-blue band of the EM spectrum due to charge transfer effect leading to colouration?

(*a*) Fe-O (*b*) Si-O
(*c*) Al-OH (*d*) Mg-OH

24. When did the supercontinent Pangaea begin to break up?

(*a*) Cenozoic (*b*) Mesozoic
(*c*) Palaeozoic (*d*) Proterozoic

25. In which of the following localities does coal deposit occur?

(*a*) Dariba (*b*) Kudremukh
(*c*) Wardha (*d*) Rudrasagar

PART-B
GEOLOGY

Q.26 - Q.55 carry two marks each.

26. Specific discharge of 1 cm per day is observed in a porous medium where hydraulic head difference is 0.5 m and flow length is 20 m. Calculate the hydraulic conductivity (in m/day).

(*a*) 0.4 (*b*) 0.8
(*c*) 1.2 (*d*) 1.6

27. A sandstone bed dipping 30° has an outcrop width of 20 m in a flat terrain. What is the true thickness (in m) of the bed?

(*a*) 5 (*b*) 10
(*c*) 20 (*d*) 30

28. Calculate the concentration (in ppm) of Ni in olivine that crystallizes from a basaltic magma containing 20 ppm Ni. The partition coefficient (solid/melt) of nickel is 5.

(*a*) 4 (*b*) 20
(*c*) 100 (*d*) 500

29. An analysis of augite yields 3 silicon atoms calculated on the basis of 12 oxygen atoms. If only Al replaces Si, calculate the number of tetrahedral-Al in the mineral.

(*a*) 1
(*b*) 2
(*c*) 3
(*d*) 4

30. Calculate the degree(s) of freedom of the assemblage orthopyroxene + clinopyroxene + plagioclase + hornblende + quartz + fluid in the chemical system $CaO–FeO–MgO–Al_2O_3–SiO_2–H_2O$ with pressure and temperature as physical variables.

(*a*) 0 (*b*) 1
(*c*) 2 (*d*) 3

31. Ca-montmorillonite is formed by the chemical weathering of

(*a*) calcite (*b*) augite
(*c*) orthoclase (*d*) forsterite

32. In which of the following crystal systems, the characteristic symmetry elements "a two-fold axis of rotation and at least two planes of symmetry" are possible?

(*a*) Tetragonal (*b*) Hexagonal
(*c*) Orthorhombic (*d*) Monoclinic

33. Determine the correctness or otherwise of the following Assertion [a] and Reason [r].

Assertion: Biaxial minerals can be pleochroic in three shades.

Reason: Biaxial minerals have three refractive indices.

(*a*) Both [a] and [r] are true and [r] is the correct reason for [a]
(*b*) [a] is true but [r] is false
(*c*) [a] is false but [r] is true
(*d*) Both [a] and [r] are true but [r] is not the correct reason for [a]

34. The correct sequence of metamorphic facies with increasing depth in a subduction zone is

(*a*) greenschist, blueschist, eclogite
(*b*) greenschist, eclogite, blueschist
(*c*) blueschist, greenschist, eclogite
(*d*) blueschist, eclogite, greenschist

35. Which one of the following basins is producing petroleum from the coal-rich reservoir rocks?

(*a*) Rajasthan Basin (*b*) Cambay Basin
(*c*) Cauvery Basin (*d*) Krishna-Godavari Basin

36. A major thrust in the Himalayas has resulted in intense shearing of a zone about 0.5 km wide on either side of the thrust leading to landslides. Which GIS function can be used to display the shear zone?

(*a*) Contiguity (adjacency)
(*b*) Spread
(*c*) Proximity (buffer)
(*d*) Search

37. Vertical exaggeration commonly occurs during stereo-viewing of aerial photographs. Where does it occur?

(*a*) In the photographs
(*b*) In the terrain
(*c*) In the stereoscope
(*d*) In the perceptor's mind

38. A potassic ultrabasic hybrid igneous rock containing macrocrysts of olivine, Cr-rich diopside, phlogopite and pyrope in a groundmass of serpentine, carbonate and perovskite can be named as

(*a*) kimberlite (*b*) ijolite
(*c*) melilitolite (*d*) harzburgite

39. Herringbone structure is generally formed in which of the following environments?

(a) Lacustrine (*b*) Fluvial
(*c*) Aeolian (*d*) Tidal

40. In a typical coal mine area affected by acid mine drainage, which one of the following acids will be dominant?

(*a*) Nitric acid (*b*) Sulphuric acid
(*c*) Hydrochloric acid (*d*) Hydrofluoric acid

41. Match the items in Group **I** with those in Group **II.**

Group I	Group II
P. Theca	1. Trilobite
Q. Midrib	2. Brachiopod
R. Deltidium	3. Glossopteris
S. Pygidium	4 .Graptolite
	5 Diatoms

(*a*) P-3, Q-4, R-5, S-1
(*b*) P-4, Q-3, R-2, S-1
(*c*) P-5, Q 3, R-2, S-1
(*d*) P-2, Q-4, R-5, S-1

42. Arrange the following formations sequentially from older to younger:

P. Sargur Schist
Q. Kajrahat Limestone
R. Cuddalore Sandstone
S. Umia Ammonite Bed

(*a*) P, S, Q, R
(*b*) P, Q, R, S
(*c*) P, Q, S, R
(*d*) Q, S, P, R

43. Which of the following statements is true?

(*a*) Transposition foliation is an indication of superposed folding

(*b*) Stratigraphic information is retained in transposition structures

(*c*) Transposition foliation develops parallel to axial plane of tight folds

(*d*) Fold closures can be well identified in transposition structures

44. Match the items in Group **I** with those in Group **II.**

Group I	Group II
P. Churching	1. Concrete gravity dam
Q. Curtain grouting	2. Tunnelling
R. Piping	3. Cement
S. Pozzolan	4. Earth dam

(*a*) P-2, Q-1, R-4, S-3 (*b*) P-4, Q-1, R-2, S-3

(*c*) P-2, Q-3, R-1, S-4 (*d*) P-1, Q-2, R-3, S-4

45. A horizontally bedded sandstone outcrop exhibits planar cross-beds at a number of places. The dip directions of the foresets of cross-beds at these locations are: N350°, N17°, N355°, N355°, N15°, N360°, N350°, N13°, N350° , N355°

Find the mean palaeocurrent direction.

(*a*) N15°

(*b*) N350°

(*c*) N355°

(*d*) N360°

46. Salinity of three different fluid inclusions in H 2 O-NaCl system is to be determined by "heating–freezing" experiments. The phase proportions of inclusions at room temperature are shown below:

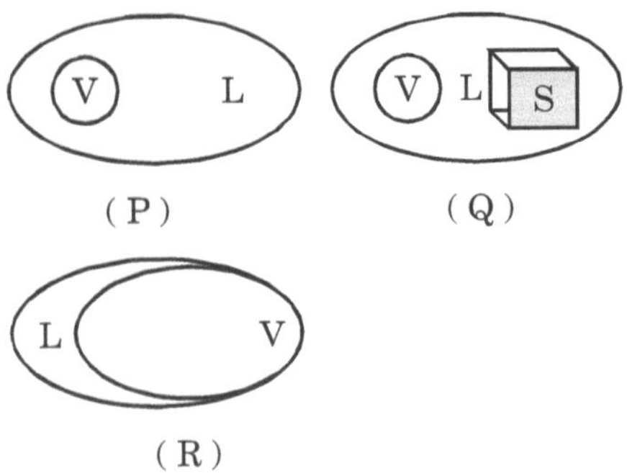

V : Vapour; L : Liquid (H_2O); S : Solid (Halite)

(*a*) heating of P, freezing of Q

(*b*) heating of Q, freezing of R

(*c*) freezing of P, heating of R

(*d*) heating of all P, Q and R

47. Study the map below showing elevation of selected locations and outcrops of sedimentary beds.

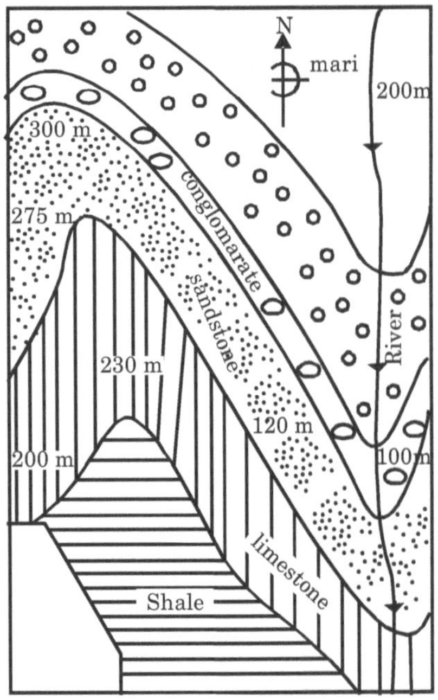

Which of the following statements is correct?

(*a*) The beds dip easterly

(*b*) The beds dip easterly

(*c*) The beds dip southerly

(*d*) The beds are folded

Common Data Questions

Common Data for Questions 48 and 49:

The figures P and Q represent schematic binary phase diagrams for solid–melt and subsolidus relations in temperature (T)–composition (X) space.

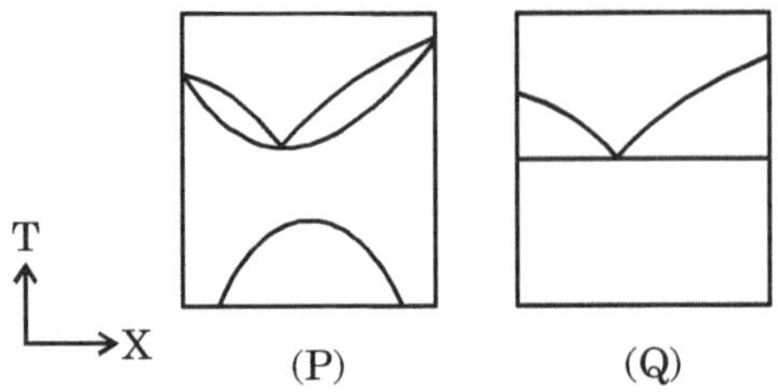

48. Which of the following statements is true?

(*a*) P shows eutectic relation and Q shows high temperature limited solid solution

(*b*) Both P and Q show high temperature limited solid solution

(*c*) Both P and Q show eutectic relation

(*d*) P shows high temperature limited solid solution and Q shows eutectic relation

49. Choose the correct statement?

(a) Solvus occurs in both P and Q

(b) Solvus is absent in both P and Q

(c) Solvus occurs in P but not in Q

(d) Solvus occurs in Q but not in P

Common Data for Questions 50 and 51:
The following figure gives Mohr envelope for a rock and Mohr circle in a particular stress condition. Fracturing occurs when the Mohr circle touches the Mohr envelope at B. involves introduction of Si and AI into dolomitic limestone.

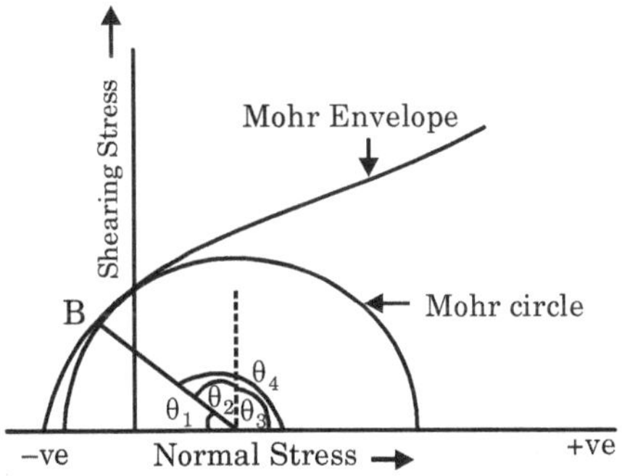

50. What type of fractures will develop in the rock?

(*a*) Extension fractures

(*b*) Conjugate shear fractures

(*c*) Columnar fractures

(*d*) Hybrid extension-shear fractures

51. What is the dihedral angle?

(*a*) θ_1 (*b*) θ_2

(*c*) θ_3 (*d*) θ_4

Linked Answer Questions

Statement for Linked Answer Questions 52 and 53:

52. Copper ore deposit with significant content of molybdenum occurs in

(*a*) thin layers of shale

(*b*) basic-ultrabasic rocks

(*c*) volcanogenic (rhyolitic) sedimentary rocks

(*d*) andesite porphyry

53. An example of the above type of copper deposit is

(*a*) Kupfersciefer, Germany

(*b*) Chuquicamata, Chile

(*c*) Kurroko, Japan

(*d*) Sudbury, Canada

Linked Answer Questions 54 and 55:

Microfossils are widely used in palaeoceanographic studies.

54. Which of the following microfossil groups is generally found in deep sea below the Carbonate Compensation Depth?

(*a*) Foraminifera (*b*) Radiolaria

(*c*) Cocoliths (*d*) Ostracods

55. What is the test composition of the microfossil group identified above?

(*a*) Carbonate (*b*) Phosphate

(*c*) Nitrate (*d*) Siliceous

GEOPHYSICS

Q.26 – Q.55 carry two marks each.

26. The average magnetic susceptibility of dolerite is 1400. What is its magnetic permeability in h/m? (Give answer up to 5 decimal places) .

(*a*) 0.00176 (*b*) 0.00176

(*c*) 0.00302 (*d*) 0.00354

27. A small scale seismic reflection survey was conducted with a shot point located at the middle of a 500 m long geophone spread. The NMO-corrected travel times at the end of the spread were found to be 1.227 s and 1.255 s. If the average seismic wave velocity above the reflector is 2500 m/s, what is the dip of the reflector? (Give the value in degrees in nearest integer)

(*a*) 4 (*b*) 6

(*c*) 8 (*d*) 10

28. The S-wave velocity in the lower continental crust is 6800 m/s and its density is 3380 kg/m^3. Find its rigidity in GPa. (Give answer up to 2 decimal places)

(*a*) 156.29 (*b*) 160.21

(*c*) 162.34 (*d*) 500

29. Given the frequency of an electromagnetic wave to be 1 kHz and ground conductivity to be 10 S/m, calculate the skin depth. (Give answer in nearest integer, in meters)

(*a*) 2 (*b*) 3

(*c*) 5 (*d*) 8

30. Based on acoustic log of a well, the transit time in a water-bearing sandstone zone is found to be 75 s/ft. The transit time of acoustic wave through the sandstone matrix and water are 50 s/ft and 200 s/ft, respectively. Determine the porosity of the sandstone. (Give answer up to 2 decimal places)

(*a*) 0.05 (*b*) 0.10

(*c*) 0.12 (*d*) 0.17

31. In frequency domain IP method, frequency effect is defined as

(*a*) $(\rho_{ac} - \rho_{dc})/\rho_{dc}$

(*b*) $(\rho_{ac} - \rho_{dc})/\rho_{ac}$

(*c*) $(\rho_{dc} - \rho_{ac})/\rho_{dc}$

(*d*) $(\rho_{dc} - \rho_{ac})/\rho_{ac}$

32. The bright spot on a seismic reflection section in a sand-shale sequence can be seen over

(*a*) fresh water-bearing sand

(*b*) saline water-bearing sand

(*c*) oil pool

(*d*) gas pool

33. The line joining the north and south magnetic dip poles misses the Earth's centre by about (in km)

(*a*) 1000 (*b*) 1100

(*c*) 1200 (*d*) 1300

34. For a three-layered earth with resistivities ρ_1, ρ_2, and ρ_3, and corresponding thicknesses h_1, h_2, and h_3 respectively, the quantity $(h_1 / \rho_1) + (h_2 / \rho_2) + (h_3 / \rho_3)$ stands for

(*a*) longitudinal conductance

(*b*) transverse resistance

(*c*) apparent conductance

(*d*) apparent resistance

35. The distance between the centre of the Earth and the barycentre (i.e. centre of mass of the Earth-Moon system) is (in km)

(*a*) 4510 (*b*) 4670

(*c*) 4810 (*d*) 4860

36. The change in gravity caused by Earth's tides on the land surface in a complete tidal cycle is in the range of (in milligal)

(*a*) 0.1 to 0.2 (*b*) 0.2 to 0.3

(*c*) 0.3 to 0.4 (*d*) 0.4to 0.5

37. Terrestrial heat flow is the product of

(*a*) thermal diffusivity and temperature

(*b*) thermal conductivity and temperature

(*c*) thermal diffusivity and temperature gradient

(*d*) thermal conductivity and temperature gradient

38. According to Archie's equation, the electrical resistivity of porous sandstone doesn't depend on:

(*a*) porosity

(*b*) nature of interstitial fluid

(*c*) tortuosity of pores

(*d*) solid matrix

39. Match the items in Group I with those in Group II.

Group I	Group II
P. Magnetic susceptibility	1. Gyromagnetic ratio
Q. Airborne magnetic survey	2. Axial dipole
R. Geomagnetic field	3. Diamagnetism
S. Proton precession magnetometer	4. Total field intensity
	5. Poisson's relation

(*a*) P-3, Q-4, R-2, S-1

(*b*) P-5, Q-2, R-4, S-3

(*c*) P-1, Q-4, R-1, S-5

(*d*) P-4, Q-3, R-3, S-1

40. The NMO of a diffraction hyperbola as compared to that of a reflection hyperbola is

(*a*) always greater (*b*) always smaller

(*c*) random (*d*) same

41. Which one of the following can be determined from the NMR log against sandstone?

(*a*) Clay content of sandstone

(*b*) Total porosity

(*c*) Water-filled porosity

d) Structured water

42. The peak in the response curves obtained from a geophone exhibits

(*a*) shift to lower frequency with increasing damping coefficient

b) shift to higher frequency with increasing damping coefficient

(*c*) no shift in frequency with increasing damping coefficient

(*d*) increase in amplitude with increasing damping coefficient

43. The solution to the purely under-determined problem Gm = d is given by

(*a*) $(G^TG)^{-1} G^Td$ (*b*) $(G^TG)^{-1} GD^T$

(*c*) $G^T(GG^T)^{-1}d$ (*d*) $G^Td(GG^T)^{-1}$

44. Given the following matrix equation:

$A_{mxn} \; X_{xx1} = b_{m\times 1}$

the nature of this system of equation is

(*a*) over-determined if m > n

(*b*) under-determined if m < n

(*c*) even-determined if m = n

(*d*) determined by the rank of the matrix A

45. Match the items in Group I with those in Group II.

Group I	Group II
P. 10^4 to 1 Hz	1. VLF
Q. 400 to 2000 Hz	2. GPR
R. 20 kHz to 25 kHz	3. MT
S. 25 MHz to 1.2 GHz	4. Slingram

(*a*) P-2, Q-1, R-4, S-3 (*b*) P-3, Q-4, R-1, S-2

(*c*) P-1, Q-4, R-3, S-2 (*d*) P-3, Q-2, R-1, S-4

46. Gamma-gamma log applied for estimation of formation density uses incident rays with energy in the range of 0.5 MeV to 2.0 MeV. The interaction of such gamma rays with rocks is governed by

(*a*) photoelectric absorption

(*b*) Compton scattering

(*c*) pair production

(*d*) secondary emission of gamma rays

47. Determine the correctness or otherwise of the following Assertion [a] and Reason [r].

Assertion: In a well-log survey using fresh-water drilling mud, an oil-bearing sandstone zone can be identified by electrical resistivity and SP logs.

Reason: Oil has high electrical resistivity and the porous nature of sandstone is indicated by negative SP.

(*a*) [a] is true but [r] is false

(*b*) [a] is false but [r] is true

(*c*) both [a] and [r] are true but [r] is not the correct reason for [a]

(*d*) both [a] and [r] are true and [r] is the correct reason for [a]

Common Data Questions

Common Data (or Questions 48 and 49:

A signal having duration of 10 seconds is sampled at a rate of 1000 samples per second. The maximum frequency of the sampled signal is 475 Hz. t slab. Q and Rare parts of the topography.

48. If the signal has been under-sampled, the maximum frequency (in Hz) of the original signal would have been

(*a*) 475 (*b*) 500

(*c*) 525 (*d*) 550

49. What is the frequency interval (in Hz) at which the spectrum of the above signal is evaluated?

(a) 0.08 (b) 0.10

(c) 0.12 (d) 0.14

Common Data for Questions 50 and 51:

In a sequence of equally thick layers in the subsurface, normally incident reflection coefficients at the three interfaces are: 0.10, 0.15 and 0.18.

50. The amplitude of primary reflection from the deepest interface is

(*a*) 0.184 (*b*) 0.174

(*c*) 0.165 (*d*) 0.156

51. The amplitude of the surface multiple that arrives along with the reflection from the deepest interface is

(*a*) 0.008 (*b*) 0.005

(*c*) 0.003 (*d*) 0.001

Linked Answer Questions

Statement for Linked Answer Questions 52 and 53:

A thick section of clean sand is identified on a suite of geophysical logs. The deep laterolog reads 4 Ohm-m in the upper part of the section and 0.1 Ohm-m in the lower part of the section. The lower part is interpreted to be 100% water-saturated. The resistivity of formation water obtained from SP log is estimated to be 0.01 Ohm-m.

52. The formation resistivity factor of the clean sand section is

(*a*) 8 (*b*) 10

(*c*) 12 (*d*) 14

53. Based on the above result, the water saturation in the top part of the sand formation is

(*a*) 0.125 (*b*) 0.158

(*c*) 0.165 (*d*) 0.184

Statement for Linked Answer Questions 54 and 55:

The seismic slip of a fault after an earthquake is measured to be 0.5 m and the fault area is estimated to be 250 km^2 . The rigidity of the medium surrounding the fault is 30 GPa.

54. The seismic moment (in Nm) of the earthquake is

(*a*) 3.75×10^{18} (*b*) 3.75×10^{16}

(*c*) 3.75×10^{14} (*d*) 3.75×10^{12}

55. Based on the above, the moment magnitude of the earthquake is

(*a*) 5.15 (*b*) 5.36

(*c*) 6.35 (*d*) 7.25

GENERA1 APTITUDE (GA)

Q.56 – Q.60 cafry one mafk each.

56. Which one of the following options is the closest in meaning to the word given below?

Pacify

(*a*) Excite (*b*) Soothe

(*c*) Deplete (*d*) Tire

57. Choose the most appropriate pair of words from the options given below to complete the following sentence:

The high level of ___ of the questions in the test was ___ by an increase in the period of time allotted for answering them.

(*a*) difficulty, compensated

(*b*) exactitude, magnified

(*c*) aptitude, decreased

(*d*) attitude, mitigated

58. Choose the grammatically **CORRECT** sentence:

(*a*) He laid in bed till 8 o'clock in the morning.

(*b*) He layed in bed till 8 o'clock in the morning

(*c*) He lain in bed till 8 o'clock in the morning.

(*d*) He lay in bed till 8 o'clock in the morning.

59. Which one of the parts (A, B, C, D) in the sentence contains an ERROR?

No sooner had the doctor seen the results of the blood test, than he suggested the patient to see the specialist.

(*a*) no sooner had

(*b*) results of the blood test

(*c*) suggested the patient

(*d*) see the specialist

60. Ten teams participate in a tournament. Every team plays each of the other teams twice. The total number of matches to be played is

(*a*) 20 (*b*) 45

(*c*) 60 (*d*) 90

Q. 61 – Q. 65 carry two marks each.

61. A value of x that satisfies the equation on log x + log (x – 7) = log (x + 11) + log 2 i is

(*a*) 1 (*b*) 2

(*c*) 7 (*d*) 11

62. Let $f(x) = x - [x]$, where $x \geq 0$ and [x] is the greatest integer not larger than x. Then $f(x)$ is a

(*a*) monotonically increasing function

(*b*) monotonically decreasing function

(*c*) linearly increasing function between two integers

(*d*) linearly decreasing function between two integers

63. Ravi is taller than Arun but shorter than Iqbal. Sam is shorter than Ravi. Mohan is shorter than Arun. Balu is taller than Mohan and Sam. The tallest person can be

(*a*) Mohan (*b*) Ravi

(*c*) Balu (*d*) Arun

64. A smuggler has 10 capsules in which five are filled with narcotic drugs and the rest contain the original medicine. All the 10 capsules are mixed in a single box, from which the customs officials picked two capsules at random and tested for the presence of narcotic drugs. The probability that the smuggler will be caught is

(*a*) 0.50 (*b*) 0.67

(*c*) 0.78 (*d*) 0.82

65. The documents expose the cynicism of the government officials – and yet as the media website reflects, not a single newspaper has reported on their existence.

Which one of the following inferences may be drawn with the greatest accuracy from the above passage?

(*a*) Nobody other than the government officials knew about the existence of the documents.

(*b*) Newspapers did report about the documents but nobody cared.

(*c*) Media reports did not show the existence of the documents.

d) The documents reveal the attitude of the government officials.

ANSWERS

PART A (Common Part)

1. (*a*) **2.** (*c*) **3.** (*d*) **4.** (*b*) **5.** (*c*) **6.** (*a*) **7.** (*b*) **8.** (*c*) **9.** (*b*) **10.** (*a*)
11. (*d*) **12.** (*d*) **13.** (*a*) **14.** (*d*) **15.** (*d*) **16.** (*d*) **17.** (*a,b,c,d*) **18.** (*c*) **19.** (*d*) **20.** (*b*)
21. (*a,b,c,d*) **22.** (*a*) **23.** (*a*) **24.** (*b*) **25.** (*c*)

PART-B (Geology)

26. (*a*) **27.** (*b*) **28.** (*c*) **29.** (*a*) **30.** (*c*) **31.** (*b*) **32.** (*c*) **33.** (*a*) **34.** (*a*) **35.** (*b*)
36. (*c*) **37.** (*d*) **38.** (*a*) **39.** (*d*) **40.** (*b*) **41.** (*b*) **42.** (*c*) **43.** (*c*) **44.** (*a*) **45.** (*d*)
46. (*b*) **47.** (*c*) **48.** (*d*) **49.** (*c*) **50.** (*d*) **51.** (*a*) **52.** (*d*) **53.** (*b*) **54.** (*b*) **55.** (*d*)

(Geophysics)

26. (*a*) **27.** (*c*) **28.** (*a*) **29.** (*c*) **30.** (*d*) **31.** (*d*) **32.** (*d*) **33.** (*c*) **34.** (*a*) **35.** (*b*)
36. (*b*) **37.** (*d*) **38.** (*d*) **39.** (*a*) **40.** (*a*) **41.** (*c*) **42.** (*a*) **43.** (*c*) **44.** (*d*) **45.** (*b*)
46. (*b*) **47.** (*d*) **48.** (*c*) **49.** (*b*) **50.** (*b*) **51.** (*d*) **52.** (*b*) **53.** (*b*) **54.** (*a*) **55.** (*c*)

(General Aptitude)

56. (*b*) **57.** (*a*) **58.** (*d*) **59.** (*c*) **60.** (*d*) **61.** (*d*) **62.** (*c*) **63.** (*c*) **64.** (*c*) **65.** (*d*)

EXPLANATIONS

PART A (COMMON PART)

1. The Mohs scale of mineral hardness is a qualitative ordinal scale characterizing scratch resistance of various minerals through the ability of harder material to scratch softer material.

Mohs hardness	Mineral	Chemical formula	Absolute hardness
1	Talc	$Mg_3Si_4O_{10}(OH)_2$	1
2	Gypsum	$CaSO_4 \cdot 2H_2O$	3
3	Calcite	$CaCO_3$	9
4	Fluorite	CaF_2	21
5	Apatite	$Ca_5(PO_4)_3(OH^-,Cl^-,F^-)$	48
6	Orthoclase feldspar	$KAlSi_3O_8$	72
7	Quartz	SiO_2	100
8	Topaz	$Al_2SiO_4(OH^-,F^-)_2$	200
9	Corundum	Al_2O_3	400
10	Diamond	C	1500

As per the table the number of silicate compositions are 4.

2. The Ganges-Brahmaputra Delta is a river delta in the Bengal region of the Indian subcontinent, consisting of Bangladesh and the Indian state of West Bengal. It is the world's largest delta and empties into the Bay of Bengal, the combined waters of several river systems, mainly those of the Brahmaputra river and the Ganges river. The Ganges Delta lies at the junction of three tectonic plates: The Indian Plate, the Eurasian Plate, and the Burma Plate. The edge of the Eocene paleo shelf runs approximately from Kolkata to the edge of the Shillong Plateau. The edge of the paleo shelf marks the transition from the thick continental crust in the northwest to the thin continental or oceanic crust in the southeast. The enormous sediment supply from the Himalayan collision has extended the delta about 400 km seaward since the Eocene. The sediment thickness southeast of the edge of the paleo shelf beneath the Ganges Delta can exceed 16 km.

3. **Unconfined compressive strength:** This is also called uniaxial compressive strength. It is the strength of a rock or soil sample when crushed in one direction (uniaxial) without lateral restraint.

   Correct order is

   Massive basalt > Mica schist > Fossiliferous limestone > Coarse- grained sandstone.

4. **Eparchaean Unconformity,** a notified National Geo-Heritage Monument is a major discontinuity of stratigraphic significance that represents a period of remarkable serenity in the geological history of the earth i.e. sudden changes and discontinuity in the rock layers in earth's crust. Eparchaean Unconformity monument indicate that this feature forms the boundary surface between Proterozoic Nagari Quartzites and Archaean granite. The time gap between the formation of the two units is at least 500 Ma.

5. A point bar is a depositional feature made of alluvium that accumulates on the inside bend of streams and rivers below the slip-off slope. Point bars are found in abundance in mature or meandering streams. They are crescent-shaped and located on the inside of a stream bend, being very similar to, though often smaller than, towheads, or river islands. A point bar is an area of deposition whereas a cut bank is an area of erosion. Point bars are formed as the secondary flow of the stream sweeps and rolls sand, gravel and small stones laterally across the floor of the stream and up the shallow sloping floor of the point bar.

6. **Polymetallic nodules**, also called manganese nodules, are rock concretions on the sea bottom formed of concentric layers of iron and manganese hydroxides around a core. The core may be microscopically small and is sometimes completely transformed into manganese minerals by crystallization. The oceanic floor consists of manganese 27-30%, Nickel 1.25- 1.5 %, Copper 1-1.4% and cobalt 0.2-0.25%. Other constituents are iron, silicon and aluminum with lesser amount of calcium, sodium, magnesium, potassium, titanium, barium, along with hydrogen and oxygen.

7. In structural geology, rake (or pitch) is formally defined as "the angle between a line and the strike line of the plane in which it is found", measured on the plane. The three-dimensional orientation of a line can be described with just a plunge and trend.

   Strike-slip fault: The movement is essentially horizontal along the strike of the fault.

   Dip-slip fault: A fault in which movement is essentially downward along the dip of fault

   Oblique slip fault: A fault in which the direction of movement is diagonal to both dip and strike of the fault.

   Transcurrent faults: Caused by the lateral trust. Tear or wrench faults belong to this group. Exhibit mainly horizontal movements.

8. Given, Scaling is 1 : 40000

If the area is scaled with given scaling on a photo, then 40000 div is converted into 1 div as follows

Area of open cast coal mine is $1km^2 = 10^{10}$ cm^2

Therefore,

$$\text{The area in } cm^2 = \frac{10^{10}}{4 \times 4 \times 10^8} \; cm^2$$

$$= 6.25 \; cm^2$$

9. Bouguer correction: An approximation of the Earth's gravitational pull as a function of elevation. The additional mass beneath an object standing on the ground at a high elevation (such as on a mountain) leads to a higher amount of gravitational force. If the strength of gravity at sea level is known, then its value at higher elevations can be approximated using the Bougeur correction. Standardly, the correction equals 0.4186 ρh, where ρ is the assumed average density of the Earth, and h is the difference in altitude between the places where the strength of gravity is known and where it is being approximated. This value is added to the value of gravity at the lower location to yield an approximation of its value at the higher one. Compare free-air correction.

10. SP log is directly used for the formation water resistivity and equivalent resistivity calculation using the relation

$$\varepsilon_c = -k \log \frac{R_{mf}}{R_w}$$

where,

ε_c is Electrochemical potential

k is constant

R_{mf} is resistivity of mud-filtarate

R_w is resistivity of formation water

11. Earth is about 147.1 million km from the Sun at perihelion around January 3 (nearest to sun), in contrast to about 152.1 million km at aphelion around July 4 (Farthest from sun), a difference of about 5.0 million km.

12. Oil bearing strata: Integrated method of seismic and well logging mostly.

Coal bearing strata: Various methods depending upon the depth of the target like magnetic, gravity, GPR, well-logging etc.

Disseminated sulphide deposit: Induced polarization method mostly.

Massive sulphide deposit: Electromagnetic method mostly, magnetotelluric, gravity etc

13. In one Mercury year, an observer on mercury surfaces rotates about the spin axis 1.5 times and thus advances by an extra half turn. Therefore, if a year started at sunrise, it will end at sunset. Thus, the observer on mercury would spend the entire 88 Earth days in day and the next year in night, thus here days are longer than year.

14. The sensitivity order for different magnetic instrument is

Optically Pumped Magnetometer > Proton Precession Magnetometer > Fluxgate Magnetometer > Magnetic Field Balance Magnetometer.

15. Electrical conductivity: Resistivity

Electromagnetic conductivity: Electromagnetic method

Seismic wave velocity: Seismic method

Electrical permeability (dielectric permittivity): GRP-Ground Penetrating Radar

16.

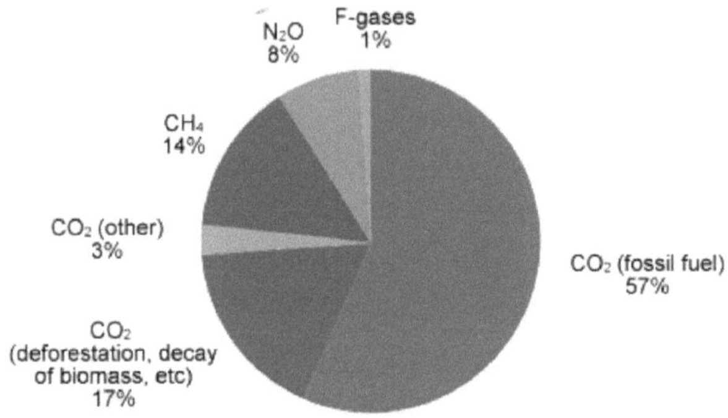

The pie chart suggest that CO_2 is the highest contributor towards the greenhouse effect on earth.

17. Depth range of transition zone associated with phase changes in Earth's mantle changes according to situations.

18.

Plutonic Rock	Volcanic Equivalent
Granite	Rhyolite
Syenite	Trachyte
Gabbro	Basalt
Granodiorite	Dacite

19. Jasper: An aggregate of microquartz- impure variety of silica, chalcedony and other mineral phases.

Coesite: Tectosilicate, repeating unit of SiO_2

Stishovite: Tetragonal, ditetragonal, dipyramidal, repeating SiO_2 unit.

Flinkite: Orthorhombic, Mn_2^{2+}, Mn^{3+} $(ASO)_4(OH)_4$

20. Aquifer: It is an underground layer of water bearing permeable rock or unconsolidated materials from which ground water can be extracted using a water well.

Aquitard: A water saturated sediment or rock whose permeability is so low that it cannot transmit any useful amount of water.

Aquiclude: An impermeable body of rock or stratum of sediment that acts as a barrier to the flow of water.

Aquifuge: A geologic formation which has no interconnected openings and cannot hold or transmit water.

21. Mark all

As per given figure it is not clear which type of fault is present in the aerial photograph.

22. A cephalopod is any member of the molluscan class Cephalopoda such as a squid, octopus or nautilus. These exclusively marine animals are characterized by bilateral body symmetry, a prominent head, and a set of arms or tentacles (muscular hydrostats) modified from the primitive molluscan foot. Cephalopods became dominant during the Ordovician period, represented by primitive nautiloids. The class now contains two, only distantly related, extant subclasses: Coleoidea, which includes octopuses, squid, and cuttlefish; and Nautiloidea, represented by Nautilus and Allonautilus.

23. A charge-transfer complex (CT complex) or electron-donor-acceptor complex is an association of two or more molecules, or of different parts of one large molecule, in which a fraction of electronic charge is transferred between the molecular entities.

24. Pangaea or Pangea was a supercontinent that existed during the late Paleozoic and early Mesozoic eras. It assembled from earlier continental units approximately 335 million years ago, and it began to break apart about 175 million years ago.

There were three major phases in the break-up of Pangaea. The first phase began in the Early-Middle Jurassic (about 175 Ma), when Pangaea began to rift from the Tethys Ocean in the east to the Pacific in the west.

The second major phase in the break-up of Pangaea began in the Early Cretaceous (150–140 Ma), when the minor supercontinent of Gondwana separated into multiple continents (Africa, South America, India, Antarctica, and Australia).

The third major and final phase of the break-up of Pangaea occurred in the early Cenozoic (Paleocene to Oligocene). Laurasia split when North America/Greenland (also called Laurentia) broke free from Eurasia, opening the Norwegian Sea about 60-55 Ma.

25. Lower Gondwana coal fields

Damadar valley region – West Bengal, Bihar

Son Mahanandi valley region – Madhya Pradesh, Orissa

Wardha Godavari valley region – Andhra Pradesh, Maharashtra

PART-B (GEOLOGY)

26. As per formula,

Specific discharge is given as,

$$q = K\frac{dh}{dl}$$

and, given that

$q = 1$ cm/day $= 0.1$ m/day

$dl = 20$ m

$dh = 0.5$ m

$$\therefore K = \frac{q \times dl}{dh} = \frac{0.01 \times 20}{0.5} = 0.4 \text{ m/sec}$$

27.

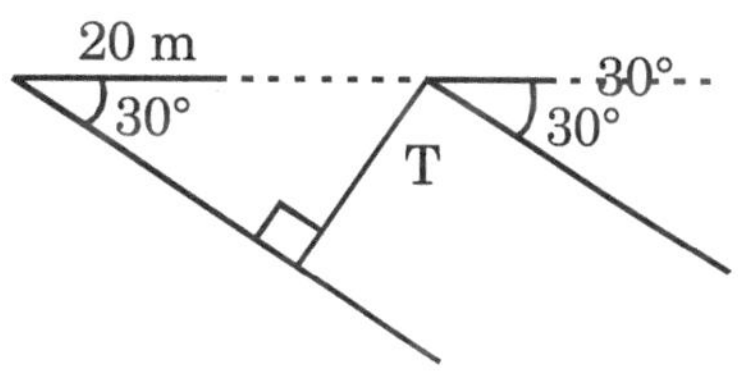

where, T is the true thickness

From figure,

$$\sin 30^o = \frac{T}{20}$$

$$\Rightarrow T = 20 \sin 30^o = 20 \times \frac{1}{2} = 10\ m$$

28. Given,

Partition coefficient = 5

Concentration of Ni in magma = 20 ppm

Now, As per formula,

$$\text{Partition coefficient} = \frac{\text{Concentration in solid}}{\text{Concentration in magma}}$$

Therefore, concentration of Ni in solid is

$$5 = \frac{\text{Concentration in solid}}{20}$$

$\Rightarrow$ Concentration in solid $= 5 \times 20 = 100$ ppm

29. Si has a valency of 4^+

Al has a valency of 3^+

Here, only Al replaces Si, therefore, the Si atoms will be replaced by 3 Al atom and the remaining 3 valency will be covered by an tetrahedral aluminum.

30. Here, the number of phases, P = 6

Number of components = 6

Applying phase rule,

P + F = C + 2 {F is degree of freedom}

F = C + 2 – P = 6 + 2 – 6 = 2

31. Augite is isomorphous with the minerals Diopside and Hedenbergite. It is an intermediary member between these minerals, forming a series, but contains additional sodium and aluminum within its chemical structure. Strictly speaking, because of the variables in its chemical structure, Augite is really more of a group then a single mineral, but it is still classified a single mineral species by the IMA. Ca-montmorillonite is formed by the weathering of augite.

32.

Crystal system	Unit cell symmetry elements
Cubic	4/m 3 2/m
Tetragonal	4/m 2/m 2/m
Hexagonal	6/m 2/m 2/m
Orthorhombic	2/m 2/m 2/m
Monoclinic	2/m
Triclinic	1

33. Biaxial minerals can be pleochroic in three shades because Biaxial minerals have three refractive indices.

34. Subduction zone facies with increasing depth Zeotite can be given as :

Prehnite Pumpelilte

↓

Greenshist

↓

Blueschist

↓

Ecologite

35. The Cambay basin, which is a part of Western Onshore Basin, is a major oil producing field of India. It is a narrow elongated rift graben situated between Saurashtra Craton on the west and Aravalli on the northeast and Deccan craton to the southeast. Till the late 90's oil companies in India were exploring hydrocarbon in the shallow Kalol sequence. Upper part of Cambay Shale formation containing siltstone was also targeted whereas the lower part which dominantly consists of shale was never thought to be a reservoir. The discovery of hydrocarbon in few wells in Cambay Basin in early 2000 changed the paradigm of exploration strategy in Cambay basin. The Olpad Formation and Lower Cambay Shale Formation are still a challenge to the explorationists in terms of petroleum prospects. This has encouraged many researchers to study the hydrocarbon potential of the above two formations. Moreover, Identification of the dual nature of source rock also has attracted much attention to the geoscientists for the hydrocarbon resource evaluation.

36. Proximity (buffer) GIS function: Proximity analysis is an analytic technique used to determine the relationship between a selected point and its relationship between a selected point and its neighbors. Proximity analysis is a crustal tool for business marketing and site selection. It measures in terms of distance and time.

37. Vertical exaggeration commonly occurs during stereo viewing in perceptor's mind, as stereo vision is different for different preceptor.

38. Kimberlite is an igneous rock, which sometimes contains diamonds. It is commonly formed by intrusion from the mantle. It contains microcrysts of olivine, Cr- rich diopside, phologopite and pyrope in a groundmass of serpentine, carbonate and perovskite.

39. Herringbone cross-stratification is a type of sedimentary structure formed in tidal areas, where the current periodically flows in the opposite direction. In tidal areas, which have bidirectional flow, structures are formed with alternating layers of cross-beds dipping in opposite directions that reflect the alternating paleocurrent. These sedimentary structures are not common because they require the current to be equal in both directions, which rarely happens in nature. The time represented by each cross-stratified layer is likely to be many years. The pattern of the structure is said to resemble the backbone structure of a herring fish.

40. Sulfuric acid will be dominant in an acidic coal mine drainage because enough sulpher is present in the coals.

41. Each graptolite colony originates from an initial individual, called the sicular zooid, from which the subsequent zooids will develop; they are all interconnected by stolons. These zooids are housed within an organic tubular structure called a theca, rhabsodome, coenoecium or tubarium, which is secreted by the glands on the cephalic shield.

Glossopteris, genus of fossilized woody plants known from rocks that have been dated to the Permian and Triassic periods (roughly 300 to 200 million years ago), deposited on the southern supercontinent of Gondwana. Glossopteris occurred in a variety of growth forms. Its most common fossil is that of a tongue-shaped leaf with prominent midrib and reticulate venation.

Deltidium: It is the triangular space between the beak and the hinge of brachiopod shells. A shelly plate usually covers it in.

The pygidium is the posterior body part or shield of crustaceans and some other arthropods, such as insects and the extinct trilobites. It contains the anus and, in females, the ovipositor. It is composed of fused body segments, sometimes with a tail, and separated from thoracic segments by an articulation.

42.

Formation	Age
Sargur schist	Archaean
Kajrahat limestone	Proterozoic
Cuddalore sandstone	Tertiary
Umia ammonite bed	Jurassic

43. Transposition foliation develops parallel to axial plane of tight folds.

44.

Group-I	Group-II
Churching	Tunnelling
Curtain grouting	Concrete gravity dam
Piping	Earth dam
Pozzolan	Cement

45. In the Northwest quadrant, the total departure from 360° that will be north is 45° and the total departure in Northeast quadrant is 45°. Therefore, the mean direction will be 360° or 0° N. By plotting rose diagram this can be easily done.

46. Heating of system Q will give the correct salinity of the system, where salt will remain in its solid form and vapour as well as liquid will be removed away by heating. Freezing of R will give correct salinity measurements.

47. River is flowing towards south. Hence, general dip direction of the beds is towards south.

48. In figure P given in the question, solid solution is limited whereas in figure Q eutectic crystallization is present.

49. A solvus is a line (binary system) or surface (ternary system) on a phase diagram which separates a homogeneous solid solution from a field of several phases which may form by exsolution or incongruent melting. The line determines a solid solubility limit which changes as a function of temperature.

50. Hybrid extension shear facture : At point B, normal stress is negative and shear stress, is also present.

51. Dihedral angle is the angle between the normal stress i.e., center and the point at which fractvring condition occur. As per given figure in the question the dihedral angle is θ_1.

52. Porphyry copper deposits are copper orebodies that are formed from hydrothermal fluids that originate from a voluminous magma chamber several kilometers below the deposit itself. Predating or associated with those fluids are vertical dikes of porphyritic intrusive rocks from which this deposit type derives its name. In later stages, circulating meteoric fluids may interact with the magmatic fluids. Successive envelopes of hydrothermal alteration typically enclose a core of disseminated ore minerals in often stockwork-forming hairline fractures and veins. Because of their large volume, porphyry orebodies can be economic from copper concentrations as low as 0.15% copper and can have economic amounts of by-products such as molybdenum, silver and gold. In some mines, those metals are the main product.

53. Chuquicamata clearly belongs to the broad class of porphyry copper deposits. Practically the entire Chuquicamata orebody is hosted by the Chuqui Porphyry Complex, made up of East, Fine Texture, West and Banco porphyries." These Cu-Mo porphyry systems formed during the Eocene-Oligocene and exhibit classic "zoned alteration-mineralization features." A regional fault zone gave rise to hydrothermal activity which concentrated metal and sulfide minerals. The West Fault is a major fault that separates Chuquicamata into two parts, west and east.

54. Radiolaria are made up of silicate skeleton. Hence, they can live below carbon compensation depth.

55. Siliceous - Radiolaria

Foraminifera – Carbonate skeleton

(GEOPHYSICS)

26. Given,

$\mu_0 = 4\pi \times 10^{-7}$ H/m

K is magnetic susceptibility

Here, K for dolerite = 1400

Magnetic permeability is a measure of the ability of a material to convey a magnetic flux.

It is given as,

$$\mu = \mu_0(1+K)$$

Therefore,

$$\mu = 4\pi \times 10^{-7}(1+1400) = 0.00176 \text{ H/m}$$

27. Given,

NMO corrected travel time for updip and downdip direction are 1.2275 and 1.2555 sec respectively

Therefore, difference in travel time

$$\Delta T_d = t_{downdip} - t_{updip} = 1.255 - 1.277 = 0.028\ s$$

Using individual travel time defined by equation

$$\Delta T_d = \frac{2x\sin\theta}{V}$$

where, x is geophone spacing from shot

θ is amount of dip

V is sesmic wave velocity

$$\therefore \sin\theta = \frac{\Delta T_d \times V}{2x} = \frac{0.028 \times 2500}{2 \times 250} = 0.14$$

$$\Rightarrow \theta = \sin^{-1}(0.14) = 8.04°$$

28. Given,

Shear wave velocity, β = 6800 m/s

Density, ρ = 3380 kg/m^3

Now,

As per given formula

$$\beta = \sqrt{\frac{\mu}{\rho}}$$

where, μ is the rigidity

$$\Rightarrow \mu = \beta^2 \times \rho = 6800^2 \times 3380 = 156.29\ GPa$$

29. Given, conductivity = 10 S/m

$$\therefore \text{Resistivity, } \rho = \frac{1}{10} = 0.1\ \Omega - m$$

Frequency, f = 1 kHz = 10^3 Hz

Now,

The skin depth is defined as

$$d = 503.8\sqrt{\frac{\rho}{f}} = \sqrt{\frac{100}{25}} = 1000\ m = 1\ km$$

30. Standard Wyllie Equation for porosity determination is

$$\phi = \frac{\Delta t_{\log}(\text{sample}) - \Delta t_{ma}(\text{matrix})}{\Delta t_f(\text{fluid/water}) - \Delta t_{ma}(\text{matrix})}$$

As per given question,

$$\phi = \frac{75\mu sft - 50\mu sft}{200\mu sft - 50\mu sft} = \frac{25}{150} = 0.16$$

31. In frequency domain IP method, two measurements are commonly made

I. Percentage frequency effect (PFE),

$$= 100 \times \frac{\rho_{dc} - \rho_{ac}}{\rho_{ac}}$$

II. Metal factor (MF) = $2\pi \times 10^5 \times \dfrac{\rho_{dc} - \rho_{ac}}{\rho_{dc} \times \rho_{ac}}$

32. Bright spot: In reflection seismology, a bright spot is a local high amplitude seismic attribute anomaly that can indicate the presence of hydrocarbons and is therefore known as a direct hydrocarbon indicator.

33. The magnetic dipole axis of the earth is tilted about 11½° from the rotation axis.

1° = 110 km

∴ 11.5° = 1265 km

34. Longitudinal conductance (S) The sum of all the thickness/resistivity ratios of n – 1 layers which overlie a semi-infinite substratum of resistivity $\bullet_n$, such that $S = h_1/\bullet 1 + h_2/\bullet_2 + h_3/\bullet_3 + \ldots + h_{n-1}/\bullet_{n-1}$ (mho), where h_1, h_2, etc. are the depths and $\bullet_1$, $\bullet_2$, etc. the resistivities, of successive layers. A knowledge of $h_i/\bullet_i$ for the ith layer when it is sandwiched between two layers of much higher resistivity is of importance in resolving the problem of equivalence.

35. The case for the Earth–Moon system, in which the barycenter is located on average 4,671 km (2,902 mi) from the Earth's center, 75% of the Earth's radius of 6,378 km (3,963 mi).

36. The change in gravity caused by Earth's tides on the land surface in a complete tidal cycle is in the range of 0.2 to 0.3 milligal.

37. Terrestrial heat flow: it is also known as heat flux and is defined as the flow of heat per unit area per second.

It is given by the equation,

$$q_z = -K\frac{dT}{dz}$$

where,

K is thermal conductivity

$\frac{dT}{dz}$ = temperature gradient

–ve sign indicates the direction of heat flow, thus there is a increase in +z direction and decrease in z– direction

38. As per Archie's law the relationship between the insitu electrical conductivity of a sedimentary rock to its porosity and rise saturation

$$C_t = \frac{1}{a} C_w \phi^m S_w^n$$

where,

C_w is electrical conductivity of the brine,

C_t is electrical conductivity of the fluid saturated rock

ϕ is porosity

m is cementation exponent ranges form 1.8 to 2

S_w is brine saturation

n is saturation exponent = 2

a is tortuosity factor

39. In electromagnetism, the magnetic susceptibility is one measure of the magnetic properties of a material. The susceptibility indicates whether a material is attracted into or repelled out of a magnetic field, which in turn has implications for practical applications. If the magnetic susceptibility is greater than zero, the substance is said to be "paramagnetic"; the magnetization of the substance is higher than that of empty space. If the magnetic susceptibility is less than zero, the substance is "diamagnetic"; it tends to exclude a magnetic field from its interior.

An airbornemagnetic survey is a kind of geophysical prospecting, which makes use of airborne geophysical surveying gauges installed in an aircraft at a certain flight height range to acquire magnetic field intensity from the subsurface.

A concept that is central to many principles of paleomagnetism is that of the geocentric axial dipole (GAD). In this model, the magnetic field produced by a single magnetic dipole at the center of the Earth and aligned with the rotation axis is considered.

A Proton Precession Magnetometer is an instrument that measures the scalar intensity of the local magnetic field and relies upon the proton-precision measurement technique. This is a well-established technique and is successfully implemented in classical proton precision magnetometers.

40. NMO of a diffraction hyperbola is always greater this is due to,

i. The curvature is greater as compared to NMO reflection hyperbolas.

ii. The apparent velocity of diffraction hyperbola is greater than NMO velocity of reflection hyperbola.

41. NMR logging, a subcategory of electromagnetic logging, measures the induced magnet moment of hydrogen nuclei (protons) contained within the fluid-filled pore space of porous media (reservoir rocks). Unlike conventional logging measurements (e.g., acoustic, density, neutron, and resistivity), which respond to both the rock matrix and fluid properties and are strongly dependent on mineralogy, NMR-logging measurements respond to the presence of hydrogen protons. Because these protons primarily occur in pore fluids, NMR effectively responds to the volume, composition, viscosity, and distribution of these fluids (oil, gas, water).

42. The peak response in the curve so obtained by geophone is governed by the equation,

$$u = \frac{A\omega^2}{\left\{\left(\omega_0^2 - \omega^2\right)^2 + 4\lambda^2\omega^2\omega_0^2\right\}^{1/2}} \cos(t - \Delta)$$

43. The minimum norm solution of a purely undermined problem is given by

$$M_{est} = \left(G^T G\right)^{-1} G^T d$$

44. The matrix equation is

$$A_{m\times n} X_{x\times 1} = b_{m\times 1}$$

Therefore, the nature of this system of equation is always determined by the rank of the matrix A as the order of the matrix changes.

45. The VLF method uses powerful remote radio transmitters set up in different parts of the world for military communications. In radio communications terminology, VLF means very low frequency, about 15 to 25 kHz.

Ground-penetrating radar (GPR) is a geophysical method that uses radar pulses to image the subsurface. This nondestructive method uses electromagnetic radiation in the microwave band (UHF/VHF frequencies) of the radio spectrum, and detects the reflected signals from subsurface structures. GPR uses high-frequency (usually polarized) radio waves, usually in the range 10 MHz to 2.6 GHz.

Magnetotellurics (MT) is an electromagnetic geophysical method for inferring the earth's subsurface electrical conductivity from measurements of natural geomagnetic and geoelectric field variation at the Earth's surface. The Earth's naturally varying electric and magnetic fields are measured over a wide range of magnetotelluric frequencies from 10,000 Hz to 0.0001 Hz.

46. Energy of gamma rays <0.5 MeV undergoes photoelectric absorption

Energy of gamma rays in the range 0.5 MeV to 2.0 MeV undergoes Compton scattering.

Higher energy is needed for pairs production and secondary emission of gamma rays.

47. **Assertion:** In a well-log survey using fresh-water drilling mud, an oil-bearing sandstone zone can be identified by electrical resistivity and SP logs.

Reason: Oil has high electrical resistivity and the porous nature of sandstone is indicated by negative SP.

Both [a] and [r] are true and [r] is the correct reason for [a]

48. Given,

Sampling rate for signal =1000 samples/sec

Therefore, sampling frequency, $f_s = 1000\ Hz$

Maximum frequency of the sampled signal, Nyquist frequency, $f_N = 475\ Hz$

If the signal is undersampled, the maximum frequency of the signal will be altered and is equal to the difference of sampling frequency and Nyquist frequency

Maximum frequency $= f_S - f_N$

$= 1000 - 475 = 525\ Hz$

49. Given,

Duration of the signal is 10 seconds

By using Fourier transform, we find out its frequency spectrum in which different frequencies exists as a function of fundamental frequency and is called harmonics

$$\text{Frequency Interval} = \frac{1}{\text{duration}} = \frac{1}{10} = 0.1\ Hz$$

50. Consider the case of three layers are a_0, a_1, a_2, a_3 the amplitude of incident, reflected and refracted waves at different interfaces.

Reflection coefficient is defined as the ratio of amplitude of reflected to the incident wave,

$$R_1 = \frac{a_1}{a_0},\ R_2 = \frac{a_2}{a_1'},\ R_3 = \frac{a_3}{a_2'}$$

Transmission coefficient is defined as ratio of amplitude of amplitude of refracted to the incident wave

$$T_1 = \frac{a_1'}{a_0},\ T_2 = \frac{a_2'}{a_1'}$$

Moreover,

$R^2 + T^2 = 1$

$\Rightarrow R_1^2 + T_1^2 = 1$

Also,

$\Rightarrow R_2^2 + T_2^2 = 1$

$\Rightarrow T_1^2 = 1 - R_1^2 = 1 - 0.1^2 = 0.99$

$\therefore T_1 = \sqrt{0.99}$

$\Rightarrow T_2^2 = 1 - R_2^2 = 1 - 0.15^2 = 0.9775$

$\therefore T_2 = \sqrt{0.9775}$

Amplitude from deepest interface is A_3 is given by

$a_0 = 1$

$a_2' = T_1 \times T_2$

and

$$R_3 = \frac{a_3}{a_2'} = \frac{a_3}{T_1 \times T_2}$$

$\Rightarrow a_3 = T_1 \times T_2 \times R_3$

$= \sqrt{0.99} \times \sqrt{0.9775} \times 0.19 = 0.178$

51. As the above question, consider the case of three layers along with surface multiples with the strength of reflection amplitude.

Therefore, the net reflection amplitude from the deepest interface and the surface multiples reaching at the geophone is the product of these amplitudes

Net amplitude = 0.01 × 0.178 = 0.00198

52. Given,

Bulk resistivity of rock fully saturated with an aqueous fluid, $R_0 = 0.1$ Ohm-m

Resistivity of aqueous fluid, $R_w = 0.01$ Ohm-m

As per Archies' first law

$$F = \frac{R_0}{R_w}$$

where, F is the formation factor

Here, $F = \frac{0.1}{0.01} = 10$

53. Given,

Bulk resistivity of rock fully saturated with an aqueous fluid, $R_t = 4$ Ohm-m

Bulk resistivity of rock partially saturated with an aqueous fluid, $R_t = 4$ Ohm-m

Now,

As per Archies' second law

The Fractional water saturation of the rock is given as

$$S_w = \sqrt[n]{\frac{R_0}{R_t}}$$

when, n is Saturation index (value lies between 1.8-2)

$$\therefore S_w = \sqrt[2]{\frac{0.1}{4}} = 0.158 \text{ [Considering } n = 2]$$

54. Given,

Sesmic slip after faulting, D = 0.5 m

Area of faulting, S = 250 km^2 = 250 × 10^6 m^2

Rigidity of the medium, m = 30 Gpa

= 30 × 10^9 N/m^2

Therefore,

The sesmic moment is given as

$$M_0 = \mu SD = 250 \times 30 \times 0.5 \times 10^{15}$$

$$= 3.75 \times 10^{18} \ Nm$$

55. Given,

$M_0 = 3.75 \times 10^{18} \ Nm$ from previous question

Now,

$$M_w = \frac{2}{3}(\log_{10} M_0 - 9.1)$$

$$\Rightarrow M_w = \frac{2}{3}\left(\log_{10}\left(3.75 \times 10^{18}\right) - 9.1\right)$$

$$\Rightarrow M_w = \frac{2}{3}(\log 3.75 + 18 \log 10 - 9.1)$$

$$= \frac{2}{3}(0.57 + 18 - 9.1) = 6.31$$

(GENERAL APTITUDE SECTION)

56. The closest meaning of pacify is soothe.

57. The high level of difficulty of the questions in the test was compensated by an increase in the period of time allotted for answering them.

58. Lay and lie are both present-tense verbs.

Lay means to put or set something down, e.g. I lay down the book.

Lie, on the other hand, is defined as, "to be, to stay or to assume rest in a horizontal position, e.g. I lie down to sleep or When I pick up a copy of my favorite magazine,

In this question "the morning" is used, so, they are talking about a specific morning so this sentence is not talking about the habit.

lay is second form of lie,

Therefore, the option is D

59. Who is the specialist here? Not clear- it must be one of the specialist for that particular disease. So, "to see a specialist" is correct.

Rest all are fine in the sentence. "No sooner had-than" means the first part happened and the second part followed immediately. The first part uses past perfect tense and the second part uses simple past tense - which is as required.

60. Let 1, 2, 3, 4, 5, 6, 7, 8, 9, 10 be teams now

first team can play with any = 9

similarly, second can play with any = 8 ...similarly 3rd team will play 7 games ...

So, $9 + 8 + 7 + \dots + 1 = \frac{n(n-1)}{2} = \frac{10 \times 9}{2} = 45$.. we are said ..to have 2 matches = 45 × 2 = 90

61. $\log m + \log n = \log mn$

$$\therefore \log x + \log(x-7) = \log(x+11) + \log 2$$

$$\Rightarrow \log x(x-7) = \log 2(x+11)$$

$$\Rightarrow x(x-7) = 2(x+11)$$

$$\Rightarrow x^2 - 9x - 22 = 0$$

$$\Rightarrow (x-11)(x+2) = 0$$

$$\therefore x = 11$$

$\because x \neq -2$, log is undefined for negative number.

62. $f(x) = x - [x]$

$f(x)$ gives nothing but the fractional part of x.

Now, as we move up the number line between two consecutive integers say a and $a + 1$.

The value of $f(a)$ starts from 0 and grows linearly till the consecutive integer and just before $x = a + 1$ (left neighborhood of $a + 1$) it tends to the value 1.

Between a and $a + 1$, the graph grows linearly from 0 to 1.

But, when at $x = a + 1$, the value comes back to 0 and same linear graph continues between the next two consecutive integers and so on.

63. Balu can be the tallest. Ravi cannot be the answer since it is clearly mentioned that he is shorter than Iqbal. Iqbal and Balu could be the tallest as no comparison is provided where these two are smaller than anyone. But Iqbal is not mentioned in options Hence, Balu is correct answer.

64. The smuggler would be caught if any one or both the randomly picked capsule contains drugs.

M represents Medicine, D represents Drugs

A– The smuggler will be caught

B– The randomly picked capsules contains M, D

C– The randomly picked capsules contains D,M

D– The randomly picked capsules contains D,D

$$P(A) = \frac{5}{10} \times \frac{5}{9} + \frac{5}{10} \times \frac{5}{9} + \frac{5}{10} \times \frac{4}{9}$$

$$= 0.278 + 0.278 + 0.222 = 0.778$$

65. Options A is wrong because in the passage they did not mention who knows or who does not know about the existence of document. Option B totally irrelevant from passage and Option C is wrong as after reading the passage you got an idea media is waiting once they got the information about existence of document then they will expose them. Whereas Option D is related to passage.

SOLVED PAPER - 2011

PART-A (Common Part)

Q. 1 – Q.25 carry one mark each.

1. The increase in the length of a day on the earth at a rate of 2.4 milliseconds/100 years is due to
   (*a*) prolate tidal bulge (*b*) tidal friction
   (*c*) spring tide (*d*) bodily earth tide

2. Which of the following rocks contributes the highest amount of radioactive heat in the earth's crust?
   (*a*) basalt (*b*) gabbro
   (*c*) dunite (*d*) granite

3. The P-wave velocity of the earth's mantle at the Mohorovicic discontinuity is
   (*a*) 5.5 km/s (*b*) 6.0 km/s
   (*c*) 7.0 km/s (*d*) 8.0 km/s

4. Variation of the geomagnetic field observed over the last 500 years indicates that the dipole moment of earth's magnetic field has been
   (*a*) decreasing (*b*) increasing
   (*c*) constant (*d*) fluctuating randomly

5. Which of the following statements is TRUE for the temperature variation with altitude in the earth's atmosphere?
   (*a*) Temperature increases in both stratosphere and mesosphere
   (*b*) Temperature decreases in stratosphere and increases in mesosphere
   (*c*) Temperature increases in stratosphere and decreases in mesosphere
   (*d*) Temperature decreases in both stratosphere and mesosphere

6. The deflection of ocean currents in the northern and southern hemispheres is due to
   (*a*) thermohaline circulation
   (*b*) Coriolis effect
   (*c*) El Nino effect
   (*d*) monsoon effect

7. Tsunamis are
   (*a*) gravity waves (*b*) acoustic waves
   (*c*) capillary waves (*d*) internal waves

8. The planet which contributes maximum to the angular momentum of the solar system is
   (*a*) Earth (*b*) Mars
   (*c*) Jupiter (*d*) Saturn

9. The depositional feature that forms where a stream emerges from a mountainous region onto a plain is called
   (*a*) alluvial fan (*b*) natural levee
   (*c*) delta (*d*) point bar

10. Hanging valleys are formed by the geological action of
    (*a*) river (*b*) glacier
    (*c*) ocean (*d*) wind

11. The surface of discontinuity between older folded sedimentary strata and younger horizontal strata is known as
    (*a*) disconformity
    (*b*) parallel unconformity
    (*c*) angular unconformity
    (*d*) nonconformity

12. The hardest oxide mineral in the Mohs' scale of hardness is
    (*a*) corundum (*b*) topaz
    (*c*) quartz (*d*) diamond

13. The dominant constituent of ultramafic rocks in the earth's mantle is
    (*a*) orthoclase (*b*) olivine
    (*c*) plagioclase (*d*) biotite

14. A highly vesicular rock formed by solidification of viscous lava is
    (*a*) tuff (*b*) obsidian
    (*c*) volcanic breccia (*d*) pumice

15. The most suitable radioactive method for dating Holocene events is
    (*a*) U – Pb (*b*) Sm – Nd
    (*c*) Rb – Sr (*d*) C – 14

16. Which of the following stratigraphic units is NOT of Proterozoic age?
    (*a*) Tipam Group (*b*) Bhima Group
    (*c*) Nallamalai Group (*d*) Semri Group

17. Rampura – Agucha in Rajasthan is known for the ore deposit of

(*a*) gold (*b*) tungsten
(*c*) zinc (*d*) iron

18. The geological age of the major hydrocarbon reservoir in the Bombay High oil field is

(*a*) Cretaceous (*b*) Holocene
(*c*) Oligocene (*d*) Miocene

19. The geophysical method for the exploration of disseminated sulfide deposits is

(*a*) induced polarization
(*b*) self- potential
(*c*) gravity
(*d*) magnetic

20. In a borehole, high pressure gas zone is identified by

(*a*) sonic logging
(*b*) resistivity logging
(*c*) temperature logging
(*d*) density logging

21. The acceleration due to gravity (g) and universal gravitational constant (G) are related by the expression (M_e and R_e are the mass and radius of the earth, respectively)

(*a*) $g = \frac{GM_e}{R_e}$ (*b*) $g = \frac{GM_e}{R_e^2}$

(*c*) $g = \frac{GR_e}{M_e}$ (*d*) $g = \frac{GR_e}{M_e^2}$

22. The metamorphic facies diagnostic of subduction zone is

(*a*) hornblende hornfels
(*b*) pyroxene hornfels
(*c*) blueschist
(*d*) granulite

23. In a formation, if the density increases and elastic constants remain unchanged, then

(*a*) both P and S wave velocities increase
(*b*) P wave velocity increases and S wave velocity decreases
(*c*) both P and S wave velocities decrease
(*d*) P wave velocity decreases and S wave velocity increases

24. The Poisson ratio (σ) for rocks in terms of Lame's constants λ and μ is

(*a*) $\sigma = \frac{1}{\lambda + \mu}$ (*b*) $\sigma = \frac{\lambda}{\lambda + \mu}$

(*c*) $\sigma = \frac{1}{2(\lambda + \mu)}$ (*d*) $\sigma = \frac{\lambda}{2(\lambda + \mu)}$

25. In seismic exploration, 'ground roll' represents

(*a*) direct wave (*b*) surface wave
(*c*) Stonely wave (*d*) shear wave

PART-B
GEOLOGY

Q.26 - Q.55 carry two marks each.

26. Choose the correct set of crystal faces for which 'c' crystallographic axis is the zone axis.

(*a*) (100), (001), $(\bar{1}00)$ (*b*) (010), (001), $(0\bar{1}0)$

(*c*) (010), $(\bar{1}10)$, $(\bar{1}00)$ (*d*) (110), (001), $(\bar{1}\bar{1}0)$

27. The twin plane in the Manebach law is

(*a*) (010) (*b*) (001)
(*c*) (100) (*d*) (021)

28. The figure below shows the pattern of increase (i) and decrease (d) in the interference colors of a mineral after insertion of mica plate. The optic sign of the mineral is

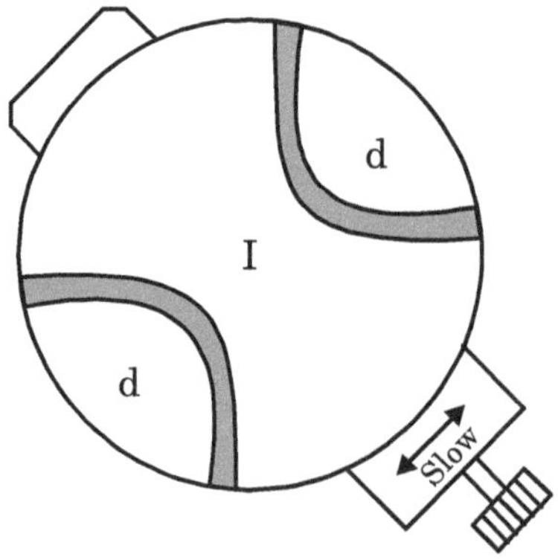

(*a*) uniaxial positive (*b*) uniaxial negative
(*c*) biaxial positive (*d*) biaxial negative

29. The igneous rock falling in the shaded field of the figure below is

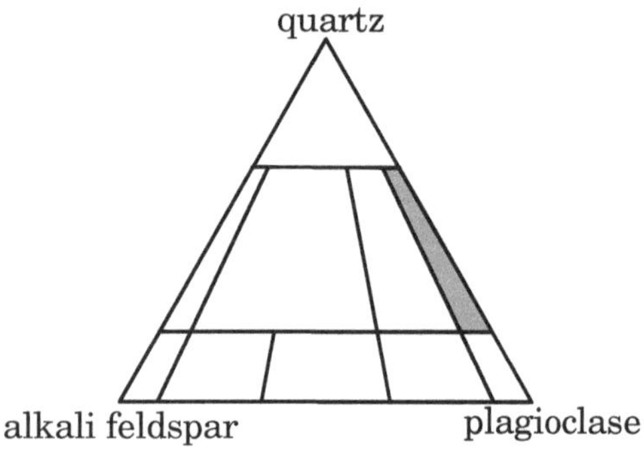

(*a*) granite
(*b*) syenite
(*c*) tonalite
(*d*) monzonite

30. The figure below is the photomicrograph of a chloritoid mica schist in which chloritoid forms porphyroblasts. The formation of porphyroblasts in the crenulated matrix is

(*a*) pre-tectonic (*b*) early syn-tectonic
(*c*) late syn-tectonic (*d*) post-tectonic

31. A pelitic rock is uplifted after high pressure metamorphism in the earth's crust. The mineral transformation due to uplift will be

(*a*) kyanite to sillimanite
(*b*) sillimanite to kyanite
(*c*) andalusite to kyanite
(*d*) andalusite to sillimanite

32. Which of the following sedimentary structures is NOT a 'tool mark'?

(*a*) prod cast (*b*) groove cast
(*c*) flute cast (*d*) bounce cast

33. The echinoids transformed from epifaunal to infaunal type in the Jurassic times. Consider the following morphological changes:

P. increase in size of spines
Q. increase in number of spines
R. development of phyllodes
S. bulging of shell

Which of the above changes were functionally advantageous in this transformation?

(*a*) P, Q, R, S (*b*) P, S only
(*c*) Q, S only (*d*) Q, R only

34. Match the Bivalvia in Group I with corresponding ecology in Group II.

Group I	Group II
P. Mytilus	1. Cemented
Q. Pecten	2. Swimmer
R. Slump	3. Bysally attached
	4. Infaunal
	5. Floating

(*a*) P - 1, Q - 2, R - 3, S - 5
(*b*) P - 3, Q - 2, R - 1, S - 4
(*c*) P - 2, Q - 3, R - 5, S - 1
(*d*) P - 2, Q - 4, R - 5, S - 3

35. Determine the correctness or otherwise of the following Assertion (a) and Reason (r).

Assertion: The Lower Gondwana rocks in Central India, containing brachiopod genera Productus, Spiriferina and Reticularia, are considered to have formed by transgression of the Tethys Sea in Peninsular India during Permian.

Reason: The brachiopods are marine organisms and the stratigraphic ranges of the brachiopod species of the formation suggest Permian age.

(*a*) Both (a) and (r) are true and (r) is the correct reason for (a)
(*b*) (a) is true but (r) is false
(*c*) (a) is false but (r) is true
(*d*) Both (a) and (r) are true but (r) is not the correct reason for (a)

36. In the following lithostratigraphic units, which of the formations are of Palaeocene and/or Eocene age?

P. Barail Formation
Q. Subathu Formation
R. Sylhet Limestone
S. Kamlial Formation

(*a*) P, Q (*b*) Q, R
(*c*) R, S (*d*) P, S

37. The microfaunal assemblages in a fining upward stratigraphic sequence are given below:

High abundance of Globigerina, Globorotalia and Orbulina (Top)

Moderate abundance of Uvigerina, Cassidulina and low abundance of Globigerina (Middle)

Moderate abundance of Ammonia, Elphidium and Quinqueloculina (Bottom)

The sequence corresponds to

(*a*) lowstand systems tract
(*b*) highstand systems tract
(*c*) transgressive systems tract
(*d*) shelf margin systems tract

38. Match the geomorphological features in Group I with corresponding characteristics in Group II.

Group I	Group II
P. Atolls	1. reefs parallel to the shore and separated by deep lagoon
Q. Mesa	2. broad flat topped hill capped by resistant rock and bounded by cliffs
R. Barchans	3. circular reefs that rim lagoons
	4. crescent shaped sand dunes

(*a*) P - 1, Q - 2, R - 3
(*b*) P - 3, Q - 2, R - 4
(*c*) P - 3, Q - 4, R - 1
(*d*) P - 3, Q - 4, R - 1

39. Match the optical properties in Group I with corresponding mineral in Group II.

Group I	**Group II**
P. internal reflections	1. galena
Q. bireflectance	2. sphalerite
R. triangular pits	3. magnetite
	4. pyrrhotite

(*a*) P - 4, Q - 3, R - 1 (*b*) P - 3, Q - 1, R - 4
(*c*) P - 2, Q - 4, R - 1 (*d*) P - 2, Q - 1, R - 4

40. Which of the following bands (in micrometre) is NOT suitable for earth observation in satellite remote sensing?
(*a*) 0.30 – 0.35 (*b*) 0.53 – 0.58
(*c*) 0.62 – 0.67 (*d*) 0.74 – 0.78

41. Thermal maturation of hydrocarbon source rocks can be determined from
(*a*) temperature of the borehole drilled into the source rock
(*b*) O^{18}/O^{16} ratio of the source rock
(*c*) Mg/Ca ratio of foraminifera in the source rock
(*d*) color of spores and pollens in the source rock

42. Determine the correctness or otherwise of the following Assertion (a) and Reason (r).

Assertion: Strontium concentration in a basic magma decreases with fractional crystallization of plagioclase.

Reason: Strontium is a compatible trace element in plagioclase during magmatic crystallization.
(*a*) Both (a) and (r) are true and (r) is the correct reason for (a)
(*b*) (a) is true but (r) is false
(*c*) (a) is false but (r) is true
(*d*) Both (a) and (r) are true but (r) is not the correct reason for (a)

43. Which of the following is TRUE for the coordination number (n) of aluminium?
(*a*) n = 4 in both plagioclase and garnet
(*b*) n = 6 in both plagioclase and garnet
(*c*) n = 4 in plagioclase and n = 6 in garnet
(*d*) n = 6 in plagioclase and n = 4 in garnet

44. If the dissociation constant of pure natural water at 50°C is $10^{-13.10}$, the pH of the water will be
(*a*) 6.00 (*b*) 6.55
(*c*) 7.00 (*d*) 7.55

45. Choose the CORRECT statement
(*a*) Sandstone forms aquifers and sandy shale forms aquifuges
(*b*) Sandstone forms aquifers and sandy shale forms aquitards
(*c*) Sandstone forms aquicludes and sandy shale forms aquifuges
(*d*) Both sandstone and sandy shale form aquifuges

46. The slow, permanent and continuous deformation of materials under constant load is called
(*a*) strain hardening (*b*) stress stiffening
(*c*) work hardening (*d*) creep

47. Which of the following lithostratigraphic units hosts lignite at Neyveli?
(*a*) Ariyalur Formation
(*b*) Cuddalore Formation
(*c*) Kamthi Beds
(*d*) Pali Beds

Common Data Questions

Common Data for Questions 48 and 49:

The figure below is the schematic geological map of a flat terrane.

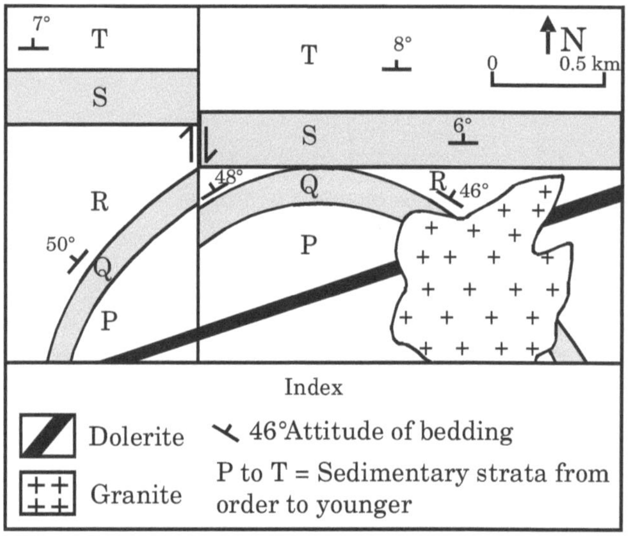

48. The strata P, Q and R have been folded into a
(*a*) north-plunging anticlinal antiform
(*b*) south-plunging anticlinal antiform
(*c*) north-plunging synclinal antiform
(*d*) south-plunging synclinal antiform

49. The granite pluton intruded
(a) before folding and faulting
(b) before faulting but after folding
(c) after development of unconformity but before faulting
(d) after development of unconformity and faulting

Common Data (or Questions 50 and 51:

Oceanic crust is generally covered by sediments. In a convergent tectonic setting, basaltic crust, along with its sedimentary cover, is subducted beneath continental plate. In such a setting, magmatism leads to the formation of a continental arc.

50. The magma series typical of the arc is

(*a*) alkaline (*b*) alkaline-shoshonitic

(*c*) tholeiitic (*d*) calc-alkaline

51. The type of sulphide mineral deposit formed in this tectonic setting is

(*a*) Porphyry copper

(*b*) Mississippi Valley lead and zinc

(*c*) Besshi copper and zinc

(*d*) Kuroko copper

Linked Answer Questions

Statement for Linked Answer Questions 52 and 53:

The modal analysis of a sandstone shows: Quartz 54%; Mica 3%; Feldspar 33%; Cement 5% and Matrix 5%

52. The sandstone belongs to the class

(*a*) Quartz wacke (*b*) Arkosic wacke

(*c*) Arkose (*d*) Quartz arenite

53. In which of the following conditions the CORRECT sandstone class in the previous question might have formed?

P. Warm arid climate

Q. Humid tropical climate

R. Long exposure and transportation

S. Quick burial without much transportation

(*a*) P, S (*b*) P, R

(*c*) Q, R (*d*) Q, S

Statement for Linked Answer Questions 54 and 55:

Lithostratigraphic units of different ages and hosting different ore deposits are exposed in Peninsular India.

54. Which of the following lithostratigraphic units is of Palaeoproterozoic age?

(*a*) Aravalli Supergroup

(*b*) Dharwar Supergroup

(*c*) Vindhyan Supergroup

(*d*) Sukma Group

55. The host rock and associated metal deposit found in the correct lithostratigraphic unit in the previous question is

(*a*) chlorite schist – copper

(*b*) dolomite – lead and zinc

(*c*) banded haematite quartzite – iron

(*d*) chlorite schist – antimony

GEOPHYSICS

Q. 26 to Q. 55 carry two marks each.

26. Rayleigh number associated with convection in the earth's interior is proportional to the ratio of

(*a*) buoyancy force to diffusive viscous force

(*b*) buoyancy force to gravitational force

(*c*) diffusive viscous force to gravitational force

(*d*) gravitational force to buoyancy force

27. Shadow zones for direct P- and S-waves lies between

(*a*) 102° to 142° for both direct P- and S-waves

(*b*) 102° to 180° for direct P- wave and 102° to 142° for direct S-wave

(*c*) 102° to 180° for both direct P- and S-waves

(*d*) 102° to 142° for direct P- wave and 102° to 180° for direct S-wave

28. Snell's law of refraction deals with which of the following properties of refracted waves?

(*a*) amplitude

(*b*) direction

(*c*) energy

(*d*) phase

29. In seismic reflection, the seismic trace is modeled as

(*a*) convolution of source wavelet with the reflection coefficient series

(*b*) multiplication of source wavelet with the reflection coefficient series

(*c*) correlation of source wavelet with the reflection coefficient series

(*d*) addition of source wavelet with the reflection coefficient series

30. From the following figure, choose the CORRECT multiple reflection events encountered in seismic exploration

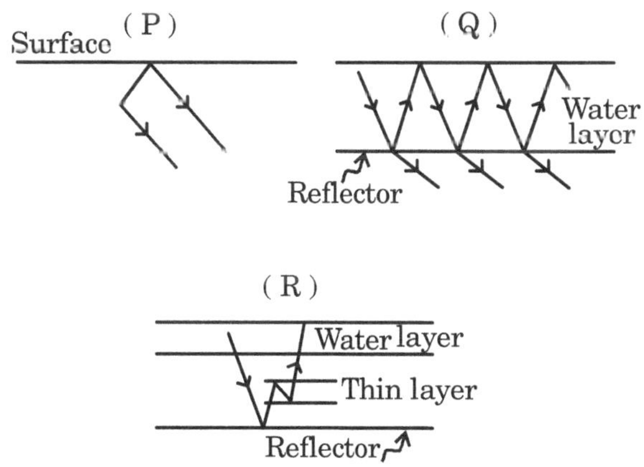

(*a*) P is peg leg multiple, Q is ghost, R is long path multiple

(*b*) P is ghost, Q is simple multiple, R is reverberation

(*c*) P is peg leg multiple, Q is simple multiple, R is reverberation

(*d*) P is ghost, Q is reverberation, R is peg leg multiple

31. The frequency of a signal sampled at 200 samples per second appears as 75 Hz. If the signal was undersampled, the frequency (in Hz) of the original signal would be

(*a*) 100 (*b*) 125

(*c*) 150 (*d*) 175

32. Match the items in Group I with those in Group II

Group I	Group II
P. correlation in frequency domain	1. reciprocal of total signal duration
Q. phase spectrum	2. aliasing
R. frequency interval	3. product of Fourier transform and its conjugate
S. undersampling	4. autocorrelation
	5. Hilbert transform

(*a*) P - 3, Q - 5, R - 1, S - 2

(*b*) P - 3, Q - 4, R - 2, S - 1

(*c*) P - 3, Q - 4, R - 1, S - 2

(*d*) P - 2, Q - 3, R - 4, S - 5

33. The derivative of the following boxcar function is

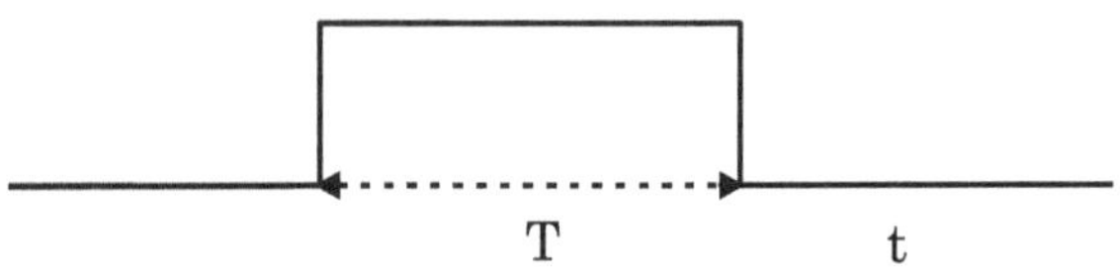

(*a*) 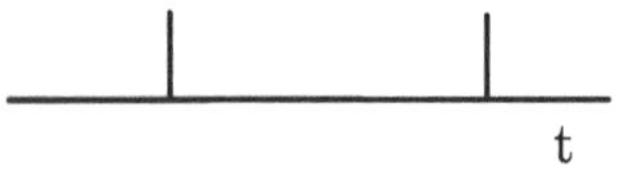

(*b*) 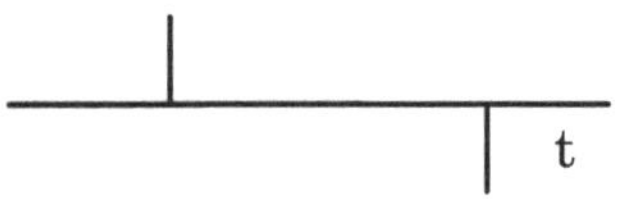

(*c*) 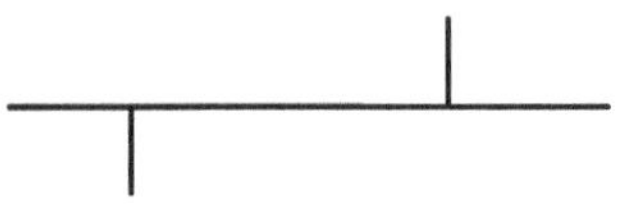

(*d*) 

34. Gravity measurement is made on a ship sailing at the speed of 6 knots in the direction N65°E at 20°N latitude. The Eotvos correction (in mGal) is

(*a*) +38.5 (*b*) +24.5

(*c*) –35.5 (*d*) –39.5

35. Isostatic residual anomaly over a mountainous terrain is due to

(*a*) gravitational effect of compensating mass

(*b*) long wavelength variations of topography

(*c*) short wavelength variations of topography

(*d*) density inhomogeneities in the upper and middle crust

36. In magnetic data reduction, the altitude correction at magnetic equator is 0.015 nT/m. Altitude correction (in nT/m) at the magnetic poles is

(*a*) 0.015 (*b*) 0.030

(*c*) 0.045 (*d*) 0.060

37. The Larmor precession frequency (in Hz) measured by proton precession magnetometer for a total field of 50,000 nT is (gyromagnetic ratio of proton $\gamma_p = 0.267513\ nT^{-1}S^{-1}$)

(*a*) 1890 (*b*) 2020

(*c*) 2130 (*d*) 2420

38. Gamma ray log measurements are used to quantify

(*a*) hydrocarbon saturation

(*b*) porosity of the formation

(*c*) density of the formation

(*d*) volume of shale in the formation

39. Free fluid index (FFI) of a formation is estimated from

(*a*) neutron log (*b*) latero log

(*c*) induction log (*d*) NMR log

40. Compton scattering takes place if the energy of gamma rays lies in the range of

(*a*) 10 KeV to 50 KeV

(*b*) 50 KeV to 100 KeV

(*c*) 100 KeV to 2.0 MeV

(*d*) 2.0 MeV to 3.5 MeV

41. Which of the following Maxwell's equations is NOT CORRECT for time varying electromagnetic field?

(*a*) $\nabla \times \vec{H} = \vec{J}$ (*b*) $\nabla \times \vec{E} = -\frac{\partial \vec{B}}{\partial t}$

(*c*) $\nabla \cdot \vec{D} = \rho$ (*d*) $\nabla \cdot \vec{B} = 0$

42. The apparent resistivity sounding curve representing the resistivity structure $\rho_1 > \rho_2 < \rho_3 < \rho_4$ is

(*a*) HK–type (*b*) HA–type

(*c*) KH-type (*d*) KQ–type

43. Forced movement of fluids through porous rocks gives rise to

(*a*) streaming potential

(*b*) Nernst potential

(*c*) mineralization potential

(*d*) liquid junction potential

44. Match the EM methods in Group I with the corresponding quantity measured by them in Group II

Group I	Group II
P. VLF	1. amplitude ratio and phase difference
Q. Two-frame	2. real and imaginary components
R. Slingram	3. dip angle
S. TURAM	4. amplitude ratio

(*a*) P - 2, Q - 4, R - 3, S - 1

(*b*) P - 3, Q - 4, R - 2, S - 1

(*c*) P - 3, Q - 4, R - 1, S - 2

(*d*) P - 2, Q - 3, R - 4, S - 1

45. Arrange the following electromagnetic methods in the decreasing order of depth of investigation.

P. Time domain EM method

Q. Magnetotelluric method

R. VLF method

S. Ground Penetrating Radar method

(*a*) P > Q > S > R (*b*) S > Q > P > R

(*c*) Q > P > R > S (*d*) Q > R > P > S

46. The least squares generalized inverse of an overdetermined problem is expressed as

(*a*) $(G^TG)^{-1}G^T$ (*b*) $(G^TG)^{-1}$

(*c*) $G^T(GG^T)^{-1}$ (*d*) $(GG^T)^{-1}$

47. The primary field (H_p) in EM prospecting is represented by $H_p = K\sin(\omega t)$. Which is the CORRECT expression for induced e.m.f. (e_s) in the subsurface conductor? (K and K ' are constants)

(*a*) $e_S = K'\sin\left(\omega t - \frac{\pi}{4}\right)$

(*b*) $e_S = K'\cos\left(\omega t - \frac{\pi}{4}\right)$

(*c*) $e_S = K'\sin\left(\omega t - \frac{\pi}{2}\right)$

(*d*) $e_S = K'\cos\left(\omega t - \frac{\pi}{2}\right)$

Common Data Questions

Common Data (or Questions 48 and 49:

Time series P and Q are given by

P = {1, –1, –2, 0, 1}

Q = {1, 0, –1}

48. The convolution of P and Q is

(*a*) {–1, 0, 3, 1, –3, –1, 1}

(*b*) {1, –1, –3, 1, 3, 0, –1}

(*c*) {1, –1, –3, –1, 3, 1, –1}

(*d*) {1, 0, 3, 1, –3, –1, 1}

49. P is similar and most out of phase to Q at a lag of

(a) 0 (b) 1

(c) 2 (d) 3

Common Data for Questions 50 and 51:

An asymmetric split spread extends from x_1 = – 400 m to x_2 = 800 m. A reflection observed on the spread yields t_1 = 0.997 s at x_1 = –400 m, t_2 = 1.025 s at x_2 = 800 m, t_0 = 1.0 s at x = 0.0 m and velocity of 2800 m/s.

50. NMO correction estimated at x_1 = –400 m and x_2 = 800 m are, respectively

(*a*) 5 and 30 ms (*b*) 8 and 35 ms

(*c*) 10 and 41 ms (*d*) 15 and 45 ms

51. The depth of the reflector at the shot point normal to the reflector is

(*a*) 700 m (*b*) 1400 m

(*c*) 2100 m (*d*) 2800 m

Linked Answer Questions

Statement for Linked Answer Questions 52 and 53:

A gravity survey is conducted over a highly compact ore deposit (spherical shape). Bouguer anomaly values reduced along a profile are given below.

Distance (m)	Gravity anomaly (mGal)
0	0.25
400	0.35
800	0.50
1200	0.80
1600	1.50
2000	2.50
2400	3.50
2800	4.00
3200	5.00
3600	4.00
4000	3.50
4400	2.50
4800	1.50
5200	0.80
5600	0.50
6000	0.35
6400	0.25

52. What is the depth to the center of the ore deposit?

(*a*) 3100 m (*b*) 1820 m

(*c*) 1560 m (*d*) 1450 m

53. What is the excess mass (in metric tons) by the deposit?

(*a*) 1.615×10^8 (*b*) 2.165×10^8

(*c*) 1.312×10^9 (*d*) 1.825×10^9

Statement for Linked Answer Questions 54 and 55:

An axial dipole-dipole configuration is given below.

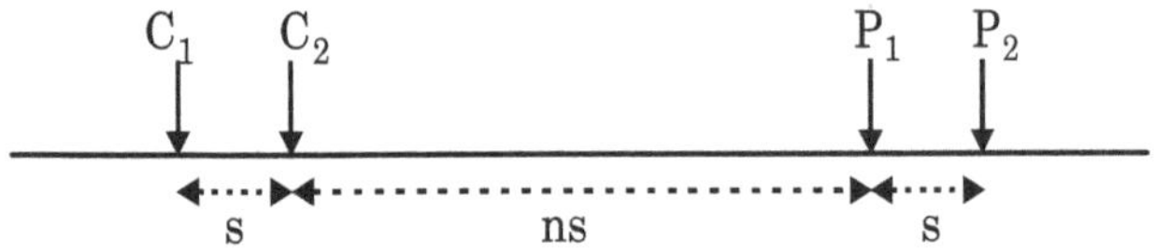

54. The geometrical factor for the above axial dipole array is

(*a*) $\pi n(n + 1)s$ (*b*) $\pi n(n + 2)s$

(*c*) $\pi(n + 1)(n + 2)s$ (*d*) $\pi n(n + 1)(n + 2)s$

55. What is the apparent resistivity (in Ωm) if 1.0 Amp current flowing between C_1 and C_2 produces 10 mV potential difference between P_1 and P_2 for s = 10 m and n = 10? (Use $\pi = 3.14$)

(*a*) 414.48 (*b*) 41.45

(*c*) 37.68 (*d*) 34.54

GENERA1 APTITUDE (GA)

Q.56 – Q.60 carry one mark each.

56. Choose the most appropriate word or phrase from the options given below to complete the following sentence.

The environmentalists hope ________ the lake to its pristine condition.

(*a*) in restoring (*b*) in the restoration of

(*c*) to restore (*d*) restoring

57. Choose the word from the options given below that is most nearly opposite in meaning to the given word:

Polemical

(*a*) imitative (*b*) conciliatory

(*c*) truthful (*d*) ideological

58. Choose the most appropriate word from the options given below to complete the following sentence.

Despite the mixture's ______ nature, we found that by lowering its temperature in the laboratory we could dramatically reduce its tendency to vaporize.

(*a*) acerbic (*b*) resilient

(*c*) volatile (*d*) heterogeneous

59. If m students require a total of m pages of stationery in m days, then 100 students will require 100 pages of stationery in

(*a*) 100 days (*b*) m/100 days

(*c*) 100/m days (*d*) m days

60. Choose the most appropriate words from the options given below to complete the following sentence.

Because she had a reputation for _________ we were surprised and pleased when she greeted us so ________.

(*a*) insolence .... irately

(*b*) insouciance .... curtly

(*c*) graciousness .... amiably

(*d*) querulousness .... affably

Q. 61 – Q. 65 carry two marks each.

61. The number of solutions for the following system of inequalities is

$X_1 \geq 0$

$X_2 \geq 0$

$X_1 + X_2 \leq 10$

$2X_1 + 2X_2 \geq 22$

(*a*) 0 (*b*) infinite

(*c*) 1 (*d*) 2

62. In a class of 300 students in an M.Tech programme, each student is required to take at least one subject from the following three:

M600 : Advanced Engineering Mathematics

C600 : Computational Methods for Engineers

E600 : Experimental Techniques for Engineers

The registration data for the M.Tech class shows that 100 students have taken M600, 200 students have taken C600 and 60 students have taken E600. What is the maximum possible number of students in the class who have taken all the above three subjects?

(*a*) 20 (*b*) 30

(*c*) 40 (*d*) 50

63. Three sisters (R, S, and T) received a total of 24 toys during Christmas. The toys were initially divided among them in a certain proportion. Subsequently, R gave some toys to S which doubled the share of S. Then S in turn gave some of her toys to T, which doubled T's share. Next, some of T's toys were given to R, which doubled the number of toys that R currently had. As a result of all such exchanges, the three sisters were left with equal number of toys. How many toys did R have originally?

(*a*) 8 (*b*) 9

(*c*) 11 (*d*) 12

64. The quality of services delivered by a company consists of six factors as shown below in the radar diagram. The dots in the figure indicate the score for each factor on a scale of 0 to 10. The standardized coefficient for each factor is given in the parentheses. The contribution of each factor to the overall service quality is directly proportional to the factor score and its standardized coefficient.

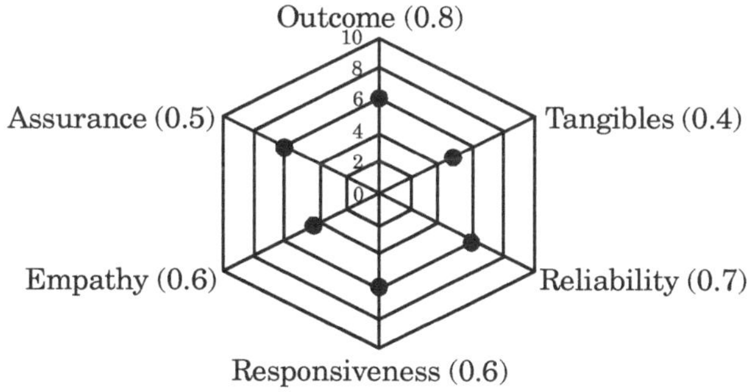

The lowest contribution among all the above factors to the overall quality of services delivered by the company is

(*a*) 10% (*b*) 20%
(*c*) 24% (*d*) 40%

65. In order to develop to full potential, a baby needs to be physically able to respond to the environment.

It can be inferred from the passage that

(*a*) Full physical potential is needed in order f or a baby to be able to respond to the environment.
(*b*) It is necessary for a baby to be able to physically respond to the environment for it to develop its full potential.
(*c*) Response to the environment of physically able babies needs to be developed to its full potential.
(*d*) A physically able baby needs to develop its full potential in order to respond to its environment.

ANSWERS

PART A (Common Part)

1. (*b*) **2.** (*d*) **3.** (*d*) **4.** (A) **5.** (*c*) **6.** (*b*) **7.** (*a*) **8.** (*c*) **9.** (*a*) **10.** (*b*)
11. (*c*) **12.** (*a*) **13.** (*b*) **14.** (*d*) **15.** (*d*) **16.** (*a*) **17.** (*c*) **18.** (*d*) **19.** (*a*) **20.** (*a,b,c,d*)
21. (*b*) **22.** (*c*) **23.** (*c*) **24.** (*d*) **25.** (*b*)

PART-B (Geology)

26. (*c*) **27.** (*b*) **28.** (*d*) **29.** (*c*) **30.** (*d*) **31.** (*a*) **32.** (*c*) **33.** (*b*) **34.** (*b*) **35.** (*a*)
36. (*b*) **37.** (*c*) **38.** (*b*) **39.** (*c*) **40.** (*a*) **41.** (*d*) **42.** (*a*) **43.** (*c*) **44.** (*b*) **45.** (*b*)
46. (*d*) **47.** (*b*) **48.** (*a*) **49.** (*d*) **50.** (*d*) **51.** (*a*) **52.** (*c*) **53.** (*a*) **54.** (*a*) **55.** (*b*)

(Geophysics)

26. (*a*) **27.** (*d*) **28.** (*b*) **29.** (*a*) **30.** (*d*) **31.** (*b*) **32.** (*c*) **33.** (*b*) **34.** (*a*) **35.** (*d*)
36. (*b*) **37.** (*c*) **38.** (*d*) **39.** (*d*) **40.** (*c*) **41.** (*a*) **42.** (*b*) **43.** (*a*) **44.** (*b*) **45.** (*c*)
46. (*a*) **47.** (*c*) **48.** (*b*) **49.** (*c*) **50.** (*c*) **51.** (*b*) **52.** (*c*) **53.** (*d*) **54.** (*d*) **55.** (*a*)

(General Aptitude)

56. (*c*) **57.** (*b*) **58.** (*c*) **59.** (*d*) **60.** (*d*) **61.** (*a*) **62.** (*c*) **63.** (*a*) **64.** (*b*) **65.** (*b*)

EXPLANATIONS

PART A (COMMON PART)

1. Mainly due to tidal effects, the Earth's rotational period is not constant, resulting in minor variations for both solar days and stellar "days". The Earth's day has increased in length over time. This phenomenon is due to tides raised by the Moon which slow Earth's rotation. Because of the way the second is defined, the mean length of a day is now about 86 400.002 seconds, and is increasing by about 1.7 milliseconds per century (an average over the last 2 700 years). The length of a day circa 620 million years ago has been estimated from rhythmists (alternating layers in sandstone) as having been about 21.9 hours. The length of day for the Earth before the moon was created is still unknown.
2. Granite could be considered a potential natural radiological hazard as, for instance, villages located over granite may be susceptible to higher doses of radiation than other communities.
3. The Mohorovici discontinuity usually referred to as the Moho, is the boundary between the Earth's crust and the mantle.

   Immediately above the Moho, the velocities of primary seismic waves (P-waves) are consistent with those through basalt (6.7-7.2 km/s), and below they are similar to those through peridotite or dunite (7.6-8.6 km/s).
4. **Dipole Field:** It exhibits secular variations of intensity and directions. It shows a nonlinear decay of the strength of the dipole moment at a rate of about 3.2 % per century, between about 1550 AD and 1900 AD. At the start of the 20th century, the decay became even faster and has averaged about 5.8 % per century during last 80 years.

5.

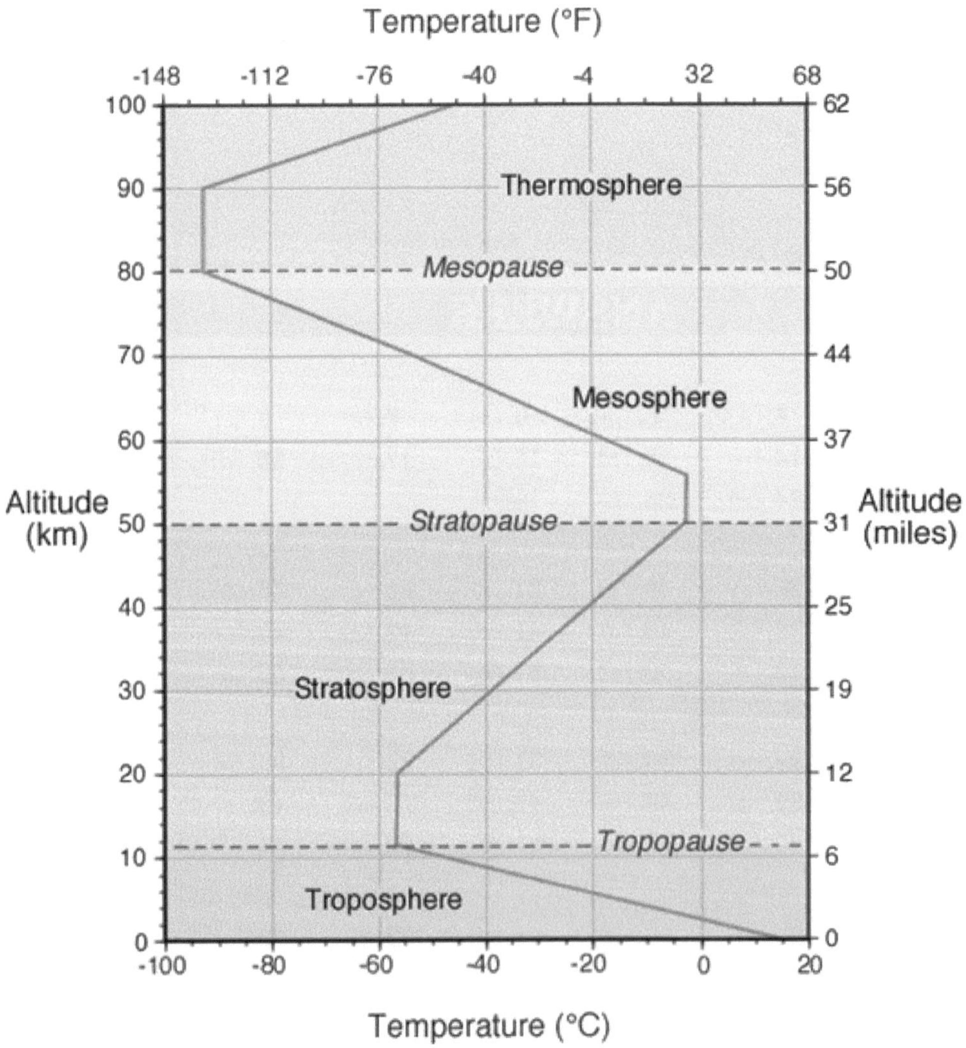

6. The Coriolis effect describes the pattern of deflection taken by objects not firmly connected to the ground as they travel long distances around and above the Earth. The Coriolis effect is responsible for many large-scale weather patterns. The Earth completes one rotation per day, so for motions of everyday objects the Coriolis force is usually quite small compared to other forces; its effects generally become noticeable only for motions occurring over large distances and long periods of time, such as large-scale movement of air in the atmosphere or water in the ocean. Such motions are constrained by the surface of the Earth, so only the horizontal component of the Coriolis force is generally important. This force causes moving objects on the surface of the Earth to be deflected to the right (with respect to the direction of travel) in the Northern Hemisphere and to the left in the Southern Hemisphere.

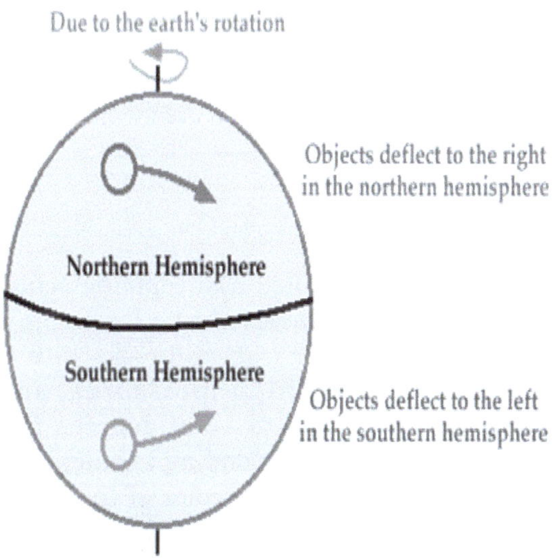

7. The principal generation mechanism (or cause) of a tsunami is the displacement of a substantial volume of water or perturbation of the sea. This displacement of water is usually attributed to either earthquakes, landslides, volcanic eruptions, glacier calving or more rarely by meteorites and nuclear tests. The waves formed in this way are then sustained by gravity.

8. Angular momentum is the measure of the tendency of a rotating body to remain rotating. Angular momentum is always conserved. The magnitude of the orbital angular momentum vector of a planet is $L = R^2 M\dot{\theta}$, where R is the orbital radius of the planet (from the barycenter), M is the mass of the planet, and $\dot{\theta}$ is its orbital angular velocity. That of Jupiter contributes the bulk of the Solar System's angular momentum, 60.3%.

9. An alluvial fan is a fan- or cone-shaped deposit of sediment crossed and built up by streams. If a fan is built up by debris flows, it is properly called a debris cone or colluvial fan. These flows come from a single point source at the apex of the fan, and over time move to occupy many positions on the fan surface. Fans are typically found where a canyon draining from mountainous terrain emerges out onto a flatter plain, and especially along fault-bounded mountain fronts.

10. Large valley glacier systems consist of numerous cirques and smaller valley glaciers that feed ice into a large trunk glacier. Because of its greater ice discharge, the trunk glacier has greater erosive capability in its middle and lower reaches than smaller tributary glaciers that join it there. The main valley is therefore eroded more rapidly than the side valleys. With time, the bottom of the main valley becomes lower than the elevation of the tributary valleys. When the ice has retreated, the tributary valleys are left joining the main valley at elevations substantially higher than its bottom. Tributary valleys with such unequal or discordant junctions are called **hanging valleys**.

11. An angular unconformity is an unconformity where horizontally parallel strata of sedimentary rock are deposited on tilted and eroded layers, producing an angular discordance with the overlying horizontal layers. The whole sequence may later be deformed and tilted by further orogenic activity. A typical case history is presented by the paleotectonic evolution of the Brianconnais realm (Swiss and French Prealps) during the Jurassic.

12. The Mohs scale of mineral hardness is a qualitative ordinal scale characterizing scratch resistance of various minerals through the ability of harder material to scratch softer material.

Mohs hardness	Mineral	Chemical formula	Absolute hardness
1	Talc	$Mg_3Si_4O_{10}(OH)_2$	1
2	Gypsum	$CaSO_4{\cdot}2H_2O$	3
3	Calcite	$CaCO_3$	9
4	Fluorite	CaF_2	21
5	Apatite	$Ca_5(PO_4)_3(OH^-,Cl^-,F^-)$	48
6	Orthoclase feldspar	$KAlSi_3O_8$	72
7	Quartz	SiO_2	100
8	Topaz	$Al_2SiO_4(OH^-,F^-)_2$	200
9	Corundum	Al_2O_3	400
10	Diamond	C	1500

The hardest oxide mineral in Mohs scale of hardness is Corundum.

13. **Ultramafic Rock:** An igneous rock with a very low silica content and rich in minerals such as hypersthene, augite, and olivine. These rocks are also known as ultrabasic rocks. Examples include: peridotite, kimberlite, lamprophyre, lamproite, dunite, and komatiite. Shown in the photo is a specimen of peridotite.

14. **Pumice** called pumicite in its powdered or dust form, is a volcanic rock that consists of highly vesicular rough textured volcanic glass, which may or may not contain crystals. It is typically light colored. Scoria is another vesicular volcanic rock that differs from pumice in having larger vesicles, thicker vesicle walls and being dark colored and denser.

15. Radiocarbon dating is the most widely used method for dating Holocene and latest Pleistocene earthquakes. The half-life of radioactive ^{14}C (5730 y) limits the application of radiocarbon dating to organic matter formed from carbon fixed within the last 50 000-60 000 y. The amount of ^{14}C in atmospheric CO_2 has varied in the past, particularly in the last few centuries due to anthropogenic emissions.

16. **Tipam Group:** This group rests conformably over the surma group. The Tipam group is composed of 3000 to 4000 m of thick secession of sandstones. The subordinate shales and clays and ranges from lower Miocene to upper Oligocene.

17. Rampura Agucha is a zinc and lead mine located on a massive sulfide deposit in the Bhilwara district of Rajasthan, India. Rampura Agucha is located 220 km from Jaipur. It is north of Bhilwara, and northwest of Shahpura. Rampura Agucha is 17 km southeast of Bijainagar on NH 79. The mine is owned by Hindustan Zinc Limited (HZL), and has the world's largest deposits of zinc and lead.

18. Bombay High is an offshore oilfield 50 km off the coast of Mumbai, India, in about 75 m of water. The oil operations are run by India's Oil and Natural Gas Corporation (ONGC). Every oil resource rock requires Structural traps which are mainly salt dome, coral reefs, fault trap and fold trap. In case of Bombay High, the structure is a "north-northwest to south-southeast trending doubly plunging Anticline with a faulted east limb", 65 km long and 23 km wide", and is the most probable reason to call it "Bombay High".

    This is a carbonate reservoir, the main producing zone, L-III, consisting of sedimentary cycles of lagoonal, algal mound, foraminiferal mound and then coastal marsh, capped by a post-middle Miocene shale.

19. Resistivity anomalies depends on the presence of continuous conductors such as ground water or massive oil bodies. If mineralization is disseminated through a rock, it may not cause a significant resistivity anomaly. The good response of the IP method for disseminated concentration of conducting ore minerals led to its development in base metal exploration, where large low grade orebodies may be commercially important.

20. **Marks to all**

    Sonic, Temperature and density logging can be used in identifying overpreassure gas zones.

21. The acceleration due to gravity (g) and universal gravitational constant (G) are related by the expression (Me and Re are the mass and radius of the earth, respectively)

    As per Newton's law of gravitation, the force of gravitation is given as,

    $$F = \frac{GM_e m}{R_e^2}$$

    Also, the force is given a F = mg

    Equating both sides

    $$mg = \frac{GM_e m}{R_e^2}$$

    $$\Rightarrow g = \frac{GM_e}{R_e^2}$$

22. Blueschist also called glaucophane schist, is a metavolcanic rock that forms by the metamorphism of basalt and rocks with similar composition at high pressures and low temperatures (200 to ~500 degrees Celsius), approximately corresponding to a depth of 15 to 30 kilometers. The blue color of the rock comes from the presence of the predominant minerals glaucophane and lawsonite. Blueschists and other high-pressure subduction zone rocks are thought to be exhumed rapidly by flow and/or faulting in accretionary wedges or the upper parts of subducted crust, or may return to the Earth's surface in part owing to buoyancy if the metabasaltic rocks are associated with low-density continental crust (marble, metapelite, and other rocks of continental margins).

23. We know that the P wave and S wave velocity is given by α and β respectively as

    $$\alpha = \sqrt{\frac{\lambda + 2\mu}{\rho}} \text{ and } \beta = \sqrt{\frac{\mu}{\rho}}$$

    where, λ and μ are Lame's constant

    Thus, α and β are inversely proportional to square roots of density Hence on increasing density P- wave and S- wave velocities decreases.

24. In continuum mechanics, the Lamé parameters are two material-dependent quantities denoted by λ and μ that arise in strain-stress relationships

The poisson ratio for rocks in terms of λ and μ is given as,

$$\sigma = \frac{\lambda}{2(\lambda + \mu)}$$

25. **Ground Roll:** It is a low frequency surface wave which creates noise in seismic data acquisition.

PART-B (GEOLOGY)

26. The correct set of crystal faces for which 'c' crystallographic axis is the zone axis is given by, $(010), (\bar{1}10), (100)$. For any axis to be a zone axis, all faces should be parallel to that axis.

27. In Manebach law, twin plane is parallel to 'a' and b axis and cut 'c' axis at unity.

29. According to the UNFC classification, it is Tonalite.

30. Chloritoid porphyroblasts are post- tectonic because they are undisturbed and oriented randomly in the deformed or crenulated matrix.

31. Kyanite, andalusite, and sillimanite are naturally occurring anhydrous aluminum silicate minerals. Each has the same chemical formula, Al_2SiO_5, but differing crystal structures, making them mineral polymorphs. Kyanite will transform to sillimanite if the pressure is reduced and temperature is maintained or increased.

32. Flute casts are scoop-shaped structures on the soles (undersides) of beds. They are features representing sediments that filled depressions on the immediately subjacent bedding plane. Flute casts form by erosive scour. The most common geologic phenomena that produce flute casts are turbidity currents (underwater sediment slides). Sedimentary rocks representing deposition by ancient turbidity currents are called turbidites. Many turbidite successions have well preserved flute casts.

33. Bulging of the shell of in faunal form occur to bear the sediment load as well as the hydrostatic pressure. It also helps in the locomotion of organisms.

34. All bivalves have the ability to secrete sticky threads known as **byssal threads**. However, most bivalves tend to use them only during infancy when they are small and require stabilization. Species such as **Mytilus** use their byssal threads into adulthood. Mytilus is an epibyssate bivalve, which means it lives on the sediment surface with its threads reaching down into the substrate for stability. Epibyssate forms tend to be squat in shape.

The colour of the body of **Pecten maximus** is pink or red with the mantle marbled brown and white. When young they are attached to the substrate by a byssus but mature animals are capable of swimming by the opening and rapid closing of the valves.

The behaviour of pediveligers of **Ostrea edulis** L. during attachment can be divided into 5 clearly defined phases. These behavioural phases are generally successive, and may be a hierarchy of fixed motor patterns which terminates in the consummatory act of cementing. During attachment, the larva utilises two different mechanisms of movement: the first, a fast, smooth, gliding action is probably due to cilia only; the second, a jerky, muscular method which becomes progressively slower as cementing is approached, is related to the burrowing movements of adult lamellibranchs.

The infaunal, suspension-feeding softshell clam i.e., **Mya arenaria** L. is a conspicuous member of the intertidal macrofauna in numerous northern temperate and boreal soft-bottom communities. Recruitment variability can affect the magnitude and scope of various ecosystem services provided by Mya arenaria, including its role as a source of food and energy for organisms at higher trophic levels.

35. Both (a) and (r) are true and (r) is the correct reason for (a)

The Lower Gondwana rocks in Central India, containing brachiopod genera Productus, Spiriferina and Reticularia, are considered to have formed by transgression of the Tethys Sea in Peninsular India during Permian is due to

The brachiopods are marine organisms and the stratigraphic ranges of the brachiopod species of the formation suggest Permian age.

36.

	Formation	Age
P	Barail	Miocene
Q	Subathu Formation	Eocene
R	Sylhet Limestone	Palaeocene
S	Kamlian Formation	Pliocene

37. **Lowstand Systems Tract:** The lowstand systems tract is the set of depositional systems active during the time of relatively low sea level following the formation of the sequence boundary. If a distinct shelf-slope break exists and relative sea level has fallen sufficiently, the lowstand systems tract may include two distinct parts, the lowstand fan and the lowstand wedge.

Highstand Systems Tract: The highstand systems tract consists of an aggradational to progradational set of parasequences that overlies the maximum flooding surface and that is overlain by the next sequence boundary. As the parasequences pass from aggradational to progradational stacking, the flooding surfaces are increasingly subdued at the expense of overall shallowing.

Transgressive Systems Tract: The transgressive systems tract consists of a retrogradational set of parasequences. It is underlain by the transgressive surface and overlain by the maximum flooding surface. As in any retrogradational set of parasequences, flooding surfaces within the transgressive systems tract are unusually prominent and display strong facies contrasts and pronounced deepening. These flooding surfaces may display variable but commonly strong degrees of sediment starvation, discussed in more detail below. Because the parasequences backstep, the transgressive systems tract displays an overall deepening-upward succession, although each component parasequence is shallowing-upward. In siliciclastic systems, much sediment is trapped in estuaries, so the continental shelf is relatively starved of sediment during major transgressions. A relatively minor amount of sand is reworked along the shoreline and little sediment is transported to the outer continental shelf. Consequently, individual parasequences of the TST are relatively thin nearshore sands with thinner offshore deposits and the TST as a whole is therefore commonly quite thin relative to other systems tracts.

Shelf-margin systems tracts are the lowstand deposits of a type 2 sequence. Type 2 sequences are deposited when relative sea level falls but not below the preceding depositional inflection. Type 1 sequences are deposited when relative sea level falls below the preceding depositional systems tract. The subsequent transgression may provide effective top seal, but the lateral seal of shelf margin systems tracts shares the same limitations as the highstand systems tract.

38. **Atolls** are coral reef enclosing a lagoon. Atolls consist of ribbons of reef that may not always be circular but whose broad configuration is a closed shape up to dozens of km across, enclosing a lagoon that may be approximately 50 m deep or more. Most of the reef itself is a submarine feature, rising from the abyssal floors of the ocean to just beneath high-tide level. Around the rim along the top of the reef, there are usually low, flat islands or more continuous strips of low, flat land. Oceanic peoples like the Maldivians, Polynesians, and Micronesians have settled some of these islands for many centuries.

Mesa is an elevated area of land with a flat top and sides that are usually steep cliffs. It takes its name from its characteristic tabletop shape. It may also be called a table hill, table-topped hill or table mountain. It is larger than a butte, which it otherwise resembles closely.

Barchans are crescent-shaped sand dune produced by the action of wind predominately from one direction. One of the commonest types of dunes, it occurs in sandy deserts all over the world. Barchans are convex facing the wind, with the horns of the crescent pointing downwind and marking the lateral advancement of the sand.

39. **Internal Reflections:** Translucent minerals, when observed under reflected light, allow light to penetrate beneath the surface and be reflected back to the observer from cracks, crystal boundaries, cleavages and other flaws within the crystal. Such light will appear as diffuse areas or patches known as internal reflections. Although visible in plane polarized light, internal reflections are best seen under crossed nicols and intense illumination using oil immersion and high power magnification. They are best seen at the edges of grains or in fine grains. It is important to note that many grains of a mineral that could show internal reflections may not exhibit them. Both the occurrence and colors of internal reflections are of diagnostic value. Example- Sphalerite gives Yellow to brown (sometimes red to green).

Bireflectance is an optical effect similar to pleochroism where the mineral appears to change in intensity as it is rotated while illuminated by plane polarized light. The polarizers are not crossed to observe bireflectance. Isotropic minerals (eg, galena, pyrite) do not show any bireflectance (or pleochroism) when rotated in plane polarized light. Minerals which are pleochroic are also bireflectant.

The presence of three or more sets of cleavages may give rise to triangular pits usually arranged in rows parallel to one set. Such pits are characteristic of galena, and may also be present in magnetite, pentlandite, gersdorffite, etc. A prismatic cleavage gives rise to diamond-shaped, triangular or rectangular patterns; a pinacoidal cleavage gives rise to a set of parallel cracks. Cleavage of a mineral may not be evident in a well polished surface, or in minerals occurring in fine grained aggregates. It is likely to be more evident in slightly weathered ores, during the earlier stages of polishing, at the margins of grains, or after etching.

40. 0.30 – 0.35 μm band corresponds to ultraviolet light which is absorbed by ozone layer.

41. Color of spore and pollens in the source rock changes with the thermal maturation of hydrocarbon source rocks.

42. Strontium has same charge and nearly same atomic radius as that of calcium. So, it is compatible to plagioclase and concentrates in plagioclase crystal during fractional crystallization.

43. Aluminum has four coordinate number in plagioclase and 6 coordinate number in garnet.

44. Given, dislocation constant $K = 10^{-13.10}$

$$H_2O \rightleftharpoons [H^+] + [OH^-]$$

For this reaction

$$K = [H^+] + [OH^-]$$

Here, $[H^+] = [OH^-]$

Therefore, $[H^+] = [H^+] = [H^+]^2$

Putting the value of K

$$10^{-13.10} = [H^+]^2$$

Taking log on both sides

$$\log 10^{-13.10} = \log\left([H^+]^2\right)$$

$$\Rightarrow -13.10 \log 10 = 2 \log[H^+]$$

$$\Rightarrow \log 10 = 1$$

Therefore, $\frac{13.10}{2} = \log[H^+]$

$$\Rightarrow -\log[H^+] = 6.55$$

$$\therefore \text{pH} = -\log[H^+]$$

$$\text{pH} = 6.55$$

45. **Aquifer:** Porous and permeable formation which contain water.

Aquitared: Formation having low porosity and very low permeability, e.g., Sandy Shale

Aquiclude: Porous but impermeable formation, e.g., Shale.

Aquifuge: Imporous, impermeable formation, e.g., Granite

46. **Strain hardening**, is the strengthening of a metal or polymer by plastic deformation. This strengthening occurs because of dislocation movements and dislocation generation within the crystal structure of the material.

Stress stiffening is a process, which brings rigidity and structural integrity in the objects.

Creep is the slow permanent and continuous deformation of materials under constant load.

47. Cuddalore formation is the host of Neyveli lignite.

48. The strata P, Q and R have folded into north plunging, anticlinal, antiform.

North plunging: Plunge of axis is towards north.

Anticlinal: Older bed in the core.

Antiform: Limbs dip away from each other.

49. Granite pluton is unaffected by folding and unconformity. Therefore, it was formed later than those of folding and unconformity. In addition, dolerite dike is unaffected by faulting. Hence, it was formed. After the fault also, granite is unaffected by the dolerite intrusion. Hence, granite was formed later than that of dolerite intrusion. Therefore, we can conclude that granite was formed after the faulting.

50. Magma series typical to the island arc and continental arc is calc alkaline.

51. Porphyry copper formed in arc system.

52. Wacke have matrix - 15% - 75 %

Sandstone have nearly 75 % of quartz and 20 - 25 % of feldspar, Matric < 15 %

Quartz Arenite have > 95 % of quartz.

53. Arkoses have generally ≥ 25% of fresh feldspar. Therefore, they generally form in warm and arid climate because feldspar is very much susceptible to chemical weathering.

54.

Group	Age
Aravalli Supergroup	Palaeoproterozoic
Dharwar Supergroup	Archaean
Vindhyan Supergroup	Neoproterozoic
Sukum Group	Archaean

55. Dolomite- lead and zinc (Zawer- Rajasthan)

(GEOPHYSICS)

26. Rayleigh number, R_a is a dimensionless number which is proportional to the ratio of the buoyancy force to diffusive viscous force given by,

$$R_a = \frac{g\rho\alpha\Delta T}{K\eta} V$$

where, g is acceleration due to gravity

ρ is density

α is coefficient of expansion

ΔT is temperature difference

V is volume involved in correction

K is thermal diffusivity

η is viscosity

27. The shadow zone is the area of the earth from angular distances of 102 to 142 degrees from a given earthquake that does not receive any direct P waves and 102 to 180 degrees for direct S waves. The shadow zone results from S waves being stopped entirely by the liquid core and P waves being bent (refracted) by the liquid core.P waves that have been converted to s-waves on leaving the outer core may be detected beyond 140 degrees.

28. Snell's law is given for two media separated by an interface having velocities V_1 and V_2 and is given by

$$\frac{\sin i}{\sin r} = \frac{V_1}{V_2}$$

Where, i and r are incident and refracted angles.

29. Modelling of seismic trace is done by the convolution of mainly source wavelet and the reflection coefficient series, but it also contains some effect due to other factors like instrument effect.

30. As per given question, it is clear that P is ghost as the reflection is from the surface inside the water and Q is reverberation as the reflection is beyond the critical angle.

31. Given, Sampling frequency, $f_s = 200$ Hz

Therefore, frequency of sampled signal = 75

Now, If the signal is undersampled, then the frequency of the original is

$$200 - 75 \text{ Hz} = 125 \text{ Hz}$$

32. According to the cross-correlation theorem: The cross-correlation between two signals is equal to the product of fourier transform of one signal multiplied by complex conjugate of fourier transform of another signal.

Frequency is the number of occurrences of a repeating event per unit of time. It is also referred to as temporal frequency, which emphasizes the contrast to spatial frequency and angular frequency. The period is the duration of time of one cycle in a repeating event, so the period is the reciprocal of the frequency.

Sometimes aliasing is used intentionally on signals with no low-frequency content, called bandpass signals. Undersampling, which creates low-frequency aliases, can produce the same result, with less effort, as frequency-shifting the signal to lower frequencies before sampling at the lower rate. Some digital channelizers exploit aliasing in this way for computational efficiency.

33. The figure B is the right choice

By simply talking the derivative at two different stages of time.

34. **Eotovos Correction**: This is the correction necessary if the instrument is on a moving platform, such as a ship or aircraft. It accounts for centrifugal acceleration due to motion on the rotating earth. The relation is

$$EC = \left(75.03V \sin\alpha \cos\phi + 0.04154V^2\right) gu$$

where, V is the speed of vehicle in knots

α is heading,

ϕ is the latitude of the observation

ImGal = 10 gu

As per given question,

V = 6 knots

$\alpha = 65^\circ$,

$\phi = 20^\circ$

35. Isostatic residual anomaly over a mountainous terrain is due to density inhomogenetics in the upper and middle crust.

36. At the magnetic equator, the field is 30,000 nT, and the altitude correction is 0.15 nTm^{-1} and at the magnetic poles, the field is 60,000 nT and the altitude correction is about 0.030 nTm^{-1}.

37. Given,

Total magnetic field, $B_t = 50000$ nT

Gyromagnetic ratio of proton,

$\gamma_p = 0.267513\ nT^{-1}S^{-1}$

For Proton-Precession magnetometer, the relation exist between Larmor precession frequency and the total field is given by,

$$B_t = \frac{2\pi}{\gamma_p} f$$

where, f is Larmor frequency

$$\text{Now, } f = \frac{B_t \times \gamma_p}{2\pi} = \frac{50000 \times 0.267513}{2\pi} = 2129 \text{ Hz}$$

38. Gamma Ray log measurement is exclusively useful for quantifying volume of shale in the formation and is given by Gamma Ray Index.

$$I_{GR} = Vsh = \frac{GR_{log} - GR_{min}}{GR_{max} - GR_{min}}$$

39. NMR log gives free fluid index (FFI).

40. Compton scattering of gamma rays takes place if the energy lies in the range of 100 KeV to 2 MeV and if energy goes below 100 KeV photoelectric is observed.

41. The maxwell's equation for time varying field are :-

$\nabla.D = \rho$

$\nabla.B = 0$

$$\nabla \times E = \frac{\partial B}{\partial t}$$

$$\nabla \times H = J + \frac{\partial D}{\partial t}$$

42. The resistivity structure $\rho_1 > \rho_2 < \rho_3 > \rho_4$ gives HA type curve. H due to $\rho_1 > \rho_2 < \rho_3$ and A due to $\rho_1 < \rho_2 < \rho_4$.

43. **Streaming Potential** originates when an electrolyte is driven by a pressure gradient through a channel or porous plug with charged walls.

44. **VLF:** The output of the described filtering results is expressed in terms of an equivalent current density at a specified depth that would cause the measured magnetic field. The most practical six-point filter gives an accuracy of 8%. The filter is an extension of the commonly used Fraser filter to process VLF dip-angle data. Filtering the same data set for various depths gives an idea about the change of current density with depth. Areas with high current-density correspond to good conductors. The conductor dip can also be determined.

Some time series exhibit seasonal movements which are regular in phase but vary in amplitude from year to year. The actual amplitude in any year, expressed as a proportion of the average amplitude taken over a long period is called the amplitude ratio.

Slingram method: A dual-coil, electromagnetic profiling system in which both the transmitter and receiver can be moved while maintaining a constant distance between them.

The **Turam method** is one of the oldest geophysical electro-magnetic methods used for mineral exploration, devised by Erik Helmer Lars Hodstrom in 1937. Its name is derived from swedish "TU" (two) and "RAM" (frame), referring to the two receiving coils.Two receiving coils are moved on lines outside of and perpendicular to the long side of the loop or grounded cable and two components of the resultant field are measured. The primary field generated by the large loop or cable interacts with the soil and subsoil and with a conductive body if present which could be a mineral and creates a resultant electromagnetic field. The electromagnetic field is measured according to two values: the Field Strength Ratio and the Phase Difference occurring between the two receiving coils. It is a fixed source horizontal loop method. Separation of the two moving coils is usually from 10 to 30 metres. Using an AC bridge (also called compensator bridge), Field Strength Ratio is measured in percent and Phase Difference in degrees. In-phase (Real) and quadrature (Imaginary) values can be calculated from these data. Observed field strength ratio readings are used to calculate reduced ratios using a formula determined by the loop size and shape or the grounded wire length and the position of the receiving coils relative to the loop or grounded wire.

45. The correct sequence of different geophysical method in terms of decreasing order of depth of investigation is

Magnetotelluric > Time domain EM > VLF > Ground Penetrating Radar

46. The least square generalized inverse of an overdetermined problem is given by,

$$M_{est} = \left(G^T G\right)^{-1} G^T d$$

47. The secondary field produced at the receiver coil encounter a phase shift of 90° from the field at transmitter coil called primary field due to the presence of conducting material inside the subsurface.

48. Given, Time series is

$P = \{1, -1, -2, 0, 1\}$

$Q = \{1, 0, -1\}$

Therefore, the convolution is $P \times Q$, is given as,

$P \times Q =$

P/Q	1	0	-1
1	1	0	-1
-1	-1	0	1
-2	-2	0	2
0	0	0	0
1	1	0	-1

= {1,-1,-3,1,3,0,-1}

49. Given, Time series is

$P = \{t_0, t_1, t_2, t_3, t_4\} = \{1, -1, -2, 0, 1\}$

$Q = \{t_0, t_1, t_2\} = \{1, 0, -1\}$

At a lag of 2, when t becomes t2 the time series Q is completely out of phase of P.

50. Give, Velocity in the layer, V = 2800 m/s

Echo time, $t_0 = 1.05$

Geophone distance from origin, x

By usig the formula for NMO correction at different travel times, we get,

As per question

For, $x_1 = -400$

$t_1 = 0.997$

$$\Delta t_n = \frac{x^2}{2V^2 t_0} = \left\{\frac{(-400)^2}{2 \times 2800^2 \times 1}\right\} = 10 \text{ msec}$$

For, x_2 = 800 m

$t_2 = 1.0245$

$$\Delta t_n = \frac{x^2}{2V^2 t_0} = \left\{\frac{(800)^2}{2 \times 2800^2 \times 1}\right\} = 41 \text{ m}$$

51. Given, V = 2800 m/s

$t_0 = 1.05$

At origin i.e., x = 0, the depth of reflector can be easily calculated as echo time,

$$t_0 = \frac{2d}{V}$$

$$\Rightarrow d = \frac{V \times t_0}{2}$$

$$= \frac{2800}{2} = 1400 \text{ m}$$

52. The depth to the center of the ore deposit can be calculated using half width method,

g_{max} = 5 mGal at x = 3200 m

Therefore, $\frac{g_{max}}{2} = 2.50$ mGal

It is found at 2000 m and 4400 m on both sides of the maximum gravity reading,

Half – width, $x_{1/2} = 4400 - 2000 = 2400$ m

Therefore, according to the formula for spherical body,

Depth to the center $z = 0.653 \times x_{1/2}$

$z = 0.652 \times 2400 = 1564.8$ m

53. The gravity anomaly due to sphere at the maximum gravity value is given by

$$g = \frac{MG}{z^2}$$

$$\Rightarrow M = \frac{gz^2}{G} = \frac{5 \times 1560^2}{6.67 \times 10^{-11}}$$

$= 1.825 \times 10^9$ metric tons

54. The apparent resistivity due to the given configuration is given by:

$$\rho_a = 2\pi \times \frac{V}{I}\left\{\left(\frac{1}{r_{c_1 p_1}} - \frac{1}{r_{c_2 p_1}}\right) - \left(\frac{1}{r_{c_1 p_2}} - \frac{1}{r_{c_2 p_2}}\right)\right\}^{-1}$$

$$\Rightarrow \rho_a = 2\pi \times \frac{V}{I}\left\{\left(\frac{1}{ns+s} - \frac{1}{ns}\right) - \left(\frac{1}{ns+2s} - \frac{1}{ns+s}\right)\right\}^{-1}$$

$$\Rightarrow \rho_a = 2\pi \times \frac{V}{I}\left\{\frac{-1}{n(n+1)} + \frac{1}{(n+1)(n+2)}\right\}^{-1}$$

$$\Rightarrow \rho_a = 2\pi \times \frac{V}{I} s \frac{n(n+1)(n+2)}{-2}$$

$$\Rightarrow \rho_a = \pi \times \frac{V}{I} s\, n(n+1)(n+2)$$

As $\rho_a = K\frac{V}{I}$ where, K is geometrical factor

Comparing with this, we get

$K = \pi n(n+1)(n+2)S$

55. From the previous question,

$$\rho_a = \pi \times \frac{V}{I} s\, n(n+1)(n+2)$$

PuttingI=1amp, V = 10 mv, s = 10, n = 10, we get

$$\rho_a = \pi \times \frac{0.01}{1} \times 10 \times 11 \times 12 \times 10 = 414.48\ \Omega\text{m}$$

(GENERAL APTITUDE SECTION)

56. The environmentalists hope to restore the lake to its pristine condition.

Pristine means original condition.

57. Polemical means a strong verbal or written attack on someone or something. Conciliatory means making someone less angry or hostile, hence the most suitable antonym for Polemical.

58. Despite the mixture's volatile nature, we found that by lowering its temperature in the laboratory we could dramatically reduce its tendency to vaporize.

Explanation: Tendency to vaporize is the nature of volatile substances.

59. As we know Men and days are inversely proportional and work and day are directly proportional

Therefore, the equation is given as

$$\frac{M_1 D_1}{W_1} = \frac{M_2 D_2}{W_2}$$

According to the question

$$\frac{m \times m}{m} = \frac{100 \times D_2}{100}$$

D_2 = m days

60. Because she had a reputation for querulousness we were surprised and pleased when she greeted us so affably.

Explanation: As the sentence reveals both the words should be contrasting in nature.

Among the options given (querulousness, affably) is the only contrasting pair.

61. $X_1 \geq 0$ ...(i)

$X_2 \geq 0$ ...(ii)

$X_1 + X_2 \leq 10$ ....(iii)

$2X_1 + 2X_2 \geq 22$ ... (iv)

Now, equation (iv) can be written as

$X_1 + X_2 \geq 11$ ...(v)

Equation (iii) and (v) cannot hold true together as $X_1 \geq 0$ and $X_2 \geq 0$

Therefore, system of inequalities can never be satisfied.

62. Let the number of students be x

As, everyone should take at least one course

Therefore, $200 - x + 100 - x + 60 - x \geq 300 - x$

$\Rightarrow 360 - 2x \geq 300$

$\Rightarrow x \leq 30$

63. We can proceed in reverse order:

R	S	T
8	8	8

Now, applying the given steps in reverse, we get,

R	S	T
4	8	12
4	14	6
11	7	6

64. As given in question

1. Contribution of outcome factor = Q × factor score × standardized coefficient=Q × 6 × 0.8 = 4.8Q = 4.8 (Here, Q the proportional constant assumed to be 1.).

   Similarly,

2. Contribution of tangibles = 5 × 0.4 = 2
3. Contribution of reliability = 6 × 0.7 = 4.2
4. Contribution of responsiveness = 6 × 0.6 = 3.6
5. Contribution of empathy = 4 × 0.6 = 2.4
6. Contribution of assurance = 6 × 0.5 = 3

Therefore, we can see here lowest contribution is "2"and total contribution is "4.8 + 2 + 4.2 + 3.6 + 2.4 + 3 = 20"

The lowest contribution among all the above factors to the overall quality of services delivered by the company $= \left(\frac{2}{20}\right) \times 100 = 10\%$

65. In order to develop to full potential, a baby needs to be physically able to respond to the environment.

Option B gives a better explanation

It is necessary for a baby to be able to physically respond to the environment for it to develop its full potential.

SOLVED PAPER - 2010

PART-A (Common Part)

Q.1 – Q.25 carry one mark each.

1. Earth's dipole field originates mainly from
   (a) mantle (b) outer core
   (c) inner core (d) crust
2. Sunspots are regions of
   (a) high pressure (b) low magnetic field
   (c) high temperature (d) high magnetic field
3. The electrical conduction mechanism in sedimentary rocks is usually
   (a) pyroelectric (b) electronic
   (c) electrolytic (d) dielectric
4. The unit of electrical reststivity is
   (a) Ohm (b) Ohm-m
   (c) Ohm-m^2 (d) Ohm-m^{-1}
5. Outcrop pattern parallel to topographic contours signifies
   (a) horizontal beds (b) vertical beds
   (c) inclined beds (d) folded beds
6. A rock with equal modal contents of quartz, plagioclase and onhoclase is known as
   (a) diorite (b) gabbro
   (c) granite (d) syenite
7. The main factors in soil-forming processes are
   (a) bedrock and time only
   (b) topography and bedrock only
   (c) climate, time and topography only
   (d) climate, topography, bedrock and time
8. Glacial drift refers to the
   (a) movement of glaciers
   (b) interglacial intervals
   (c) erosional landforms produced by glaciers
   (d) sediments deposited by glaciers
9. Sand dunes are long ridges whose alignment is
   (a) always parallel to the prevailing wind direction
   (b) always perpendicular to the prevailing wind direction
   (c) either parallel or perpendicular to the prevailing wind direction
   (d) not related to the prevailing wind direction
10. The oldest rocks in India are
    (a) more tban 3 billion years old
    (b) between 2.5 and 3 billion years old
    (c) between 2 and 2.5 billion years old
    (d) less than 2 billion years old
11. The sequential placement of geological events, as determined by their position in the rock record is known as
    (a) relative dating
    (b) correlation
    (c) absolute dating
    (d) uniformitarianism
12. Time equivalence of rock units in different areas can be established primarily by considering similarity in
    (a) lithology
    (b) fossil assemblages
    (c) sedimentary structures
    (d) mineral assemblages
13. Which of the following volcanic events has been suggested as a major cause of the extinction of dinosaurs?
    (a) Panjal volcanism
    (b) Deccan volcanism
    (c) Rajmahal volcanism
    (d) Malani volcanism
14. Bode's law expresses the approximate distance between
    (a) earth and other planets
    (b) moon and sun
    (c) planets and sun
    (d) moon and earth
15. India's northward drift from Gondwanaland is believed to have started approximately (in million years ago, Ma)
    (a) 50 Ma (b) 150 Ma
    (c) 300 Ma (d) 400 Ma
16. Which of the following instruments contains piezoelectric material?
    (a) hydrophone (b) geophone
    (c) gravimeter (d) magnetometer

17. If the average crustal thickness is 35 km and the height of a mountain is 5 km above mean sea level the crustal thickness based on Airy's model beneath the mountain will he approximately

(a) 35 km (b) 40 km
(c) 50 km (d) 70 km

18. The equipotential surface over which the gravitational field has equal value is known as

(a) geoid (b) spheroid
(c) ellipsoid (d) mean sea level

19. The angle between the present geographic north and geomagnetic north is

(a) 1.5° (b) 7.5°
(c) 11.5° (d) 23.5°

20. Among the following, the best reconnaissance method for determining basement configuration of sedimentary basins is

(a) gravity method
(b) self potential method
(c) seismic method
(d) electromagnetic method

21. Cooling of basaltic lava under water will lead to the formation of

(a) lava tunnel
(b) pillow structure
(c) columnar jointing
(d) cumulus texture

22. What rock would you expect to find at the base of a typical oceanic plate?

(a) Basalt (b) Diorite
(c) Gabbro (d) Peridotite

23. Major coal deposits of India are found in the

(a) Cuddapah Supergroup
(b) Vindhyan Supergroup
(c) Gondwana Supergroup
(d) Dharwar Supergroup

24. Which of the following is a product of residual weathering process?

(a) Placer gold (b) Banded iron ore
(c) Bauxite (d) Porphyry copper

25. Choose the correct combination of ore and location of its deposit.

(a) Uranium - Jaduguda
(b) Lcad - Khetri
(c) Gold - Panna
(d) Iron - Malanjkhand

PART-B
GEOLOGY

Q.26 - Q.55 carry two marks each.

26. The age of the oldest rocks in present-day ocean basins is

(a) Devonian
(b) Jurassic
(c) Eocene
(d) Pennian

27. Silicon to oxygen ratio in the following silicate structure is

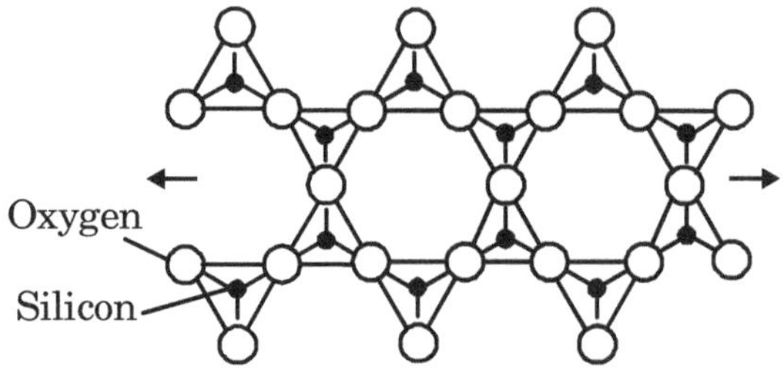

(a) 1 : 2 (b) 2 : 5
(c) 4 : 11 (d) 1 : 3

28. Direct precipitation of uraninite from a mineralizing solution containing UO_2^{2+} ions can take place due to

(a) increase in Eh
(b) decrease in Eh
(c) increase in pH
(d) decrease in pH

29. Match the optical properties in Group I with approprtate minerals in Group II.

Group I	Group II
P. Twinkling	1. Quartz
Q. Pleochroic haloes	2. Nepheline
R. Anomalous interference colour	3. Calcite
	4. Chlorite
S. Uniaxial positive	5. Biotite

(a) P - 4, Q - 5, R - 3, S - 2
(b) P - 3, Q - 4, R - 5, S - 2
(c) P - 3, Q - 5, R - 4, S - 1
(d) P - 3, Q - 4, R - 5, S - 1

30. Wall-rock alteration producing epidote, albite and chlorite around an ore body is called

(a) argillic alteration
(b) propylitic aheration
(c) potassic-oilicate alteration
(d) sericite alteration

31. Match the textures/structures in Group I with appropriate processes in Group II.

Group I	Group II
P. Cumulus texture	1. Cavity filling
Q. spinifex texture	2. Gravity settling
R. Oriented intergrowth	3. Annealing
S. Comb structure	4. Quenching
	5. Coherent exsolution

(*a*) P - 2, Q - 4, R - 5, S - I
(*b*) P - 3, Q - l, R - 2, S - 5
(*c*) P - 1, Q - 5, R - 4, S - 3
(*d*) P - 2, Q - 5, R - 4, S - 1

32. An area shows linear erosional depression, sag pond, spring and offset stream along with sub-horizontal slickensides. The prominent structure indicated by these features is

(*a*) strike-slip fault (*b*) horst and graben
(*c*) klippe (*d*) nappe

33. Match the ore types in Group I with appropriate path-finder elements in Group II.

Group I	Group II
P. Porphyry Cu ore	1. As
Q. Vein type Au ore	2. Hg
R. Pb-Zn-Ag ores	3. Cr
	4. Mo
	5. Ni

(*a*) P - 4, Q - l, R - 2 (*b*) P - 3, Q - 2, R - l
(*c*) P - 4, Q - 3, R - 5 (*d*) P - 5, Q - 4, R - 2

34. Match the name of mass movements listed in Group I with the evidences listed in Group II.

Group I	Group II
P. Creep	1. Tounge-shaped mass movment
Q. Earth flow	2. Curved tree trunks
R. Slump	3. Scree formation at the base
	4. Curved surface of rupture

(*a*) P - 2, Q - 1, R - 4 (*b*) P - 1, Q - 3, R - 4
(*c*) P - 4, Q - 2, R - 1 (*d*) P - 4, Q - 3, R - 2

35. Which of the following metamorphic facies is characterized by the pyrope rich garnet + omphacite assemblage?

(*a*) Blueschist (*b*) Eclogite
(*c*) Greenschist (*d*) Granulite

36. Match the gemstones in Group I with corresponding minerals in Group II.

Group I	Group II
P. peridote	1. Beryl
Q. Emerald	2. Feldspar
R. Amazonite	3. Corundum
S. Ruby	4. Olivine

(*a*) P - 4, Q - 1, R - 2, S - 3
(*b*) P - 1, Q - 3, R - 2, S - 4
(*c*) P - 2, Q - 4, R - 1, S - 3
(*d*) P - 3, Q - 4, R - 1, S - 2

37. Which of the following statements is NOT correct with regard to a perched water table?

(*a*) It is within an area where a local aqviclude occurs within a larger aquifer
(*b*) It lies above the main water table
(*c*) It is found in the main woe of saturation
(*d*) It is occasionally associated with springs

38. The spatial resolution of IRS LISS-Ill multi-spectral sensor for Near Infra-Red (NIR) band is

(*a*) 5.8 m × 5.8 m (*b*) 23.5 m × 23.5 m
(*c*) 70 m × 70 m (*d*) 72.5 m × 72.5 m

39. Which of the following combinations of extinction events and extinct organisms is NOT correct?

(*a*) Cretaceous end-Dinosaurs
(*b*) Triassic end-Conodonts
(*c*) Permian end- Trilobites
(*d*) Miocene end-Ammonites

40. In India, marine fossiliferous rocks of lower Paleozoic age are mainly found in the

(*a*) Gondwana
(*b*) Higher Himalaya
(*c*) Outer Himalaya
(*d*) Tethys Himalaya

41. Which of the following pain; of rock formations and characteristic fossils is correct?

(*a*) Raniganj - Elephas
(*b*) Pinjor - Titamosaurus
(*c*) Lameta - Glossopteris
(*d*) Subathu - Nummulites

42. Which of !he following group; of rock formations is NOT arranged from older to younger?

(*a*) Uttatur - Trichinopoly - Ariyalur - Niniyur
(*b*) Paleham - Katrol - Chari - Umia
(*c*) Talchir - Damuda - Panchet - Mahadev
(*d*) Semri - Kaimur - Rewa - Bhander

43. Choose the correct combination of geologcial agents and associated features

(*a*) River - Spit

(*b*) Glacier - Yardang

(*c*) Longshore current - Esker

(*d*) Wind - Ventifact

44. A sedimentary sequence donunated by large scale (5-10 m thick) cross beds, well-sorted and well-rounded quartz-rich sand with no fine matrix is most likely to be a

(*a*) deltaic deposit (*b*) lagoonal deposit

(*c*) colian deposit (*d*) outer shelf deposit

45. An invertebrate in which the plane of symmetry bisects the shell through the mid-point of the hinge is a

(*a*) Pelecypod (*b*) Brachiopod

(*c*) Gastropod (*d*) Caphalopod

46. The oldest marrunals and birds are known, respectively, from

(*a*) Cretaceous and Paleocene

(*b*) Silurian and Devonian

(*c*) Triassic and Jurassic

(*d*) Oligocene and Miocene

47. Allochems in a limestone consist of

(*a*) micrite only (*b*) spar only

(*c*) ooids only (*d*) bioclasts and ooids

Common Data Questions

Common Data for Questions 48 and 49:

The following geological map exposes three beds, of which the bed P is the oldest and the bed R the youngest.

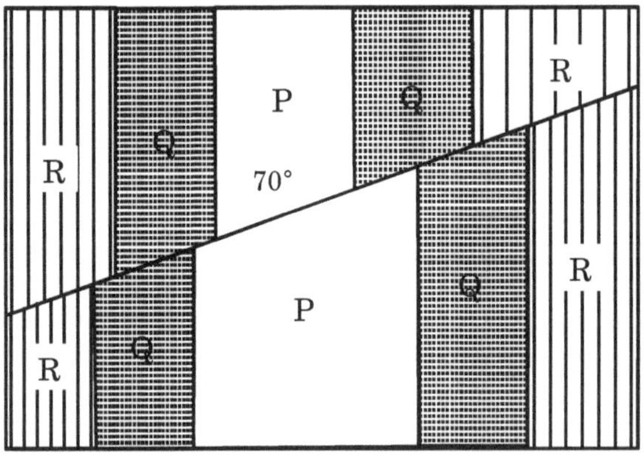

48. What type of structure does the map depict?

(*a*) Faulted anticline

(*b*) Folded strike-slip fault

(*c*) Faulted syncline

(*d*) Folded normal fault

49. Why is bed P wider in the area south of fault?

(a) Erosion has removed most of bed P to the north of fault

(b) Folding has caused thinning of bed P to the north of fault

(c) Deeper level of bed P is exposed due to faulting and erosion to the south of fault

(d) Bed P had a variable thickness prior to faulting

Common Data (or Questions (50 and 51:

A sequence of shale and limestone is intruded by an igneous pluton. Metasomatic interaction between pluton and the country rocks involves introduction of Si and Al into dolomitic limestone.

50. Which pair of rock types best describes tile products of metamorphism in the contact aureole?

(*a*) Slate and schist (*b*) Schist and bomfels

(*c*) Schist and skarn (*d*) Hornfels and skarn

51. The mineral which is NOT expected in assemblages in the metamorphosed dolomitic limestone is

(*a*) grossular (*b*) anorhite

(*c*) diopside (*d*) andalusite

Linked Answer Questions

Statement for Linked Answer Questions 52 and 53:

A pluton of iron-poor basic magma containing trace concentrations of Ni, Rb, Sr and V undergoes crystallization upon cooling.

52. The first mineral to crystallize will be

(*a*) augite (*b*) hornblende

(*c*) olivine (*d*) oligoclase

53. The trace element that will be preferentially incorporated in the correct mineral in Q. 52 is

(*a*) Ni (*b*) Rb

(*c*) Sr (*d*) V

Linked Answer Questions 54 and 55:

54. Silica-undersaturated minerals are

(*a*) nepheline and albite

(*b*) olivine and enstatite

(*c*) leucite and orthoclase

(*d*) olivine and leucire

55. The Hermann-Mauguin symbols of crystallographic notation for the correct minerals in Q. 54 are

(*a*) 2/m2/m2/m and 4/m

(*b*) 2/m2/m2/m for both

(*c*) 4/m and 2/m

(*d*) 6 and I

GEOPHYSICS

Q.26 – Q.55 carry two marks each.

26. The gravity value measured at the base of a 10 m tall building is 40 mGal. The value at the top of the bullding ignoring its mass is close to

(*a*) 20 mGal (*b*) 37 mGal

(*c*) 40 mGal (*d*) 43 mGal

27. Upward continuation technique filters ________ wavelength anomalies and ____ their amplitudes.

(*a*) short, reduces (*b*) long, enhances

(*c*) long, reduces (*d*) short, enhances

28. The relative intensities of induced and remanent magnctiution are commonly expressed in terms of

(*a*) susceptibility (*b*) gyromagnetic ratio

(*c*) Poisson's ratio (*d*) Konigsberger ratio

29. In electrical resistivity method, which among the following is correct with reference to Geometric Factor (Gf)?

(*a*) GF varies for profiling and remains constant for sounding

(*b*) GF remains constant for both profiling and sounding

(*c*) GF remains constant for profiling and varies for sounding

(*d*) GF varies for both profiling and sounding

30. If in a magnetic dipole 'm' represents poles of equal strength and 'l' represents the distance between the two poles, then the magnetic moment of dipole is

(*a*) lm (*b*) $\frac{l}{m}$

(*c*) 2 lm (*d*) $\frac{lm}{2}$

31. Energy in radioactive decay with respect to time follows

(*a*) normal distribution

(*b*) Poisson distribution

(*c*) chi-squared distribution

(*d*) binomial distribution

32. The logging technique that uses non-conductive drilling fluids is

(*a*) SP logging (*b*) Resistivity logging

(*c*) Induction logging (*d*) Radiometric logging

33. Unguided random-walk inversion technique signifies

(*a*) Genetic algorithm

(*b*) Simulated annealing

(*c*) Monte Carlo inversion

(*d*) Metropolis algorithm

34. The compressional wave velocity V_p, within a wild with adiabatic bulk modulus K_f, rigidity modulus G and density ρ is given by

(*a*) $V_p = \sqrt{\frac{K_s + (5/3)G}{\rho}}$ (*b*) $V_p = \sqrt{\frac{K_s + (2/3)G}{\rho}}$

(*c*) $V_p = \sqrt{\frac{K_s + (1/3)G}{\rho}}$ (*d*) $V_p = \sqrt{\frac{K_s + (4/3)G}{\rho}}$

35. The number of independent elements of the 4th order stiffness tensor required to characterize general elastic media is

(*a*) 2 (*b*) 21

(*c*) 36 (*d*) 81

36. The seismic energy released in an earthquake of magnitude M_1 = 7.0 is about ________ times that released in an earthquake of M_s = 6.0.

(*a*) 10 (*b*) 32

(*c*) 64 (*d*) 100

37. In the figure given below "–" represents dilatation and "+" represents compression. The fault plane solution of an earthquake with strike-slip mechanism is represented by

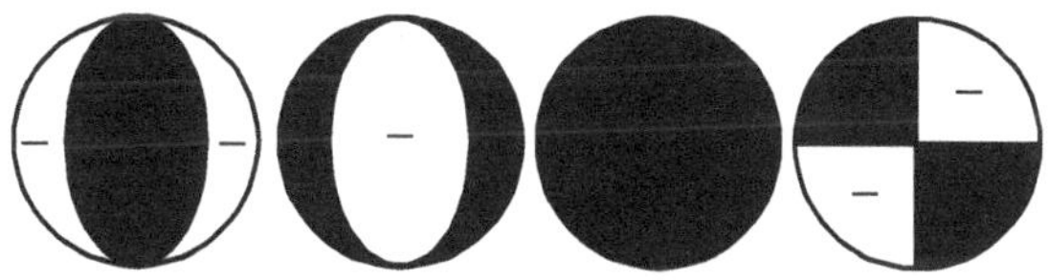

(P) (Q) (R) (S)

(*a*) P (*b*) Q

(*c*) R (*d*) S

38. The anelastic attenuation of seismic energy depends on

(*a*) quality factor (*b*) particle acceleration

(*c*) stress drop (*d*) particle velocity

39. The seismic wave travelling in low velocity layer and critically incident at the discontinuity between low and high velocity layers

(*a*) will be diffracted

(*b*) will be reflected

(*c*) will propagate along the discontinuity

(*d*) will be absorbed

40. An input signal {–1, 1, 0.2}, after passmg through a delay operator z, will be

(*a*) $-z^2 + z^3 + 2z^3$ (*b*) {0, –1, 1, 0, 2}

(*c*) {0, 2, 0, 1, –1} (*d*) $-z + z^2 + 2z^4$

41. If m represents the number of model parameters, d the number of data points and p the rank of matrix to be inverted, then which of the following defines an under determined system?

(*a*) m < d and p = d (*b*) m > d and p = d

(*c*) m = d and p = d (*d*) m < d and p ≠ d

42. A unit amplitude of an electromagnetic wave at thrice the skin-depth will be reduced to

(*a*) –3e (*b*) $\frac{3}{e}$

(*c*) $\frac{e}{3}$ (*d*) e^{-3}

43. The Hilbert transform of a function $f(t)$ is denoted by H (f(1)). If $f(t) = \sin t$, then H {H(f(t))} is

(*a*) –sin t (*b*) – cost t

(*c*) sin t (*d*) cos t

44. The rectangular function π(t) is defined as

$$\pi(t) = 1|t| \le 1/2 = 0|t| > 1/2$$

The convolution of π(t) with itself will be

(*a*) a triangular function Λ(t)

(*b*) π(t) again

(*c*) a unit-step function u(t)

(*d*) a delta function δ(t)

45. Given $A = e^{-y}(\cos xa_x - \sin xa_y)$, where ax and ay denote the unit vectors in x- and y-directions, respectively. Then ∇.{∇ × A) is equal to

(*a*) e^{-y} (*b*) 0

(*c*) e^{-y} (cos x) (*d*) e^{-y} (sin x)

46. Match the items in Group I with those in Group II.

Group I	Group II
P. Convolution in time domain	1. $\frac{1}{2\Delta t}$
Q. Nyquist frequency	2. Flat spectrum
R. Aliasing	3. Multiplication in frequency domain
S. White noise	4. Frequency folding
	5. Autocorrelation function

(*a*) P - 3, Q - 1, R - 4, S - 2

(*b*) P - 2, Q - 1, R - 5, S - 4

(*c*) P - 3, Q - 1, R - 2, S - 1

(*d*) P - 2, Q - 4, R - 1, S - 5

47. In magnetic materials, the relation between magnetic penneability μ and susceptibility K (in Sl units) is

(*a*) μ = 1/K (*b*) μ = 1 – K

(*c*) μ = 1 + K (*d*) μ = 1 – 2 πK

Common Data Questions

Common Data (or Questions 48 and 49:

The terrain correction in gravity method accounts for topographic relief in the vicinity of the observation point. The Bouguer slab assumes the topography around the observation point to be flat. In the figure below, the Bouguer slab thickness is h and the hollow portion P lies within the Bouguer slab. Q and Rare parts of the topography.

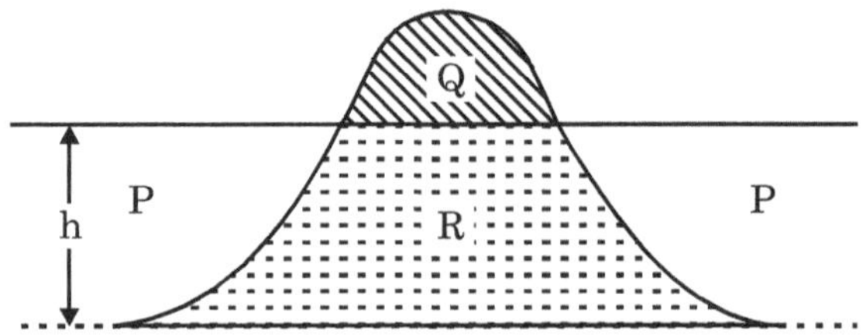

48. In the region P, the terrain correction is

(*a*) half of that in R (*b*) negative

(*c*) zero (*d*) positive

49. In the region Q, the terrain correction is required to account for

(a) hollow portion P

(b) reduced gravity due to excess mass in portion Q

(c) increased gravity due to excess mass in portion Q

(d) over-correction of Bouguer slab

Common Data for Questions 50 and 51:

For an input x_n, the output of a digital filter y_n is given by $y_n = 1.5x_n - 2x_{n-1} + 2.5y_{n-2}$.

50. The order of the digital filter is

(*a*) 4 (*b*) 3

(*c*) 2 (*d*) 1

51. The transfer function of the digital filter is

(*a*) $\frac{y_n}{x_n} = \frac{1.5 - 2z}{1 - 2.5z}$ (*b*) $\frac{y_n}{x_n} = \frac{1.5 - 2z}{1 - 2.5z^2}$

(*c*) $\frac{y_n}{x_n} = \frac{1 - 2.5z^2}{1.5 - 2z}$ (*d*) $\frac{y_n}{x_n} = \frac{1.5 - 2z}{1 + 2.5z^2}$

Linked Answer Questions

Statement for Linked Answer Questions 52 and 53:

In a two-layer earth model, the values of seismic velocity and density of first and second layers, respectively are V_{p1} = 4000 m/s. ρ_1 = 2500 Kg/ m³, and V_{p2} = 4500 m/s. ρ_2 = 2600 Kg/m¹.

52. The acoustic impedance of the first layer in Sl units at normal incidence is

(*a*) 10^3 (*b*) 10^4

(*c*) 10^5 (*d*) 10^7

53. The transmission coefficient for a wave at normal incidence at the boundary of first and second layer is

(*a*) 0.46 (*b*) 0.58

(*c*) 0.92 (*d*) 1.07

Statement for Linked Answer Questions 54 and 55:

Consider a magnetotelluric (MT) field set up. A plane electromagnetic wave with a time dependence factor $e^{-i\omega t}$ is travelling venically downwards (t-direction) into the Earth with an angular frequency ω. The electric field is polarized in the x-direction (strike).

54. The electromagnetic field components considered in this mode are

(a) E_t, H_v and H_z (b) E_z, H_v, H_z

(c) E_t, H_v and E_z (d) E_v, H_t and H_z

55. Which of the following equations represents the above mode?

(a) $E_t = \frac{-1}{i\omega\mu}\frac{\partial H_z}{\partial_z}$ (b) $H_z = \frac{-1}{i\omega\mu}\frac{\partial E_z}{\partial_z}$

(c) $H_v = \frac{1}{i\omega\mu}\frac{\partial E_v}{\partial_z}$ (d) $H_v = \frac{1}{i\omega\mu}\frac{\partial E_t}{\partial_z}$

GENERAL APTITUDE (GA)

Q.56 – Q.60 carry one mark each.

56. Choose the most appropriate word from thc options given below to complete the following sentence:

His rather casual remarks on politics __________ his lack of seriousness about the subject.

(a) masked (b) belied

(c) betrayed (d) suppressed

57. Which of the following options is the closest in meaning to the word below:

Circuitous

(a) cyclic (b) indirect

(c) confusing (d) crooked

58. Choose the most appropriate word from the options given below to complete the following sentence:

If we manage to _________ our natural resources, we would leave a better planet for our children.

(a) uphold (b) restrain

(c) cherish (d) conserve

59. 25 persons are in a room. 15 of them play hockey 17 of them play football and 10 of them play both hockey and football. Then the number of persons playing neither hockey nor football is:

(a) 2 (b) 17

(c) 13 (d) 3

60. The question below consists of a pair of related words followed by four pairs of words. Select the pair that best expresses the relation in the original pair.

Unemployed : Worker

(a) fallow : land (b) unaware : sleeper

(c) wit : jester (d) renovated : house

Q. 61 – Q. 65 carry two marks each.

61. If 137 + 276 = 435 how much is 731 + 672?

(a) 534 (b) 1403

(c) 1623 (d) 1513

62. Hari (H), Gila (G), lrfan (I) and Saira (S) are siblings (i.e. brothers and sisters). All were born on 1st January. The age difference between any two successive siblings (that is born one after another) is less than 3 years. Given the following facts:

i. Hari' s age + Gita' s age > lrfan's age + Saira' s age.

ii. The age dtfference between Gita and Saira is I year. However, Gita is not the oldest and Saira is not the youngest.

iii. There are no twins.

In what order were they born (oldest first)?

(a) HSIG (b) SGHI

(c) IGSH (d) IHSG

63. Modern warfare has changed from large scale clashes of armies to suppression of civillian populations. Chemical agents that do their wort silently appear to be suited to such warfare; and regretfully, there exist people in military establishments who think that chemical agents are useful tools for their cause.

Which of the following statements best sums up the meaning of the above passage:

(a) Modem warfare has resulted in civil strife.

(b) Chemical agents are useful in modem warfare.

(c) Use of chemical agents in warfare would be undesirable.

(d) People in military establishments like to use chemical agents in war.

64. 5 skilled workers can build a wall in 20 days; 8 semi-skilled workers can build a wall in 25 days; 10 unskilled workers can build a wall in 30 days. If a team has 2 skilled, 6 semi-skilled and 5 unskilled workers, how long will it take to build the wall?

(a) 20 days (b) 18 days

(c) 16 days (d) 15 days

65. Given digits 2, 2, 3, 3, 3, 4, 4, 4, 4 how many distinct 4 digit numbers greater than 3000 can be formed?

(a) 50 (b) 51

(c) 52 (d) 54

ANSWERS

PART A (Common Part)

1. (*b*)	**2.** (*d*)	**3.** (*c*)	**4.** (*b*)	**5.** (*a*)	**6.** (*c*)	**7.** (*d*)	**8.** (*b*)	**9.** (*c*)	**10.** (*a*)
11. (*a*)	**12.** (*b*)	**13.** (*b*)	**14.** (*c*)	**15.** (*b*)	**16.** (*a*)	**17.** (*c*)	**18.** (*a*)	**19.** (*c*)	**20.** (*a*)
21. (*b*)	**22.** (*c*)	**23.** (*c*)	**24.** (*c*)	**25.** (*a*)					

PART-B (Geology)

26. (*b*)	**27.** (*c*)	**28.** (*b*)	**29.** (*c*)	**30.** (*b*)	**31.** (*a*)	**32.** (*b*)	**33.** (*a*)	**34.** (*a*)	**35.** (*b*)
36. (*a*)	**37.** (*c*)	**38.** (*b*)	**39.** (*d*)	**40.** (*b*)	**41.** (*b*)	**42.** (*b*)	**43.** (*d*)	**44.** (*c*)	**45.** (*a*)
46. (*c*)	**47.** (*d*)	**48.** (*b*)	**49.** (*c*)	**50.** (*b*)	**51.** (*d*)	**52.** (*b*)	**53.** (*a*)	**54.** (*d*)	**55.** (*a*)

(Geophysics)

26. (*b*)	**27.** (*a*)	**28.** (*d*)	**29.** (*d*)	**30.** (*a*)	**31.** (*b*)	**32.** (*c*)	**33.** (*c*)	**34.** (*d*)	**35.** (*b*)
36. (*b*)	**37.** (*d*)	**38.** (*a*)	**39.** (*c*)	**40.** (*d*)	**41.** (*b*)	**42.** (*d*)	**43.** (*a*)	**44.** (*a*)	**45.** (*b*)
46. (*a*)	**47.** (*c*)	**48.** (*d*)	**49.** (*b*)	**50.** (*c*)	**51.** (*b*)	**52.** (*d*)	**53.** (*c*)	**54.** (*a*)	**55.** (*d*)

(General Aptitude)

56. (*c*)	**57.** (*b*)	**58.** (*d*)	**59.** (*d*)	**60.** (*a*)	**61.** (*c*)	**62.** (*b*)	**63.** (*a*)	**64.** (*d*)	**65.** (*b*)

EXPLANATIONS

PART A (COMMON PART)

1. Earth's magnetic field, also known as the geomagnetic field, is the magnetic field that extends from the Earth's interior out into space, where it meets the solar wind, a stream of charged particles emanating from the Sun. Its magnitude at the Earth's surface ranges from 25 to 65 microteslas (0.25 to 0.65 gauss). Approximately, it is the field of a magnetic dipole currently tilted at an angle of about 11 degrees with respect to Earth's rotational axis, as if there were a bar magnet placed at that angle at the center of the Earth.The magnetic field is generated by electric currentsdue to the motion of convection currents of molten iron in the Earth's outer core driven by heat escaping from the core, a natural process called a geodynamo.
2. Sunspots are temporary phenomena on the Sun's photosphere that appear as spots darker than the surrounding areas. They are regions of reduced surface temperature caused by concentrations of magnetic field flux that inhibit convection. Sunspots usually appear in pairs of opposite magnetic polarity.
3. The electrical conduction mechanism in sedimentary rocks is usually electrolytic due to the movement of ions through the pores.
4. The SI unit of electrical resistivity is the ohm?metre (Ωm). It is commonly represented by the Greek letter ρ, rho.
5. Horizontal beds give outcrop pattern which is parallel to topographic contour while vertical beds cut the topographic contour vertically.
6. Granite is classified according to the QAPF diagram for coarse grained plutonic rocks and is named according to the percentage of quartz, alkali feldspar (orthoclase, sanidine, or microcline) and plagioclase feldspar on the A-Q-P half of the diagram. True granite (according to modern petrologic convention) contains both plagioclase and alkali feldspars. When a granitoid is devoid or nearly devoid of plagioclase, the rock is referred to as alkali feldspar granite.
7. The main factors leading to the formation of soil (combination of minerals, organic matter, water and air) are climate, topography, bedrock and time.
8. Glacial Drift is the name for all materials of glacial origin found anywhere at land or at sea including sediment and large rocks (glacial erratic). Glacial origin refers to erosion, transportation and deposition by glaciers
9. A sand dune is a hill of loose sand built by aeolian processes (wind) or the flow of water. Dunes occur in different shapes and sizes, formed by interaction with the flow of air or water. Most kinds of dunes are longer on the stoss (upflow) side, where the sand is pushed up the dune, and have a shorter "slip face" in the lee side. The valley or trough between dunes is called a slack. A "dune field" or erg is an area covered by extensive dunes.

10. The oldest rocks in India are more than 3 billion years old, which is about 3.8 Ga.

11. Relative dating is the science of determining the relative order of past events (i.e., the age of an object in comparison to another), without necessarily determining their absolute age, (i.e. estimated age). Though relative dating can only determine the sequential order in which a series of events occurred, not when they occurred, it remains a useful technique.

12. **Fossil assemblages:** It is a group of associated animal fossils found together in a given stratum. The principle of faunal succession is used in biostratigrophy to determine each biostratigraphic unit or biozone which in turn gives the time equivalence of rock in different areas.

13. **Panjal volcanism:** It is a large igneous province (LIP) that erupted during the Early-Middle Permian in what is now northwestern India. The Panjal Traps are associated with the opening of the Neo-Tethys Ocean, which resulted in the dispersal of the Cimmerian continental blocks from the northeastern margin of Gondwana and possibly the break-up of this old and large continent. In the Zanskar-Spliti-Lahaul area (in the north-western Himalayas and south-east Ladakh) the 30-150 m thick basalts of the Panjal Traps are mostly exposed as massive (terrestrial) lava flows, but also as (marine) pillow lavas and hyaloclastites.

    Deccan volcanism: It leads to formation of deccan traps which is made up of lava flows of basic composition. The age of lava flows ranges from Upper Cretarecous to lower lower Eocene. Deccan volcanism along with other volcanism and the impact of asteroids or comets are thought to be the prime suspect of dinosaurs extinctions.

    Rajmahal volcanism: Volcanic activity during Rajmahal time (UpperGondwana period) led to the formation of Rajmahal traps.

    Malani volcanism: It includes acid volcanic rocks such as rhyolites and tuffs. They cover enormous areas around Jodhpur in Rajasthan. This formation is regarded as of lower Vindhyan age.

14. Bode's law, also called Titius-Bode law, empirical rule giving the approximate distances of planets from the Sun. It was first announced in 1766 by the German astronomer Johann Daniel Titius but was popularized only from 1772 by his countryman Johann Elert Bode. Once suspected to have some significance regarding the formation of the solar system, Bode's law is now generally regarded as a numerological curiosity with no known justification.

15. The Indian plate is a major tectonic plate straddling the equator in the eastern hemisphere originally a part of the ancient Gondwana. India broke away from the other fragments of Gondwana 400 million years ago and began moving north.

16. **Hydrophone** is a microphone designed to be used underwater for recording or listening to underwater sound. Most hydrophones are based on a piezoelectric transducer that generates electricity when subjected to a pressure change.

    Geophone is a device that converts ground movement (velocity) into voltage, which may be recorded at a recording station. The deviation of this measured voltage from the base line is called the seismic response and is analyzed for structure of the earth.

    Gravimeter is an instrument used to measure gravitational acceleration. Every mass has an associated gravitational potential. The gradient of this potential is an acceleration. A gravimeter measures this gravitational acceleration.

    Magnetometer or magnetic sensor is an instrument that measures magnetism-either the magnetization of a magnetic material like a ferromagnet, or the direction, strength, or relative change of a magnetic field at a particular location. A compass is a simple type of magnetometer, one that measures the direction of an ambient magnetic field.

17. Given, $\rho_c = 2.7\ \text{gm/cm}^3$

    $\rho_m = 3.3\ \text{gm/cm}^3$

    $H = 5$ km

    According to Airy's hypothesis, the root underneath the mountain is given by

    $$r_0 = \left(\frac{\rho_c}{\rho_m - \rho_c}\right) \times h = \left(\frac{2.7}{3.3 - 2.7}\right) \times 5 = 22.5\ \text{km}$$

    Therefore,

    The total crustal thickness is $(35 + 22.5) = 57.5$ km

18. All points on a geoid surface have the same effective potential (the sum of gravitational potential energy and centrifugal potential energy). The force of gravity acts everywhere perpendicular to the geoid, meaning that plumb lines point perpendicular and water levels parallel to the geoid if only gravity and rotational acceleration were at work.

19. The angle between geographic north and geomagnetic north is defined as magnetic declination. It changes over time.

20. The best reconnaissance method for determining basement configuration of sedimentary basins is gravity and magnetic method as they are cheap and fast method of all the methods for a regional survey.

21. Pillow lavas are lavas that contain characteristic pillow-shaped structures that are attributed to the extrusion of the lava under water, or subaqueous extrusion. Pillow lavas in volcanic rock are characterized by thick sequences of discontinuous pillow-shaped masses, commonly up to one metre in diameter. They form the upper part of Layer 2 of normal oceanic crust.

22. Oceanic crust is the uppermost layer of the oceanic portion of a tectonic plate. It is composed of the upper oceanic crust, with pillow lavas and a dike complex, and the lower oceanic crust, composed of troctolite, gabbro and ultramafic cumulates. The crust overlies the solidified and uppermost layer of the mantle. The crust and the solid mantle layer together constitute oceanic lithosphere.

23. The Gondwana rocks are the biggest source of COAL deposits in India. Peninsular India bears great evidence of these accumulations that are spread over vast areas of Bengal, Bihar, Orissa, Madhya Pradesh and Maharashtra. The rocks form a composite group, in stratigraphical sense, rather than a single system, in as much as it contains rocks belonging to more than one true system, that is, of Triassic system, Jurassic system and Cretaceous system.

24. Weathering not only disintegrates a rock but also by removing the undesirable constituents in it, concentrates the residual useful substance, which forms an economic deposit.

The effects of weathering usually do not extend deeper than a couple of meters extends but occasionally reach 30 to 60 meters. It is most active in tropical and sub-tropical climates. In such climates, rock decay is carried further; leaching is more complete; the silicates are thoroughly broken down and surface water readily removes the silica, thus bringing about the concentration of the residual material which, when useful, forms valuable mineral deposits.

Bauxite is an important example of this kind. Valuable deposits of clay have been formed by removal in solution of the lime in a limestone bed. The removing by weathering of the useless constituents has brought about the concentration of the sparse nickel content in ultra basic rocks to form valuable deposits of the metal.

25. The Jaduguda Mine is a uranium mine in Jaduguda village in the PurbiSinghbhum district of the Indian state of Jharkhand.

PART-B (GEOLOGY)

26. The oldest oceanic crust dated back to Jurassic. The rock of earlier ages than Jurassic are destroyed by subduction.

27.

Silicate structures	S:O ratio
Neso silicate/orthasilicate/island silicate	1:04
Ring silicate	1:03
Double chain silicate (Inosilicates)	4:11
Single chain silicates (Inosilicates)	1:03
Sheet silicate (Phyllosilicates)	2:05
Framework silicates	1:02
Orosilicate	2:07

28. In nature, uranium occurs in two valence states, as the Uranus (U^{4+}) ion and the uranyl (U^{6+}) ion. In the magnetic environment, uranium occurs essentially as U^{4+} and in this form is a highly incompatible trace element that occurs in only a few accessory minerals (zircon, monazite, apatite, sphene) and is concentrated into residual. It can precipitate in the reducing environment i.e., Eh.

29. **Twinkling** In mineral optics, the effect observed in plane-polarized light when a thin section of an anisotropic mineral with widely differing refractive indices is rotated rapidly on the stage. The 'twinkling' appearance is caused by the rapid changes in relief. Calcite is a well-known example.

Pleochroic halo, ring of colour produced around a radioactive impurity included in a mineral by alpha particles emitted from the radioactive elements in the inclusion. Because most of the energy of an alpha particle is absorbed at the end of its path length in a mineral, these colourcentres are produced most intensely around the inclusion. The halos exhibit different colours when viewed in different directions because they differentially absorb light that vibrates in different directions. Pleochroic halos are commonly found in the minerals biotite, fluorite, and amphiboles; the most common inclusions are the minerals zircon, xenotime, apatite, and monazite.

Anomalous interference colors tend to be dark. Blue, violet, green and brown are all-possible. These are actually useful diagnostic features. Chlorite tends to show anomalous greens and browns. Epidote commonly shows a dark "denim" blue color near extinction. When combined with its normal bright yellow and red interference colors, the effect is quite colorful.

Quartz is a uniaxial hexagonal-rhombohedral positive mineral with extremely low birefringence. It is easy to determine on account of its lack of alteration, absence of cleavage or twinning. It is also one of the most common rock-forming minerals.

30. **Propylitic alteration** is the chemical alteration of a rock, caused by iron and magnesium bearing hydrothermal fluids, altering biotite or amphibole within the rock groundmass. It typically results in epidote-chlorite-albite alteration and veining or fracture filling with the mineral assemblage along with pyrite. The alteration occurs due to hot fluids that have a high sodium ion composition. This is typically due to fluids that have lost potassium ions in potassic alteration and gained sodium ions.

31. Igneous rocks formed by sedimentation are termed cumulates, and characteristically display **cumulate textures**. The classification of cumulate textures should be non-genetic, but retains the terminology for the textures.These descriptions remain valid, but the genetic interpretation that influenced this terminology remains a matter for conjecture, largely because the role of gravity settling is critically dependent on magma viscosity and the relative densities of crystals and parental liquid, which in the case of plagioclase feldspars and basaltic liquid often remain to be demonstrated.

One of the first names for spinifex texture in komatiite lavas was "crystalline quench texture". spinifex as a texture characteristic of komatiite, and they noted that the morphology of the dominant minerals resembled those of crystals that form when molten olivine basalt is cooled rapidly.

Many ore minerals undergo compositional and textural readjustments in the form of exsolution or inversion as they cool. In exsolution one phase is expelled from another, often in a characteristic pattern.The form of the exsolved phase varies with the minerals involved, their relative proportions, and the postdepositional cooling history of the ore.Theexsolution process results from diffusion (usually of metal ions through a sulfur or oxygen lattice), the nucleation of crystallites, and the growth of crystallites to crystals.Similarities of srystal structure and chemical bonding between host and exsolved phase (particularly the matching of atomic arrangements in specific layers resulting in a shared plane of atoms) dictates that exsolution is crystallographically controlled.Such exsolutions are called **Coherent Exsolutions**.

Cavity filling and the resulting deposits: Ore solutions when deposited in a cavity of whatever type, exhibit method and order. A vein filling where nearly sub parallel crystals have grown almost at right angles to the wall cavity constitutes a comb structure due to its resemblance to the teeth of a comb.

32. Horst and graben refer to regions that lie between normal faults and are either higher or lower than the area beyond the faults. A horst represents a block pushed upward relative to the blocks on either side by the faulting, and a graben is a block generally long compared to its width that has been lowered relative to the blocks on either side due to the faulting. Horst and grabenare formed when normal fault of opposite dip occur in pair with parallel strike lines. Horst and grabenare always formed together. Grabenare usually represented by low-lying areas such as rifts and river valleys whereas horsts represent the ridges between or on either side of these valleys.

33. **Porphyry copper deposits** are copper orebodies that are formed from hydrothermal fluids that originate from a voluminous magma chamber several kilometers below the deposit itself. Predating or associated with those fluids are vertical dikes of porphyritic intrusive rocks from which this deposit type derives its name. In later stages, circulating meteoric fluids may interact with the magmatic fluids. Successive envelopes of hydrothermal alteration typically enclose a core of disseminated ore minerals in often stockwork-forming hairline fractures and veins. Because of their large volume, porphyry orebodies can be economic from copper concentrations as low as 0.15% copper and can have economic amounts of by-products such as molybdenum, silver and gold. In some mines, those metals are the main product.

Vein type Au ore: Many outcrops of good looking veins are barren of gold or other ore minerals, but rich ore shoots may occur unexposed on surface, either down dip or along strike.

Therefore, geochemical pathfinders are required. These include arsenic, antimony, or mercury which may be enriched in the rocks adjacent to the gold ore, either within the vein structure or in adjacent country rocks, producing a "halo".

The Caijiaying Pb-Zn-Ag deposits consist of five zones of mineralization occurring in hornblende-plagioclase granulite. Alithogeochemical survey was carried out within the area of the ore deposits; very strong primary anomalies of Pb, Zn, Ag, Cd,As, Sb, Hg and B, and weak anomalies of I, Cu, Co and Bi were found.

34. **Tree trunks** are often curved as a result of external factors including catastrophic events, the availability of light, and soil creep. Where trees with curved trunks due to soil creep can be recognized, they may provide a useful indication of slope instability. Trees with trunks, which are curved downslope to resemble catenaries probably, owe their shape to downslope soil creep. Sharp curves in tree trunks are usually the result of catastrophic events, but snow/ice pressure may cause trees to bow with gentle curves.

    Transporting of earth materials downslope due to gravity, without the aid of a transporting medium such as water or ice. **Earthflows** are fluid movements of relatively fine-grained materials such as soils, weathered shales and clays. Earthflows may be active for days, months or years. An earthflow generally has a long, narrow tongue-like shape with a rounded, bulging front. Earthflows typically range in size from several meters long to over 1 km long.

    Slump moves materials as a large block along a curved surface . Slumps often happen when a slope is undercut, with no support for the overlying materials, or when too much weight is added to an unstable slope.

35. **Ecologitefacies:** It is a high pressure, high temperature metamorphic facies having index minerals. Pyrope + Omphacite.

36. **Peridot** is gem-quality olivine, which is a silicate mineral with the formula of $(Mg, Fe)_2SiO_4$. As peridot is the magnesium-rich variety of olivine, the formula approaches Mg_2SiO_4. Olivine, of which peridot is a type, is a common mineral in mafic and ultramafic rocks, and it is often found in lavas and in peridotite xenoliths of the mantle, which lavas carry to the surface; but gem quality peridot occurs in only a fraction of these settings. Peridotscan also be found in meteorites.

    Beryl is a mineral composed of beryllium aluminum cyclosilicate with the chemical formula $Be_3Al_2(Si_6O_{18})$. Well-known varieties of beryl include emerald and aquamarine. Naturally, occurring, hexagonal crystalsof beryl can be up to several meters in size, but terminated crystals are relatively rare. Pure beryl is colorless, but it is frequently tinted by impurities; possible colors are green, blue, yellow, red (the rarest), and white. Beryl is also an ore source of beryllium.

    Amazonite also known as Amazonstone is a green tectosilicate mineral made from microcline. It has the chemical formula $K(AlSi_3O_8)$. Amazonite is a beautiful green variety of microcline feldspar.Feldspars can be alkali or they can be plagioclase. Amazonite is the pure potassium end member of the alkali group. It crystallizes at relatively low temperatures.

    Corundum is a crystalline form of aluminum oxide (Al_2O_3) typically containing traces of iron, titanium, vanadium and chromium. It is a rock-forming mineral. It is also a naturally transparent material, but can have different colors depending on the presence of transition metal impurities in its crystalline structure. Corundum has two primary gem varieties, ruby and sapphire. Rubies are red due to the presence of chromium, and sapphires exhibit a range of colors depending on what transition metal is present.

37. Perched water table always found above the zone of saturation. It forms the local aquifers.

38. Data set specification of IRS LISS-III

    Temporal Coverage - 2003- 12 - 31 to current day.

    Spatial coverage - 90°N, 90°S, 180°W, 180°E

    Data type - multispectral radiometry high resolution

    ESRIM - Horizontal Resolution - 23.5 m × 23.5 m

39. Last species of ammonites were died out in cretraceaus- Paleogene extinction.

40. Higher Himalaya has lower polaeozoic marine fossiliferous rocks in salt range, Spiti Himalaya.

41. Pinjor-Titanosaurus.

42. Patcham

    Katrol

    Chari

    Umia

43. Wind - ventifacts

    Wind sculptured pebbles are known as ventifacts.

44. **Eolian processes** pertain to wind activity in the study of geology and weather and specifically to the wind's ability to shape the surface of the Earth (or other planets). Winds may erode, transport, and deposit materials and are effective agents in regions with sparse vegetation, a lack of soil moisture and a large supply of unconsolidated sediments. Although water is a much more powerful eroding force than wind, eolian processes are important in arid environments such as deserts.

45. Pelecypod (Bivalvia) -shows bilateral symmetry so called bivalvia i.e., having two valves.

46. **Triassic**-Oldest mammal, first dinosaurs.

    Jurassic-First birds, dinosaurs diversity.

47. **Bioclasts:** Shell fragments of dead organism.

    Ooids: Spherical to octave to subspherical in shape having a nucleus in the center.

48. The map clearly depicts folded normal fault
49. As per figure, deeper level of bed P is exposed due to faulting and erosion to the south of fault. Therefore, bed P is wider in the area south of fault.
50. Harnfels and skarns are contact aureole rocks. Therefore, these pair of rock types describes the best products of metamorphism in the contact aureole.
51. Andalusite is free of Ca (Al_2SiO_5) whereas all other three minerals have Ca in their composition.
52. If iron poor basic magma undergoes cooling olivine Magnesium rich is most likely to crystallize first.
53. Olivine generally incorporates Ni preferentially.
54. Olivine and leucite

    Silica under saturated-Minerals having lack of silica.
55. Hermann-Mauguin symbol for olivine and leucite is 2/m2/m2/m and 4/m .

(GEOPHYSICS)

26. Given,

    Gravity value at the base of 10 m tall building = 40 mGal

    Therefore, free air gravity at the top of 10 m tall building is $0.3086 \times 10 = 3.086$ mGal

    Thus, the net gravity at the top of the building is $(40 - 3.086)$ mGal $= 36.914$ mGal
27. **Upward continuation techniques:** These techniques are generally employed in potential field method to enhance the deep-seated features by filtering short wavelength anomalies and reducing their amplitudes.
28. **Konigsberger ratio** (Q, Q_n) Originally the ratio (Q) of the intensity of natural remanent magnetization (NRM) of an igneous rock to the intensity of magnetization induced at room temperature in a magnetic field the same as that in which the original NRM was acquired. Now it usually means the ratio (Q_n) of the intensity of NRM to that induced in a magnetic field of 50μT at room temperature.
29. **Geometrical factor (GF):** GF in resistivity surveying method is a function of current electrode spacing and potential electrode spacing thus resulting in different values for both profiling and sounding.
30. **Magnetic Dipole Moment:** It is defined at the product of magnetic pole strength (m) with the distance between them, l

    $$\bar{m} = ml$$
31. Energy in radioactive decay with respect to time follows Gaussian to Poisson distribution. In addition, the Gaussian distributions can approximate Poisson distribution very well at high-count rates.
32. **Induction logging** was originally developed to measure formation resistivities in boreholes containing oil-based muds and in air-drilled boreholes because electrode devices could not work in these nonconductive boreholes. However, because the tools were easy to run and required much less in the way of chart corrections than laterals or normals, induction tools were used in a wide range of borehole salinity soon after their introduction.
33. Monte Carlo method is an unguided random walk technique without any artificial intelligence. Monte Carlo inversion needs more than one million forward problem computations.
34. The bulk modulus of rigidity is defined in terms of Lame's constant is given as,

    $$K = \lambda + \frac{2}{3}\mu$$

    where μ is rigidity modulus

    Replacing μ by G, we get,

    $$K = \lambda + \frac{2}{3}G$$

    $$\Rightarrow \lambda = K - \frac{2}{3}G$$

    Now, Compressional wave velocity, V_p in terms of Lame's constant is given by,

    $$V_P = \sqrt{\frac{\lambda + 2G}{\rho}}$$

    where ρ is the density

    Putting the value of λ in the above, we get

    $$V_P = \sqrt{\frac{K - \frac{2}{3}G + 2G}{\rho}} = \sqrt{\frac{K + \frac{4}{3}G}{\rho}}$$
35. For 4th order stiffness tensor, the number of total clements required to characterize general elastic media is $3^4 = 81$ and independent element is 21.
36. Gutenberg devised an empirical formula, which relates the seismic energy released E to the surface wave magnitude MS.

    $$\log_{10} E = 4.8 + 1.5M_s$$

    Now, as per question,

    $$\log_{10} E_7 = 4.8 + 1.5M_7$$

    $$\log_{10} E_6 = 4.8 + 1.5M_6$$

$\Rightarrow \log_{10} E_7 = 4.8 + 1.5 \times 7$ ...(i)

$\log_{10} E_6 = 4.8 + 1.5 \times 6$ ....(ii)

Dividing (i) by (ii)

$$\frac{\log_{10} E_7}{\log_{10} E_6} = \frac{15.3}{13.8}$$

$$\frac{\log_{10} E_7}{\log_{10} E_6} = \frac{15.3}{13.8}$$

$$\Rightarrow E_7 = 32E_6$$

37. The fault plane solution of given different figures depicts different faults

Figure P depicts Reverse fault.

Figure Q depicts Normal faults

Figure R depicts Strike-slip fault

38. **Anelastic attenuation:** There is another factor that affects seismic amplitudes. This is the energy loss due to anelastic processes or internal friction during wave propagation. This is called intrinsic or anelastic attenuation. Intrinsic attenuation occurs mostly during shear wave motion associated with lateral movements of lattice and grain boundaries.When traveling through subsurface, an elastic wave's mechanical energy is converted to heat energy due to friction and changes in viscosity. It occurs at interface boundaries such as water, gas, formation and grain boundaries. This transformation results in decrease in amplitude and pulse broadening. As the wave travels away from the source, the pulse broadens with increasing distances.

39. For a critically incident seismic wave at a discontinuity, it will propagate along the discontinuity and called as head waves.

40. Given, The input signal $x(t) = \{-1, 1, 0, 2\}$

The z-transform of this signal is

$$X(z) = -1 + z + 0 \times z^2 + 2z^3$$

If we multiply the X(z) by z, we delayed it by unit delay

Therefore,

$$Y(z) = z \times (z)$$

$$\Rightarrow Y(z) = z(-1 + z + 0 \times z^2 + 2z^3)$$

$$\Rightarrow Y(z) = 2z^4 + z^2 - z$$

41. For an underdetermined problem,
m > d and p = d

42. The depth of penetration/skin depth, d can be defined as the depth at which the amplitude of the field A_d is decreased by a factor e^{-1} compared with its surface amplitude A_o

$$A_d = A_o e^{-1}$$

Therefore, for the amplitude decay at thrice the skin depth is

$$A_{3d} = A_o e^{-3}$$

$$A_o = 1$$

$$\therefore A_d = e^{-3}$$

43. Given, $f(t) = \sin(t)$

Now, as per Hilbert transform having a phase difference of $\frac{\pi}{2}$ with the function, we get

$$H\{f(t)\} = \sin\left(t - \frac{\pi}{2}\right) = -\cos t$$

$$\Rightarrow H[H\{f(t)\}] = H[-\cos t]$$

$$\Rightarrow H\left[-\cos\left(t - \frac{\pi}{2}\right)\right]$$

$$\Rightarrow H[H\{f(t)\}] = -\sin t$$

44. As per question,

$$\pi(t) = \begin{cases} 1, -1/2 < t < 1/2 \\ 0, (t) > 1/2 \end{cases}$$

Convolution of two function is defined by,

$$(f \times g)(t) = \int_{-\infty}^{\infty} f(u) g(t-u) du$$

$$= \begin{cases} \int_{t_{1/2}}^{t_{-1/2}} 1.1du, & -1 < t < 1 \\ \int_{t_{-1/2}}^{t_{1/2}} 1.1du, & 0 < t < 2T_0 \end{cases} = \begin{cases} 1(t+1), & -1 < t < 0 \\ 1(t-1), & 0 < t < 1 \\ 0, & |t| > 0 \end{cases}$$

45. Given,

$$\vec{A} = e^{-y}(\cos x a_x - \sin x a_y)$$

therefore,

$$\vec{\nabla} \times \vec{A} = \begin{vmatrix} a_x & a_y & a_z \\ \frac{\partial}{\partial x} & \frac{\partial}{\partial y} & \frac{\partial}{\partial z} \\ e^{-y} \cos x & e^{-y} \sin x & 0 \end{vmatrix}$$

$$\vec{\nabla} \times \vec{A} = a_x(0+0) - a_y(0+0) + a_z (-e^{-y} \cos x + e^{-y} \cos x)$$

$$\vec{\nabla}(\vec{\nabla} \times \vec{A}) = \left(\frac{\partial}{\partial x} a_x + \frac{\partial}{\partial y} a_y + \frac{\partial}{\partial z} a_z\right).0 = 0$$

46. **The convolution theorem** states that under suitable conditions the Fourier transform of a convolution of two signals is the pointwise product of their Fourier transforms. In other words, convolution in one domain (e.g., time domain) equals point-wise multiplication in the other domain (e.g., frequency domain).

The Nyquist frequency is the bandwidth of a sampled signal, and is equal to half the sampling frequency of that signal. If the sampled signal should represent a continuous spectral range starting at 0 Hz (which is the most common case for speech recordings), the Nyquist frequency is the highest frequency that the sampled signal can unambiguously represent.

Aliasing is an interesting (and usually unwanted) phenomenon that happens when a signal is sampled at less than the double of the highest frequency contained in the signal. Related to this concept are the Nyquist-Shannon sampling theorem, Nyquist frequency, frequency folding, anti-aliasing filter and others.

An infinite-bandwidth white noise signal is a purely theoretical construction. The bandwidth of **white noise** is limited in practice by the mechanism of noise generation, by the transmission medium and by finite observation capabilities. Thus, random signals are considered "white noise" if they are observed to have a flat spectrum over the range of frequencies that are relevant to the context.

47. The relation between B field, H-field and magnetization M is given by

$$\vec{B} = \mu_0(\vec{H} + \vec{M})$$

As, $\vec{M} = k\vec{H}$

where, k = magnetic susceptibility

$$\Rightarrow \vec{B} = \mu_0\vec{H}(1+k)$$

$$\Rightarrow \vec{B} = \mu_0 M\vec{H}$$

48. In the region P, the gravity values recorded is reduced due to attracting nature of terrain part Q. Hence, to compensate for the reduce in gravity at P, terrain correction is positive at P.

49. In region Q, due to the attracting nature of the terrain, portion Q results in reduced gravity. Hence, we require terrain correction in region Q.

50. The given filter is, $y_n = 1.5x_n - 2x_{n-1} + 2.5y_{n-2}$

Therefore, The order of filter is 2.

51. The transfer function of the given digital filter is given by the ratio of z- transform of y_n and x_n

i.e., $H(z) = \dfrac{Y(z)}{X(z)}$

As per given question the equation is

$y_n = 1.5x_n - 2x_{n-1} + 2.5y_{n-2}$

After z- transformation it becomes

$Y(z) = 1.5X(z) - 2zX(z) + 2.5z^2(z)$

$$\frac{Y(z)}{X(z)} = \left(\frac{1.5 - 2z}{1 - 2.5z^2}\right)$$

52. Given,

$V_1 = 4000$ m/s

$\rho_1 = 2500$ kg/m^3

Therefore, Acoustic Impedence of first layer Z is

$Z_1 = \rho_1 V_1 = 2500 \times 4000 = 10^7$ kg/m^2/s

53. Given,

$V_1 = 4000$ m/s

$\rho_1 = 2500$ kg/m^3

$V_2 = 4500$ m/s

$\rho_2 = 2600$ kg/m^3

Therefore,

Reflection coefficient,

$$R = \frac{\rho_2 V_2 - \rho_1 V_1}{\rho_2 V_2 + \rho_1 V_1}$$

$$= \frac{26 \times 45 \times 10^4 - 25 \times 40 \times 10^4}{26 \times 45 \times 10^4 + 25 \times 40 \times 10^4} = 0.07$$

Therefore, Tranmission coefficient,

$T = 1 - R = 1 - 0.017 = 0.9216$

54. **B-polarization:** When the magnetic field is polarized in x-direction (strike direction), the electromagnetic field component considered in this model is H_x, E_y and E_z.

E-polarization: When the electric field is polarized in x-direction (strike direction), the electromagnetic field component considered in this model is E_x, H_y and H_z.

55. **E-polarization:** The different electromagnetic equations governing this mode are:

When $B_y = B_0 e^{i\omega t}$

$$\frac{\partial E_x}{\partial y} = \frac{\partial B_z}{\partial t} = i\omega B_z$$

$$\frac{\partial E_x}{\partial Z} = \frac{\partial B_y}{\partial t} = -i\omega B_y$$

$$\frac{\partial B_z}{\partial y} - \frac{\partial B_y}{\partial z} = \mu\sigma E_x$$

B-polarization: The different electromagnetic equations governing this mode are:

When $B_y = B_0 e^{i\omega t}$

$$\frac{\partial B_x}{\partial y} = \mu_0 \sigma E_Z$$

$$\frac{\partial B_x}{\partial z} = \mu_0 \sigma E_y$$

$$\frac{\partial E_z}{\partial y} - \frac{\partial E_y}{\partial z} = i\omega B_x$$

(GENERAL APTITUDE SECTION)

56. His father casual remarks on politics betrayed his lack of seriousness about the subject.

    Betrayed here means unintentionally reveal, be evidence of.

57. Circuitous means not being forthright or direct in language or action. Here, the closest meaning is indirect.

58. If we manage to conserve our natural resources, we would leave a better planet for our children.

    Conserve means protect (something, especially something of environmental or cultural importance) from harm or destruction.

59. No. of person in room = 25

    Play hockey = 15

    Play football =17

    Play both = 10

    Therefore, No. of persons playing neither hockey or football is

    $25-[(17+15)-10]=3$

60. No. of persons who play either football or hockey

    $= 15 + 17 - 10 = 22$

    No. of persons playing neither hockey nor football

    $= 25 - 22 = 3$

61. $(137)_8+(276)_8=(435)_8$

    So basically the number are given in octal base.

    Similarly, addition of 731,672 gives 1623 in octal.

62. Given that,

    - H + G > S + I
    - No twins,
    - And either G = S + 1 or S = G + 1
    - G is not the oldest and S is not the youngest.

      Let us analyze each case,

Case 1:

G = S + 1,

It implies, H > I – 1H > I – 1, since twins are not possible H > I

Case 2:

G = S – 1,

It implies H > I + 1

Therefore, both cases imply H is older than I, also G and S must be placed successively.

Only option B satisfies these implications.

63. As per the passage the appropriate sentence is

    Modern warfare has resulted in civil strife.

64. 1 skilled person can do $120\times 5=\frac{1}{100}$ of work in 1 day, so 2 skilled person do $\frac{2}{100}$ of work in a day.

    Similarly, 6 semi-skilled and 5 unskilled person can do $\frac{6}{200}$ and $\frac{5}{300}$ of work respectively in 1 day.

    So, together they do $\frac{2}{100}+\frac{6}{200}+5300=\frac{1}{15}$ of work together in 1 day, which gives required number of day to complete the work =15.

65. Let first digit is 3 now rest 3 digits can be from 2,2,3,3,4,4,4,4 but in this no of 2's and 3's are only 2 so 222 and 333 is not possible so the possible no

    $3\times3\times3-2=25$

    In second condition the First no is 4 now rest three digits can be 2,2,3,3,3,4,4,4 so here no of 2's is also two so possible numbers is

    $3 \times 3 \times 3 - 1 = 26$

    $25 + 26 = 51$

SOLVED PAPER - 2009

PART-A (Common Part)

Q. 1 – Q. 20 carry one mark each.

1. The Gutenberg discontinuity is located at a depth of around

(*a*) 35 km (*b*) 150 km

(*c*) 2900 km (*d*) 5000 km

2. What is the age of the "Barail Series" ?

(*a*) Jurassic (*b*) Paleocene

(*c*) Oligocene (*d*) Miocene

3. Thermohaline circulation in the oceans is driven by

(*a*) only salinity gradients

(*b*) both temperature and salinity gradients

(*c*) only temperature gradients

(*d*) only density difference

4. Which one of the following minerals cannot be used as an abrasive?

(*a*) Garnet (*b*) Corundum

(*c*) Quartz (*d*) Gypsum

5. Which one of the following lakes is interpreted to be of meteoritic impact origin?

(*a*) Lonar Lake (*b*) Chilka Lake

(*c*) Kolleru Lake (*d*) Pulicate Lake

6. Which of the following geomorphic features is not related to desert environments?

(*a*) yardang (*b*) bajada

(*c*) hamada (*d*) esker

7. Which of the following is located closest to the Ninety-East Ridge?

(*a*) Bombay High

(*b*) Lakshwadweep Islands

(*c*) Andarnan and Nicobar Islands

(*d*) Maldives

8. LPG (Liquefied Petroleum Gas) consists mainly of

(*a*) propane and butane

(*b*) methane and ethane

(*c*) methane and butane

(*d*) ethane and propane

9. Who proposed the principle "the present is the key to the past"?

(*a*) Carl von Linnaeus

(*b*) James Hutton

(*c*) William Smith

(*d*) Alcide d'Orbigny

10. Of the following, which is an ore of nickel?

(*a*) Pentlandite (*b*) Cinnabar

(*c*) Cassiterite (*d*) Scheelite

11. Over a three layered earth, comprising of top dry soil followed by saturated weathered layer and hard rock basement, a resistivity sounding experiment is performed. The obtained VES curve is

(*a*) K-type (*b*) A-type

(*c*) H-type (*d*) Q-type

12. The logging tool for direct determination of permeability is

(*a*) induction (*b*) litho-density

(*c*) sonic (*d*) NMR

13. Which of the following parameters is uniquely resolved by residual gravity anomaly data?

(*a*) lateral density contrast

(*b*) excess/deficit mass

(*c*) absolute density

(*d*) geometric dimensions of geophysical model

14. Crude oil density, in degree API (American Petroleum Institute), is a measure of viscosity. The value of 10 API is of

(*a*) water (*b*) heavy crude

(*c*) average crude (*d*) light crude

15. For perfectly conducting medium, skin depth (m) is

(*a*) 10^5 (*b*) 100

(*c*) 10 (*d*) 0

16. If a planet revolves around the Sun with a period of 8 years, then its distance from the Sun would be (in terms of distance between Earth and Sun)

(*a*) two times (*b*) four times

(*c*) six times (*d*) eight times

17. A vast majority of earthquake sources are often linked to

(*a*) inner core

(*b*) outer core

(*c*) brittle part of the earth's crust

(*d*) molten part of earth's mantle

18. In paleomagnetism, detrital magnetization is an important process for study of

(*a*) sedimentary rocks

(*b*) metamorphic rocks

(*c*) basic igneous rocks

(*d*) acidic igneous rocks

19. A Geiger-Muller counter is used for measuring

(*a*) gamma radiation

(*b*) alpha particles

(*c*) beta particles

(*d*) both alpha and beta particles

20. The presence of crustal root beneath a mountain chain can be best explained by

(*a*) Pratt's model

(*b*) Airy's model

(*c*) Vening Meinesz model

(*d*) Plume model

PART-B
GEOLOGY

Q. 21 to Q. 60 carry two marks each.

21. Which one of the following is a typical Lower Gondwana plant assemblage?

(*a*) Glossapteris, Ptilophyllum, Nilssonia, Bucklandia

(*b*) Glossopteris, Gangamopteris, Schizoneura, Sphenophyllum

(*c*) Gangamopteris, Lycopodites, Brachyphyllum, Nilssonia

(*d*) Vertebraria, Alethopteris, Otozamites, Glossopteris

22. Which of the following is not correct for a Pelecypod shell?

(*a*) Pedicle is present.

(*b*) Pallial sinus, if present, is on the posterior side.

(*c*) Lunule is towards anterior.

(*d*) Both the valves have teeth and sockets.

23. Match the following:

	Group I		Group II
P.	Muschelkalk	1.	Cambrian
Q.	Katrol Formation	2.	Miocene
R.	Uttatur Stage	3.	Middle Triassic
S.	Baripada beds	4.	Cretaceous
		5.	Pleistocene
		6.	Late Jurassic

(*a*) P - 3, Q - 6, R - 5, S - 1

(*b*) P - 1, Q - 2, R - 3, S - 4

(*c*) P - 3, Q - 6, R - 4, S - 2

(*d*) P - 6, Q - 3, R - 1, S - 2

24. Match the following:

	Group I		Group II
P.	Pelagic	1.	Open ocean
Q.	Pycnocline	2.	Cold sphere
R.	Psychrosphere	3.	North Atlantic
S.	Humboldt Current	4.	Density
		5.	Thermocline
		6.	East Pacific

(*a*) P - 1, Q - 4, R - 3, S - 6

(*b*) P - 6, Q - 2, R - 1, S - 5

(*c*) P - 5, Q - 6, R - 1, S - 3

(*d*) P - 1, Q - 4, R - 2, S - 6

25. Match the following:

	Group I		Group II
P.	Globigerina	1.	Lower Cambrian
Q.	Olenellus bulloides	2.	Echinodermata
R.	Ambulancrum	3.	Graptolites
S.	Nema	4.	Upwelling
		5.	Coelenterata
		6.	Silurian

(*a*) P - 1, Q - 6, R - 2, S - 5

(*b*) P - 5, Q - 6, R - 2, S - 3

(*c*) P - 4, Q - 1, R - 2, S - 3

(*d*) P - 2, Q - 4, R - 5, S - 6

26. Dinosaurs can be distinguished from the other Mesozoic reptiles by

(*a*) Large size

(*b*) Carnivorous habit

(*c*) Erect stance

(*d*) Sprawling stance

27. Which of the following is a polar planktic formanifer?

(*a*) Globigerenoides rubber

(*b*) Neogloboquadrina pachyderma

(*c*) Globorotalia menardii

(*d*) Orbulina universa

28. Which one of the following mass-wasting processes is designated as a slow flowage type?

(*a*) Mudflow (*b*) Solifluction

(*c*) Slump (*d*) Rockslide

29. Which of the following accurately describes the rock 'phonolite'?

(*a*) Undersaturated ultramafic volcanic rock

(*b*) Undersaturated mafic plutonic rock

(*c*) Undersaturated ultrabasic volcanic rock

(*d*) Intermediate alkaline plutonic rock

30. Match the assemblages in Group I with the corresponding metamorphic facies in Group II:

Group I	Group II
P. Albite-jadeite-glaucophane-lawsonite	1. Greenschist
Q. Garnet-ortho-pyroxene-clinopyr-oxene-plagioclase	2. Blueschist
R. Garnet-muscovite-biotite-sillimanite-quartz	3. Granulite
S. Albite-chlorite-epidote-actinolite	4. Amphibolite
	5. Zeolite
	6. Prehnite-pumpelJyite

(*a*) P - 1, Q - 6, R - 2, S - 5

(*b*) P - 5, Q - 1, R - 3, S - 4

(*c*) P - 2, Q - 3, R - 4, S - 1

(*d*) P - 3, Q - 2, R - 1, S - 6

31. When underplated by mafic magmas, and with no erosion, lower crustal rocks will experience ______ during metamorphism.

(*a*) isobaric heating followed by isothermal decompression

(*b*) isothermal compression followed by isobaric heating

(*c*) isobaric heating followed by isothermal compression

(*d*) isobaric heating-cooling trajectory

32. Match the minerals in Group I with their characteristic optical properties in Group II:

Group I	Group II
P. Biotite	1. Uniaxial negative
Q. Sodalite	2. Mottled extinction
R. Nepheline	3. Uniaxial positive
S. Quartz	4. Isotropic, low relief
	5. Isotropic, high relief
	6. Biaxial negative

(*a*) P - 5, Q - 1, R - 3, S - 6

(*b*) P - 6, Q - 2, R - 5, S - 1

(*c*) P - 3, Q - 2, R - 4, S - 5

(*d*) P - 2, Q - 4, R - 1, S - 3

33. A single slice of rock bound by thrust faults on all sides is called a

(*a*) horse (*b*) pop-up structure

(*c*) duplex (*d*) graben

34. A strike-slip dip fault strikes 30°N, and dips 45°SE. The net slip of the fault plunges

(*a*) 30° towards 45°N (*b*) 0° towards 30°N

(*c*) 45° towards 120°N (*d*) 90° towards 30°N

35. The boundary between the Indian and Eurasian plates is the

(*a*) Main Central Thrust

(*b*) Main Boundary Thrust

(*c*) South Tibetan Detachment Zone

(*d*) Indus-Tsangpo Suture Zone

36. Plagioclase feldspars belong to the ______ crystal system.

(*a*) Triclinic (*b*) Monoclinic

(*c*) Orthorhombic (*d*) Rhombic

37. The plane by which twinned crystals are united is called the

(*a*) mirror plane (*b*) twin plane

(*c*) glide plane (*d*) composition plane

38. In satellite remote-sensing, the spectral bands near 1.4 μm and 1.9 μm are avoided because of

(*a*) absorption due to H20 and C02 in the atmosphere

(*b*) absorption due to ozone layer in the atmosphere

(*c*) absorption due to nitrogen in the atmosphere

(*d*) absorption by vegetation

39. Formation of chromitite from a basaltic magma can be explained by

(*a*) liquid immiscibility

(*b*) assimilation

(*c*) magma mixing

(*d*) Soret effect

40. Match the following economic deposits in Group I with their places of occurrences in Group II:

Group I	Group II
P. Bauxite	1. Naliya
Q. Phosphorite	2. Maldeota
R. Magnesite	3. Pahalgam
S. Barite	4. Salem
	5. Mangampeta
	6. Belgaum

(*a*) P - 1, Q - 2, R - 4, S - 5
(*b*) P - 2, Q - 3, R - 4, S - 6
(*c*) P - 3, Q - 1, R - 6, S - 5
(*d*) P - 6, Q - 2, R - 4, S - 5

41. What is the host rock for sulphide mineralization in Rampura-Agucha belt?
(*a*) Graphitic mica schist
(*b*) Gametiferous mica schist
(*c*) Graphitic biotite-sillimanite gneiss
(*d*) Oametiferous sillimanite-feldspar gneiss

42. Which of the following is the correct order of decreasing permeability?
(*a*) silty sandstone > siltstone > sandstone > pebbly sandstone
(*b*) siltstone > silty sandstone > sandstone > pebbly sandstone
(*c*) pebbly sandstone > sandstone > silty sandstone > siltstone
(*d*) pebbly sandstone > sandstone > siltstone > silty sandstone

43. Which of the following varieties of coal has the least H/C ratio?
(*a*) peat (*b*) lignite
(*c*) bituminous (*d*) anthracite

44. What is the age of the reservoir rock in the Cambay basin?
(*a*) Eocene (*b*) Oligocene
(*c*) Miocene (*d*) Paleocene

45. Which one of the following can be considered the best cap rock for oil and gas traps?
(*a*) chert (*b*) evaporite
(*c*) sandstone (*d*) shale

46. A negative Eu anomaly will develop in a fractionating magma following separation of
(*a*) garnet (*b*) olivine
(*c*) plagioclase (*d*) orthopyroxene

47. In which of the following islands is the Mid-oceanic ridge exposed above sea-level?
(*a*) Japan (*b*) Seychelles
(*c*) Hawaii (*d*) Iceland

48. _____ dams are constructed where the foundation rock is strong.
(*a*) Gravity (*b*) Arch
(*c*) Buttress (*d*) Earth

49. Which type of cross-bedding is a definite indicator of tidal currents?
(a) epsilon cross-bedding
(b) herring-bone cross-bedding
(c) hummocky cross-bedding
(d) trough cross-bedding

50. Which type of sedimentary basin is formed close to continent-continent collisional settings?
(*a*) Fore-arc basin
(*b*) Peripheral foreland basin
(*c*) Back-arc basin
(*d*) Retro-arc foreland basin

Common Data Questions

Common Data for Questions 51 and 52:

A rock contains 65% forsterite (Fo), 27% enstatite (En) and 8% pigeonite (Pig) and its melting relationships at 1 bar can be represented by the figure given below:

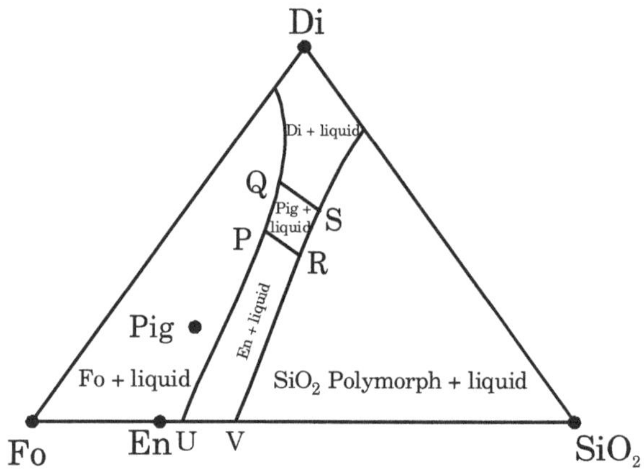

51. The name of the rock is
(*a*) Lherzolite (*b*) Harzburgite
(*c*) Wehrlite (*d*) Dunite

52. On partially melting this rock, the first melt will have the composition of point
(*a*) P
(*b*) Q
(*c*) R
(*d*) S

Common Data for Questions 53 and 54:

An unfossiliferous sedimentary succession is characterized by the following features -

(i) sandstone-shale alternation, with sheet-like geometry of the sandstone beds; (ii) the sandstones exhibit graded bedding; (iii) erosional structures under the sandstone beds; (iv) convolute lamination, and (v) ripple marks on the sandstone beds.

53. Which depositional environment is indicated for the above sedimentary succession?

(*a*) Fluvial (*b*) Eolian

(*c*) Intertidal (*d*) Deep marine

54. What type of paleocurrent pattern is expected from the erosional structures in the succession?

(*a*) Unimodal (*b*) Bimodal

(*c*) Bimodal-bipolar (*d*) Polymodal

Common Data for Questions 55 and 56:

Examine the given geological section, which contains sedimentary successions interrupted by a dyke, and which contains no tectonic discontinuities.

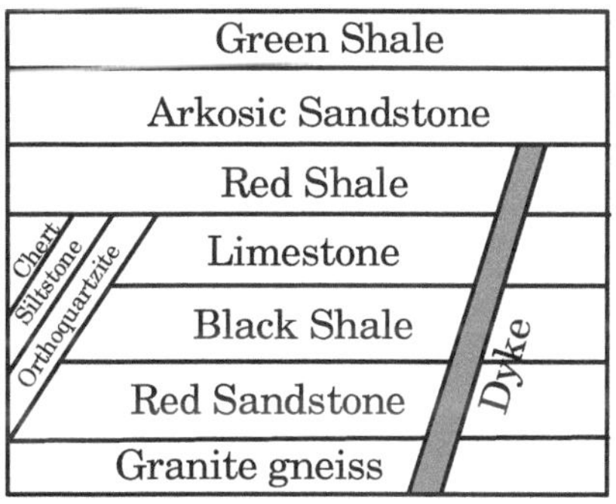

55. How many unconformities can be identified in the section?

(*a*) 3 (*b*) 4

(*c*) 5 (*d*) 6

56. Which of the following contacts is a nonconformity?

(*a*) Granite gneiss - Red Sandstone

(*b*) Black Shale - Limestone

(*c*) Limestone - Red Shale

(*d*) Red Shale - Arkosic Sandstone

Linked Answer Questions

Statement for Linked Answer Questions 57 and 58:

Microfossils may have different test composition.

57. Which of the following is a siliceous microfossil group?

(*a*) Conodonts (*b*) Radiolaria

(*c*) Dinoflagellates (*d*) Foraminifera

58. What is the preferred microhabitat of the wicrofossil group that is the correct answer in Q.57?

(*a*) Benthic (*b*) Planktic

(*c*) Nektic (*d*) Nektobenthic

Statement for Linked Answer Questions 59 and 60:

Pb-Zn sulphide deposits can form in different types of host rocks.

59. Of the following, where do we get predominantly carbonate-hosted Pb-Zn sulphide deposits?

(*a*) Mochia - Zawar (*b*) Sargipalli

(*c*) Pur - Banera (*d*) Sindesar - Khurd

60. What is the age of the host rock to the correct answer in Q.59?

(*a*) Neoproterozoic (*b*) Mesoproterozoic

(*c*) Paleoproterozoic (*d*) Archean

GEOPHYSICS

Q. 21 to Q. 60 carry two marks each.

21. Match the following functions in time-domain with their fourier spectra:

	Group I		**Group II**
P.	$\Pi(t) = \begin{cases} 1, -1/2 \le t \le 1/2 \\ 0, t < -1/2 \text{ and } t > 1/2 \end{cases}$	1.	1
Q.	Dirac delta function, $\delta(t)$	2.	$\frac{\sin(\pi f)}{f}$, where f is frequency
R.	$x(t) = e^{-\lvert t \rvert}$	3.	$\frac{2}{1+4\pi^2 f^2}$, where f is frequency
S.	$A(t) = \begin{cases} 1+t, -1 < t < 0 \\ 1-t, 0 < t < 1 \\ 0, \text{otherwise} \end{cases}$	4.	$\frac{\sin^2(\pi f)}{f^2}$, where f is frequency

(*a*) P - 2, Q - 3, R - 1, S - 4

(*b*) P - 1, Q - 3, R - 2, S - 4

(*c*) P - 1, Q - 4, R - 2, S - 3

(*d*) P - 2, Q - 1, R - 3, S - 4

22. The teleseismic rays are those that arrive at a seismometer for a distance greater than

(*a*) 18° (*b*) 28°

(*c*) 38° (*d*) 48°

23. Match the following seismic source generated noise type with its appearance on the seismogram:

Group I	Group II
P. Reverberation	1. Coherent hyperbolic events
Q. Multiples	2. Tails on reflected events
R. Guided waves	3. Events paralleling first breaks
S. Diffractions	4. Reflections at even time intervals after the primary reflections

(*a*) P - 1, Q - 3, R - 2, S - 4
(*b*) P - 3, Q - 4, R - 2, S - 1
(*c*) P - 2, Q - 4, R - 3, S - 1
(*d*) P - 4, Q - 1, R - 3, S - 2

24. Which is the parameter for measuring the size of the earthquake that does not need an instrumental record?

(*a*) Richter Magnitude (*b*) Intensity
(*c*) Moment (*d*) M_w

25. The standard form of wave equation for propagation of cubical dilatation (θ) is

$$\rho\frac{\partial^2\theta}{\partial t^2} = (\lambda + 2\mu)\nabla^2\theta.$$

The compressional wave velocity is given by

(*a*) $\sqrt{\frac{2\lambda+\mu}{\rho}}$ (*b*) $\sqrt{\frac{\lambda+2\mu}{2\rho}}$

(*c*) $\sqrt{\frac{\lambda+\mu}{\rho}}$ (*d*) $\sqrt{\frac{\lambda+2\mu}{\rho}}$

26. PKIKP is a seismic body wave which travels through

(*a*) upper mantle
(*b*) upper and lower mantle
(*c*) mantle, outer core and inner core
(*d*) mantle and outer core

27. A seismic signal is recorded in a frequency band, 50-100 Hz. The sampling interval (ms) to avoid aliasing would be

(*a*) 5 (*b*) 10
(*c*) 15 (*d*) 20

28. The minimum appreciable amplitude recorded by a seismometer is 0.2 mm and the maximum one is 20.0 cm, then the dynamic range in dB is

(*a*) 80 (*b*) 60
(*c*) 40 (*d*) 20

29. Match the following:

Group I	Group II
P. Primary wave	1. Propagate along surface of the medium
Q. Secondary wave	2. Particle motion is orthogonal to direction of propagation
R. Rayleigh wave	3. Particle motion describes a a retrograde ellipse
S. Love wave	4. Particle motion in the direction of propagation

(*a*) P - 3, Q - 4, R - 1, S - 2
(*b*) P - 1, Q - 4, R - 2, S - 3
(*c*) P - 1, Q - 3, R - 2, S - 4
(*d*) P - 4, Q - 2, R - 3, S - 1

30. Which of the following is a minimum-phase wavelet? The first value in each case is at time zero.

(*a*) {–2, 5, –2} (*b*) {–2, 5, 2}
(*c*) {6, –1, –2} (*d*) {3, 4, –4}

31. In a gas zone, true porosity ϕ_t, neutron log ϕ_n and density derived porosity ϕ_d are related as

(*a*) $\phi_n < \phi_d > \phi_t$
(*b*) $\phi_n > \phi_d > \phi_t$
(*c*) $\phi_n > \phi_d = \phi_t$
(*d*) $\phi_n < \phi_d = \phi_t$

32. Identify the equation for formation water resistivity (Rw_e) estimation from SP Jog, wherein SSP, K(T) and Rmf_e are respectively static SP, temperature dependent coefficient and mudfiltrate resistivity.

(*a*) $SSP = -Rw_e \log\left(\frac{K(T)}{Rmf_e}\right)$

(*b*) $SSP = -K(T)\log\left(\frac{Rw_e}{Rmf_e}\right)$

(*c*) $SSP = -Rmf_e \log\left(\frac{K(T)}{Rw_e}\right)$

(*d*) $SSP = -K(T)\log\left(\frac{Rmf_e}{Rw_e}\right)$

33. Gamma ray detected in density log is

(*a*) natural gamma present in the formation
(*b*) gamma ray from epithermal neutron source
(*c*) gamma ray scattered from the formation
(*d*) gamma ray emitted from neutron capture reaction

34. In Turam method, one measures the reduced field ratio of the amplitude and of the phase difference between the two coils. In the absence of subsurface conducting body, the response is characterized as

(*a*) the successive reduced field ratio is equal to 1.0 and phase difference is 0°

(*b*) the successive reduced field ratio is equal to 1.0 and phase difference is 45°

(*c*) the successive reduced field ratio is equal to 0.5 and phase difference is 90°

(*d*) the successive reduced field ratio is equal to 0.5 and phase difference is 60°

35. Electric field $(\vec{E})$ through a polarizable dielectric medium with polarization vector $(\vec{P})$, electric susceptibility (χ_e) and dielectric permittivity (ε_0). The electric displacement vector $(\vec{D})$ for the medium can be written as

(*a*) $\vec{D} = \varepsilon_0 (1 + \chi_e)$ (*b*) $\vec{D} = \varepsilon_0 \vec{E} - \vec{P}$

(*c*) $\vec{D} = \varepsilon_0 \vec{E} + \chi_e$ (*d*) $\vec{D} = \varepsilon_0 \vec{E} + \vec{P}$

36. Using different electrodes configuration, maximum depth of investigation is achieved in

(*a*) Schlumberger (*b*) dipole

(*c*) tri-electrodes (*d*) Wenner

37. Relevant differential equation to study low frequency electromagnetic prospecting for a conducting target can be written in the form of

(*a*) Wave equation

(*b*) Laplace's equation

(*c*) Helmholtz equation

(*d*) Poisson's equation

38. In a layered medium, if the basement is perfectly conducting, magnetotelluric phase response asymptotically approaches to

(*a*) 0° (*b*) 45°

(*c*) 60° (*d*) 90°

39. Magnetotelluric spectral impedance can be defined as

(*a*) the ratio of the spatial spectrum from mutually orthogonal horizontal components of the electric and magnetic field

(*b*) the ratio of the spatial spectrum of the vertical component to the horizontal component of magnetic field

(*c*) the ratio of the spatial spectrum of the vertical component to the horizontal component of electric magnetic field

(*d*) the ratio of the spatial spectrum of the two horizontal components of electric field

40. Following four electrodes array: Pl, P2 are measuring electrodes and Cl, C2 are current electrodes used in resistivity measurement. Inter-electrode separation is also shown in figure.

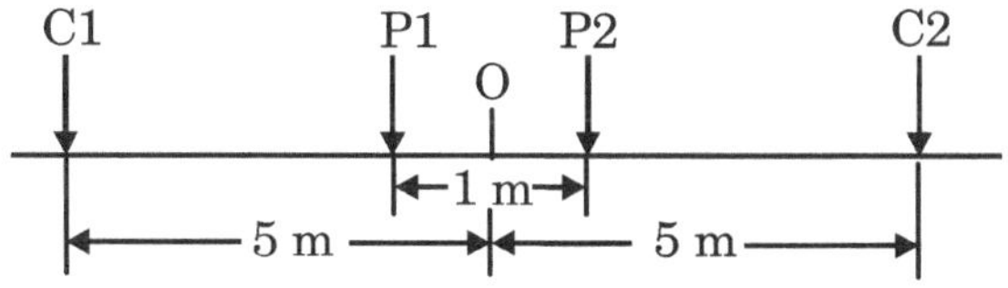

The above electrode configuration is

(*a*) radial dipole (*b*) parallel dipole

(*c*) Schlumberger (*d*) Wenner

41. In DC resistivity method, direct filter coefficients are used to compute

(*a*) apparent resistivity data from resistivity transform

(*b*) resistivity transform from apparent resistivity data

(*c*) apparent resistivity from measured potential difference

(*d*) apparent resistivity from one electrode configuration to other electrode configuration

42. A counting rate of 15,100 counts per minute is recorded by a radiation counter having a dead time of 300 J.l.Sec. The count rate (counts per minute) in the absence of dead time would be

(*a*) 13,333 (*b*) 14,333

(*c*) 15,333 (*d*) 16,333

43. The output of a linear and invariant system for a unit input is {3, 1}. Then what would be the output for an input {–2, 1} ?

(*a*) {–6, 1, 1} (*b*) {–1, 1, 6}

(*c*) {–1, 6, 1} (*d*) {1, –1, 6}

44. Geophysical inverse problems are described by

(*a*) Fredholm's integral equation of first kind

(*b*) Fredholm's integral equation of second kind

(*c*) Volterra's equation of second kind

(*d*) Legendre equation

45. Spot the ANN method from the following:

(*a*) Singular value decomposition

(*b*) monte-carlo technique

(*c*) Ridge regression procedure

(*d*) Back propagation technique

46. The concept of resolving kernel is used in

(*a*) Tikhonov's regularization method

(*b*) Ridge regression method

(*c*) Backus-Gilbert method

(*d*) Simulated annealing method

47. For underwater gravity measurements, the following correction is needed:

(*a*) Prey correction (*b*) Free-air correction

(*c*) Bouguer correction (*d*) Isostatic correction

48. The source of magnetic anomalies extend up to

(*a*) upper mantle (*b*) core-mantle boundary

(*c*) lower mantle (*d*) Curie-point isotherm

49. In magnetic prospecting scalar magnetometers are used. Then, the prime assumption involved in magnetic data acquisition is

(a) remnant magnetization is predominant

(b) both remnant and induced magnetization are responsible

(c) induced magnetization plays a dominant role

(d) only diamagnetic sources are responsible

50. Source of main geomagnetic field is best represented by

(*a*) a system of electric currents at core-mantle boundary

(*b*) a system of dipoles, quadrupoles, octupoles and multipoles

(*c*) an inclined geomagnetic dipole at center of earth

(*d*) a system of currents in the ionosphere

Common Data Questions

Common Data for Questions 51 and 52:

In a resistivity sounding experiment using Schlumberger configuration the apparent resistivity function asymptotically approaches a sloping straight line of slope 45 with abscissa

51. From the above data it can be inferred that the basement is

(*a*) Perfectly conducting

(*b*) Relatively resistive

(*c*) Relatively conducting

(*d*) Perfectly resistive

52. If the intercept at ρ_a = 1 ohm-m is 5 and resistivity of top layer is 10 ohm-m, then the depth of basement is

(*a*) 50.0 m (*b*) 5.0 m

(*c*) 2.0 m (*d*) 0.5 m

Common Data for Questions 53 and 54:

In a seismic refraction experiment involving a two-layered earth of P-wave velocities, 3 km/sec and 4.5 km/sec the delay time is found to be 49.69 m sec.

53. From the above data, the depth to the interface is given by

(*a*) 150 m (*b*) 120 m

(*c*) 100 m (*d*) 50 m

54. Using the above depth, the computed critical distance (m) would be

(*a*) 151.20 (*b*) 178.88

(*c*) 221.67 (*d*) 169.87

Common Data for Questions 55 and 56:

The peak gravity anomaly over a 2-D line mass of circular cross-section (horizontal cylinder) of density contrast 500 kg/m^3 is 1.674 mgal. The anomaly decreases to 0.837 mgal at a distance of 500 m along a principal profile. The universal gravitation constant, G = 6.6667 × 10^{-11} m^3 sec^{-2} kg^{-1}.

55. The depth (m) to center of line mass and radius (m) of the horizontal cylinder are =

(*a*) 500, 199.80 (*b*) 200, 150.93

(*c*) 200, 100.33 (*d*) 100, 60.37

56. Hence compute the excess mass per unit length (kg/m) of the line mass

(*a*) 11.0 × 10^7 (*b*) 9.0 × 10^7

(*c*) 6.27 × 10^7 (*d*) 3.67 × 10^7

Linked Answer Questions

Statement for Linked Answer Questions 57 and 58:

Resistivity log recorded using normal device with measuring electrode, M, is situated close to the current electrode, A, in logging device placed in borehole. A constant current, I, injected from current electrode into the formation.

57. If the spacing between A and M is r, and the potential difference ΔV is measured between the measuring electrode, M and remotely placed surface electrode. Then the expression for the apparent resistivity can be written as

(*a*) $\rho_a = \frac{2\pi r}{I}\Delta V$ (*b*) $\rho_a = \frac{4\pi r^2}{I}\Delta V$

(*c*) $\rho_a = \frac{2\pi r^2}{I}\Delta V$ (*d*) $\rho_a = \frac{4\pi r}{I}\Delta V$

58. If r = 0.40 m; I = 0.02 amp ; ΔV = 0.04 volt, then the measured apparent resistivity will be

(*a*) 1 Ωm (*b*) 5 Ωm

(*c*) 10 Ωm (*d*) 20 Ωm

Statement for Linked Answer Questions 59 and 60:

Given the wavelets, a = {3, –2} and b = { 1, –2}

59. The cross-correlation, φ_{ab} is given by

(*a*) {–6, 7, –2} (*b*) {–6, 10, –12}

(*c*) {–4, –11, –6} (*d*) {–6, 11, –4}

60. The inverse of wavelet 'a', W_a^{-t} is given by

(*a*) {4/3, 16/9, 17/7, 64/81}

(*b*) { 1/3, 2/9, 4/27, 8/81}

(*c*) {4/9, 1/3, 64/81, 16/27}

(*d*) {16/27, 64/81, 4/9, 1/3}

ANSWERS

PART A (Common Part)

1. (*c*)	**2.** (*c*)	**3.** (*b*)	**4.** (*d*)	**5.** (*a*)	**6.** (*d*)	**7.** (*c*)	**8.** (*a*)	**9.** (*b*)	**10.** (*a*)
11. (*c*)	**12.** (*d*)	**13.** (*a*)	**14.** (*b*)	**15.** (*d*)	**16.** (*b*)	**17.** (*c*)	**18.** (*a*)	**19.** (*c*)	**20.** (*b*)

PART-B (Geology)

21. (*b*)	**22.** (*a*)	**23.** (*c*)	**24.** (*a*)	**25.** (*c*)	**26.** (*c*)	**27.** (*b*)	**28.** (*b*)	**29.** (*c*)	**30.** (*c*)
31. (*a*)	**32.** (*d*)	**33.** (*a*)	**34.** (*b*)	**35.** (*a*)	**36.** (*a*)	**37.** (*d*)	**38.** (*a*)	**39.** (*d*)	**40.** (*d*)
41. (*a*)	**42.** (*c*)	**43.** (*d*)	**44.** (*a*)	**45.** (*b*)	**46.** (*c*)	**47.** (*d*)	**48.** (*a*)	**49.** (*b*)	**50.** (*b*)
51. (*b*)	**52.** (*a*)	**53.** (*a*)	**54.** (*a*)	**55.** (*a*)	**56.** (*a*)	**57.** (*b*)	**58.** (*b*)	**59.** (*a*)	**60.** (*c*)

(Geophysics)

21. (*d*)	**22.** (*a*)	**23.** (*d*)	**24.** (*b*)	**25.** (*d*)	**26.** (*c*)	**27.** (*a*)	**28.** (*b*)	**29.** (*d*)	**30.** (*c*)
31. (*a*)	**32.** (*d*)	**33.** (*c*)	**34.** (*a*)	**35.** (*d*)	**36.** (*c*)	**37.** (*b*)	**38.** (*b*)	**39.** (*a*)	**40.** (*c*)
41. (*b*)	**42.** (*d*)	**43.** (*a*)	**44.** (*d*)	**45.** (*d*)	**46.** (*c*)	**47.** (*c*)	**48.** (*d*)	**49.** (*b*)	**50.** (*b*)
51. (*d*)	**52.** (*a*)	**53.** (*c*)	**54.** (*b*)	**55.** (*a*)	**56.** (*c*)	**57.** (*d*)	**58.** (*c*)	**59.** (*a*)	**60.** (*b*)

EXPLANATIONS

PART A (COMMON PART)

1. The CMB (Core-Mantle Boundary) has also been referred to as the Gutenberg discontinuity. It is a seismic discontinuity occurs within Earth's interior at a depth of about 2,900 km (1,800 mi) below the surface, where there is an abrupt change in the speed of seismic waves (generated by earthquakes or explosions) that travel through Earth. At this depth, primary seismic waves (P waves) decrease in velocity while secondary seismic waves (S waves) disappear completely. S waves shear material, and cannot transmit through liquids, so it is thought that the unit above the discontinuity is solid, while the unit below is in a liquid or molten form.

2. The term 'Barail Series' was applied to the strata, mostly of Oligocene Age, overlying either 'Disang or Jaintia Series' and underlying either 'Surma Series' or 'TipamSeries'. Bulk of oil and gas discovered in Upper Assam till late 1980s has been found in the Barial Group of Upper Eocene to lower Oligocene age and Tipam Group of upper Miocene age.

3. Winds drive ocean currents in the upper 100 meters of the ocean's surface. However, ocean currents also flow thousands of meters below the surface. These deep-ocean currents are driven by differences in the water's density, which is controlled by temperature (thermo) and salinity (haline). This process is known as thermohaline circulation.

4. Mined gypsum is a somewhat abrasive material. As a result, robust equipment must be used when processing gypsum ore. Rotary dryers are an ideal solution for many types of ore, as they are rugged pieces of equipment easily customized with heavy-duty linings that defend against erosion. Rotary dryers are also beneficial in applications that require a reduction in the gypsum ore's moisture content. The tumbling movement rounds and dries the gypsum, preparing the material for future processing steps.

5. **Lonar Lake**, also known as Lonar crater, is a notified National Geo-heritage Monument saline soda lake located at Lonar in Buldhana district, Maharashtra, India, which was created by a meteor impact during the Pleistocene Epoch and it is the only known hyper velocity impact crater in basaltic rock anywhere on Earth.

Chilika Lake is a brackish water lagoon, spread over the Puri, Khurda and Ganjam districts of Odisha state on the east coast of India, at the mouth of the Daya River, flowing into the Bay of Bengal, covering an area of over 1,100 square km. It is the largest coastal lagoon in India and the second largest coastal lagoon in the world.

Kolleru Lake is one of the largest freshwater lakes in India located in state of Andhra Pradesh and forms the largest shallow freshwater lake in Asia, 15 kilometers away from the city of Eluru. Kolleru is located between Krishna and Godavari deltas.Kolleru spans into two districts - Krishna and West Godavari. The lake is fed directly by water from the seasonal Budameru and Tammileru streams, and is connected to the Krishna and Godavari irrigation systems by over 67 major and minor irrigation canals.

Pulicat Lake is considered to be the second largest brackish water body in India measuring 759 square km. The Lagoon is one the three important wetlands to attract North-East Monsoon rain clouds during October to December season to Tamil Nadu.

6. **Yardang** is a streamlined protuberance carved from bedrock or any consolidated or semiconsolidated material by the dual action of wind abrasion by dust and sand, and deflation, which is the removal of loose material by wind turbulence.

   Bajada consists of a series of coalescing alluvial fans along a mountain front. These fan-shaped deposits form from the deposition of sediment within a stream onto flat land at the base of a mountain. The usage of the term in landscape description or geomorphology derives from the Spanish word bajada, generally having the sense of "descent" or "inclination".

   Hamada is a type of desert landscape consisting of high, largely barren, hard rocky plateaus, where most of the sand has been removed by deflation.

   Esker is a long, winding ridge of stratified sand and gravel, examples of which occur in glaciated and formerly glaciated regions of Europe and North America. Eskers are frequently several kilometres long and, because of their peculiar uniform shape, are somewhat like railway embankments.

7. The Ninety East Ridge is a linear structure on the Indian Ocean floor named for its near-parallel strike along the 90th meridian at the center of the Eastern Hemisphere. It is approximately 5,000 kilometres (3,100 mi) in length and can be traced topographically from the Bay of Bengal southward towards the Southeast Indian Ridge (SEIR), though the feature continues to the north where it is hidden beneath the sediments of the Bengal Fan. The ridge extends between latitudes 33°S and 17°N and has an average width of 200 km.The ridge divides the Indian Ocean into the West and East Indian Ocean. Andaman and Nicobar Islands are located closed to this ridge.

8. Liquefied petroleum gas (LPG), also referred to as simply propane or butane, are flammable mixtures of hydrocarbon gases used as fuel in heating appliances, cooking equipment, and vehicles.

9. In the mid-seventeenth century, biblical scholar and Archbishop James Ussher determined that the earth had been created in the year 4004 B.C. Just over a century later, James Hutton, known as the father of geology, suggested that the earth was much older and that processes occurring in the present were the same processes that had operated in the past, and would be the processes that operate in the future. This concept became known as uniformitarianism and can be summarized by the phrase "the present is the key to the past."

10. Pentlandite is an iron-nickel-sulfide, (Fe, Ni, Si). Pentlandite has a narrow variation range in Ni:Fe but it is usually described as having a Ni:Fe of 1:1. It also contains minor cobalt, usually at low levels as a fraction of weight.Pentlandite forms isometric crystals, but it is foundnormally in massive granular aggregates. It is brittle with a hardness of 3.5 - 4 and specific gravity of 4.6 - 5.0 and is non-magnetic. It has a yellowish bronze color.

11. Top dry soil is relatively higher resistive than saturated weathered layer which is in turn lower resistive than hard rock basement thus giving the nature of curve as $\rho_{dry} > \rho_{weathered} < \rho_{rock}$ basement which is a H-type curve.

12. NMR logging, a subcategory of electromagnetic logging, measures the induced magnet moment of hydrogen nuclei (protons) contained within the fluid-filled pore space of porous media (reservoir rocks). Unlike conventional logging measurements (e.g., acoustic, density, neutron, and resistivity), which respond to both the rock matrix and fluid properties and are strongly dependent on mineralogy, NMR-logging measurements respond to the presence of hydrogen protons. Because these protons primarily occur in pore fluids, NMR effectively responds to the volume, composition, viscosity, and distribution of these fluids, for example:
    - Oil
    - Gas
    - Water

13. Residual gravity anomaly data gives the lateral density contrast within the subsurface which is then used for locating orebodies.

14. Oil viscosity is inversely proportional to API gravityAPI gravities more than 40 is Light oil.

    API gravities less than 10 is heavy oil.

15. The skin depth is defined as

$$m = 503\sqrt{\frac{\rho}{f}}$$

where f = frequency

and ρ = resistivity of medium

For perfectly conducting medium

$$\rho = 0$$

$$\therefore \quad m = 0$$

16. As per Kepler's third law

$$T^2 = \frac{4\pi^2 a^3}{GM}$$

$$\therefore \quad T^2 \propto a^3$$

where, T is the time period and a is the semi-major axis

For T= 8 years, the distance between sun and planet is given as

$$\frac{a_p}{a_e} = \left(\frac{T_p}{T_e}\right)^{2/3}$$

where, a_p is distnace between planet and sun

a_e is distance between earth and sun

T_p is period of planet around sun

a_p is period of earth around sun

$$\therefore \quad a_p = 8^{2/3} \times a_e$$

$$= 4a_e$$

17. A vast majority of earthquake sources is related to tectonic process in the Earth's crust which is taken due to the brittle part of the rocks that lies in the earth's crust.

18. The paleomagnetism of sediments is known as detrital remanent magnetism (DRM), and it arises from the collective alignment with the Earth's magnetic field of small magnetic carriers in the sediment. In general, the magnetic carriers that contribute most to the paleomagnetic signal are smaller than 10 μ across. Except where the sediment itself is derived from older material containing hematite grains, the primary magnetic mineral is fine-grained magnetite (or titanomagnetite). In a typical situation, the magnetite weathers out of parent rock material and is carried by water into a relatively quiet sedimentary environment where it is deposited with the sediment. As a magnetic carrier settles through the water column, the magnetic moment of the carrier tends to rotate to become parallel to the Earth's magnetic field.

19. A Geiger counter is an instrument used for detecting and measuring ionizing radiation. Also known as a Geiger-Mueller (G.M) counter it is widely used in applications such as radiation dosimetry, radiological protection, experimental physics, and the nuclear industry.It detects ionizing radiation such as alpha particles, beta particles, and gamma rays using the ionization effect produced in a G.M tube, which gives its name to the instrument. In wide and prominent use as a hand-held radiation survey instrument, it is perhaps one of the world's best-known radiation detection instruments.

20. Three principal models of isostasy are used:

The Airy-Heiskanen model - where different topographic heights are accommodated by changes in crustal thickness, in which the crust has a constant density

The Pratt-Hayford model - where different topographic heights are accommodated by lateral changes in rock density.

The VeningMeinesz, or flexural isostasy model - where the lithosphere acts as an elastic plate and its inherent rigidity distributes local topographic loads over a broad region by bending.

Airy and Pratt isostasy are statements of buoyancy, whereas flexural isostasy is a statement of buoyancy when deflecting a sheet of finite elastic strength.

PART-B (GEOLOGY)

21. The Lower Gondwana plant assemblage is represented by

Glossopteris communis,

Phyllothecaindica,

Schizoneurea

Gangamopterisangustifolia,

Noeggrrathiopisishislopi

Buriadiasewardi

Taenioperisdanaeoides

Spenofhyllumseciosum

Seeds of Cordaicarpuszeilleri

Equisetaceous stems.

22. Pedicle: The largest valve on a brachiopod is the pedicle valve and contains a hole (pedicle opening) where the pedicle would have been attached, this then would have been attached to the sea floor or rock.

23. The **Muschelkalk** is a sequence of sedimentary rock strata in the geology of central and Western Europe. It has a Middle Triassic (240 to 230 million years) age and forms the middle part of the tripartite Germanic Trias, which give the Triassic its name, lying above the older Buntsandstein and below the younger Keuper.

The **Katrol Formation** is a Mesozoic geologic formation in India. Fossil sauropod tracks have been reported from the formation. These sedimentary rocks represent a phase of marine transgression along the western part of India during the Jurassic Period.

The lower stage named after the village Uttatur, lying at thr western margin of Cretaceous basin. A thin ferrugineous bed sepratesGondwana from the overlying Cretaceous strata. The Uttatur sediments range in thickness from 300 to 600 m. Albian to Turonian have been recognised in the in the **Uttatur Formation**.

Baripada Marine Beds (BMB) have been studied extensively in terms of its mega fossil content. However, not much has been discussed about the foraminiferal content and the organic matter assemblage in these beds. The fossiliferous sequence of BMB consists of sandstone, shale and limestone units.Several coprolites from the Lower Miocene Baripada Beds in Mayurbhanj District, Orissa. Most of the coprolites that we collected are characterized by their teardrop, ovoid, cylindrical and spindle shapes. The sizes and shapes of these coprolites combined with fish teeth inclusion in some of them strongly point towards a crocodilian source.

24. The **pelagic zone** consists of the water column of the open ocean, and can be further divided into regions by depth. The word "pelagic" is derived from Greek, meaning 'open sea'. The pelagic zone can be thought of in terms of an imaginary cylinder or water column that goes from the surface of the sea almost to the bottom.

The physical properties in a **pycnocline** driven by density gradients also affect the flows and vertical profiles in the ocean. These changes can be connected to the transport of heat, salt, and nutrients through the ocean and the pycnocline diffusion controls upwelling.

Psychrosphere is the deep, relatively cold layer of the ocean that lies beneath the warmer water of the thermosphere, example North Atlantic.

The **Humboldt Current** is a cold, low-salinity ocean current. It flows north along the west coast of South America from the southern tip of Chile to northern Peru (East Pacific). Also called the 'Peru Current', it flows in the direction of the equator. It extends 1,000 kilometers offshore.

25. **Globigerina bulloides** is a species of heterotrophic planktonic foraminifer with a wide distribution in the photic zone of the world's oceans. It is able to tolerate a range of sea surface temperatures, salinities and water densities, and is most abundant at high southern latitudes (up to 40°S), certain high northern latitudes (up to 80°N), and in low-latitude upwelling regions.

Olenellus is an extinct genus of redlichiid trilobites, with species of average size (about 5 centimetres or 2.0 inches long). It lived during the Botomian and Toyonian stages (Olenellus-zone), 522 to 510 million years ago (Lower Cambrian), in what is currently North America, part of the paleocontinentLaurentia.

An **ambulacrum** is an elongated area of the shell of an echinoderm in which rows of tube feet are arranged. It is pluralized as ambulacra. The area on the shell between ambulacra is known as an interambulacrum.

Graptolites are an extinct group of Paleozoic colonial organisms, most often found as thin carbonized films in various shales or limestones from the Cambrian to the Carboniferous. It is believed that they were either planktonic (floating) or benthonic (bottom dwelling) in habit.In some genera of graptolites, the individual stipes are strung together by a whip-like structure called the nema.

26. Dianosaurs became quadrupedal but retained the erect stance of their bipedal ancestors by which they can be easily distinguished from other Mesozoic reptiles

27. Neogloboquadrinapachyderma dominates assemblages in transitional to polar water masses and occurs in low frequencies in warm subtropical and tropical environments. The species has broad tolerances for sea surface temperature and preferences for low sea surface salinities with little seasonal change. Its preferences for dense surface waters with low vertical temperature gradients and little stratification reflect its preferred high latitude habitats.

28. Classification of slope failures based on type of material and type of motion

Failure Type	Type of Material	Type of Motion	Rate of Motion
Rock fall	Rock fragments	Vertical or near-vertical fall (plus bouncing in many cases)	Very fast (>10s m/s)
Rock slide	A large rock body	Motion as a unit along a planar surface (translational sliding)	Typically very slow (mm/y to cm/y), but some can be faster
Rock avalanche	A large rock body that slides and then breaks into small fragments	Flow (at high speeds, the mass of rock fragments is suspended on a cushion of air)	Very fast (>10s m/s)
Creep or solifluction	Soil or other overburden; in some cases, mixed with ice	Flow (although sliding motion may also occur)	Very slow (mm/y to cm/y)
Slump	Thick deposits (m to 10s of m) of unconsolidated sediment	Motion as a unit along a curved surface (rotational sliding)	Slow (cm/y to m/y)
Mudflow	Loose sediment with a significant component of silt and clay	Flow (a mixture of sediment and water moves down a channel)	Moderate to fast (cm/s to m/s)

29. Phonolite is an uncommon volcanic rock, of intermediate chemical composition between felsic and mafic, with texture ranging from aphanitic (fine-grain) to porphyritic (mixed fine- and coarse-grain).Unusually, phonolite forms from magma with a relatively low silica content, generated by low degrees of partial melting (less than 10%) of highly aluminous rocks of the lower crust such as tonalite, monzonite and metamorphic rocks. Melting of such rocks to a very low degree promotes the liberation of aluminium, potassium, sodium and calcium by melting of feldspar, with some involvement of mafic minerals. Because the rock is silica-undersaturated, it has no quartz or other silica crystals, and is dominated by low-silica feldspathoid minerals more than feldspar minerals.

30. **Blueschist**, as a rock type, is defined by the presence of the minerals glaucophane + (lawsonite or epidote) +/- jadeite +/- albite or chlorite +/- garnet +/- muscovite in a rock of roughly basaltic composition.

Blueschist often has a lepidoblastic, nematoblastic or schistose rock microstructure defined primarily by chlorite, phengitic white mica, glaucophane, and other minerals with an elongate or platy shape.

Granulites form at crustal depths, typically during regional metamorphism at high thermal gradients of greater than 30°C/km.[2] In continental crustal rocks, biotite may break down at high temperatures to form orthopyroxene + potassium feldspar + water, producing a granulite. Other possible minerals formed at dehydration melting conditions include sapphirine, spinel, sillimanite, and osumilite. Some assemblages such as sapphirine + quartz indicate very high temperatures of greater than 90°C.

Metamorphic rocks composed primarily of **amphibole**, plagioclase, with subordinate epidote, zoisite, chlorite, quartz, titanite, and accessory leucoxene, ilmenite and magnetite, which have a protolith of an igneous rock,are known as Orthoamphibolite.

Para-amphibolite will generally have the same equilibrium mineral assemblage as orthoamphibolite, with more biotite, and may include more quartz, plagioclase, and depending on the protolith, more calcite/aragonite and wollastonite.

Greenschist faciesis determined by the particular temperature and pressure conditions required to metamorphose basalt to form the typical greenschistfacies minerals chlorite, actinolite, and albite. Greenschistfacies results from low temperature, moderate pressure metamorphism. Metamorphic conditions, which create typical greenschistfacies assemblages,are called the BarrovianFacies Sequence, and the lower-pressure AbukumaFacies Series. Temperatures of approximately 400 to 500°C (750 to 930°F) and depths of about 8 to 50 kilometres (5 to 31 miles) are the typical envelope of greenschistfacies rocks.

31. When underplated by mafic magmas, and with no erosion, lower crustal rock will experience isobaric heating followed by isothermal decomposition during metamorphism.

32. **Biotite** or black mica is a member of the mica group within the sheet silicates. Its general formula is $K(Mg, Fe)_3(AlSi_3O_{10})(OH)_2$. Biotite is usually a solid solution of several minerals, mostly Fe-rich annite, $KFe3(AlSi_3O_{10})(OH)_2$, and Mg-rich phlogopite, $KMg_3(AlSi_3O_{10})(OH)_2$; the exact composition of a sample is variable and has to be determined through a thorough analysis. A distinguishing Featuresis resembles muscovite but has smaller 2V and darker color. Mottled "birds-eye" extinction helps distinguish from similar minerals outside the mica family. Has moderate to high relief in thin section. Has micaceous habit and dark color.

Sodalite ($Na_8(AlSiO_4)6Cl_2$) is a rather uncommon mineral restricted to alkaline igneous rocks, and is commonly associated with other feldspathoids. It is colourless to pale blue in plane light and is isotropic, with a low refractive index (n = 1.48-1.49), which gives it negative relief relative to nepheline or feldspars with which it commonly occurs.

Nepheline occurs in both volcanic and plutonic alkaline igneous rocks. In hand specimen, Nepheline is difficult to distinguish from the feldspars, and thus must usually be identified by its association with other alkalic minerals. Nepheline has a yellowish colored alteration product, called cancrinite. Nepheline is hexagonal, and thus uniaxial, making it easy to distinguish from the feldspars. Furthermore, it is optically negative, making it distinguishable from quartz. It usually shows no cleavage, has low birefringence and low relief (refractive indices are smaller than the feldspars). The only other common mineral with which nepheline could be confused is apatite, which is also uniaxial negative. Apatite, however, shows much higher relief than does nepheline.

Quartz is a uniaxial hexagonal-rhombohedral positive mineral with extremely low birefringence. It is easy to determine on account of its lack of alteration, absence of cleavage or twinning. It is also one of the most common rock-forming minerals.

33. In duplex structure, a rock body that is bounded by thrust faults from all the sides is called Horse.

34. The net slip of the fault plunges 0o towards 30°N.

35. The **Main Central Thrust** is a major geological fault where the Indian Plate has pushed under the Eurasian Plate along the Himalaya. The fault slopes down to the north and is exposed on the surface in a NW-SE direction (strike). It is a thrust fault that continues along 2200 km of the Himalaya mountain belt. The generally accepted definition of the Main Central Thrust is that it is a ductile shear zone along which the High-grade Great Himalayan Crystalline complex was placed above the low-grade to unmetamorphosed Lesser Himalayan Sequence.

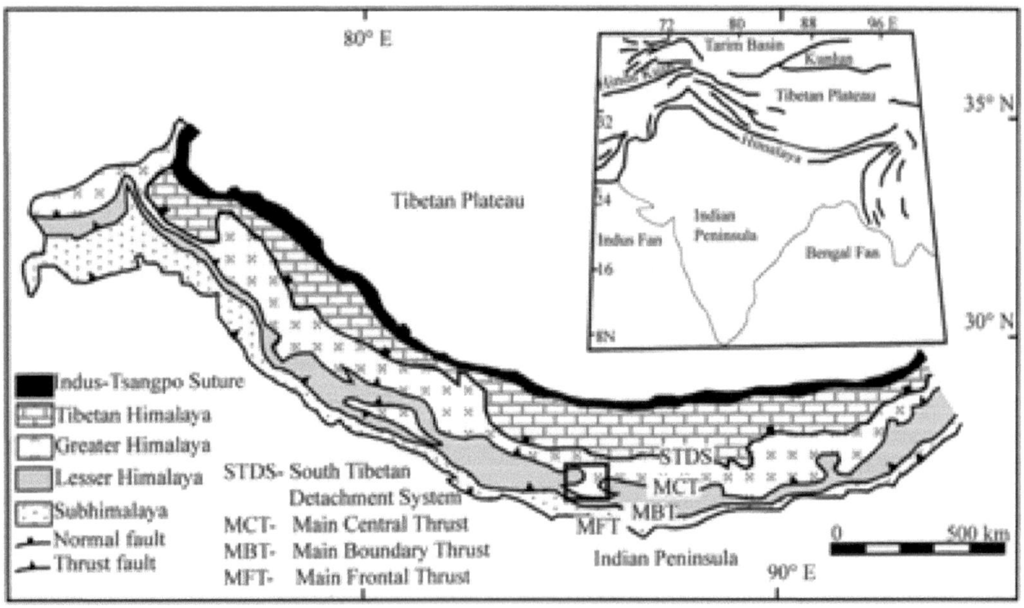

36. **Plagioclase** is a series of tectosilicate (framework silicate) minerals within the feldspar group. Rather than referring to a particular mineral with a specific chemical composition, plagioclase is a continuous solid solution series, more properly known as the plagioclase feldspar series.

The composition of a plagioclase feldspar is typically denoted by its overall fraction of anorthite (An) or albite (Ab), and readily determined by measuring the plagioclase crystal's refractive index in crushed grain mounts, or its extinction angle in thin section under a polarizing microscope.

- Anorthite was named by Gustav Rose in 1823 from the Ancient Greek meaning oblique, referring to its triclinic crystallization. Anorthite is a comparatively rare mineral but occurs in the basic plutonic rocks of some orogenic calc-alkaline suites.
- Albite is named from the Latin albus, in reference to its unusually pure white color. It is a relatively common and important rock-making mineral associated with the more acid rock types and in pegmatite dikes, often with rarer minerals like tourmaline and beryl.

37. The surface that separates two individuals (domains) in a twin is called composition surface or, when it has the regular shape of a plane, composition plane. The former is characteristic of penetration twins, the latter of contact twins. In the majority of twins the composition plane is parallel to the twin plane (for reflection twins) or normal to the twin axis (for rotation twins) but exceptions do exist

38. 1.4 μm and 1.9 μm belongs to infrared light, which is absorbed by the greenhouse gases mostly H_2O and CO_2.

39. The soret effect is where small light molecules and large heavy molecules separate under a temperature gradient. Usually this effect is important where more than one chemical species is present under a very large temperature gradient such as CVD problems and chemical reactors. This effect is found when solving the species mass fraction equations.

40. Belgaum is city with rich deposits of Bauxite are found in Belgaum district and have led to the creation of the Indian aluminium-producing company Hindalco Industries of the Aditya Birla Group.

The phosphorites of Durmala and Maldeota blocks of Mussoorie may be classified into five distinct varieties on the bases of their megascopic characters as platy, laminated, granular, lenticular, nodular and pelletal.

The most prominent deposit of Magnesite is located in Chalk hills of Salem over an area of 17 Sq. Kms and estimated to be 44 million tonnes.

The barite mining area of Mangampeta (Lat. 14 •01 N; Long. 79 •19 E), which is located in the Kodur Mandal of Cuddapah District, Andhra Pradesh, India. The important geological formations in this area are quartzites (quartz veins), carbonaceous tuff and dolomites.

41. Rampura-Aguha base metal sulfide deposits is metamorphic house along with the host rock graphite bearing mica schists. The area has undergone three phases of deformation. The deposits occur in a doubly plunging synformal structure. Rampura-Aguha lead zinc (sulfides) deposits is located in the Bhilwara district, Rajasthan.

42. Sandstones, pebbly sandstones and conglomerates can be distinguished from all other rock types by their grainy appearance.

Pebbly sandstones > sandstones > silty sandstones > siltstone

43. Composition of H/C

Varieties of coal	H in %	C in %
Anthracite	2	90-95
Bituminous	2-Mar	75-90
Lignite	5	65-72

44. The Cambay rift Basin, a rich Petroleum Province of India, is a narrow, elongated rift graben, extending from Surat in the 7south to Sanchor in the north. In the north, the basin narrows, but tectonically continues beyond Sanchor to pass into the Barmer Basin of Rajasthan. On the southern side, the basin merges with the Bombay Offshore Basin in the Arabian Sea.The Early Tertiary sediments ranging in age from Paleocene to Early Eocene represent syn-rift stage of deposition that was controlled by faults and basement highs in an expanding rift system. These sediments are characterised by an assortment of illsorted, high energy trap derived materials. Subsidence of the basin resulted in the accumulation of a thick sequence of euxinic black shales with subordinate coarser clastics. The Middle Eocene witnessed a regressive phase with oscillating conditions of deposition and development of deltaic sequences in the entire basin. There was a regional southward tilt of the entire rift basin during Late Eocene and it is marked by a regional marine transgression extending far to the north upto Sanchor basin

45. Caprock or cap rock is a harder or more resistant rock type overlying a weaker or less resistant rock type.Common types of caprock are sandstone and mafic rock types. An analogy of caprock could be the outer crust on a cake that is a bit harder than the underlying layer. Common caprock locations are escarpments, mesa formations, and salt domes. In the petroleum industry, caprockis generalized to any nonpermeable formation that may prevent oil, gas, or water from migrating to the surface.

46. Plagioclase is compatible for Eu, hence shows positive Eu anomaly. Therefore, open separation of plagioclase melt will be depleted in Eu

47. Iceland represents the largest portion of the mid-Atlantic ridge exposed above sea level. Formed from volcanic eruptions on the Mid-Atlantic ridge, about 24 million years ago, it is one of the few places where you can stand on the ridge on dry land. This makes Iceland very special and a popular place for geologists and scientists.

48. **Gravity dam** is a dam constructed from concrete or stone masonry and designed to hold backwater by primarily using the weight of the material alone to resist the horizontal pressure of water pushing against it. Gravity dams are designed so that each section of the dam is stable, independent of any other dam section. Gravity dams generally require stiff rock foundations of high bearing strength (slightly weathered to fresh); although they have been built on soil foundations in rare cases. The bearing strength of the foundation limits the allowable position of the resultant, which influences the overall stability. In addition, the stiff nature of the gravity dam structure is unforgiving to differential foundation settlement; which can induce cracking of the dam structure.

49. Herringbone cross-stratification is a type of sedimentary structure formed in tidal areas, where the current periodically flows in the opposite direction.In tidal areas, which have bidirectional flow, structures are formed with alternating layers of cross-beds dipping in opposite directions that reflect the alternating paleocurrent. These sedimentary structures are not common because they require the current to be equal in both directions, which rarely happens in nature. The time period represented by each cross-stratified layer is likely to be many years.

50. Foreland basin is a structural basin that develops adjacent and parallel to a mountain belt. Foreland basins form because the immense mass created by crustal thickening associated with the evolution of a mountain belt causes the lithosphere to bend, by a process known as lithospheric flexure.

Foreland basins can be divided into two categories:

- Peripheral foreland basins - related to continent-continent collision (e.g. the Indo-Ganges basin and the North Alpine basin)
- Retro-arc foreland basins - related to the subduction of oceanic lithosphere (e.g. the Late Mesozoic-Cenozoic Rocky Mountain basins)

51. Harzburgite, an ultramafic, igneous rock, is a variety of peridotite consisting mostly of the two minerals, olivine and low-calcium (Ca) pyroxene (enstatite); it is named for occurrences in the Harz Mountains of Germany. It commonly contains a few percent chromium-rich spinel as an accessory mineral. Garnet-bearing harzburgite is much less common, found most commonly as xenoliths in kimberlite.

52. On partially melting this rock, the first melt will have the composition of point P.

53. In the above sedimentary succession the Fluvial depositional environment is indicated.

54. Based on the above depositional process the fluvial depositional environment mainly follow Unimodal paleocurrent pattern.

55. As per the given geological section in the question 3, unconformities can be identified in the section.

56. The Granite Gneiss-Red Sandstone contacts is a non- conformity. A non-conformity is characterized by igneous or metamorphic succession below and sedimentary succession above it.

57. **Siliceous microfossils** are protists with shells constructed of opaline (amorphous) silica. There is no intense dissolution of siliceous remains in the deep ocean. Sediments deposited below the carbonate compensation depth are commonly enriched in silica by removal of the carbonate, sometimes to the point of forming siliceous oozes. With subsequent remobilization of the silica, deep-sea chertsmay be formed. Siliceous microfossils are subject to burial diagenesis and become rare at great well depths except when recrystallized, preserved in nodules or concretions, or replaced by pyrite or calcite. There are three major groups of siliceous microfossils: radiolarians, diatoms, and silicoflagellates.

58. Radiolarians are planktonic (planktic) protists that occur primarily in open marine, deep-water settings. They are useful time indicators and are found in rocks of Cambrian to Holocene age. They may be the only common microfossils in abyssal environments, commonly forming radiolarian oozes. Radiolarian chert, the product of silica diagenesis, is widespread in the geologic record. Radiolarians are common in some marine source rocks.

59. Dolomite is the main host rock of Pb-Zn deposits in Mochia -Zawar.

60. Paleoproterozoic

(GEOPHYSICS)

21. P-2

Q-1

R-3

S-4

22. Teleseismic rays are the rays that arrive at a seismometer at a seismometer at distance greater than 18°.

23. The **reverberant** sound in an auditorium dies away with time as the sound energy is absorbed by multiple interactions with the surfaces of the room. In a more reflective room, it will take longer for the sound to die away and the room is said to be 'live'. In an absorbent room, the sound will die away quickly and the room will be described as accoustically 'dead'.

The Coherent hyperbolic events generate **multiples** on the seismograms

Guided waves is created by events paralleling first break.

Tails on reflected events create **diffractions**.

24. The intensity is a number describing the severity of an earthquake in terms of its effects on the earth's surface and on humans and their structures. Several scales exist, but the ones most commonly used in the United States are the Modified Mercalli scale and the Rossi-Forel scale. There are many intensities for an earthquake, depending on where you are, unlike the magnitude, which is one number for each earthquake. Intensity is the more appropriate parameter for describing the severity of its effect on mankind and the environment.

25. The P- wave equation,in terms of cubical dilatation, θ is given as

$$\frac{\partial^2\theta}{\partial t^2} = \alpha^2\nabla^2\theta$$

Now, comparing with the wave equation for propagation

$$\rho\frac{\partial^2\theta}{\partial t^2} = (\lambda+2\mu)\nabla^2\theta$$

We get,

$$\alpha^2 = \frac{\lambda+2\mu}{\rho}$$

$$\therefore \alpha = \sqrt{\frac{\lambda+2\mu}{\rho}}$$

26. A P-wave that travels, through mantle, fluid core and inner core is labelled as PKIKP while reflection of P-wave from the inner core after travelling mantle, fluid core is labeled as PKiKP.

27. Sesmic signal is recorded in a frequency band, 50-100 Hz.

As per Nyquist frequency for the sampling to avoid the aliasing is given as twice the highest recorded frequency,

$$f_N = 2\times100 \text{ Hz} = 200 \text{ Hz}$$

Therefore, Sampling interval, ms = $\frac{1}{200} = 5$

28. Dynamic range, abbreviated DR, DNR, or DYR is the ratio between the largest and smallest values that a certain quantity can assume. It is often used in the context of signals, like sound and light. It is defined as

$$DR = 20\log_{10}\left(\frac{A_{max}}{A_{min}}\right)\text{dB}$$

where,

A_{max} = Maximum recoverable amplitude

A_{min} = Minimum recoverable amplitude

As per the questions

A_{max} = 20 cm

A_{min} = 0.2 mm = 0.02 cm

$$DR = 20\log_{10}\left(\frac{20}{0.02}\right)\text{dB} = 60 \text{ dB}$$

29. Types of seismic waves, one can make a broad distinction between body waves, which travel through the Earth, and surface waves, which travel at the Earth's surface.

Body waves

Primary waves: Particle motion consists of alternating compression and dilation. Particle motion is parallel to the direction of propagation (longitudinal). Material returns to its original shape after wave passes.

Secondary waves: Particle motion consists of alternating transverse motion. Particle motion is perpendicular to the direction of propagation (transverse). Transverse particle motion shown here is vertical but can be in any direction. However, Earth's layers tend to cause mostly vertical (SV; in the vertical plane) or horizontal (SH) shear motions. Material returns to its original shape after wave passes.

Rayleigh waves: Particle motion consists of elliptical motions (generally retrograde elliptical) in the vertical plane and parallel to the direction of propagation. Amplitude decreases with depth. Material returns to its original shape after wave passes.

Love waves: Particle motion consists of alternating transverse motions. Particle motion is horizontal and perpendicular to the direction of propagation (transverse). To aid in seeing that the particle motion is purely horizontal, focus on the Y axis (red line) as the wave propagates through it. Amplitude decreases with depth. Material returns to its original shape after wave passes.

30. A minimum phase digital signal have all its energy concentrated towards time 0 more than any other.

31. **Neutron Porosity:** Hydrocarbon gas has a much lower hydrogen index resulting from its low density and its presence gives rise to underestimations in porosity.

Density Derived Porosity: In a gas zone density derived porosity is overestimated. The density of gases is very low compared to aqueous fluids. This gas will reduce the mean fluid density of invaded zones and will cause overestimation of the porosity.

32. The equation for the formation of water resistivity estimation from SP log is given as

$$SSP = -K(T)\log\left(\frac{R_{mfe}}{Rw_e}\right)$$

where,

SSP is static SP

K(T) is temperature dependent coefficient

Rw_e is water resistivity

R_{mfe} is mudfiltrate

33. Density logging is another application of gamma rays in gathering data about subsurface formations. Density logging tools rely on gamma-gamma scattering or on photoelectric (PE) absorption.A density-logging tool sends gamma rays into a formation and detects those that are scattered back.

34. The **Turam method** is one of the oldest geophysical electro-magnetic methods used for mineral exploration. An insulated cable a few hundred meters to several kilometers long is laid parallel to the geological strike direction. The cable is either grounded at both ends or laid out in a large loop, and energized at low frequencies (less than 1 kHz). Two receiving coils are moved on lines outside of and perpendicular to the long side of the loop or grounded cable and two components of the resultant field are measured. The primary field generated by the large loop or cable interacts with the soil and subsoil and with a conductive body if present which could be a mineral and creates a resultant electromagnetic field. For a non-conducting subsurface, reduced field ratio is 1 and phase difference is $0°$.

35. As per given question

The relationship between the electric displacement vector $\vec{D}$, electric field $\vec{E}$ and polarization vector $\vec{P}$ is $\vec{D} = \varepsilon_0\vec{E} + \vec{P}$

36. The maximum depth of investigation is achieved in tri-electrodes configuration.

37. Electromagnetic induction surveying is usually carried out at frequencies below 10^4 Hz, for which the magnitude ratio is much less than unity in both good and bad conductors. At these frequencies, the electromagnetic signal passes through the ground in a diffusive manner by conversion of the changing magnetic field to electric current and vice versa. High frequency surveying employs radar signals with frequencies around 10^8 Hz. Under these conditions, the EM signal propagate like a wave, and so is subject to diffraction, reflection and reflection.

Relevant differential equation to study low frequency electromagnetic prospecting for a conducting target can be written in the form of Laplace's equation.

38. The magnetotelluric phase response for the basement wheather it is perfectly conducting or perfectly resistive, the phase asymptotically approaches to $45°$.

39. Magnetotelluric spectral impedenceis defined as the ratio of the spatial spectrum from mutually orthogonal horizontal components of the electric and magnetic field. For five component data recorded in the field Ex, Ey, Hx, Hy, and Hz the magnetotelluric spectral impedence is given by

$$Z_{xy} = \left(\frac{Ex}{Hy}\right)$$

$$Z_{yz} = \left(\frac{Ey}{Hz}\right)$$

40. For the Schlumberger electrode configuration in resistivity method, it is always taken care that the potential electrode difference is about 1/5 of the current electrode difference.

41. In resistivity surveying, information about the subsurface distribution of electrical conductivity is obtained by examining howcurrents flow in the earth. DC (direct current) resistivity methods involve injecting a steady state electrical current into the ground and observing the resulting distribution of potentials (voltages) at the surface or within boreholes. The direct filter coefficients are used to compute for resistivity transform from apparent resistivity data.

42. Given,

Measured count rate, M = 15,100

Dead time, τ = 300 msec

Therefore,

Count rate in absense of dead time, N is

$$N = \frac{M}{1-\tau M} = \frac{15,100}{1-\frac{300}{60}\times10^{-6}\times15,100}$$

= 16333.1 count/min

43. Given,

The output of a linear and invariant system for a unit impulse is {3,1}.

Also, the output for an input {-2,1} is the convolution between {-2,1} and {3,1}

Therefore, Output = {-2,1} × {3,1} = {-6,1,1}.

44. Legendre Equation plays a vital role in many problems of mathematical Physics and in the theory of quadratures (as applied to Numerical Integration).

$$(1-x^2)y'' - 2xy' + p(p+1)y = 0, -1 < x < 1$$

where $p \in \mathbb{R}$ is called a legendre equation of order p.

Geophysical inverse problems are described legendre equation.

45. Artificial neural networks (ANN) or connectionist systems are computing systems vaguely inspired by the biological neural networks that constitute animal brains. The neural network itself is not an algorithm, but rather a framework for many different machine-learning algorithms to work together and process complex data inputs.

A key trigger for renewed interest in neural networks and learning was Werbos's (1975) backpropagation algorithm that effectively solved the exclusive-or problem by making the training of multi-layer networks feasible and efficient. Backpropagation distributed the error term back up through the layers, by modifying the weights at each node.

46. Backus-Gilbert method is a regularization method for obtaining meaningful solutions to ill-posed inverse problems.Backus-Gilbert instead seeks to impose stability constraints, so that the solution would vary as little as possible if the input data were resampled multiple times. In practice, and to the extent that is justified by the data, smoothness results from this.

47. For underwater gravity measurement, Bouguer correction ia applied

The Bouguer reduction for a Bouguer plate of thickness H is

$$\delta g_B = 2\pi\rho GH$$

where ρ is the density of the material and G is the constant of gravitation. On Earth, the effect on gravity of elevation is 0.3086 mGalm^{-1} decrease when going up, minus the gravity of the Bouguer plate, giving the Bouguer gradient of 0.1967 mGalm^{-1}.

48. The base of the magnetic crust is interpreted as the position of the Curie point isotherm. A zone of shallow Curie depth (~10 km) in a belt, about 60 km wide, running through the center of the state.

49. Scalar Magnetometers measures the total magnetic field which is generally involved with both remnant and induced magnetization of the rock body.

50. Source of main geomagnetic field is best represented by a system of dipoles, quadrapoles, octupoles and multipoles. Gauss concluded that the field of external origin was insignificant and that the field of external origin was predominantly that of a dipole. Later on, Gauss and Schmidt gives the multipole expression of the geomagnetic potential.

51. As per given question, it can beinferred that the basement is perfectly resistive.

52. The intersection of the straight line with the abscissa at ρ_a = 1 Ωm gives the value of the total longitudinal conductance 'S' of the section.

For a basement of high resistivity ($\rho_2 = \infty$), the depth of the basement is given as

$$h_1 = \rho_1 s$$

$$h_1 = 10\times5 \quad [\because \rho_1 = 10\,\Omega m \text{ and } S = 5\,\Omega m]$$

$$h_1 = 50 \text{ m}$$

53. Given,

Velocity of P – wave in 1st medium, V_1 = 3 km/s

Velocity of P – wave in 2nd medium, V_2 = 4.5 km

time delay, t = 49.69 msec

The time delay equation for sesmi refraction is given as

$$t = 2d\frac{\sqrt{V_2^2 - V_1^2}}{V_1V_2}$$

$$\Rightarrow d = \frac{t\times V_1\times V_2}{2\times\sqrt{V_2^2-V_1^2}} = \frac{49.69\times4.5\times3}{2\times\sqrt{4.5^2-3^2}} = 100 \text{ m}$$

54. The critical distance (x_c) for a sesmic refraction survey is

$$x_c = 2d \tan i_c$$

where d is depth of the refractor

From, snell's law

$$\sin(i_c) = \frac{V_1}{V_2} = \frac{3}{4.5} = 0.67 = 41.8^\circ$$

$$\therefore x_c = 2 \times 100 \times \tan 41.8^\circ = 178.88 \text{ m}$$

[d = 100 m (from previous question)

55. Given, Gravitational constant,

$$G = 6.67 \times 10^{-11} \text{ m}^3\text{s}^{-2}\text{kg}^{-1}$$

$$\Delta\rho = 500 \text{ kg/m}^3$$

$$\Delta g_0 = 1.67 \text{ mgal}$$

the depth to the center of a horizontal cylinder is

Z = 0.5 W

where, W = half-height width

$$W = 500 \times 2 = 1000 \text{ m}$$

$$Z = 0.5 \times 100 = 500 \text{ m}$$

Now, The central peak value of the gravity (Δg_0) of a horizontal cylinder is

$$\Delta g_0 = 2\pi G\left(\frac{\Delta\rho R^2}{Z}\right)$$

$$R = \sqrt{\frac{\Delta g_0 \times Z}{2\pi G\Delta\rho}} = \sqrt{\frac{1.674 \times 500 \times 10^{-5}}{2 \times \pi \times 6.67 \times 10^{-11} \times 500}} = 197.98 \text{ m}$$

56. The central peak value of the gravity (Δg_0) of a horizontal cylinder is

$$\Delta g_0 = 2\pi G\left(\frac{\Delta\rho R^2}{Z}\right)$$

Let, L be the length of the cylinder.

$$\Delta m = \Delta\rho \times \pi R^2 L$$

Putting the value of $(\Delta\rho \times \pi R^2)$ in equation, we get

$$\Delta g_0 = 2G\left(\frac{\Delta m}{LZ}\right)$$

$$\frac{\Delta m}{L} = \frac{\Delta g_0 \times Z}{2G} = \frac{1.67 \times 500 \times 10^{-5}}{2 \times 6.67 \times 10^{-11}}$$

$$= 6.27 \times 10^7 \text{ kg/m}$$

57. When measuring electrode is at surface and the current electrode inside a borehole the surface covered by the current is a sphere and the current density (τJ) is

$$J = \frac{I}{4\pi r^2}$$

where I si the current injected

The electric field is

$$E = \rho J$$

$$\Rightarrow E = \frac{\rho I}{4\pi r^2}$$

Therefore, the electric potential is

$$V = \frac{\rho I}{4\pi r}$$

$$\Rightarrow \rho = \frac{4\pi r V}{I}$$

The apparent resistivity is given by

$$\rho = \frac{4\pi r \Delta V}{I}$$

where ΔV is the potential difference between A and M.

58. Given

$$r = 0.40 \text{ m}$$

$$I = 0.02 \text{ amp}$$

$$V = 0.04 \text{ V}$$

As per formula

$$\rho_a = \frac{4\pi r \Delta V}{I} = \frac{4 \times 3.14 \times 0.40 \times 0.04}{0.02}$$

$$\Rightarrow \rho_a = 10.048 \text{ }\Omega\text{m}$$

59. Given,

wavelet, a = {3, –2}

b = (1, 2}

a/b	1	–2
3	3	–6
–2	–2	4

$$y_0 = -6, y_1 = 7, y_2 = -2$$

$$\Rightarrow y = \{-6, 7, -2\}$$

60. Given,

wavelet, $a = \{3, -2\}$

the z- transform of a is $(3, -2z)$

Therefore, the inverse of a is W_a^{-1} is given as

$$W_a^{-1} = \frac{1}{(3-2z)} = \frac{1}{3}\left(1 - \frac{2}{3}z\right)^{-1}$$

$$= \frac{1}{3}\left\{1 + \frac{2}{3}z + \frac{4}{9}z^2 + \frac{8}{27}z^3 + \frac{16}{81}z^4 + \ldots\right\}$$

$$\therefore W_a^{-1} = \left\{\frac{1}{3}, \frac{2}{9}, \frac{4}{27}, \frac{8}{81}\right\}$$

Printed by Libri Plureos GmbH in Hamburg,
Germany

9 788193 975688